21st Century African American Social and Popular Cultural Issues

A Reader

Anita K. McDaniel, Ph.D.
University of North Carolina at Wilmington

Clyde O. McDaniel, Jr., Ph.D.
University of North Carolina at Wilmington

THOMSON
★
™
CUSTOM PUBLISHING

Editor: Kristin Cunningham
Publishing Services Supervisor: Christina Smith
Manufacturing Supervisor: Donna M. Brown
Project Coordinator: Jessica Obermeyer
Graphic Designer: Krista Pierson
Rights and Permissions Specialist: Kalina Ingham Hintz
Marketing Manager: Sara L. Hinckley

Thomson Custom Publishing
5191 Natorp Blvd.
Mason, Ohio 45040
USA

For information about our products, contact us:
1-800-355-9983
http://www.thomsoncustom.com

International Headquarters
Thomson Learning
International Division
290 Harbor Drive, 2nd Floor
Stamford, CT 06902-7477
USA

UK/Europe/Middle East/South Africa
Thomson Learning
Berkshire House
168-173 High Holborn
London WCIV 7AA

Asia
Thomson Learning
60 Albert Street, #15-01
Albert Complex
Singapore 189969

Canada
Nelson Thomson Learning
1120 Birchmount Road
Toronto, Ontario MIK 5G4
Canada
United Kingdom

Visit us at www.thomsoncustom.com and learn more about this book and other titles published by Thomson Learning Custom Publishing.

ISBN 0-759-33695-4

The Adaptable Courseware Program consists of products and additions to existing Custom Publishing products that are produced from camera-ready copy. Peer review, class testing, and accuracy are primarily the responsibility of the author(s).

Table of Contents

PART 5: RELIGION

APPENDIX

ACKNOWLEDGEMENTS

21st Century African American Social and Popular Cultural Issues: A Reader

Preface

The purpose of this book is to present some of the key perennial issues that are inherent in various sociological and popular definitions and expressions of African American culture. These issues can be seen in the often contrasting notions that others have of African Americans and the notions that black people have of themselves. From a black person's point of view, "who 'they' say we are *versus* who 'we' say we are" is a valid existential question of self representation and/or group identification. Often, consensus obtains between the sociological and the general popular culture points of view, but frequently they both diverge from actual black cultural experiences.

This is our third book that attempts to tackle this problem, and it differs from previous versions in two major ways. First, this one focuses on African American *cultural* issues rather than on African American *racial* issues. Earlier versions were concerned with issues related to racial differences between African Americans and others—defining African Americans according to several ostensible physical features (like skin color) and sociological dimensions and extrapolating behavioral correlates of them. The approach followed tradition by assuming that racial differences are real and continuous and that they lead to differences in

experiences. As a result, the earlier books were compilations of voices that spoke with authority on who African Americans are and what being African American means.

Whereas our earlier books **assumed a persistence of racial distinctions,** it appears that in the 21st century (with racial blending occurring at an ever increasing rate coincidentally with a trend toward cultural pluralism) one must look past physiology, **assume, instead, a persistence of African American ethnicity** (see Carl Hancock-Rux's article, "The New White Negro," in the Appendix), and target its **culture** and the destiny that is linked to it. The latter assumption of persistence is born out historically and contemporaneously as African American culture is routinely appropriated and incorporated (often comodified) into the mainstream of American general popular culture. So, the present book moves directly to actual **African American cultural experiences** and issues with which they must contend now and, by implication, throughout the 21st century. As was the case with our earlier books, the selections are organized systematically within the contexts of the five basic social institutions (family, education, economics, government/ politics, and religion). In these contexts, this version of our book provides a forum for voices that describe the issues involved in African

Americans' "doing what African Americans do" distinctly.

The second difference between this edition and the previous ones is that both sociological *and* popular selections are included. This is justified by the foregoing assumption that African Americans comprise an ethnic group, and that their culture can be understood only via the intersection of two complementary perspectives or approaches: the "objective" and the "subjective." The "objective" approach is appropriate for discovering ethnic boundaries and describing component institutions—that is, for studying and understanding the evolved structure of an ethnic group. This is almost purely sociological. However, it is clear that contemporary sociological notions of African American culture are limited unless they are infused with realistic references to **black popular life** or **culture** (i.e., the realm of actual experience where the rules of subjectivity and expedience obtain). The "objective" perspective cannot yield an understanding of the lived experience of black ethnic membership. This is because while black ethnicity presupposes an identifiable group with a common history, it is manifested only as a common set of *experiences* and *interpretations,* i.e., a common black culture. To explicate this is the role of the "subjective" (black popular culture) approach.

We invoked the "objective/subjective" approaches in order to describe African American culture from the points of view of both. That is, we included selections that parameterize basic African American institutions and structures (i.e., family, education, religion, etc.) as well as selections on actual black life taken from popular sources (i.e., *Essence, Black Enterprise,* and *ABC.com*) that provide the internal, more experiential ("from the inside looking out") perspective of African American culture. Hence, the book presents African American social issues from both "objective" and "subjective" points of view.

Consistent with the five basic social institutions *and* the "objective/subjective" organizing frameworks, we allowed for a dialogue to take place within each set of selections. That is, we assigned our over-all group of textual selections on African American cultural issues to five sections according to the five basic social institutions of a society with four or five complementary or competing selections in each section. Further, each section contains at least one selection that anchors the discussion within it. That is, it provides a historical, empirical, and/or conceptual foundation for the social or popular cultural issue—almost purely "objective." Then the remaining selections within each section add color to the discussion—they interpret the foundational piece(s) by offering more "subjective" treatments of the social or popular cultural issues. This strategy was used to engage the reader on both scholarly and non-scholarly levels.

The first section of the book explores the African American **family.** Traditionally, one of the essential roles of the family has been to socialize the young. The four articles and two dialogues included in this section address the issues that complicate the socialization process for African Americans. The first dialogue is between McDaniel and Lareau wherein McDaniel highlights the adaptability of African American families from slavery to the present, and Lareau discusses the contemporary influence of social class on child rearing. The second dialogue deals with the subject of interracial dating and the influence of African American familial pressures on one's decision to date (and mate) outside of one's race. Kennedy details the ultimate effect of close and intimate association between blacks and whites after the black power movement of the 1960s in spite of the oppositional stance that some African American mothers take to interracial dating as presented by Edwards.

The second section of the book explores some of the functions of **education** for African

Americans. Generally, one of the main functions is to create a formal awareness of a group's cultural heritage on levels K thru Ph.D. The two dialogues included herein describe varying perspectives on multicultural education and the reality facing African Americans in higher education. Given the salience of issues concerning cultural pluralism in America today, Jackson discusses the difficulties involved in defining and implementing multicultural education programs that adequately serve the needs of African American school-aged children. Placier, Hall, Benson Kendall, and Cockrell present a perfect illustration of the difficulties described by Jackson. The second dialogue offers competing views of African Americans in higher education. The selection from the National Urban League's *The State of Black America 2000* gives a positive view of the increasing number of African Americans earning Ph.D. degrees and teaching at institutions of higher learning. However, the selection from *Black Issues in Higher Education* presents an unsettling look at the career of one young African American academic, John Whorton, leaving readers to wonder if some scholars do more harm than good to the black cultural heritage once they achieve high status (like college professor). A review of Whorten's controversial book, *Losing the Race,* is included to add to the dialogue.

The third section of the book deals with **economics** and African American culture. Frequently, economics discussions in the U.S. explore the various aspects of production and distribution of goods and services in a capitalistic society. Our book looks at the increasing trend toward African Americans' really cashing in on the opportunities inherent in capitalistic enterprises via entrepreneurship. The four selections included are meant to engage the reader in conversations about attaining and maintaining success in the business world. The first textual conversation explores the enter-

tainment field as an arena of continued success for African Americans. An interview with Harry Edwards, sports sociologist, reveals the pitfalls as well as the possibilities for economic gain and social influence available to African Americans who choose to become athletes and rap artists. The second textual conversation is actually a debate—when minority businesses look for opportunities to develop and/or grow, to whom should they turn for help? Adebayo, Adekoya and Ayadi suggest that historically black colleges should play a larger role, whereas an article from *Black Enterprise* suggests that mergers with major white corporations point the way.

The fourth section of the book discusses **government and/or politics** and African American social and popular cultural issues. Of the five institutional arenas in which African American culture is presented in this book, the government and/or politics arena is the most contentious because it involves means of social control. As such, we present four selections with competing views about who possesses the power to control the dialogue about African American social and popular cultural issues. The first pair debates the subject of reparations and whose view of slavery should prevail. Both articles hail from *The Black Scholar* and present pro and con views of the revisionist take on the African American experience. The second pair presents competing views on how to address racism in America. Williams and Simms advocate strengthening the political power base among African Americans, whereas Moon and Flores advocate eliminating perceptions of privilege and victimage based on race and engaging in a more productive exchange about class. In essence, the debate between these two becomes: "Should African Americans rely on black or white America to solve the problem of racism?"

The fifth section of the book addresses issues concerning the role of **religion** for African Americans. In this section, we turn to the function of religion as a social institution responsible for creating meaning for a group and as a way of coping with adversity. The five selections presented revolve around two of the concepts that help to define African American culture—spirituality and gospel music. The first two, from the *Journal of Black Psychology*, use spirituality to describe African Americans from within. Mathis interviews African American women in order to discover how they define spirituality and religiosity and explain how it works in their lives. Christian and Barbarin continue with the theme of spirituality by investigating how it is being used as a coping mechanism for African American children. The remaining three use gospel music to define African Americans from the outside. Two selections, from *The Atlanta Journal and Constitution* and *The Tampa Tribune*, carry on a dialogue about the public face of gospel music and how, to some, it becomes virtually synonymous with African American culture, past and present. The last selection by Johnson uses ethnographic methods to challenge this symbiotic relationship between performing gospel music and performing "being African American" by documenting the evolution of The Café of the Gate of Salvation—a white Australian gospel group.

Finally, an **appendix** and a list of relevant **websites** are included in the book to provide additional resource and reference material. In the appendix can be found the most recent statement (2002) from the American Sociological Association on the importance of collecting data and doing scientific research (particularly, with regard to the use of ethnography) on race and culture in America. Also, the appendix includes the previously mentioned article by Carl Hancock-Rux that clearly illustrates one of the themes of this book: that black culture persists through its appropriation and often comodification (regardless of physiology). The websites are available for those who wish to pursue further any of the subject areas covered in this book. They are (and provide other) valuable links to government, professional, civil rights, academic, research, and social policy and action sources.

Part 1: Family

The 21st Century African American Family

Clyde O. McDaniel, Jr.

INTRODUCTION

Since the publication of E. Franklin Frazier's book on the matriarchal black family in 1939, and especially since the publication of the infamous *Moynihan Report* in 1967, the African American family has been the subject of much debate. These seminal works used the classic structural-functional approach and wound up casting the black family in a negative light (that has persisted until today) by focusing on some of its structural abnormalities and dysfunctions. In line with subsequent attempts to rectify the situation (Hill, 1972; 1999), to clear the fog a bit, it seems that a different approach—the situational/adaptive approach—is more appropriate (see, for example, Boss, Doherty, LaRossa, Schumm, and Steinmetz, 1993), for it allows one to discuss the African American family more objectively in its own, as well as in broader, historical and contemporary contexts. Clearly, this allows one to pay more attention to the essential emotional, physical, and social survival tasks that the black family addresses.

While the general American family in the 21st century is a mosaic of contemporary perceptions and tailor-made ("designer") social units, it echoes a traditional framework that the general population inheres. As a result, any serious discussion of the 21st century African American family should not dispense with the idea of *"the"* family as an ideal. But the one-size-fits-all notion does deserve scrutiny in light of the more contemporary concept of family as dynamic interactional processes between/among human beings (African Americans, in particular) as they form unions on the basis of different values and expectations that are imposed by different social constraints and/or inducements (for example, history and contemporary demographics—age, sex and gender ratios, sexual preference, and/or socio-economic status). Scholars of the African American family in the 21st century should be aware of the resonance role of the traditional model, but they should not be distracted with the value-laden issues of structural and functional deviations from it as a "norm"; they should be concerned, on the other hand, with the different **adaptive** relationships that blacks operationalize.

While the traditional notion of *"family"* is socially constructed, it is idealized and does not reflect reality. Its utility resides in the fact that it, like other social constructs, serves as a prescriptive guideline that encompasses only a few of the more prominent (and, by implication, socially approved) features of actual family life: for instance, it does not reflect diversity based on environmental presses and psychological and social need. Such a construction streamlines thinking and directs attention, but it does not determine behavior: social exigencies do that. This social construction *does not represent the wide range of actual social con-*

nections that comprise either historical or contemporary African American families. Even though it does help to classify information and make generalizations, it tends to overlook specificity, particularly those relationships that are important, psychologically and socially, to African American family members.

This paper discusses the African American family as an evolving coping strategy. It proceeds on the basis of four fundamental assumptions: (1) that the African American family cannot be understood apart from its dynamic social context; (2) that some of the familial patterns that were functional in the past are probably dysfunctional today; (3) that those that are operative today will change; and (4) that those patterns that are functional for one African American socio-demographic group may not be functional for another. Thus, after defining African American family in general, and assessing the impacts of the agricultural (rural), industrial/technology (urban), and post-industrial/hi-tech (information) contexts, assessments of present-day (and future) socio-demographic patterns are offered, and key references are listed.

DEFINITION OF THE AFRICAN AMERICAN FAMILY

Generally, according to Andrew Billingsley (1992), the African American family is:

> …an intimate association of persons who are related to one another by a variety of means including blood, marriage, formal adoption, informal adoption, and appropriation; (often) sustained by common residence and deeply embedded in a social network of social structures both internal and external to itself. Numerous interlocking elements come together, forming this extraordinarily **resilient** institution.

Billingsley discusses, in detail, **twelve** different African American family types, but his primary emphasis is on the process and function (i.e., "intimate association" whether positive or negative) of relationships in the different types of family groups. Others focus more directly on actual structural arrangements (Eitzen and Bacca-Zinn, 2002, p. 377) from single person and one generation units to large multi-generation units, sometimes related by blood and sometimes not, even (more recently) to the extent of embracing the notion of mere **household** (a residential and economic social unit) as a family (Osbmond and Thorne, 1993:603; Rapp, 1982). Together, the two points of view acknowledge the fact that the contemporary African American family is a source of personal intensity and adaptive variety (i.e., **resilience**).

HISTORICAL CONTEXTS

Some of the major trends operative in the American society today are: globalization, an expansion of women's public roles, and a triumph of the individual over the group (Naisbitt, 1990; 2001 and Toffler, 1990). They affect the American family in general and the African American family in particular, because, inherently, their emphases are both bi-focal and myopic. Since they focus globally *and* toward the individual, they tend to marginalize traditional intermediate group affiliations (like the traditional extended family and the community) as sources of identity and gratification. These trends, particularly the long overdue one regarding more flexibility of women's public roles, call for special familial adaptive responses.

Others that are occurring in America may offset the possible dis-equilibrating effects of these trends but, again, they are global—that is, they are sweeping the earth as the American culture becomes, via push and pull forces, the enviable and predominant lifestyle of the world. These trends evolved in stages that reflect the history of the country with the predominant values, race relations policies, and African American family relationships that obtained within them. They are: the **Agricultural Stage** (mostly rural settings wherein manual labor, land, things, and people-as-property were valued; provincial in-group norms guided behavior); the **Industrial/Technology Stage** (more urban, mobile, heterogeneous, and antagonistically cooperative settings wherein machinery and machine-like human behavior—with wages as incentives—were valued; later automation replaced much manual labor and people became less valuable than property); and the **(Contemporary) Hi-Tech/Information Stage** (rural, urban metropolitan, national, and global settings wherein information and service are valued with the goal of ego gratification; in effect, America now is a globally-oriented, information, hi-tech, egocentric, networking, multi-option society.

In these contexts, the situational/adaptive approach is used to show the intimate connections between social structure and African American family relationships that developed and elaborated during and since slavery in the United States. This evolution will be discussed in yearly intervals during: the **Agricultural Stage** (Up to 1865: Slavery, 1866–1877: Reconstruction, and 1877–1920s: Post Reconstruction); the **Industrial/Technology Stage** (1930s: Black Migration from the South, 1930s–1960s: Depression to Revolution, and 1960s: The Revolution); and the **Hi-Tech/Information Stage** (1970s–Present: Post Revolution).

From a historical point of view, the actual African American family has evolved, and discussions of it as *nuclear, extended,* and *augmented* can provide insights regarding change over the above-mentioned stages. The *nuclear* family is composed of a couple (whether legally married or not) and their dependent children living together, and is considered a close-knit unit. The *extended* family is composed of the nuclear family plus relatives, and is considered to have several advantages over the nuclear family. Advantages like shared resources, including wealth and power, protection of property rights, education and care of the young assured the survival of the kinship group. The *augmented* family, which is composed of nuclear and extended family members, also includes non-relatives. It may be important to note that in general, and especially in the African American community, these basic types may be fragmented (as in a single parent nuclear family) or not bound by blood or law (as in cohabitation).

AGRICULTURAL STAGE FAMILIES

Up to 1865: Slavery. Until 1865, blacks, as slaves, had no political or civil rights: they could not sue or testify against whites; they could neither own property nor make wills, nor could they enter into contracts (marital or otherwise). State laws called Black Codes were passed to protect slaves as property, to maintain racial discipline, and to provide security for whites. These laws regulated slave assemblies, controlled slave movements, forbade teaching slaves to read or write (except in Maryland and Kentucky), and established special slave patrols and courts (Simpson and Yinger, 1953). One can only characterize the race relations policy of this period as *subjugation,* and the most crucial issue facing blacks at the time was the abolition of slavery without provoking severe white retaliation, because any attempts by blacks or whites in the South to initiate abolition would have meant catastrophe for those who were responsible. In the North, however, abolitionists were quite active, attempting to use moral persuasion, via the freedoms of speech and press, to get slaveholders to repent and initiate voluntary emancipation of the slaves (Duberman, 1965). Obviously, any other strategy even in the North, would have been abortive. It was alleged, by abolitionists, that slavery was a sin and that it ought to be abolished immediately. Even so, the majority of blacks were southern and rural.

1866–1877: Reconstruction. From 1866 to 1877, the economic status of blacks in the South changed for the worse. During the Civil War, the use of slave labor persisted, and blacks were supported by their masters, but during Reconstruction, with no more slave labor and a shortage of money, staple crop production was resumed on plantations via the sharecropping system (Franklin, 1961). Yet even in virtual economic peonage, the political/legal status of blacks changed for the better, since the South was *forced* to free, enfranchise, and attempt to protect the newly given civil rights of the ex-slaves via the supervision of the Freedmen's Bureau and the union officers. Until 1865, even most Northern states had denied the franchise to blacks, but when black enfranchisement came to be seen as a means of ensuring the ascendancy of Republicans and Northern businessmen, expedience seemed to override prejudice and blacks were given the franchise (Franklin, 1961). The Northerners did not give blacks economic independence through land reform, but they did change their legal and political statuses through the Thirteenth, Fourteenth, and Fifteenth Amendments, revised Southern state constitutions, two Civil Rights Acts, the Freedmen's Bureau, and the Force Acts. Reforms also came in education, prisons, criminal codes, and social services (Franklin, 1961). This was a period of *forced tolerance* of blacks' mandated freedom, and it appears that the main task facing blacks was to attain social and economic integration via their status as legal and politic equals.

As a result of the foregoing, some states that had white majorities in the population had black majorities in the electorate, while others had their white majorities drastically reduced (Franklin, 1961). The enfranchised blacks immediately elected delegates to constitutional conventions and obtained full-scale political participation in all aspects of state and local offices. That most of the black officials had less education, less political experience, and less property than whites was obvious. But, their appearance at the polls and elsewhere was spectacular (Franklin, 1961).

1877–1920s: Post-Reconstruction. The withdrawal of federal troops from the last Southern states and the resumption of home rule by Southern whites in 1877 probably signaled the end of Reconstruction (Lyons, 1971). Increasing urbanization and industrialization in the North during the 1880s and 1890s intensified agricultural depression in the South, which made the black and white farmers economic competitors for scarce resources; and blacks became scapegoats. From 1877 through the 1920s, both legal and extralegal forms of intimidation and suppression of blacks occurred with increasing frequency (Lyons, 1971). For instance, from 1889–1919, recorded lynchings averaged one every 32 days with a high of 232 in 1892, and a rash of race riots occurred all over the country. This, along with conservative victories at the polls, initiated a movement to disfranchise blacks, which grew rapidly, with all levels of whites joining in the effort. By 1910, all the ex-Confederate states passed laws or amended their state constitutions with a qualifying "grandfather clause" that had the net effect of disfranchising blacks at the polls (Lyons, 1971). This was a period of extreme *de jure re-segregation,* and the most crucial issue facing blacks at this time was survival.

In this context, blacks opted for a policy of *extreme* accommodation and conciliation (*a la* Booker T. Washington), not one of protest and agitation. Apparently, Washington saw this strategy as one of practicality and the only feasible one under the circumstances. Actually, Washington enunciated a strategy that dominated black thought at the turn of the century, and it set the terms for the debate on black programs for the next two decades. Largely blaming black people themselves for their condition, and describing Southern whites as the black man's "best friends," Washington minimized the extent of racial prejudice and discrimination, accepted segregation and the separate-but-equal doctrine, deprecated political activity, favored vocational training and working with the hands at the expense of higher education and the professions, and recommended economic accumulation and the cultivation of Christian character as the best methods for advancing the status of blacks in America. The strategy sacrificed enfranchisement and equal interaction with whites since they seemed to be bones of contention with whites, but it salvaged education (although a technical variety) and self-reliance.

Implications for the Family. During slavery, the African American family was, for all intents and purposes, a contrivance of convenience imposed and, sometimes, allowed by the slavery system. However, after slavery, when the country was still mostly rural and non-industrial, although all three types of families could be found among African Americans, the extended and augmented family models served as guideposts and were quite evident in many cases. Also, for most African American families, their unions were the result of economic conditions and tradition. Numerous exchanges and mutually supportive relations with other kin existed in extended and augmented family relationships.

Another way of looking at black families during this stage is in terms of who dominated the family system. The majority of agricultural stage African American families were organized around female lineage and matriarchy. Family authority and power were vested in the hands of females, with the oldest female having the greatest power. By implication, others in the family, especially males, had less authority in the family and in the public in general. But, beyond decision making, the instrumental division of labor in the family was quite clear—both males and females played necessary, mutually exclusive, but interdependent roles.

Since most blacks in America right after slavery were still pretty much rural southerners, severely subordinated to white society, and uprooted from their close ties back on the slavery-era plantation, their new families became, for the most part, simple nuclear and extended units (some large, some small) initially. Each of these units served fundamental **economic** (to supplement subsistence generated from working for whites), **psycho-emotional,** and **social** needs, wherein, with regard to the latter, the home—along with the church—was a refuge from blatant racism. Also, frequently the "extended and augmented family" model was operationalized on a community-wide or black town-wide basis by black families' combining their nuclear units cooperatively (by "swapping" labor) to perform large-scale agricultural tasks and provide mutual support. Collective welfare was essential, so family unions and demeanor were ethnocentrically and morally monitored by the rural black community or black town church (Rothman and Rothman, 1972). Often, personal and individual decisions and interests were subordinate to community interests.

During Reconstruction and Post-Reconstruction, with the economically necessary migration of many black males to urban southern cities like Atlanta, Charleston, Birmingham, New Orleans, Baltimore, Norfolk, Richmond, and Nashville, the family units to which they were connected were altered significantly (contributing, in some cases, to separation and fragmentation with the dominant female assuming an even larger parental and/or head of household role back in the rural environment). But even when the separation involved long distances, black people's familial values continued to connote extended kinship ties (until they re-established or established actual on-site extended families of their own).

INDUSTRIAL/TECHNOLOGY STAGE FAMILIES

1920s: Black Migration to the North. As far back as 1905, Washington's accommodation was challenged by a small group of black intellectuals in the urban North who advocated a pluralistic brand of integration. The group, which was led by W. E. B. DuBois (1868–1963), formed the Niagara Movement that held whites directly responsible for the race problem, and denounced segregation, the separate but equal doctrine, and the disfranchisement laws that they held to be incompatible with black economic progress. Finally, they insisted that the only way for blacks to gain their rights was through verbal agitation and complaints. In 1910, the group evolved into the NAACP whose explicit goal was to use *legalisms* to obtain constitutional rights for blacks (Meier, *et. al.,* 1965) and during the following decade, the NAACP was able to get the Courts to declare the "grandfather clause" and residential segregation ordinances unconstitutional (Meier, *et. al.,* 1965).

During the late 19-teens and the 1920s, the situation was such that many social and political changes occurred for blacks, principally resulting from the mass migration of blacks to the North, World War I, and Wilsonian Idealism. Yet the same years saw the rebirth of the Ku Klux Klan, racial tensions in the military, problems of post-war demobilization and job competition, and extensive race riots during the summer of 1919 (Osofsky, 1966). From 1910 to 1920, the black population of New York City, for instance, increased by 66 percent; and from 1920 to 1930, it increased by 115 percent (Osofsky, 1966). Most of these immigrants were black Southerners who were disenchanted with the South and who came North to seek "a better life." By 1930, fewer than 25 percent of the city's blacks had been born in New York (Osofsky, 1966). There were more blacks in New York City in 1930 than in Birmingham, Memphis, and St. Louis combined (Osofsky, 1966). This pattern was duplicated in other northern cities as blacks sought and gained employment in the various factory systems, and it caused whites to react with fear, increased *de facto segregation,* and hostility.

One of the black responses to this situation was an increased interest in black nationalism. The Harlem Renaissance (Cruse, 1967) was launched by black intellectuals and artisans, and the Garvey movement had an especial appeal to the masses. Both promoted black consciousness, black unity, and black pride. However, the Garvey movement also rejected white stereotypes of black life and white control of black institutions and communities, and it went on to glorify black people, their culture and history, and it subscribed to the belief that *separation* offered an attractive alternative to integration or accommodation wherein blacks everywhere would have a sense of identity, prestige, and protection (Cornon, 1955).

1930s–1960s: From the Depression to the Revolution. During the depression of the 1930s (which was economic catastrophe for blacks), Hoover's failure to curb the depression became a primary reason for blacks' massive shift from the Republican Party to the New Deal Democratic Party that benefited black people. Also, the Democratic Party, under Roosevelt, selected a "Black Cabinet," as many blacks were appointed to significant federal posts (20,000 by 1946) and their advice was sought and heeded (Lyons, 1971). However, the New Deal social and economic programs, in some respects, continued discriminatory practices in the form of farm payments that often went to landlords rather than to black tenants and sharecroppers, government-sanctioned wage differentials that favored whites, federal housing programs that increased segregation, and minimum wage, maximum hours, and Social Security legislation that exempted domestics, farm workers, and other menials, thus excluding many blacks (Lyons, 1971).

Additionally, during the 1930s, the old problems of Southern disfranchisement, *de jure segregation,* lynchings, economic subordination, discrimination, and Northern ghettos remained. So during the 1940s and 1950s, Truman, by executive order, established a Committee on Civil Rights that developed a report for a comprehensive civil rights bill. Although Congress turned down the bill, the *report* became a blueprint for civil rights reformers for the next two decades (Meier, 1965). Later, in 1948, Truman issued another executive order to end segregation in the armed forces (that was fully implemented during the Korean War) and an order for fair employment in the federal government. While Eisenhower relaxed on civil rights during the 1950s (being preoccupied with the Korean War), schools were integrated, and during the early 1960s, Kennedy again relied on executive orders to combat discrimination in housing and employment until public opinion, in 1963, finally stirred congressional action on a significant scale (Meier, 1965). In all, this was a period of gradual *desegregation* and rising expectations as blacks enjoyed more and more social, economic, and political freedoms. The critical issues, therefore, facing blacks concerned desegregation; i.e., to attack the *de jure* and *de facto* barriers to equality.

The depression and the New Deal produced, among blacks a deep concern for economic problems. Also, in the favorable atmosphere of the New Deal, the NAACP broadened the scope of its legalisms to include educational discrimination concentrating on black-white teacher salary differentials and the absence of graduate and professional schools for blacks in Southern states (Meier, 1965). During the 1950s, the NAACP won many victories in the courts (significantly, public school integration in 1954), successfully attacking racially restrictive covenants in housing, segregation in

interstate transportation, and discrimination in publicly owned recreational facilities.

Consistent with NAACP legalisms, in 1941, employment was secured for blacks in the discriminatory defense industries via organizing and threatening non-violent direct action (Meier, 1965), and CORE was organized in 1942 to use non-violent direct action (such as interracial-group sit-ins) to attack discrimination in places of public accommodation in the cities of the Northern and border states (Meier, 1965). This growing use of direct action heightened during and after the Montgomery, Alabama bus boycott of 1955–56, which was led by local blacks, and catapulted Martin Luther King, Jr. into national prominence. King's leadership of the civil rights' movement, especially through SCLC from the mid 1950s through the 1960s, was facilitated by mass media coverage, but his role in the Montgomery bus boycott, the Selma March, the 1963 March on Washington, and others, signaled the emergence, especially in the South, of a new militant orientation on the part of black people that stressed integration, but that, tactically, stressed *immediacy* (rather than the old NAACP gradualist approach), and that physically resisted injustice, yet left the resister morally blameless.

1960s: The Revolution. During the revolution of the 1960s, the whole process of social change in race relations was speeded up, and the barriers standing against the recognition of blacks' constitutional rights were largely destroyed. This seemed to have turned blacks toward a deeper concern with the economic and social problems that particularly affected the masses: discrimination in employment opportunities and the quality of education and housing. Blacks obtained desegregation of public accommodations in the South, and thousands of jobs in retail stores and consumer-oriented industries in the North. They obtained the passage of the Civil Rights Act of 1964 and the Voting Rights Act of 1965, but they met white resistance in using strikes, school boycotts, and demonstrations against discrimination in the building trades unions. Progress was being made, but it was not keeping pace with rising expectations, and genuine equality appeared as distant as ever.

The 1964 Anti-poverty Act accelerated the shift from an emphasis on national legislative programs to grass roots action by the poor themselves, but it seemingly increased the frustration and discontent among the black poor by further escalating expectations while delivering nothing substantial. Paradoxically, the War on Poverty, in stressing that government programs should be initiated and administered by people at the grass roots level, but failing to solve the problems of the poor, led to a heightened militancy among them and set the stage for the dramatic appearance of the slogan "black power."

"Black power," first articulated by SNCC, signaled a mood rather than a program—disillusionment and alienation from white America, race pride, self-respect, and black consciousness (Haskins, 1972). The precipitating occasion was James Meredith's march from Memphis to Jackson in the early summer of 1966, but the slogan expressed tendencies that had been present for a long time. In political terms, "black power" meant independent action: black control of the political power of the black ghettos and its conscious use to better the slum dwellers' conditions. With escalating expectations among blacks, it seems that the primary issue was political control of their destiny for further social and economic improvement, especially in areas where blacks were in the numerical majority. This is a variant of *pluralism.*

SCLC, the Southern college student sit-ins, and the formation of SNCC in 1960 initiated events that made direct action temporarily preeminent as a civil rights technique and ended NAACP's dominance. But it also started a

steady radicalization of tactics among blacks: from legalism to direct action to black power; from guaranteeing the protection of blacks' constitutional rights to securing economic policies that would ensure the welfare of the disadvantaged in a progressively automated society; from appeal to whites' sense of fair play to demands based on power in the black ghetto; from concentrating in the South to concentrating nationwide; from participation by the upper and middle classes to mass action by all classes.

The number of black leaders proliferated and became more associated with organizations that, in turn, became more militant, inclusive, far-reaching in their demands, and urgent in their attitudes (Haskins, 1972). So by 1965, non-violent direct action had waned. New goals embraced pluralism, integration, and separation. However, the different groups that espoused these goals differed far more substantially on tactical grounds (Meier, 1965). For instance, SNCC applauded guerrilla warfare and saw riots as rebellions for political independence; CORE saw riots as natural explosions, urged violence only in self defense, and advocated working within the Democratic Party for economic gains. Black Muslims also advocated violence only in self-defense but eschewed political action; and others were revolutionary separatists, variously advocating armed resistance, reparations, territorial separation, and/or complete control of the central cities.

Implications for the Family. By the late 1800s, industrialization, along with precipitous urbanization, was in full swing. During this time, the northeastern cities of America were being flooded with European immigrants and erstwhile indigenous rural dwellers. This flood was curtailed drastically in 1924 by the passage of the Immigration and Naturalization Act. However, a great migration of African Americans to northeastern cities in the late 1890s began to overlap European immigration.

It escalated in the 19-teens and 1920s, subsided in the 1930s, but regained speed in the 1950s. Again, while all three types of African American families could be found, most of those in urban areas were nuclear and/or nuclear/ augmented (in some cities, for example, as much as a fifth of families had live-in boarders and/or other relatives—Glasco, 1977). Both men and women worked outside the home. The demand for cheap labor ensured that most of those who were strong and healthy could meet their basic needs by earning a salary in the voracious labor market, but the typical African American still lived on the margins of viability in the crowded makeshift slums of large northeastern cities (Flanagan, 2001). In their racially homogeneous residential areas, the families were in constant face-to-face contact with others in very close proximity, but the demands of the labor force often pushed them into the public racially and ethnically diverse arena. Clearly, in this urban environment, cultural diffusion obtained, and the two-parent type of family structure was solidified as the ideal, but in actuality, among African Americans, the ideal was being eroded more and more as black females in the inner city were becoming single-parent heads of households with independent sources of income.

With hard-earned affluence in the early and middle parts of the 20th century came upward social mobility for many. While this meant urban de-concentration—suburbanization—for whites, it meant more intense urban concentration for African Americans in the residential areas of inner cities that were occupied previously by whites. There seemed to be progressive disaffection for formal marriage, and those who did marry opted for smaller families. The African American socio-economic class structure became quite diverse, but, for the most part, they all remained confined residentially to the inner city. The white social classes, on the other hand, began to separate geographically with middle and upper classes suburbanizing. In these white suburban families, the wives or domestic partners started to gain ground insofar as obtaining more privileges than traditional wives (Allan, 1986). The same pattern was stark but less traumatic in inner city African American families because they already had a history of matriarchy. The escalating role shift was precipitated by America's participation in World Wars I and II and the Korean War (with surges of women in the domestic workforce and family decision making while their husbands were at war), war economies, the expansion of transportation and communication capabilities, the invention of modern conveniences, the movement of industry away from the central city, significant civil rights gains, and a shift in the moral code of the country (for example, making divorce easier and more acceptable, and flexibility of sexual standards).

Since these suburbs tended to be racially, ethnically, and socio-economically homogeneous, according to Sennett (1970), the white families who resided there harbored conceptions and attitudes about other people (especially about African American people) that rarely got tested by the actual experience of face-to-face contact. The suburbanites had retreated into the private world of home and small, copycat families, with only superficial contact even with next-door neighbors. Clearly, the old neighborhoods of the inner city (that were now being occupied more and more by African Americans) provided richer opportunities for extended family and meaningful interactions (whether positive or negative) than the suburban housing tracts that later came to symbolize the typical American residential setting.

These white suburban areas, families, and homes were neatly packaged and presented to the public in a fashion similar to the way food service is packaged in the fast foods industry (Ritzer, 2002). These "formulaic families" prided themselves in their adherence to standards of social conformity such that they all looked and acted alike. So, society had become the reference source, not the neighborhood community; and, **to some extent, those African Americans who became affluent but still lived in the inner city adopted this value also. Later, when some of them were able to break the barriers of residential segregation and suburbanize, they were already pre-socialized to operationalize the value.**

HI-TECH/INFORMATION STAGE

1970s: Post-Revolution. Since the 1970s, blacks have been returning to the South in droves, but mostly to urban and suburban areas that had been occupied previously by whites. Even so, blacks today enjoy full legal citizenship, access to public accommodations, and the opportunity" to enjoy a relatively moderate level of affluence. American institutions are being *forced* to comply with (formal and informal) affirmative action, equal employment opportunity, fair housing, and school desegregation guidelines, etc. However, starting in the 1970s, while many blacks could be classified as middle class, the proportion of middle-class blacks then and today is not at parity with whites (National Urban League, 2000). With the demise of emphasis on black power (perhaps because most black power advocates were either imprisoned, killed, forced out of the country or co-opted), the life styles of affluent blacks are becoming more indistinguishable from the life styles of whites, but poor blacks remain severely disadvantaged and challenged (National Urban League, 2000).

This may be the result of institutionalized racism via prejudice, which cannot be ignored. Most blacks recognize the fact that prejudice cannot be legislatively controlled. Therefore, blacks are faced with the inevitable problems (that today result from the prejudicial, organi-

zational implementation of ostensibly just city, state, and national statutes) of *de facto* segregation, extremely high unemployment, disproportionate representation in the criminal justice system, a progressively widening gap in economic status between blacks and whites, increased urbanization (and, therefore, increased ghettoization), of blacks, a de-emphasis on social services and welfare, a conservative trend in higher education toward tightening admission and performance standards, a de-emphasis on formal black culture programs (e.g., black studies), and a decline in emphasis on massive reform programs like OEO and Model Cities (National Urban League, 2000).

In the early part of this stage, more and more blacks began verbalizing the need for cultural pluralism **and** integration via public office and political participation, but as a conservative trend in race relations policy set in (and the fact that Hispanics were becoming, and, in 2003, did become the largest minority group of color in this country) particularly regarding economic concerns (which was exacerbated by the recent recession and current inflation), blacks have been forced to defer the focus on cultural pluralism to black intellectuals and artisans while concentrating their main efforts on economic and social parity with whites. Therefore, education and training emphases were increased. Since blacks and whites (as well as other minorities) now are competing with each other for residential, economic, employment and other resources that used to be mediated under the duress of affirmative action, integration, as a goal, still seems to be as distant as ever as a race relations policy. With affirmative action removed, now institutionalized racism is unleashed to victimize blacks directly. It seems that the current race relations policy in the country as again one of social *tolerance* of blacks who are kept from attaining full equality via economic and social constraints. Therefore, the critical task facing blacks now in this high-tech, information stage is to look around and step over and/or circumvent the subtle and overt forms of institutionalized racism by **using technical, hi-tech, and information generating skills to explore the world as a resource pool** pursuant to the attainment of economic and social parity.

The latter point was underscored by the Joint Center for Political Studies in Washington as early as 1975 when it released a report on the numbers of black elected officials in the United States. The report indicated that 3,503 of the 500,000 persons in elected offices as of May 1975 were black (Black World, 1975). Many, many more are in these kinds of positions today. Also, it is quite evident that many blacks across the country occupy important non-political positions that carry executive responsibility and/or are entrepreneurs with abilities to exercise networking options across the world. And many private African American homes have computers, faxes, Internet web access, other information sources, and a global perspective. Today, the responsibility for determining the average African American individual's destiny and the task of acquiring the requisite abilities to do so are very much in his/her own hands. Fortunately, the inclination to operationalize these capabilities is becoming more and more distributed throughout the black population.

Implications for the Family. With the shift from the agricultural to the industrial to the present-day service oriented hi-tech/information economy, families in general and African American families in particular have adapted in many unique ways. Essentially, now *"family"* really has become more of a social process than a social object to subscribe or react to. While the predominant family type ideals among African Americans are extended and nuclear, they are quite fragmented. Many different structures and functions are operative today. The entire American culture has shifted toward individual gratification and personal

achievement with the whole world becoming a resource pool.

With socially prescribed formulaic family structures and functions having been jettisoned, personal preferences and decision-making now serve as guideposts for optimum family relationships and interactions, and African American families and "temporarily committed relationships" are entered into in this regard. For instance, there are those who contemplate getting together with others or marrying merely in order to maximize their chances of a personally gratifying relationship. In these cases, each person who wishes to be involved looks, on an ad hoc basis, for a good deal, a bargain, if possible, in which their assets and liabilities are compared with those of potential mates. And once entered into a relationship, it is continued on the basis of the assumption that each member will get as much, if not more, out of it than it will cost. Those potential mates who are construed as incongruous, or not potentially gratifying in the exchange, are likely to be out of luck. Complementary desires theory suggests that people select others for relationships to make up for, balance, or supply features that they do not themselves have. Some of these may be quite superficial and not sustaining. Thus, the talker may look for a listener; the eater may look for a cook.

Each person feels that, in terms of relationships, there is no need or excuse to go lacking, for there are enough resources in the black community and, indeed, in the world, and available information about them, to grant him/her (resources permitting) relative immunity from loneliness, stress, and unhappiness. With this selfish orientation, one feels that he/she is not locked into an all-encompassing group with exclusive dependencies and attachments. Instead, they feel that they can be involved, instrumentally, in a number of well-defined groups sequentially, segmentally, and/or superficially. This possibility of multifaceted, hi-tech, ad hoc involvement in a variety of circles often contributes to a heightened sense of self consciousness and self awareness; this segmentation often brings about a sense of uniqueness and can serve as a precondition for the emergence of a perception of individual independence. While this situation appears to be indicative of extreme independence, in reality, it is one of **multiple dependencies** (rather than exclusive dependence on one source, e.g., one's special individual, the community, the family). And since these patterns imply reciprocity, they reflect **interdependence** also.

As a matter of fact, social networking theory suggests that the information era liberates "intimate associations" from local residential space, indicating that black people now can associate on the basis of ad hoc interests rather than within neighborhood boundaries. Since modern technologies allow interaction without proximity, spatial agglomeration becomes only one of the ways black family members can gain access to one another. Further, the ultimate domain within which potential family members may meet, interact, and, ultimately, "commit" to each other is not the rural town, the urban community, the suburban complex, or the national society. It is now the international web and, on it, one can find the greatest number and intensity of subgroups of interest providing support for the greatest variety of traditionally unconventional thoughts and behaviors. All types of virtual families are possible. One can give and take ideas on the web, and exchange those ideas with new partners at any distance. In this context, one is safe by remoteness, where one's persona is shielded by anonymity, perhaps promoting a sense of daring that might otherwise become inconvenient or uncomfortable if uttered or practiced within a local town or community. This provokes each African American member of a family to be more experimental in his/her mode of self-expression than he/she would otherwise be, and so forth.

DEMOGRAPHIC CONTEXTS: OVERVIEW OF AFRICAN AMERICANS

As can be seen from the historical sketches outlined above, it is clear that the 21st century inheres the kind of significant and swift changes in relationships and communities that are quite different from what obtained a few decades ago. Clearly, they challenge ideas about normalcy or having a single referent or standard by which to think about and evaluate families.

Also, according to the following analyses taken from statistical databases at the U.S. Bureau of the Census, the U.S. Department of Education, the U.S. Department of Health and Human Services, the U.S. Department of Justice, and the U.S. Department of Labor, there are other quite contemporary reasons for variation in family life in the black community. As the 20th century came to a close, the United States had a population of about 281 million people, and it is projected to reach close to 400 million by the middle of the 21st century. Even though a surprising number of those in the 2000 census (7 million) indicated multiracial identities (Barefoot, 2002, p.61), 12.1 percent of the population was black. The latter percentage is expected to increase in the years 2025 and 2050 to 14.2 and 15.4 respectively (U.S. Bureau of the Census, 2000).

Also, over the years, the proportion of females in the country, across the races, has increased until, now, they comprise about 51–52 percent of the population (with a considerably higher percentage of females in the black population), with most of them working outside the home and their earning capacities are approaching parity with men. In 1996, 60 percent of African American women were officially in the labor force (U. S. Department of Labor). Obviously, these numbers radically underestimate the true size of the black female labor force, for they do not include those who work sporadically, those whose names do not appear on official work lists, or women who work in "cottage industries," at home, or on contractual bases.

The educational attainment levels of the unemployed in 1999 was as follows: 12 percent of blacks had dropped out of high school (only 6 percent of whites); those with a high school education: 6 percent for blacks, 3 percent for whites; those with some college education: 5 percent for blacks, 3 percent for whites; and those who had graduated from college: 3 percent for blacks, and 2 percent for whites. In 1977, 42 percent of black men had BA degrees: it fell to 38 percent in 1987, and all the way down to 36 percent in 1997 (for white men the percentages are a little higher 54, 47, and 45 respectively). Also in 1997, the total enrollment of black women in higher education was much higher then it was for black men: almost a million for black women and about 600,000 for black men. In graduate and professional schools, females also outnumbered males by wide margins: there were 85,000 black females enrolled in graduate schools and 10,000 in professional schools; for males, it was 40,000 and 13,000 respectively.

The five most popular bachelor degrees for both blacks and whites in 1996–97 were: (1) business, (2) social sciences, (3) education, (4) psychology, and (5) health sciences. Incidentally, the fourth and fifth choices for blacks and whites changed places: blacks' fourth choice was psychology. In 1999, there were not too many black faculty members at institutions of higher education in the United States. They comprised about 7 percent altogether, with about 4–5 percent of them in the highest ranking liberal arts colleges, and about 3 percent in the highest ranking research institutions.

The number of black children in school is expected to increase from 1995 to 2005 by 8 percent, but this is not nearly as much as the expected percentages increase among Asian and Hispanic children (39 percent and 30 percent respectively). In fact, the actual number of Hispanics in the country and the number of their children in particular moved past those of blacks in 2003, and are expected to greatly exceed those of blacks in the coming years.

African American families vary by socio-economic status (SES), and the income and wealth disparities among them in the country have widened. In fact, SES confers different connections with the broader local, national, and international social environment and different ways of acquiring the necessities of life from the worldwide resource pool. Upper class African American families have boundaries that are quite open. They tend to be nuclear and extended, living in multiple homes. They have direct national and international institutional linkages, and their life chances are significantly enhanced as a result if it. Middle and upper middle class African American families tend to be nuclear with tight boundaries but with crucial links (principally *via* occupations) to nonfamily institutions. Many of their two-parent families have been able to sustain their status by the wife working also. Clearly, this places a hardship on child rearing and other functions of the home, but these families do, however, survive by virtue of their broad involvement in the public sector.

Working class African American families, whose resources depend primarily on their wages, have expanded notions of the family in order to call upon and use friends and sometimes neighbors to help out when there is a need for, for example, baby-sitting, moving, or borrowing money. Resources are pooled when connections with outside opportunities are tenuous (e.g., when the job folds). The family boundaries are flexible for expedience purposes and reflect a network of sharing and support that even extends to indirect social and human capital sources that sometimes traverse national boundaries. Whereas poverty rates are highest among blacks who dropped out of high school, it is particularly acute for those who are also single parent heads of households. Further, at age 65 and older, the poverty rate is over two and a half times that of whites. For those who were 65+ and who were near poor or highly vulnerable in 1995 (and who were likely to wind up being poverty stricken ten years later), the percentage is staggering: 57 percent.

In a recent analysis of census data, 9 percent of those who were 65+ indicated that their health was excellent; 15 percent that their health was very good; 31 percent that their health was good; 27 percent that their health was fair; and only 18 percent that their health was poor. These and other statistics imply that older blacks are expected to live a good distance into the 21st century. In fact, the life expectancy tables for blacks indicate that, at 65, black females can expect to live another 17–18 years and black males, another 13–14 years. At 75, they can expect another 11 and 9 years respectively.

As of 2000, the death rate for black males was much higher than it was for black females for all causes except cerebrovascular diseases and diabetes mellitus. Further, as a culprit, prostate cancer (at a rate of 180.6 per 1,000) loomed larger than other diseases for black males; for black females, breast cancer (at a rate of 95.4 per 1,000) loomed larger. Between 64 and 74 years of age, both black males and black females contract diabetes at about the same high rate (171.8 per 1,000). After 74, the rate drops precipitously for males (120.6 per 1,000), but rises for females (173.5 per 1,000).

Cohabitation among blacks has been accepted privately for a long time, but now, at the start of the 21st century, it is more acceptable publicly before marriage, and, sometimes, instead of marriage. At the start of the 20th century, nearly all children lived with both parents, but by the 1970s, it was down. At present, significantly less than half live with both of their par-

ents. At the same time, in actual hours, parents are spending more time with their children now than at the start of the 20th century. Divorce is increasing in frequency such that recent divorce rates show that the chances of a first marriage ending in divorce are about 1 in 2. Black people are postponing marriage, with many opting instead for living alone, single hood and/or cohabitation (actually, cohabitation rates are increasing phenomenally) even after widowhood. Since many do not want children either (U.S. Bureau of the Census, 1995), single hood and childlessness seem to be increasing.

Even though in the past three decades, homosexuality has become more tolerated and visible in America; and gay and lesbian marriages or "legal domestic partnerships" are recognized in one state and several counties and cities across the nation (Eitzen and Baca-Zinn), blacks tend to be somewhat less tolerant of it than whites (Staples, 1999).

The racial disparities in involvement with drugs and the criminal justice system are interesting. Approximately two thirds of crack users are white or Hispanic, yet the vast majority of persons convicted of possession in federal court in the 1990s were African American. About 85 percent of the defendants convicted of crack possession were African American compared to 10 percent for whites and 5 percent for Hispanics. Trafficking offenders were 4 percent white, 88 percent black and 7 percent Hispanic. Powder cocaine offenders were racially mixed. Defendants convicted of powder possession were 58 percent white, 27 percent black, and 15 percent Hispanic. The powder trafficking offenders were 32 percent white, 28 percent black, and 39 percent Hispanic.

The result of the combined difference in sentencing laws and racial disparities is that more black men and women are apprehended, incarcerated, and are serving longer prison sentences than white men and women. As of 2000, there were about 117,995 federal, 1,136,582 state, and 605,943 local jail inmates. Most of them were male but, tragically, over 40 percent of them were black.

CONCLUSION

At no time in history have *all* African American families been alike, but in the 21st century remarkable variety obtains for all races. This is, in part, due to individualism and technology; but it is also due to demographic patterns. It is clear that, in response to the continuous simultaneous globalization and individualization of the American society, the actual American family in general and the actual African American family in particular are becoming fragmented both structurally and functionally. These orientations mean that it can overstep and/or circumvent local racism in efforts to gratify explicitly the purely personal and individual (rather than social) needs and desires of its members while now being able to use the world (with all its diversification) as a resource pool. Further, African American family members feel even freer now to jettison, serially and at their discretion, previously chosen, socially approved, and mutually beneficial familial patterns in preference for others that appear to be more satisfying personally. Accordingly, many different family structures and functions obtain in the African American community in the 21st century (Billingsley, 1992). And it is important to note, as implied above, that this variety is a clear indication that the African American family, like any other social institution, is adaptive (McDaniel and McDaniel, 2000, viii).

REFERENCES

Allan, G. (1986). *Family life: domestic roles and social organization.* New York: Basal Blackwell, Inc.

Billingsley, A. (1992). *Climbing jacob's ladder.* New York: Simon and Schuster.

Cornon, D. E. (1955). Marcus garvey: one aim! one god! one destiny! *Black moses: the story of marcus garvey and the universal improvement association.* Madison, Wisconsin: University of Wisconsin Press.

Cruse, H. (1967). *The crisis of the negro intellectual.* New York: William Morrow and Co., Inc.

Duberman, M. B. (1965). *The anti-slavery vanguard: new essays on the abolitionists.* Princeton, NJ: Rutgers University Press.

Eitzen, S. and M. Bacca-Zinn (2000). *Social problems* (8th Ed.). Boston: Allyn and Bacon.

Flanagan, W. G. (2001). *Urban sociology* (4th Ed.). Boston: Allyn and Bacon.

Franklin, J. H. (1961). The south's new leaders. In J. H. Franklin, *Reconstruction after the civil war.* (Chicago: University of Chicago Press (pp. 85–103).

Frazier, E. F. (1939). (Revised 1966). *The Negro family in the united states.* Chicago, IL: University of Chicago Press.

Genovese, E. D. (1965). *The political economy of slavery: studies in the economy and society of the slave south.* Princeton, NJ: Rutgers University Press.

Glasco, L. A. (1977). The life cycles and household structure of American ethnic groups: irish, german, and native born whites in buffaloe, new york, 1855. In T. K. Hareven (Ed.), *Family and kin in urban communities, 1700–1930* (pp. 122–143). New York: New Viewpoints.

Haskins, J. (1972). *Profiles in black power.* New York: Doubleday and Co., Inc. (p. 11).

Hicks, L. (2002). Changing and continuity since 1900. In N. Smith (Ed.), *Changing U.S. demographics* (pp. 5–13). New York: The H. W. Wilson Company.

Hill, R. B. (1972). *The strengths of black families.* New York: Emerson Hall.

Hill, R. B. (1999). *The strengths of african american families: twenty-five years later.* Lanham, MD: University Press of America.

Lyons, T. T. (1971). *Black leadership in american history.* Menlo Park, California: Addison Wesley Publishing Company.

Meier, A., E. Rudwick, and F. L. Broderick (1965). *Black protest thought in the twentieth century.* Indianapolis: Bobbs-Merril Co., Inc. (p. xxvi).

McDaniel, A. K. and C. O. McDaniel (2000). *21st century African American social issues: a Reader.* Fort Worth, Texas: Harcourt Publishing Co.

Moynihan, D. P. (1967). The negro family: a case for national action. In Lee Rainwater and William L. Yancy (Eds.), *The moynihan report and the politics of controversy* (pp. 41–124). Cambridge, MA: The MIT Press.

Naisbitt, John and P. Aburdene (1990). *Megatrends 2000.* New York: William and Morrow Company, Inc.

Naisbitt, John (2001). *High Tech/High Touch.* London: Nicholas Braely Publishing.

National Urban League (2000). *The state of black america 2000.* New York: National Urban League.

Olson, D., Sprenkle, D., & Russell, C. (1979). Circumplex model of marital and family systems 1: Cohesion and adaptability dimensions, family types and clinical applications. *Family Process,* 18, 3–28

Osmond, M. W. and B. Thorne (1993). Feminist theories: the social construction of gender in families and society. In P. G. Boss, W. Doherty, R. LaRossa, W. R. Schumm, and S. K. Steinmetz (Eds.), *Sourcebook of family theories and methods: a contextual approach* (pp. 591–623). New York: Plenum Press.

Osofsky, G. (1966). Come out from among them: negro migration and settlement, 1890–1914. *Harlem: the making of a ghetto.* New York: Harper and Row (pp. 17–24, 33–34).

Perspectives. *Black world* (October, 1975), p. 49.

Rapp, Rayna (1982). Families and class in contemporary america. In B. Thorne and M. Valon (Eds.), *Rethinking the family: some feminist questions* (pp. 167–187). New York: Longman.

Ritzer, G. (2000). *The mcdonaldization of society* (New Century Edition). Thousand Oaks, CA: Pine Forge Press.

Scholnick, A. S. and J. H. Scholnick (1997). *Family transition* (9th Ed.). New York: Longman.

Sennett, R. (1970). *The uses of disorder: personal identity and city life.* New York: Random House.

Staples, R.(1999). Patterns of change in the post-industrial black family. In R. Staples (Ed.). *Black family: essays and studies* (pp. 281–290). Belmont, CA: Wadsworth.

Simpson, G. and M. Yinger (1953). *Racial and cultural minorities.* New York: Harper and Brothers.

Toffler, A. (1991). *The third wave.* New York: Bantam Books.

U.S. Bureau of the Census (1995). Population profile of the united states, 1995. *Current population reports,* pp. 23–189. Washington, D.C.: U.S. Government Printing Office (p. 9, p. 22).

U.S. Bureau of the Census (2000c). Educational attainment in the united states: march 2000. *Current population reports:* Series P-20-536. Washington, D.C.: U.S. Government Printing Office.

U.S. Department of Education (2001). *Digest of the education statistics 2000.* NCES 2001–034. Washington, D.C.: U.S. Government Printing Office.

U.S. Department of Health and Human Services (DHSS) (1999). *Health, united states 1999.* DHSS publication 99–1232. Washington, D.C.: U.S. Government Printing Office.

U.S. Department of Justice (2000). State court sentencing of convicted felons. *Bureau of justice statistics.* Washington, D.C.: U.S. Government Printing Office.

U.S. Department of Labor, Bureau of Labor Statistics (2001). *Employment and earnings 2001.* Washington, D.C.: U.S. Government Printing Office.

Invisible Inequality: Social Class and Childrearing in Black Families and White Families

Annette Lareau

Although family life has an important impact on children's life chances, the mechanisms through which parents transmit advantages are imperfectly understood. An ethnographic data set of white children and black children approximately 10 years old shows the effects of social class on interactions inside the home. Middle-class parents engage in concerted cultivation *by attempting to foster children's talents through organized leisure activities and extensive reasoning. Working-class and poor parents engage in the* accomplishment of natural growth, *providing the conditions under which children can grow but leaving leisure activities to children themselves. These parents also use directives rather than reasoning. Middle-class children, both white and black, gain an emerging sense of entitlement from their family life. Race had much less impact than social class. Also, differences in a cultural logic of childrearing gave parents and their children differential resources to draw on in their interactions with professionals and other adults outside the home. Middle-class children gained individually insignificant but cumulatively important advantages. Working-class and poor children did not display the same sense of entitlement or advantages. Some areas of family life appeared exempt from the effects of social class, however.*

In recent decades, sociological knowledge about inequality in family life has increased dramatically. Yet, debate persists, especially about the transmission of class advantages to children. Kingston (2000) and others question whether disparate aspects of family life cohere in meaningful patterns. Pointing to a "thin evidentiary base" for claims of social class differences in the interior of family life, Kingston also asserts that "class distinguishes neither distinctive parenting styles or distinctive involvement of kids" in specific behaviors (p. 134).

One problem with many studies is that they are narrowly focused. Researchers look at the influence of parents' education on parent involvement in schooling *or* at children's time spent watching television *or* at time spent visiting relatives. Only a few studies examine more than one dynamic inside the home. Second, much of the empirical work is descriptive. For example, extensive research has been done on time use, including patterns of women's labor force participation, hours parents spend at work, and mothers' and fathers' contributions to childcare (Hertz and Marshall 2001; Jacobs and Gerson 1998; Menaghan 1991). Time parents spend with children also has been examined (Bianchi 2000; Bianchi and Robinson 1997; Marsiglio 1991; Presser 1989; Zick and Bryant 1996), as well as patterns of children's time use (Hofferth and Sandberg 2001b; Juster and Stafford 1985; Sandberg and Hofferth 2001). But these works have not given sufficient attention to the meaning of events or to the ways different family contexts may affect how a given task is executed (but see Daley 2001; Rubin 1976; Thorne 2001).

Third, researchers have not satisfactorily explained how these observed patterns are produced. Put differently, *conceptualizations* of the *social processes* through which families differ are underdeveloped and little is known about how family life transmits advantages to children. Few researchers have attempted to integrate what is known about behaviors and attitudes taught inside the home with the ways in which these practices may provide unequal resources for family members outside the home. A key exception is the work by Kohn and colleagues (e.g., Kohn and Schooler 1983), where the authors argue that middle-class parents value self-direction while working-class parents place a premium on "conformity to external authority." These researchers did not investigate, however, how parents go about translating these beliefs into actions.

Fourth, little is known about the degree to which children adopt and enact their parents' beliefs. Sociologists of the family have long stressed the importance of a more dynamic model of parent-child interaction (Skolnick 1991), but empirical research has been slow to emerge (but see Hess and Handel 1974). Ethnographers' efforts to document children's agency have provided vivid but highly circumscribed portraits (Shehan 1999; Waksler 1991), but most of the case studies look at only one social class or one ethnic group. Moreover, ethnographers typically do not explicitly examine how social class advantages are transmitted to children.

I draw on findings from a small, intensive data set collected using ethnographic methods. I map the connections between parents' resources and their children's daily lives. My first goal, then, is to challenge Kingston's (2000) argument that social class does not distinguish parents' behavior or children's daily lives. I seek to show empirically that social class does indeed create distinctive parenting styles. I demonstrate that parents differ by class in the ways they define their own roles in their children's lives as well as in how they perceive the nature of childhood. The middle-class parents, both white and black, tend to conform to a cultural logic of childrearing I call "concerted cultivation." They enroll their children in numerous age specific organized activities that dominate family life and create enormous labor, particularly for mothers. The parents view these activities as transmitting important life skills to children. Middle-class parents also stress language use and the development of reasoning and employ talking as their preferred form of discipline. This "cultivation" approach results in a wider range of experiences for children but also creates a frenetic pace for parents, a cult of individualism within the family, and an emphasis on children's performance.[1]

The childrearing strategies of white and black working-class and poor parents emphasize the "accomplishment of natural growth."[2] These parents believe that as long as they provide love, food, and safety, their children will grow and thrive. They do not focus on developing their children's special talents. Compared to the middle-class children, working-class and poor children participate in few organized activities and have more free time and deeper, richer ties within their extended families. Working-class and poor parents issue many more directives to their children and, in some households, place more emphasis on physical discipline than do the middle-class parents. These findings extend Kohn and Schooler's (1983) observation of class differences in parents' values, showing that differences also exist in the *behavior* of parents *and* children.

Quantitative studies of children's activities offer valuable empirical evidence but only limited ideas about how to conceptualize the mechanisms through which social advantage is transmitted. Thus, my second goal is to offer "conceptual umbrellas" useful for making comparisons across race and class and for assessing the role of social structural location in shaping daily life.[3]

Last, I trace the connections between the class position of family members-including children-and the uneven outcomes of their experiences outside the home as they interact with professionals in dominant institutions. The pattern of concerted cultivation encourages an *emerging sense of entitlement* in children. All parents and children are not equally assertive, but the pattern of questioning and intervening among the white and black middle-class parents contrasts sharply with the definitions of how to be helpful and effective observed among the white and black working-class and poor adults. The pattern of the accomplishment of natural growth encourages an *emerging sense of constraint*. Adults as well as children in these social classes tend to be deferential and outwardly accepting in their interactions with professionals such as doctors and educators. At the same time, however, compared to their middle-class counterparts, white and black working-class and poor family members are more distrustful of professionals. These are differences with potential long-term consequences. In an historical moment when the dominant society privileges active, informed, assertive clients of health and educational services, the strategies employed by children and parents are not equally effective across classes. In sum, differences in family life lie not only in the advantages parents obtain for their children, but also in the skills they transmit to children for negotiating their own life paths.

METHODOLOGY

STUDY PARTICIPANTS

This study is based on interviews and observations of children, aged 8 to 10, and their fami-

lies. The data were collected over time in three research phases. Phase one involved observations in two third-grade classrooms in a public school in the Midwestern community of "Lawrenceville."[4] After conducting observations for two months, I grouped the families into social class (and race) categories based on information provided by educators. I then chose every third name, and sent a letter to the child's home asking the mother and father to participate in separate interviews. Over 90 percent of parents agreed, for a total of 32 children (16 white and 16 African American). A black graduate student and I interviewed all mothers and most fathers (or guardians) of the children. Each interview lasted 90 to 120 minutes, and all took place in 1989–1990.

Phase two took place at two sites in a northeastern metropolitan area. One school, "Lower Richmond," although located in a predominantly white, working-class urban neighborhood, drew about half of its students from a nearby all-black housing project. I observed one third-grade class at Lower Richmond about twice a week for almost six months. The second site, "Swan," was located in a suburban neighborhood about 45 minutes from the city center. It was 90 percent white; most of the remaining 10 percent were middle-class black children.[5] There, I observed twice a week for two months at the end of the third grade; a research assistant then observed weekly for four more months in the fourth grade.[6] At each site, teachers and parents described their school in positive terms.[7] The observations took place between September 1992 and January 1994. In the fall of 1993, I drew an interview sample from Lower Richmond and Swan, following the same method of selection used for Lawrenceville. A team of research assistants and I interviewed the parents and guardians of 39 children. Again, the response rate was over 90 percent but because the classrooms did not generate enough black middle-class children and white poor children to fill the analytical categories, interviews were also conducted with 17 families with children aged 8 to 10. (Most of these interviews took place during the summers of 1996 and 1997.)[8] Thus, the total number of children who participated in the study was 88 (32 from the Midwest and 56 from the Northeast).

FAMILY OBSERVATIONS

Phase three, the most intensive research phase of the study, involved home observations of 12 children and their families in the Northeast who had been previously interviewed (see Table 1).[9] Some themes, such as language use and families' social connections, surfaced mainly during this phase. Although I entered the field interested in examining the influence of social class on children's daily lives, I incorporated new themes as they "bubbled up" from the field observations. The evidence presented here comes mainly from the family observations, but I also use interview findings from the full sample of 88 children where appropriate.[10]

Nine of the 12 families came from the Northeastern classroom sample. The home observations took place, one family at a time, from December 1993 to August 1994. Three 10-year-olds (a black middle-class boy and girl and a white poor boy) who were not part of the classroom sample were observed in their homes during the summer of 1995.[11]

The research assistants and I took turns visiting the participating families daily, for a total of about 20 visits to each home, often in the space of one month.[12] The observations went beyond the home: Fieldworkers followed children and parents as they participated in school

Table 1. Frequency Distribution of Children in the Study by Social Class and Race

SOCIAL CLASS	WHITE	BLACK	TOTAL
Middle class[a]	18 (Garrets Tallinger) (Melanie Handlon)	18 (Alexander Williams) (Stacey Marshall)	36
Working class[b]	14 (Billy Yanelli) (Wendy Driver)	12 (Tyrec Taylor) (Jessica Irwin)[c]	26
Poor[d]	12 (Karl Greeley) (Katie Brindle)	14 (Harold McAllister) (Tara Carroll)	26
Total sample	44	44	88

Note: The names in each cell of the table indicate the children selected to take place in the family-observation phase of the study.

[a]Middle-class children are those who live in households in which at least one parent is employed in a position that either entails substantial managerial authority or that draws upon highly complex, educationally certified skills (i.e., college-level).

[b]Working-class children are those who live in households in which neither parent is employed in a middle-class position and at least one parent is employed in a position with little or no managerial authority and that does not draw on highly complex, educationally certified skills. This category includes lower-level white-collar workers.

[c]An inter-racial girl who has a black father and a white mother.

[d]Poor children are those who live in households in which parents receive public assistance and do not participate in the labor force on a regular, continuous basis.

activities, church services and events, organized play, visits to relatives, and medical appointments. Observations typically lasted three hours, but sometimes much longer (e.g., when we observed an out-of-town funeral, a special extended family event, or a long shopping trip). Most cases also involved one overnight visit. We often carried tape recorders and used the audiotapes for reference in writing field notes. Writing field notes usually required 8 to 12 hours for each two- or three-hour home visit. Participating families each were paid $350, usually at the end of the visits.

We worked in teams of three. One fieldworker visited three to four times per week; another visited one to two times per week; and I visited once or twice per week, except for the two families for which I was lead fieldworker. The research teams' composition varied with the race of the family. Two white graduate students and I (a middle-aged white woman) visited the white families; for the black families, the teams included one white graduate student, one black graduate student, and me. All black families with male children were visited by teams that included a black male fieldworker. A white male fieldworker observed the poor family with the white boy; the remaining white fieldworkers were female. Team members met regularly to discuss the families and to review the emerging analytic themes.

Our presence altered family dynamics, especially at first. Over time, however, we saw signs of adjustment (e.g., yelling and cursing increased on the third day and again on the tenth). The children, especially, seemed to enjoy participating in the project. They reported it made them feel "special." They were visibly happy to see the fieldworkers arrive and reluctant to let them leave. The working-class and poor black boys were more comfortable with the black male fieldworkers than with the white female ones, especially at first.[13] Overall, however, family members reported in exit interviews that they had not changed their behavior significantly, or

they mentioned very specific alterations (e.g., "the house got cleaner").

A NOTE ON CLASS

I undertook field observations to develop an intensive, realistic portrait of family life. Although I deliberately focused on only 12 families, I wanted to compare children across gender and race. Adopting the fine-grained differentiations characteristic of current neo-Marxist and neo-Weberian empirical studies was not tenable.[14] Further limitations were imposed by the school populations at the sites I selected. Very few students were children of employers or of self-employed workers. I decided to focus exclusively on those whose parents were employees. Authority in the workplace and "credential barriers" are the criteria most commonly used to differentiate within this heterogeneous group. I assigned the families to a working-class or middle-class category based on detailed information that each of the employed adults provided about the work they did, the nature of the organization that employed them, and their educational credentials. I also included a category traditionally excluded from class groupings: families not involved in the labor market. In the first school I studied, many children were from households supported by public assistance. Omitting them would have restricted the scope of the study arbitrarily.[15]

The three class categories conceal important internal variations. The Williams family (black) and the Tallinger family (white) have very high incomes, both in excess of $175,000; the median income among the middle-class parents was much lower.[16] Income differences among the middle-class families were not associated with differences in childrearing methods. Moreover, no other data in the study showed compelling intraclass divisions. I consider the use of one term—middle class—to be reasonable.

CONCERTED CULTIVATION AND NATURAL GROWTH

The interviews and observations suggested that crucial aspects of family life cohered. Within the concerted cultivation and accomplishment of natural growth approaches, three key dimensions may be distinguished: the organization of daily life, the use of language, and social connections. ("Interventions in institutions" and "consequences" are addressed later in the paper.) These dimensions do not capture all important parts of family life, but they do incorporate core aspects of childrearing (Table 2). Moreover, our field observations revealed that behaviors and activities related to these dimensions dominated the rhythms of family life.

Conceptually, the organization of daily life and the use of language are crucial dimensions.

Both must be present for the family to be described as engaging in one childrearing approach rather than the other. Social connections are significant but less conceptually essential.

All three aspects of childrearing were intricately woven into the families' daily routines, but rarely remarked upon. As part of everyday practice, they were invisible to parents and children. Analytically, however, they are useful means for comparing and contrasting ways in which social class differences shape the character of family life. I now examine two families in terms of these three key dimensions. I "control" for race and gender and contrast the lives of two black boys—one from an (upper) middle-class family and one from a family on public assistance. I could have focused on almost any of the other 12 children, but this pair seemed optimal, given the limited

Table 2. Summary of Differences in Childrearing Approaches

	Childrearing Approach	
Dimension Observed	Concerted Cultivation	Accomplishment of Natural Growth
Key elements of each approach	Parent actively fosters and assesses child's talents, opinions, and skills	Parent cares for child and allows child to grow
Organization of daily life	Multiple child leisure activities are orchestrated by adults	Child "hangs out" particularly with kin
Language use	Reasoning/directives	Directives
	Child contestation of adult statements	Rare for child to question or challenge adults
	Extended negotiations between parents and child	General acceptance by child of directives
Social connections	Weak extended family ties	Strong extended family ties
	Child often in homogenous age groupings	Child often in heterogeneous age groupings
Interventions in institutions	Criticisms and interventions on behalf of child	Dependence on institutions
	Training of child to intervene on his or her own behalf	Sense of powerlessness and frustration
		Conflict between childrearing practices at home and at school
Consequences	Emerging sense of entitlement on the part of the child	Emerging sense of constraint on the part of the child

number of studies reporting on black middle-class families, as well as the aspect of my argument that suggests that race is less important than class in shaping childrearing patterns.

DEVELOPING ALEXANDER WILLIAMS

Alexander Williams and his parents live in a predominantly black middle-class neighborhood. Their six-bedroom house is worth about $150,000.[17] Alexander is an only child. Both parents grew up in small towns in the South, and both are from large families. His father, a tall, handsome man, is a very successful trial lawyer who earns about $125,000 annually in a small firm specializing in medical malpractice cases. Two weeks each month, he works very long hours (from about 5:30 A.M. until midnight) preparing for trials. The other two weeks, his workday ends around 6:00 p.m. He rarely travels out of town. Alexander's mother, Christina, is a positive, bubbly woman with freckles and long, black, wavy hair.[18] A high-level manager in a major corporation, she has a corner office, a personal secretary, and responsibilities for other offices across the nation. She tries to limit her travel, but at least once a month she takes an overnight trip.

Alexander is a charming, inquisitive boy with a winsome smile. Ms. Williams is pleased that Alexander seems interested in so many things:

> Alexander is a joy. He's a gift to me. He's very energetic, very curious, loving, caring person, that, um…is outgoing and who, uh, really loves to be with people. And who loves to explore, and loves to read and…just do a lot of fun things.

The private school Alexander attends[19] has an on-site after-school program. There, he participates in several activities and receives guitar lessons and photography instruction.

Organization of Daily Life. Alexander is busy with activities during the week and on weekends (Table 3). His mother describes their Saturday morning routine. The day starts early with a private piano lesson for Alexander downtown, a 20-minute drive from the house:

> It's an 8:15 class. But for me, it was a tradeoff. I am very adamant about Saturday morning TV. I don't know what it contributes. So…it was…um…either stay at home and fight on a Saturday morning [laughs] or go do something constructive.…Now Saturday mornings are pretty booked up. You know, the piano lesson, and then straight to choir for a couple of hours. So, he has a very full schedule.

Ms. Williams's vehement opposition to television is based on her view of what Alexander needs to grow and thrive. She objects to TV's passivity and feels it is her obligation to help her son cultivate his talents. Sometimes Alexander complains that "my mother signs me up for everything!" Generally, however, he likes his activities. He says they make him feel "special," and without them life would be "boring." His sense of time is thoroughly entwined with his activities: He feels disoriented when his schedule is not full. This unease is clear in the following field-note excerpt. The family is driving home from a Back-to-School night. The next morning, Ms. Williams will leave for a work-related day trip and will not return until late at night. Alexander is grumpy because he has nothing planned for the next day. He wants to have a friend over, but his mother rebuffs him. Whining, he wonders what he will do. His mother, speaking tersely, says:

> You have piano and guitar. You'll have some free time. [Pause] I think you'll survive for one night. [Alexander does not respond but seems mad. It is quiet for the rest of the trip home.]

Alexander's parents believe his activities provide a wide range of benefits important for his development. In discussing Alexander's piano lessons, Mr. Williams notes that as a Suzuki student,[20] Alexander is already able to read music. Speculating about more diffuse benefits of Alexander's involvement with piano, he says:

awareness of who Beethoven was. And is that Bach or Mozart? I don't know the difference between the two! I don't know Baroque from Classical—but he does. How can that not be a benefit in later life?

> I don't see how any kid's adolescence and adulthood could not but be enhanced by an

Table 3. Participation in Activities Outside of School: Boys

Boy's Name/Race/Class	Activities Organized by Adults	Informal Activities
Middle Class		
Garrett Tallinger (white)	Soccer team	Plays with siblings in yard
	Traveling soccer team	Watches television
	Baseball team	Plays computer games
	Basketball team (summer)	Overnights with friends
	Swim team	
	Piano	
	Saxophone (through school)	
Alexander Williams (black)	Soccer team	Restricted television
	Baseball team	Plays outside occasionally
	Community choir	with two other boys
	Church choir	Visits friends from school
	Sunday school	
	Piano (Suzuki)	
	School plays	
	Guitar (through school)	
Working Class		
Billy Yanelli (white)	Baseball team	Watches television
		Visits relatives
		Rides bike
		Plays outside in the street
		Hangs out with neighborhood kids
Tyrec Taylor (black)	Football team	Watches television
	Vacation Bible School	Plays outside in the street
	Sunday school (off/on)	Rides bikes with neighborhood
		boys
		Visit relatives
		Goes to swimming pool
Poor		
Karl Greeley (white)	Goes to swimming pool	Watches television
	Walks dogs with neighbor	Plays Nintendo
		Plays with siblings
Harold McAllister (black)	Bible study in neighbor's	Visits relatives
	house (occasionally)	Plays ball with neighborhood kids
	Bible camp (1 week)	Watches television
		Watches videos

I'm convinced that this rich experience will make him a better person, a better citizen, a better husband, a better father—certainly a better student.

Ms. Williams sees music as building her son's "confidence" and his "poise." In interviews and casual conversation, she stresses "exposure." She believes it is her responsibility to broaden Alexander's worldview. Childhood activities provide a learning ground for important life. skills:

> Sports provide great opportunities to learn how to be competitive. Learn how to accept defeat, you know. Learn how to accept winning, you know, in a gracious way. Also it gives him the opportunity to learn leadership skills and how to be a team player....Sports really provides a lot of really great opportunities.

Alexander's schedule is constantly shifting; some activities wind down and others start up. Because the schedules of sports practices and games are issued no sooner than the start of the new season, advance planning is rarely possible. Given the sheer number of Alexander's activities, events inevitably overlap. Some activities, though short-lived, are extremely time consuming. Alexander's school play, for example, requires rehearsals three nights the week before the opening. In addition, in choosing activities, the Williamses have an added concern—the group's racial balance. Ms. Williams prefers that Alexander not be the only black child at events. Typically, one or two other black boys are involved, but the groups are predominantly white and the activities take place in predominantly white residential neighborhoods. Alexander is, however, part of his church's youth choir and Sunday School, activities in which all participants are black.

Many activities involve competition. Alex must audition for his solo performance in the school play, for example. Similarly, parents and children alike understand that participation on "A," "B," or "All-Star" sports teams signal different skill levels. Like other middle-class children in the study, Alexander seems to enjoy public performance. According to a field note, after his solo at a musical production in front of over 200 people, he appeared "contained, pleased, aware of the attention he's receiving."

Alexander's commitments do not consume *all* his free time. Still, his life is defined by a series of deadlines and schedules interwoven with a series of activities that are organized and controlled by adults rather than children. Neither he nor his parents see this as troublesome.

Language Use. Like other middle-class families, the Williamses often engage in conversation that promotes reasoning and negotiation. An excerpt from a field note (describing an exchange between Alexander and his mother during a car ride home after summer camp) shows the kind of pointed questions middle-class parents ask children. Ms. Williams is not just eliciting information. She is also giving Alexander the opportunity to develop and practice verbal skills, including how to summarize, clarify, and amplify information:

> As she drives, [Ms. Williams] asks Alex, "So, how was your day?"
>
> Alex: "Okay. I had hot dogs today, but they were burned! They were all black!"
>
> Mom: "Oh, great. You shouldn't have eaten any."
>
> Alex: "They weren't *all* black, only half were. The rest were regular."
>
> Mom: "Oh, okay. What was that game you were playing this morning?..."
>
> Alex: "It was [called] 'Whatcha doin?'"
>
> Mom: "How do you play?"

Alexander explains the game elaborately—fieldworker doesn't quite follow. Mom asks Alex questions throughout his explanation, saying, "Oh, I see," when he answers. She asks him about another game she saw them play; he again explains….She continues to prompt and encourage him with small giggles in the back of her throat as he elaborates.

Expressions of interest in children's activities often lead to negotiations over small, home-based matters. During the same car ride, Ms. Williams tries to adjust the dinner menu to suit Alexander:

> Alexander says, "I don't want hot dogs tonight."
>
> Mom: "Oh? Because you had them for lunch."
>
> Alexander nods.
>
> Mom: "Well, I can fix something else and save the hot dogs for tomorrow night."
>
> Alex: "But I don't want any pork chops either."
>
> Mom: "Well, Alexander, we need to eat something. Why didn't you have hamburgers today?"
>
> Alex: "They don't have them any more at the snack bar."
>
> Mom asks Alexander if he's ok, if he wants a snack. Alexander says he's ok. Mom asks if he's sure he doesn't want a bag of chips?

Not all middle-class parents are as attentive to their children's needs as this mother, and none are *always* interested in negotiating. But a general pattern of reasoning and accommodating is common.

Social Connections. Mr. and Ms. Williams consider themselves very close to their extended families. Because the Williams's aging parents live in the South, visiting requires a plane trip. Ms. Williams takes Alexander with her to see his grandparents twice a year. She speaks on the phone with her parents at least once a week and also calls her siblings several times a week. Mr. Williams talks with his mother regularly by phone (he has less contact with his

stepfather). With pride, he also mentions his niece, whose Ivy League education he is helping to finance.

Interactions with cousins are not normally a part of Alexander's leisure time. (As I explain below, other middle-class children did not see cousins routinely either, even when they lived nearby.) Nor does he often play with neighborhood children. The huge homes on the Williams's street are occupied mainly by couples without children. Most of Alexander's playmates come from his classroom or his organized activities. Because most of his school events, church life, and assorted activities are organized by the age (and sometimes gender) of the participants, Alexander interacts almost exclusively with children his own age, usually boys. Adult-organized activities thus define the context of his social life.

Mr. and Ms. Williams are aware that they allocate a sizable portion of time to Alexander's activities. What they stress, however, is the time they *hold back*. They mention activities the family has chosen *not* to take on (such as traveling soccer).

Summary. Overall, Alexander's parents engaged in concerted cultivation. They fostered their son's growth through involvement in music, church, athletics, and academics. They talked with him at length, seeking his opinions and encouraging his ideas. Their approach involved considerable direct expenses (e.g., the cost of lessons and equipment) and large indirect expenses (e.g., the cost of taking time off from work, driving to practices, and foregoing adult leisure activities). Although Mr. and Ms. Williams acknowledged the importance of extended family, Alexander spent relatively little time with relatives. His social interactions occurred almost exclusively with children his own age and with adults. Alexander's many activities significantly shaped the organization of daily life in the family. Both parents' leisure time was tailored to their son's commitments.

Mr. and Ms. Williams felt that the strategies they cultivated with Alexander would result in his having the best possible chance at a happy and productive life. They couldn't imagine themselves *not* investing large amounts of time and energy in their son's life. But, as I explain in the next section, which focuses on a black boy from a poor family, other parents held a different view.

SUPPORTING THE NATURAL GROWTH OF HAROLD MCALLISTER

Harold McAllister, a large, stocky boy with a big smile, is from a poor black family. He lives with his mother and his 8-year-old sister, Alexis, in a large apartment. Two cousins often stay overnight. Harold's 16-year-old sister and 18-year-old brother usually live with their grandmother, but sometimes they stay at the McAllister's home. Ms. McAllister, a high school graduate, relies on public assistance (AFDC). Hank, Harold and Alexis's father, is a mechanic. He and Ms. McAllister have never married. He visits regularly, sometimes weekly, stopping by after work to watch television or nap. Harold (but not Alexis) sometimes travels across town by bus to spend the weekend with Hank.

The McAllister's apartment is in a public housing project near a busy street. The complex consists of rows of two- and three-story brick units. The buildings, blocky and brown, have small yards enclosed by concrete and wood fences. Large floodlights are mounted on the corners of the buildings, and wide concrete sidewalks cut through the spaces between units. The ground is bare in many places; paper wrappers and glass litter the area.

Inside the apartment, life is humorous and lively, with family members and kin sharing in the daily routines. Ms. McAllister discussed, disdainfully, mothers who are on drugs or who abuse alcohol and do not "look after" their children. Indeed, the previous year Ms. McAllister called Child Protective Services to report her twin sister, a cocaine addict, because she was neglecting her children. Ms. McAllister is actively involved in her twin's daughters' lives. Her two nephews also frequently stay with her. Overall, she sees herself as a capable mother who takes care of her children and her extended family.

Organization of Daily Life. Much of Harold's life and the lives of his family members revolve around home. Project residents often sit outside in lawn chairs or on front stoops, drinking beer, talking, and watching children play. During summer, windows are frequently left open, allowing breezes to waft through the units and providing vantage points from which residents can survey the neighborhood. A large deciduous tree in front of the McAllister's apartment unit provides welcome shade in the summer's heat.

Harold loves sports. He is particularly fond of basketball, but he also enjoys football, and he follows televised professional sports closely. Most afternoons, he is either inside watching television or outside playing ball. He tosses a football with cousins and boys from the neighboring units and organizes pick-up basketball games. Sometimes he and his friends use a rusty, bare hoop hanging from a telephone pole in the housing project; other times, they string up an old, blue plastic crate as a makeshift hoop. One obstacle to playing sports, however, is a shortage of equipment. Balls are costly to replace, especially given the rate at which they disappear—theft of children's play equipment, including balls and bicycles, is an ongoing problem. During a field observation, Harold asks his mother if she knows where the ball is. She replies with some vehemence, "They stole the blue and yellow ball, and they stole the green ball, and they stole the other ball."

Hunting for balls is a routine part of Harold's leisure time. One June day, with the temperature and humidity in the high 80s, Harold and his cousin Tyrice (and a fieldworker) wander around the housing project for about an hour, trying to find a basketball:

> We head to the other side of the complex. On the way....we passed four guys sitting on the step. Their ages were 9 to 13 years. They had a radio blaring. Two were working intently on fixing a flat bike tire. The other two were dribbling a basketball.

> Harold: "Yo! What's up, ya'll."

> Group: "What's up, Har." "What's up? "Yo."

> They continued to work on the tire and dribble the ball. As we walked down the hill, Harold asked, "Yo, could I use your ball?"

> The guy responded, looking up from the tire, "Naw, man. Ya'll might lose it."

Harold, Tyrice, and the fieldworker walk to another part of the complex, heading for a makeshift basketball court where they hope to find a game in progress:

> No such luck. Harold enters an apartment directly in front of the makeshift court. The door was open....Harold came back. "No ball. I guess I gotta go back."

The pace of life for Harold and his friends ebbs and flows with the children's interests and family obligations. The day of the basketball search, for example, after spending time listening to music and looking at baseball cards, the children join a water fight Tyrice instigates. It is a lively game, filled with laughter and with efforts to get the adults next door wet (against their wishes). When the game winds down, the kids ask their mother for money, receive it, and then walk to a store to buy chips and soda. They chat with another young boy and then amble back to the apartment, eating as they walk. Another afternoon, almost two weeks later, the children—Harold, two of his cousins, and two children from the neighborhood—and

the fieldworker play basketball on a makeshift court in the street (using the fieldworker's ball). As Harold bounces the ball, neighborhood children of all ages wander through the space.

Thus, Harold's life is more free-flowing and more child-directed than is Alexander Williams's. The pace of any given day is not so much planned as emergent, reflecting child-based interests and activities. Parents intervene in specific areas, such as personal grooming, meals, and occasional chores, but they do not continuously direct and monitor their children's leisure activities. Moreover, the leisure activities Harold and other working-class and poor children pursue require them to develop a repertoire of skills for dealing with much older and much younger children as well as with neighbors and relatives.

Language Use. Life in the working class and poor families in the study flows smoothly without extended verbal discussions. The amount of talking varies, but overall, it is considerably less than occurs in the middle-class homes.[21] Ms. McAllister jokes with the children and discusses what is on television. But she does not appear to cultivate conversation by asking the children questions or by drawing them out. Often she is brief and direct in her remarks. For instance, she coordinates the use of the apartment's only bathroom by using one-word directives. She sends the children (there are almost always at least four children home at once) to wash up by pointing to a child, saying one word, "bathroom," and handing him or her a washcloth. Wordlessly, the designated child gets up and goes to the bathroom to take a shower.

Similarly, although Ms. McAllister will listen to the children's complaints about school, she does not draw them out on these issues or seek to determine details, as Ms. Williams would. For instance, at the start of the new school year, when I ask Harold about his teacher, he tells me she is "mean" and that "she lies." Ms. McAllister, washing dishes, listens to her son, but she does not encourage Harold to support his opinion about his new teacher with more examples, nor does she mention any concerns of her own. Instead, she asks about last year's teacher, "What was the name of that man teacher?" Harold says, "Mr. Lindsey?" She says, "No, the other one." He says, "Mr. Terrene." Ms. McAllister smiles and says, "Yeah. I liked him." Unlike Alexander's mother, she seems content with a brief exchange of information.

Social Connections. Children, especially boys, frequently play outside. The number of potential playmates in Harold's world is vastly higher than the number in Alexander's neighborhood. When a fieldworker stops to count heads, she finds 40 children of elementary school age residing in the nearby rows of apartments. With so many children nearby, Harold could choose to play only with others his own age. In fact, though, he often hangs out with older and younger children and with his cousins (who are close to his age).

The McAllister family, like other poor and working-class families, is involved in a web of extended kin. As noted earlier, Harold's older siblings and his two male cousins often spend the night at the McAllister home. Celebrations such as birthdays involve relatives almost exclusively. Party guests are not, as in middle-class families, friends from school or from extra-curricular activities. Birthdays are celebrated enthusiastically, with cake and special food to mark the occasion; presents, however, are not offered. Similarly, Christmas at Harold's house featured a tree and special food but no presents. At these and other family events, the older children voluntarily look after the younger ones: Harold plays with his 16-month-old niece, and his cousins carry around the younger babies.

The importance of family ties—and the contingent nature of life in the McAllister's world—is clear in the response Alexis offers when asked what she would do if she were given a million dollars:

Oh, boy! I'd buy my brother, my sister, my uncle, my aunt, my nieces and my nephews, and my grandpop, and my grandmom, and my mom, and my dad, and my friends, not my friends, but mostly my best friend—I'd buy them all clothes…and sneakers. And I'd buy some food, and I'd buy my mom some food, and I'd get my brothers and my sisters gifts for their birthdays.

Summary. In a setting where everyone, including the children, was acutely aware of the lack of money, the McAllister family made do. Ms. McAllister rightfully saw herself as a very capable mother. She was a strong, positive influence in the lives of the children she looked after. Still, the contrast with Ms. Williams is striking. Ms. McAllister did not seem to think that Harold's opinions needed to be cultivated and developed. She, like most parents in the working-class and poor families, drew strong and clear boundaries between adults and children. Adults gave directions to children. Children were given freedom to play informally unless they were needed for chores. Extended family networks were deemed important and trustworthy.

THE INTERSECTION OF RACE AND CLASS IN FAMILY LIFE

I expected race to powerfully shape children's daily schedules, but this was not evident (also see Conley 1999; Pattillo-McCoy 1999). This is not to say that race is unimportant. Black parents were particularly concerned with monitoring their children's lives outside the home for signs of racial problems.[22] Black middle-class fathers, especially, were likely to stress the importance of their sons understanding "what it means to be a black man in this society" (J. Hochschild 1995). Mr. Williams, in summarizing how he and his wife orient Alexander, said:

[We try to] teach him that race unfortunately is the most important aspect of our national life. I mean people look at other people and they see a color first. But that isn't going to define who he is. He will do his best. He will succeed, despite racism. And I think he lives his life that way.

Alexander's parents were acutely aware of the potential significance of race in his life. Both were adamant, however, that race should not be used as "an excuse" for not striving to succeed. Mr. Williams put it this way:

I discuss how race impacts on my life as an attorney, and I discuss how race will impact on his life. The one teaching that he takes away from this is that he is never to use discrimination as an excuse for not doing his best.

Thus far, few incidents of overt racism had occurred in Alexander's life, as his mother noted:

Those situations have been far and few between....I mean, I can count them on my fingers.

Still, Ms. Williams recounted with obvious pain an incident at a birthday party Alexander had attended as a preschooler. The grandparents of the birthday child repeatedly asked, "Who is that boy?" and exclaimed, "He's so dark!" Such experiences fueled the Williams's resolve always to be "cautious":

We've never been, uh, parents who drop off their kid anywhere. We've always gone with him. And even now, I go in and—to school in the morning—and check [in]....The school environment, we've watched very closely.

Alexander's parents were not equally optimistic about the chances for racial equality in this country. Ms. Williams felt strongly that, especially while Alexander was young, his father should not voice his pessimism. Mr. Williams complained that this meant he had to "watch" what he said to Alexander about race relations. Still, both parents agreed about the need to be vigilant regarding potential racial problems in Alexander's life. Other black parents reported experiencing racial prejudice and expressed a similar commitment to vigilance.

Issues surrounding the prospect of growing up black and male in this society were threaded through Alexander's life in ways that had no equivalent among his middle-class, white male peers. Still, in fourth grade there were no signs of racial experiences having "taken hold" the way that they might as Alexander ages. In terms of the number and kind of activities he participated in, his life was very similar to that of Garrett Tallinger, his white counterpart (see Table 3). That both sets of parents were fully committed to a strategy of concentrated cultivation was apparent in the number of adult-organized activities the boys were enrolled in, the hectic pace of family life, and the stress on reasoning in parent-child negotiations. Likewise, the research assistants and I saw no striking differences in the ways in which white parents and black parents in the working-class and poor homes socialized their children.

Others (Fordham and Ogbu 1986) have found that in middle school and high school, adolescent peer groups often draw sharp racial boundaries, a pattern not evident among this study's third- and fourth-grade participants (but sometimes present among their older siblings). Following Tatum (1997:52), I attribute this to the children's relatively young ages (also see "Race in America," *The New York Times,* June 25, 2000, p. 1). In sum, in the broader society, key aspects of daily life were shaped by racial segregation and discrimination. But in terms of enrollment in organized activities, language use, and social connections, the largest differences between the families we observed were across social class, not racial groups.

DIFFERENCES IN CULTURAL PRACTICES ACROSS THE TOTAL SAMPLE

The patterns observed among the Williams and McAllister families occurred among others in the 12-family subsample and across the larger group of 88 children. Frequently, they also echoed established patterns in the literature. These patterns highlight not only the amount of time spent on activities but also the quality of family life and the ways in which key dimensions of childrearing intertwine.

ORGANIZATION OF DAILY LIFE

In the study as a whole, the rhythms of family life differed by social class. Working-class and poor children spent most of their free time in informal play; middle-class children took part in many adult-organized activities designed to develop their individual talents and interests. For the 88 children, I calculated an average score for the most common adult-directed, organized activities[23] based on parents' answers to interview questions.[24] Middle-class children averaged 4.9 current activities ($N = 36$), working-class children averaged 2.5 activities ($N = 26$), and poor children averaged 1.5 ($N = 26$).[25] Black middle-class children had slightly more activities than white middle-class children, largely connected to more church involvement, with an average of 5.2 ($N = 18$) compared with 4.6 activities for whites ($N = 18$). The racial difference was very modest in the working-class group (2.8 activities for black children [$N = 12$] and 2.3 for white children [$N = 14$]) and the poor group (1.6 activities for black children [$N = 14$] and 1.4 for white children [$N = 12$]). Middle-class boys had slightly more activities than middle-class girls (5.1 versus 4.7, $N = 18$ for both) but gender did not make a difference for the other classes. The type of activity did however. Girls tended to participate in dance, music, and Scouts, and to be less active in sports. This pattern of social class differences in activities is comparable to other, earlier reports (Medrich et al. 1982). Hofferth and Sandberg's (2001a, 2000b) recent research using a representative national sample suggests that the number of children's organized activities increases with parents' education and that children's involvement in organized activities has risen in recent decades.

The dollar cost of children's organized activities was significant, particularly when families had more than one child. Cash outlays included paying the instructors and coaches who gave lessons, purchasing uniforms and performance attire, paying for tournament admission and travel to and from tournaments, and covering hotel and food costs for overnight stays. Summer camps also were expensive. At my request, the Tallingers added up the costs for Garrett's organized activities. The total was over $4,000 per year. Recent reports of parents' expenditures for children's involvement in a single sport (e.g., hockey) are comparably high (Schemari 2002). Children's activities consumed time as well as money, co-opting parents' limited leisure hours.

The study also uncovered differences in how much time children spent in activities controlled by adults. Take the schedule of Melanie Handlon, a white middle-class girl in the fourth grade (see Table 4). Between December 8 and December 24, Melanie had a piano lesson each Monday, Girl Scouts each Thursday, a special Girl Scout event one Monday night, a special holiday musical performance at school one Tuesday night, two orthodontist appointments, five special rehearsals for the church Christmas pageant, and regular Sunday commitments (an early church service, Sunday

Table 3. Participation in Activities Outside of School: Boys

Girl's Name/Race/Class	Activities Organized by Adults	Informal Activities
Middle Class		
Melanie Handlon (white)	Girl Scouts	Restricted television
	Piano	Plays outside with neighborhood
	Sunday school	kids
	Church	Bakes cookies with mother
	Church pageant	Swims (not on swim team)
	Violin (through school)	Listens to music
	Softball team	
Stacey Marshall (black)	Gymnastics lessons	Watches television
	Gymnastic teams	Plays outside
	Church	Visits friends from school
	Sunday school	Rides bike
	Youth choir	
Working Class		
Wendy Driver (white)	Catholic education (CCD)	Watches television
	Dance lessons	Visits relatives
	School choir	Does housework
		Rides bike
		Plays outside in the street
		Hangs out with cousins
Jessica Irwin (black father/	Church	Restricted television
white mother)	Sunday school	Reads
	Saturday art class	Plays outside with neighborhood
	Schoolband	kids
		Visit relatives
Poor		
Katie Brindle (white)	School choir	Watches television
	Friday evening church group	Visits relatives
	(rarely)	Plays with Barbies
		Rides bike
		Plays with neighborhood kids
Tara Carroll (black)	Church	Watches television
	Sunday school	Visits relatives
		Plays with dolls
		Plays Nintendo
		Plays with neighborhood kids

school, and youth choir). On weekdays she spent several hours after school struggling with her homework as her mother coached her step-by-step through the worksheets. The amount of time Melanie spent in situations where her movements were controlled by adults was typical of middle-class children in the study.

The schedule of Katie Brindle, a white fourth-grader from a poor family, contrasts sharply, showing few organized activities between December 2 and 24. She sang in the school choir. This involved one after-school rehearsal on Wednesdays; she walked home by herself after these rehearsals. Occasionally, Katie attended a Christian youth group on Friday nights (i.e., December 3). Significantly, all her activities were free. She wanted to enroll in ballet classes, but they were prohibitively expensive. What Katie did have was unstructured leisure time. Usually, she came home after school and then played outside with other children in the neighborhood or watched television. She also regularly visited her grandmother and her cousins, who lived a few minutes away by bus or car. She often spent weekend nights at her grandmother's house. Overall, Katie's life was centered in and around home. Compared with the middle-class children in the study, her life moved at a dramatically less hectic pace. This pattern was characteristic of the other working-class and poor families we interviewed.

In addition to these activities, television provided a major source of leisure entertainment. All children in the study spent at least some free time watching TV, but there were differences in when, what, and how much they watched. Most middle-class parents we interviewed characterized television as actually or potentially harmful to children; many stressed that they preferred their children to read for entertainment. Middle-class parents often had rules about the amount of time children could spend watching television.[26] These concerns did not surface in interviews with working-class and poor parents. Indeed, Ms. Yanelli, a white working-class mother, objected to restricting a child's access to television, noting, "You know, you learn so much from television." Working-class and poor parents did monitor the content of programs and made some shows off-limits for children. The television itself, however, was left on almost continuously (also see Robinson and Godbey 1997).

LANGUAGE USE

The social class differences in language use we observed were similar to those reported by others (see Bernstein 1971; Hart and Risley 1995; Heath 1983). In middle-class homes, parents placed a tremendous emphasis on reasoning. They also drew out their children's views on specific subjects. Middle-class parents relied on directives for matters of health and safety, but most other aspects of daily life were potentially open to negotiation: Discussions arose over what children wore in the morning, what they ate, where they sat, and how they spent their time. Not all middle-class children were equally talkative, however. In addition, in observations, mothers exhibited more willingness to engage children in prolonged discussions than did fathers. The latter tended to be less engaged with children overall and less accepting of disruptions (A. Hochschild 1989). In working-class and poor homes, most parents did not focus on developing their children's opinions, judgments, and observations. When children volunteered information, parents would listen, but typically they did not follow up with questions or comments. In the field note excerpt below, Wendy Driver shares her new understanding of sin with the members of her white working-class family. She is sitting in the living room with her brother (Willie), her mother, and her mother's live-in boyfriend (Mack). Everyone is watching television:

Wendy asks Willie: "Do you know what mortal sin is?"

Willie: "No."

Wendy asks Mom: "Do you know what mortal sin is?"

Mom: "What is it?"

Wendy asks Mack: "Do you know what it is?"

Mack: "No."

Mom: "Tell us what it is. You're the one who went to CCD [Catholic religious education classes]."

Wendy: "It's when you know something's wrong and you do it anyway."

No one acknowledged Wendy's comment. Wendy's mother and Mack looked at her while she gave her explanation of mortal sin, then looked back at the TV.

Wendy's family is conversationally cooperative, but unlike the Williamses, for example, no one here perceives the moment as an opportunity to further develop Wendy's vocabulary or to help her exercise her critical thinking skills.

Negotiations between parents and children in working-class and poor families were infrequent. Parents tended to use firm directives and they expected prompt, positive responses. Children who ignored parental instructions could expect physical punishment. Field notes from an evening in the home of the white, working-class Yanelli family capture one example of this familiar dynamic. It is past 8:00 p.m. Ms. Yanelli, her son Billy, and the fieldworker are playing *Scrabble*. Mr. Yanelli and a friend are absorbed in a game of chess. Throughout the evening, Billy and Ms. Yanelli have been at odds. She feels Billy has not been listening to her. Ms. Yanelli wants her son to stop playing *Scrabble,* take a shower, and go to bed.

Mom: "Billy, shower. I don't care if you cry, screams."

Billy: "We're not done with the Scrabble game."

Mom: "You're done. Finish your homework earlier." That evening, Billy had not finished his homework until 8:00 p.m. Billy remains seated.

Mom: "Come on! Tomorrow you've got a big day." Billy does not move.

Mom goes into the other room and gets a brown leather belt. She hits Billy twice on the leg.

Mom: "Get up right now! Tomorrow I can't get you up in the morning. Get up right now!"

Billy gets up and runs up the steps.

Ms. Yanelli's disciplinary approach is very different from that of the middle-class parents we observed. Like most working-class and poor parents we observed, she is directive and her instructions are nonnegotiable ("Billy, shower" and "You're done."). Using a belt may seem harsh, but it is neither a random nor irrational form of punishment here. Ms. Yanelli gave Billy notice of her expectations and she offered an explanation (it's late, and tomorrow he has "a big day"). She turned to physical discipline as a resource when she felt Billy was not sufficiently responsive.[27]

SOCIAL CONNECTIONS

We also observed class differences in the context of children's social relations. Across the sample of 88 families, middle-class children's involvement in adult-organized activities led to mainly weak social ties. Soccer, photography classes, swim team, and so on typically take place in 6 to 8 week blocks, and participant turnover rates are relatively high. Equally important, middle-class children's commitment to organized activities generally preempted visits with extended family. Some did not have relatives who lived nearby, but even among those who did, children's schedules made it difficult to organize and attend regular extended-family gatherings. Many of the middle-class children visited with relatives only on major holidays.[28]

Similarly, middle-class parents tended to forge weak rather than strong ties. Most reported having social networks that included professionals: 93 percent of the sample of middle-class parents had a friend or relative who was a teacher, compared with 43 percent of working-class parents and 36 percent of poor families. For a physician friend or relative, the pattern was comparable (70 percent versus 14 percent and 18 percent, respectively).[29] Relationships such as these are not as deep as family ties, but they are a valuable resource when parents face a challenge in childrearing.

Working-class and poor families were much less likely to include professionals in their social networks but were much more likely than their middle-class counterparts to see or speak with kin daily. Children regularly interacted in casually assembled, heterogeneous age groups that included cousins as well as neighborhood children. As others have shown (Lever 1988), we observed gender differences in children's activities. Although girls sometimes ventured outside to ride bikes and play ball games, compared with boys they were more likely to stay inside the house to play. Whether inside or outside, the girls, like the boys, played in loose coalitions of kin and neighbors and created their own activities.

Interactions with representatives of major social institutions (the police, courts, schools, and government agencies) also appeared significantly shaped by social class. Members of white *and* black working-class and poor families offered spontaneous comments about their distrust of these officials. For example, one white working-class mother described an episode in which the police had come to her home looking for her ex-husband (a drug user). She recalled officers "breaking down the door" and terrifying her eldest son, then only three years old. Another white working-class mother reported that her father had been arrested. Although by all accounts in good spirits, he had been found dead in the city jail, an alleged suicide. Children listened to and appeared to absorb remarks such as these.

Fear was a key reason for the unease with which working class and poor families approached formal (and some informal) encounters with officials. Some parents worried that authorities would "come and take our kids away." One black mother on public assistance interviewed as part of the larger study was outraged that school personnel had allowed her daughter to come home from school one winter day without her coat. She noted that if she had allowed that to happen, "the school" would have reported her to Child Protective Services for child abuse. Wendy Driver's mother (white working-class) complained that she felt obligated to take Wendy to the doctor, even when she knew nothing was wrong, because Wendy had gone to see the school nurse. Ms. Driver felt she had to be extra careful because she didn't want "them" to come and take her kids away.[30] Strikingly, no middle class parents mention similar fears about the power of dominant institutions.

Obviously, these three dimensions of childrearing patterns—the organization of daily life, language use, and social connections—do not capture all the class advantages parents pass to their children. The middle-class children in the study enjoyed relatively privileged lives. They lived in large houses, some had swimming pools in their backyards, most had bedrooms of their own, all had many toys, and computers were common. These children also had broad horizons. They flew in airplanes, they traveled out of state for vacations, they often traveled an hour or two from home to take part in their activities, and they knew older children whose extracurricular activities involved international travel.

Still, in some important areas, variations among families did *not* appear to be linked to social class. Some of the middle-class children had learning problems. And, despite their relatively privileged social-class position, neither middle-class children nor their parents were insulated from the realities of serious illness and premature death among family and friends. In addition, some elements of family life seemed relatively immune to social class, including how orderly and tidy the households were. In one white middle-class family, the house was regularly in a state of disarray. The house was cleaned and tidied for a Christmas Eve gathering, but it returned to its normal state shortly thereafter. By contrast, a black middle-class family's home was always extremely tidy, as were some, but not all, of the working-class and poor homes. Nor did certain aspects of parenting, particularly the degree to which mothers appeared to "mean what they said," seem linked to social class. Families also differed with respect to the presence or absence of a sense of humor among individual members, levels of anxiety, and signs of stress-related illnesses they exhibited. Finally, there were significant differences in temperament and disposition among children in the same family. These variations are useful reminders that social class is not fully a determinant of the character of children's lives.

IMPACT OF CHILDREARING STRATEGIES ON INTERACTIONS WITH INSTITUTIONS

Social scientists sometimes emphasize the importance of reshaping parenting practices to improve children's chances of success. Explicitly and implicitly, the literature exhorts parents to comply with the views of professionals (Bronfenbrenner 1966; Epstein 2001; Heimer and Staffen 1998). Such calls for compliance do not, however, reconcile professionals' judgments regarding the intrinsic value of current childrearing standards with the evidence of the historical record, which shows regular shifts in such standards over time (Aries 1962; Wrigley 1989; Zelizer 1985). Nor are the stratified, and limited, possibilities for success in the broader society examined.

I now follow the families out of their homes and into encounters with representatives of dominant institutions—institutions that are directed by middle-class professionals. Again, I focus on Alexander Williams and Harold McAllister. (Institutional experiences are summarized in Table 2.) Across all social classes, parents and children interacted with teachers and school officials, healthcare professionals, and assorted government officials. Although they often addressed similar problems (e.g., learning disabilities, asthma, traffic violations), they typically did not achieve similar resolutions. The pattern of concerted cultivation fostered an *emerging sense of entitlement* in the life of Alexander Williams and other middle-class children. By contrast, the commitment to nurturing children's natural growth fostered an *emerging sense of constraint* in the life of Harold McAllister and other working-class or poor children. (These consequences of childrearing practices are summarized in Table 2.)

Both parents and children drew on the resources associated with these two childrearing approaches during their interactions with officials. Middle-class parents and children often customized these interactions; working-class and poor parents were more likely to have a "generic" relationship. When faced with problems, middle-class parents also appeared better equipped to exert influence over other adults compared with working-class and poor parents. Nor did middle-class parents or children display the intimidation or confusion we witnessed among many working-class and poor families when they faced a problem in their children's school experience.

EMERGING SIGNS OF ENTITLEMENT

Alexander Williams's mother, like many middle-class mothers, explicitly teaches her son to be an informed, assertive client in interactions with professionals. For example, as she drives Alexander to a routine doctor's appointment, she coaches him in the art of communicating effectively in healthcare settings:

Alexander asks if he needs to get any shots today at the doctor's. Ms. Williams says he'll need to ask the doctor....As we enter Park Lane, Mom says quietly to Alex: "Alexander, you should be thinking of questions you might want to ask the doctor. You can ask him anything you want. Don't be shy. You can ask anything."

Alex thinks for a minute, then: "I have some bumps under my arms from my deodorant."

Mom: "Really? You mean from your new deodorant?"

Alex: "Yes."

Mom: "Well, you should ask the doctor."

Alexander learns that he has the right to speak up (e.g., "don't be shy") and that he should prepare for an encounter with a person in a position of authority by gathering his thoughts in advance.

These class resources are subsequently *activated* in the encounter with the doctor (a jovial white man in his late thirties or early forties). The examination begins this way:

Doctor: "Okay, as usual, I'd like to go through the routine questions with you. And if you have any questions for me, just fire away." Doctor examines Alex's chart: "Height-wise, as usual, Alexander's in the ninety-fifth percentile."

Although the physician is talking, to Ms. Williams, Alexander interrupts him:

Alex: "I'm in the what?"

Doctor: "It means that you're taller than more than ninety-five out of a hundred young men when they're, uh, ten years old."

Alex: "I'm not ten."

Doctor: "Well, they graphed you at ten...they usually take the closest year to get that graph."

Alex: "Alright."

Alexander's "Alright" reveals that he feels entitled to weigh-in with his own judgment. A few minutes later, the exam is interrupted when the doctor is asked to provide an emergency consultation by telephone. Alexander listens to the doctor's conversation and then uses what he has overheard as the basis for a clear directive:

Doctor: "The stitches are on the eyelids themselves, the laceration?...Um....I don't suture eyelids....um...Absolutely not!... Don't even touch them. That was very bad judgment on the camp's part....[Hangs up.] I'm sorry about the interruption."

Alex: "Stay away from my eyelids!"

Alexander's comment, which draws laughter from the adults, reflects this fourth grader's tremendous ease interacting with a physician.

Later, Ms. Williams and the doctor discuss Alexander's diet. Ms. Williams freely admits that they do not always follow nutritional guidelines. Her honesty is a form of capital because it gives the doctor accurate information on which to base a diagnosis. Feeling no need for deception positions mother and son to receive better care:

Doctor: Let's start with appetite. Do you get three meals a day?"

Alex: "Yeah."

Doctor: "And here's the important question: Do you get your fruits and vegetables too?"

Alex: "Yeah."

Mom, high-pitched: "Ooooo...."

Doctor: "I see I have a second opinion." [laughter]

Alex, voice rising: "You give me bananas and all in my lunch every day. And I had cabbage for dinner last night."

Doctor: "Do you get at least one or two fruits, one or two vegetables every day?"

Alex: "Yeah."

Doctor: "Marginally?"

Mom: "Ninety-eight percent of the time he eats pretty well."

Doctor: "OK, I can live with that...."

Class resources are again activated when Alexander's mother reveals she "gave up" on a medication. The doctor pleasantly but clearly instructs her to continue the medication. Again, though, he receives accurate information rather than facing silent resistance or defiance, as occurred in encounters between healthcare professionals and other (primarily working-class and poor) families. The doctor acknowledges Ms. Williams's relative power: He "argues for" continuation rather than directing her to execute a medically necessary action:

Mom: "His allergies have just been, just acted up again. One time this summer and I had to bring him in."

Doctor: "I see a note here from Dr. Svennson that she put him on Vancinace and Benadryl. Did it seem to help him?"

Mom: "Just, not really. So, I used it for about a week and I just gave up." Doctor, sitting forward in his chair: "OK, I'm actually going to argue for not giving up. If he needs it, Vancinace is a very effective drug. But it takes at least a week to start...."

Mom: "Oh. OK...."

Doctor: "I'd rather have him use that than heavy oral medications. You have to give it a few weeks...."

A similar pattern of give and take and questioning characterizes Alexander's interaction with the doctor, as the following excerpt illustrates:

Doctor: "The only thing that you really need besides my checking you, um, is to have, um, your eyes checked downstairs."

Alex: "Yes! I love that, I love that!"

Doctor laughs: "Well, now the most important question. Do you have any questions you want to ask me before I do your physical?"

Alex: "Um...only one. I've been getting some bumps on my arms, right around here [indicates underarm]."

Doctor: "Underneath?"

Alex: "Yeah."

Doctor: "OK....Do they hurt or itch?"

Alex: "No, they're just there."

Doctor: "OK, I'll take a look at those bumps for you. Um, what about you—um..."

Alex: "They're barely any left."

Doctor: "OK, well, I'll take a peek....Any questions or worries on your part? [Looking at the mother]

Mom: "No....He seems to be coming along very nicely."[31]

Alexander's mother's last comment reflects her view of him as a project, one that is progressing "very nicely." Throughout the visit, she signals her ease and her perception of the exam as an exchange between peers (with Alexander a legitimate participant), rather than a communication from a person in authority to his subordinates. Other middle-class parents seemed similarly comfortable. During Garrett Tallinger's exam, for example, his mother took off her sandals and tucked her legs up under her as she sat in the examination room. She also joked casually with the doctor.

Middle-class parents and children were also very assertive in situations at the public elementary school most of the middle-class children in the study attended. There were numerous conflicts during the year over matters small and large. For example, parents complained to one another and to the teachers about the amount of homework the children were assigned. A black middle-class mother whose daughters had not tested into the school's gifted program negotiated with officials to have the girls' (higher) results from a private testing company accepted instead. The parents of a fourth-grade boy drew the school superintendent into a battle over religious lyrics in a song scheduled to be sung as part of the holiday program. The superintendent consulted the district lawyer and ultimately "counseled" the principal to be more sensitive, and the song was dropped.

Children, too, asserted themselves at school. Examples include requesting that the classroom's blinds be lowered so the sun wasn't in their eyes, badgering the teacher for permission to retake a math test for a higher grade, and demanding to know why no cupcake had been saved when an absence prevented attendance at a classroom party. In these encounters, children were not simply complying with adults' requests or asking for a repeat of an earlier experience. They were displaying an emerging sense of entitlement by urging adults to permit a customized accommodation of institutional processes to suit their preferences.

Of course, some children (and parents) were more forceful than others in their dealings with teachers, and some were more successful than others. Melanie Handlon's mother, for example, took a very "hands-on" approach to her daughter's learning problems, coaching Melanie through her homework day after day. Instead of improved grades, however, the only result was a deteriorating home environment marked by tension and tears.

EMERGING SIGNS OF CONSTRAINT

The interactions the research assistants and I observed between professionals and working-class and poor parents frequently seemed cautious and constrained. This unease is evident, for example, during a physical Harold McAllister has before going to Bible camp. Harold's mother, normally boisterous and talkative at home, is quiet. Unlike Ms. Williams, she seems wary of supplying the doctor with accurate information:

Doctor: "Does he eat something each day—either fish, meat, or egg?"

Mom, response is low and muffled: "Yes."

Doctor, attempting to make eye contact but mom stares intently at paper: "A yellow vegetable?"

Mom, still no eye contact, looking at the floor: "Yeah."

Doctor: "A green vegetable?" Mom, looking at the doctor: "Not all the time." [Fieldworker has not seen any of the children eat a green or yellow vegetable since visits began.]

Doctor: "No. Fruit or juice?"

Mom, low voice, little or no eye contact, looks at the doctor's scribbles on the paper he is filling out: "Ununh humn."

Doctor: "Does he drink milk everyday?" Mom, abruptly, in considerably louder voice: "Yeah."

Doctor: "Cereal, bread, rice, potato, anything like that?"

Mom, shakes her head: "Yes, definitely." [Looks at doctor.]

Ms. McAllister's knowledge of developmental events in Harold's life is uneven. She is not sure when he learned to walk and cannot recall the name of his previous doctor. And when the doctor asks, "When was the last time he had a tetanus shot?" she counters, gruffly, "What's a tetanus shot?"

Unlike Ms. Williams, who urged Alexander to share information with the doctor, Ms. McAllister squelches eight-year-old Alexis's overtures:

Doctor: "Any birth mark?"

Mom looks at doctor, shakes her head no.

Alexis, raising her left arm, says excitedly: "I have a birth mark under my arm!"

Mom, raising her voice and looking stern: "Will you cool out a minute?" Mom, again answering the doctor's question: "No."

Despite Ms. McAllister's tension and the marked change in her everyday demeanor, Harold's whole exam is not uncomfortable. There are moments of laughter. Moreover, Harold's mother is not consistently shy or passive. Before the visit begins, the doctor comes into the waiting room and calls Harold's and Alexis's names. In response, the McAllisters (and the fieldworker) stand. Ms. McAllister then beckons for her nephew Tyrice (who is about Harold's age) to come along *before* she clears this with the doctor. Later, she sends Tyrice down the hall to observe Harold being weighed; she relies on her nephew's report rather than asking for this information from the healthcare professionals.

Still, neither Harold nor his mother seemed as comfortable as Alexander had been. Alexander was used to extensive conversation at home; with the doctor, he was at ease initiating questions. Harold, who was used to responding to directives at home, primarily answered questions from the doctor, rather than posing his own. Alexander, encouraged by his mother, was assertive and confident with the doctor. Harold was reserved. Absorbing his mother's apparent need to conceal the truth about the range of foods he ate, he appeared cautious, displaying an emerging sense of constraint.

We observed a similar pattern in school interactions. Overall, the working-class and poor adults had much more distance or separation from the school than their middle-class counterparts. Ms. McAllister, for example, could be quite assertive in some settings (e.g., at the start of family observations, she visited the local drug dealer, warning him not to "mess with" the black male fieldworker).[32] But throughout the fourth-grade parent-teacher conference, she kept her winter jacket zipped up, sat hunched over in her chair, and spoke in barely audible tones. She was stunned when the teacher said that Harold did not do homework.

Sounding dumbfounded, she said, "He does it at home." The teacher denied it and continued talking. Ms. McAllister made no further comments and did not probe for more information, except about a letter the teacher said he had mailed home and that she had not received. The conference ended, having yielded Ms. McAllister few insights into Harold's educational experience.[33]

Other working-class and poor parents also appeared baffled, intimidated, and subdued in parent-teacher conferences. Ms. Driver, who was extremely worried about her fourth-grader's inability to read, kept these concerns to herself. She explained to us, "I don't want to jump into anything and find it is the wrong thing." When working-class and poor parents did try to intervene in their children's educational experiences, they often felt ineffectual. Billy Yanelli's mother appeared relaxed and chatty in many of her interactions with other adults. With "the school," however, she was very apprehensive. She distrusted school personnel. She felt bullied and powerless. Hoping to resolve a problem involving her son, she tried to prepare her ideas in advance. Still, as she recounted during an interview, she failed to make school officials see Billy as vulnerable:

Ms. Yanelli: I found a note in his school bag one morning and it said, "I'm going to kill you...you're a dead mother-f-er...." So, I started shaking. I was all ready to go over there. [I was] prepared for the counselor....They said the reason they [the other kids] do what they do is because Billy makes them do it. So they had an answer for everything.

Interviewer: How did you feel about that answer?

Ms. Yanelli: I hate the school. I hate it.

Working-class and poor children seemed aware of their parents' frustration and witnessed their powerlessness. Billy Yanelli, for example, asserted in an interview that his mother "hate[d]" school officials.

At times, these parents encouraged their children to resist school officials' authority.

The Yanellis told Billy to "beat up" a boy who was bothering him. Wendy Driver's mother advised her to punch a male classmate who pestered her and pulled her ponytail. Ms. Driver's boyfriend added, "Hit him when the teacher isn't looking."

In classroom observations, working-class and poor children could be quite lively and energetic, but we did not observe them try to customize their environments. They tended to react to adults' offers or, at times, to plead with educators to repeat previous experiences, such as reading a particular story, watching a movie, or going to the computer room. Compared to middle-class classroom interactions, the boundaries between adults and children seemed firmer and clearer. Although the children often resisted and tested school rules, they did not seem to be seeking to get educators to accommodate their own *individual* preferences.

Overall, then, the behavior of working-class and poor parents cannot be explained as a manifestation of their temperaments or of overall passivity; parents were quite energetic in intervening in their children's lives in other spheres. Rather, working-class and poor parents generally appeared to depend on the school (Lareau 2000a), even as they were dubious of the trustworthiness of the professionals. This suspicion of professionals in dominant institutions is, at least in some instances, a reasonable response.[34] The unequal level of trust, as well as differences in the amount and quality of information divulged, can yield unequal *profits* during an historical moment when professionals applaud assertiveness and reject passivity as an inappropriate parenting strategy (Epstein 2001). Middle-class children and parents often (but not always) accrued advantages or profits from their efforts. Alexander Williams succeeded in having the doctor take his medical concerns seriously. Ms. Marshall's children ended up in the gifted program, even though they did not technically qualify. Middle-class children expect institutions to be responsive to *them* and to accommodate their individual needs. By contrast, when Wendy Driver is told to hit the boy who is pestering her (when the teacher isn't looking) or Billy Yanelli is told to physically defend himself, despite school rules, they are not learning how to make bureaucratic institutions work to their advantage. Instead, they are being given lessons in frustration and powerlessness.

WHY DOES SOCIAL CLASS MATTER?

Parents' economic resources helped create the observed class differences in childrearing practices. Enrollment fees that middle-class parents dismissed as "negligible" were formidable expenses for less affluent families. Parents also paid for clothing, equipment, hotel stays, fast food meals, summer camps, and fund-raisers. In 1994, the Tallingers estimated the cost of Garrett's activities at $4,000 annually, and that figure was not unusually high.[35] Moreover, families needed reliable private transportation and flexible work schedules to get children to and from events. These resources were disproportionately concentrated in middle-class families.

Differences in educational resources also are important. Middle-class parents' superior levels of education gave them larger vocabularies that facilitated concerted cultivation, particularly in institutional interventions. Poor and working-class parents were not familiar with key terms professionals used, such as "tetanus shot." Furthermore, middle-class parents' educational backgrounds gave them confidence when criticizing educational professionals and intervening in school matters. Working-class and poor parents viewed educators as their social superiors.

Kohn and Schooler (1983) showed that parents' occupations, especially the complexity of their work, influence their childrearing beliefs. We found that parents' work mattered, but also saw signs that the experience of adulthood itself influenced conceptions of childhood. Middle-class parents often were preoccupied with the pleasures and challenges of their work lives.[36] They tended to view childhood as a dual opportunity: a chance for play, and for developing talents and skills of value later in life. Mr. Tallinger noted that playing soccer taught Garrett to be "hard nosed" and "competitive," valuable workplace skills. Ms. Williams mentioned the value of Alexander learning to work with others by playing on a sports team. Middle-class parents, aware of the "declining fortunes" of the middle class, worried about their own economic futures and those of their children (Newman 1993). This uncertainty increased their commitment to helping their children develop broad skills to enhance their future possibilities.

Working-class and poor parents' conceptions of adulthood and childhood also appeared to

be closely connected to their lived experiences. For the working class, it was the deadening quality of work and the press of economic shortages that defined their experience of adulthood and influenced their vision of childhood. It was dependence on public assistance and severe economic shortages that most shaped poor parents' views. Families in both classes had many worries about basic issues: food shortages, limited access to healthcare, physical safety, unreliable transportation, insufficient clothing. Thinking back over their childhoods, these parents remembered hardship but also recalled times without the anxieties they now faced. Many appeared to want their own youngsters to concentrate on being happy and relaxed, keeping the burdens of life at bay until they were older.

Thus, childrearing strategies are influenced by more than parents' education. It is the interweaving of life experiences and resources, including parents' economic resources, occupational conditions, and educational backgrounds, that appears to be most important in leading middle-class parents to engage in concerted cultivation and working-class and poor parents to engage in the accomplishment of natural growth. Still, the structural location of families did not fully determine their childrearing practices. The agency of actors and the indeterminacy of social life are inevitable.

In addition to economic and social resources, are there other significant factors? If the poor and working-class families' resources were transformed overnight so that they equaled those of the middle-class families, would their cultural logic of childrearing shift as well? Or are there cultural attitudes and beliefs that are substantially independent of economic and social resources that are influencing parents' practices here? The size and scope of this study preclude a definitive answer. Some poor and working-class parents embraced principles of concerted cultivation: They wished (but could not afford) to enroll their children in organized activities (e.g., piano lessons, voice lessons), they believed listening to children was important, and they were committed to being involved in their children's schooling. Still, even when parents across all of the classes seemed committed to similar principles, their motivations differed. For example, many working-class and poor parents who wanted more activities for their children were seeking a safe haven for them. Their goal was to provide protection from harm rather than to cultivate the child's talents per se.

Some parents explicitly criticized children's schedules that involved many activities. During the parent interviews, we described the real-life activities of two children (using data from the 12 families we were observing). One schedule resembled Alexander Williams's: restricted television, required reading, and many organized activities, including piano lessons (for analytical purposes, we said that, unlike Alexander, this child disliked his piano lessons but was not allowed to quit). Summing up the attitude of the working-class and poor parents who rejected this kind of schedule,37 one white, poor mother complained:

I think he wants more. I think he doesn't enjoy doing what he's doing half of the time (light laughter). I think his parents are too strict. And he's not a child.

Even parents who believed this more regimented approach would pay off "job-wise" when the child was an adult still expressed serious reservations: "I think he is a sad kid," or, "He must be dead-dog tired."

Thus, working-class and poor parents varied in their beliefs. Some longed for a schedule of organized activities for their children and others did not; some believed in reasoning with children and playing an active role in schooling and others did not. Fully untangling the effects of material and cultural resources on parents and children's choices is a challenge for future research.[38]

DISCUSSION

The evidence shows that class position influences critical aspects of family life: time use, language use, and kin ties. Not all aspects of family life are affected by social class, and there is variability within class. Still, parents do transmit advantages to their children in patterns that are sufficiently consistent and identifiable to be described as a "cultural logic" of childrearing. The white and black middle-class parents engaged in practices I have termed "concerted cultivation"—they made a deliberate and sustained effort to stimulate children's development and to cultivate their cognitive and social skills. The working-class and poor parents viewed children's development as spontaneously unfolding, as long as they were provided with comfort, food, shelter, and other basic support. This commitment, too, required ongoing effort; sustaining children's natural growth despite formidable life challenges is properly viewed as an accomplishment.

In daily life, the patterns associated with each of these approaches were interwoven and mutually reinforcing. Nine-year-old middle-class children already had developed a clear sense of their own talents and skills, and they differentiated themselves from siblings and friends. They were also learning to think of themselves as special and worthy of having adults devote time and energy to promoting them and their leisure activities. In the process, the boundaries between adults and children sometimes blurred; adults' leisure preferences became subordinate to their children's. The strong emphasis on reasoning in middle-class families had similar, diffuse effects. Children used their formidable reasoning skills to persuade adults to acquiesce to their wishes. The idea that children's desires should be taken seriously was routinely realized in the middle-class families we interviewed and observed. In many subtle ways, children were taught that they were entitled. Finally, the commitment to cultivating children resulted in family schedules so crowded with activities there was little time left for visiting relatives. Quantitative studies of time use have shed light on important issues, but they do not capture the interactive nature of routine, everyday activities and the varying ways they affect the texture of family life.[39]

In working-class and poor families, parents established limits; within those limits, children were free to fashion their own pastimes. Children's wishes did not guide adults' actions as frequently or as decisively as they did in middle-class homes. Children were viewed as subordinate to adults. Parents tended to issue directives rather than to negotiate. Frequent interactions with relatives rather than acquaintances or strangers created a thicker divide between families and the outside world. Implicitly and explicitly, parents taught their children to keep their distance from people in positions of authority, to be distrustful of institutions, and, at times, to resist officials' authority. Children seemed to absorb the adults' feelings of powerlessness in their institutional relationships. As with the middle class, there were important variations among working-class and poor families, and some critical aspects of family life, such as the use of humor, were immune to social class.

The role of race in children's daily lives was less powerful than I had expected. The middle-class black children's parents were alert to the potential effects of institutional discrimination on their children. Middle-class black parents also took steps to help their children develop a positive racial identity. Still, in terms of how children spend their time, the way parents use language and discipline in the home, the nature of the families' social connections, and the strategies used for intervening in institutions, white and black middle-class parents engaged

in very similar, often identical, practices with their children. A similar pattern was observed in white and black working-class homes as well as in white and black poor families. Thus my data indicate that on the childrearing dynamics studied here, compared with social class, race was less important in children's daily lives.[40] As they enter the racially segregated words of dating, marriage, and housing markets, and as they encounter more racism in their interpersonal contact with whites (Waters 1999), the relative importance of race in the children's daily lives is likely to increase.

Differences in family dynamics and the logic of childrearing across social classes have long-term consequences. As family members moved out of the home and interacted with representatives of formal institutions, middle-class parents and children were able to negotiate more valuable outcomes than their working-class and poor counterparts. In interactions with agents of dominant institutions, working-class and poor children were learning lessons in constraint while middle-class children were developing a sense of entitlement.

It is a mistake to see either concerted cultivation or the accomplishment of natural growth as an intrinsically desirable approach. As has been amply documented, conceptions of childhood have changed dramatically over time (Wrigley 1989). Drawbacks to middle-class childrearing, including the exhaustion associated with intensive mothering and frenetic family schedules and a sapping of children's naivete that leaves them feeling too sophisticated for simple games and toys (Hays 1996), remain insufficiently highlighted.

Another drawback is that middle-class children are less likely to learn how to fill "empty time" with their own creative play, leading to a dependence on their parents to solve experiences of boredom. Sociologists need to more clearly differentiate between standards that are intrinsically desirable and standards that facilitate success in dominant institutions. A more critical, and historically sensitive, vision is needed (Donzelot 1979). Here Bourdieu's work (1976, 1984, 1986, 1989) is valuable.

Finally, there are methodological issues to consider. Quantitative research has delineated population-wide patterns; ethnographies offer rich descriptive detail but typically focus on a single, small group. Neither approach can provide holistic, but empirically grounded, assessments of daily life. Multi-sited, multi-person research using ethnographic methods also pose formidable methodological challenges (Lareau 2002). Still, families have proven themselves open to being studied in an intimate fashion. Creating penetrating portraits of daily life that will enrich our theoretical models is an important challenge for the future.

Annette Lareau is Associate Professor in the Department of Sociology at Temple University. She is the author of Home Advantage (Rowman and Littlefield, 2000) and with Jeff Shultz is editor of Journeys through Ethnography (Westview, 1996). She has received grants from the Spencer Foundation and the Alfred P. Sloan Foundation. The research reported in this article is discussed more fully in her forthcoming book, Unequal Childhoods: Class, Race, · and Family Life (University of California Press, forthcoming).

REFERENCES

Aries, Philippe. 1962. *Centuries of Childhood: A Social History of the Family.* Translated by R. Baldick. London, England: Cape.

Bernstein, Basil. 1971. *Class, Codes, and Control: Theoretical Studies towards a Sociology of Language.* New York: Schocken Books.

Bianchi, Suzanne M. 2000. "Maternal Employment and Time with Children: Dramatic Change or Surprising Continuity." *Demography* 37:401–14.

Bianchi, Suzane and John Robinson. 1997. "What Did You Do Today? Children's Use of Time, Family Composition, and Acquisition of Social Capital." *Journal of Marriage and the Family* 59:332–44.

Bourdieu, Pierre. 1976. "Marriage Strategies as Strategies of Social Reproduction." pp. 117–44 in *Family and Society,* edited by R. Forster and O. Ranum. Baltimore, MD: Johns Hopkins University Press.

———. 1984. *Distinction: A Social Critique of the Judgment of Taste.* Cambridge, MA: Harvard University Press.

———. 1986. "The Forms of Capital." pp. 241–58 in *Handbook of Theory and Research for the Sociology of Education,* edited by J. C. Richardson. New York: Greenwood.

———. 1989. *The State Nobility: Elite Schools in the Field of Power.* Stanford, CA: Stanford University Press.

Bronfenbrenner, Urie. 1966. "Socialization and Social Class through Time and Space." pp. 362–77 in *Class, Status and Power,* edited by R. Bendix and S. M. Lipset. New York: Free Press.

Burawoy, Michael, Alice Burton, Ann Arnett Ferguson, and Kathryn J. Fox, eds. 1991. *Ethnography Unbound: Power and Resistance in the Modern Metropolis.* Berkeley, CA: University of California Press.

Chidekel, Dana. 2002. *Parents in Charge.* New York: Simon and Schuster.

Conley, Dalton. 1999. *Being Black, Living in the Red: Race, Wealth, and Social Policy in America.* Berkeley, CA: University of California Press.

Corsaro, William A. 1997. *The Sociology of Childhood.* Thousand Oaks, CA: Pine Forge.

Crouter, Ann C., Heather Helms-Erikson, Kimberly Updegraff, and Susan M. McHale. 1999. "Conditions Underlying Parents' Knowledge about Children's Daily Lives in Middle Childhood: Between—and within—Family Comparisons." *Child Development* 70:246–59.

Daley, Kerry J. 2001. "Deconstructing Family Time: From Ideology to Lived Experience." *Journal of Marriage and the Family* 63:238–94.

Donzelot, Jacques. 1979. *The Policing of Families.* Translated by R. Hurley. New York: Pantheon.

Epstein, Joyce. 2001. *Schools, Family, and Community Partnerships.* Boulder, CO: Westview.

Erikson, Robert, and John H. Goldthorpe. 1993. *The Constant Flux: A Study of Class Mobility in Industrial Societies.* Oxford, England: Clarendon.

Fischer, Claude. 1982. *To Dwell among Friends.* Chicago: University of Chicago Press.

Fordham, Signithia and John U. Ogbu. 1986. "Black Students' School Success: Coping with the 'Burden of Acting White.'" *The Urban Review* 18:176–206.

Gordon, Linda. 1989. *Heroes of Their Own Lives: The Politics and History of Family Violence.* New York: Penguin.

Halbfinger, David M. 2002. "A Hockey Parent's Life: Time, Money, and Yes,—Frustration." *New York Times,* January 12, p. 29.

Hart, Betty and Todd Risley. 1995. *Meaningful Differences in the Everyday Experience of Young American Children.* Baltimore, MD: Paul Brooks.

Hays, Sharon. 1996. *The Cultural Contradictions of Motherhood.* New Haven, CT: Yale University Press.

Heath, Shirley Brice. 1983. *Ways with Words.* London, England: Cambridge University Press.

Reimer, Carol A. and Lisa Staffen. 1998. *For the Sake of the Children: The Social Organization of Responsibility in the Hospital and at Home.* Chicago, IL: University of Chicago Press.

Hertz, Rosanna and Nancy L. Marshall, eds. 2001. *Working Families: The Transformation of the American Home.* Berkeley, CA: University of California Press.

Hess, Robert and Gerald Handel. 1974. *Family Worlds: A Psychosocial Approach to Family Life.* Chicago, IL: University of Chicago Press.

Hochschild, Arlie Russell. 1989. *The Second Shift: Working Parents and the Revolution at Home.* New York: Viking.

Hochschild, Jennifer L. 1995. *Facing Up to The American Dream.* Princeton, NJ: Princeton University Press.

Hofferth, Sandra L. 1999. "Family Reading to Young Children: Social Desirability and Cultural Biases in Reporting" (Working paper no. 005–99, May 13, 1999). Institute for Survey Research, Center for Ethnography of Everyday Life, University of Michigan, Ann Arbor, MI. (http://www.ethno.isr.umich.edu/06papers.html).

Hofferth, Sandra and John Sandberg. 2001a. "Changes in American Children's Time, 1981–1997." Pp. 193–232 in *Advances in Life Course Research,* vol. 6, *Children at the Millennium: Where Have We Come From, Where Are We Going?,* edited by S. Hofferth and T. Owens. Oxford, England, Eslevier Science Ltd.

———. 2001b. "How American Children Spend Their Time." *Journal of Marriage and the Family* 63:295–308.

Jacobs, Jerry and Kathleen Gerson. 1998. "Who Are the Overworked Americans?" *Review of Social Economy* 56:442–59.

Juster, F. Thomas and Frank P. Stafford, eds. 1985. *Time, Goods, and Well-Being.* Ann Arbor, MI: Survey Research Center, Institute for Social Research.

Kingston, Paul. 2000. *The Classless Society.* Stanford, CA: Stanford University Press.

Kohn, Melvin and Carmi Schooler, eds. 1983. *Work and Personality: An Inquiry into the Impact of Social Stratification.* Norwood, NJ: Ablex.

Kropp, Paul. 2001. *I'll Be the Parent, You Be the Child.* New York: Fisher Books.

Lamont, Michele. 2000. *The Dignity of Working Men: Morality and the Boundaries of Race, Class, and Immigration.* Cambridge, MA: Harvard University Press.

Lareau, Annette. Forthcoming. *Unequal Childhood: Class, Race, and Family Life.* Berkeley, CA: University of California Press.

———. 2002. "Doing Multi-Person, Multi-Site 'Ethnographic' Work: A Reflective, Critical Essay." Department of Sociology, Temple University, Philadelphia, PA. Unpublished manuscript.

———. 2000a. *Home Advantage: Social Class and Parental Intervention in Elementary Education.* 2d ed. Lanham, MD: Rowman and Littlefield.

———. 2000b. "My Wife Can Tell Me Who I Know: Methodological and Conceptual Issues in Studying Fathers." *Qualitative Sociology* 23:407–33.

Lever, Janet. 1988. "Sex Differences in the Complexity of Children's Play and Games." Pp. 324–44 in *Childhood Socialization,* edited by G. Handel. New York: Aldine de Gruyter.

Marsiglio, William. 1991. "Paternal Engagement Activities with Minor Children." *Journal of Marriage and the Family* 53:973–86.

Massey, Douglas and Nancy Denton. 1993. *American Apartheid.* Cambridge, MA: Harvard University Press.

McLanahan, Sara and Gary Sandefur. 1994. *Growing Up with a Single Parent: What Hurts, What Helps.* Cambridge, MA: Harvard University Press.

Medrich, Elliot, Judith Roizen, Victor Rubin, and Stuart Buckley. 1982. *The Serious Business of Growing Up.* Berkeley, CA: University of California Press.

Menaghan, Elizabeth G. 1991. "Work Experiences and Family Interaction Processes: The Long Reach of the Job?" *Annual Review of Sociology* 17:419–44.

Newman, Kathleen. 1993. *Declining Fortunes: The Withering of the American Dream*. New York: Basic Books.

Pattillo-McCoy, Mary 1999. Black *Picket Fences: Privilege and Peril among the Black Middle-class*. Chicago, IL: University of Chicago Press.

Presser, Harriet B. 1989. "Can We Make Time for Children? The Economy, Work Schedules, and Child Care." *Demography* 26:523–13.

Robinson, John P. and Geoffry Godbey. 1997. *Time for Life: The Surprising Ways Americans Use Their Time*. University Park, PA: The Pennsylvania State Press.

Rubin, Lillian 1976. *Worlds of Pain: Life in a Working-class Family*. New York: Basic Books.

Sandberg, John F. and Sandra L. Hofferth. 2001. "Changes in Children's Time with Parents, U.S., 1981–1997." *Demography* 38:423–36.

Shehan, Constance L., ed. 1999. *Through the Eyes of the Child: Re-Visioning Children as Active Agents of Family Life*. New York: JAI Press.

Schemari, James. 2002. "Practice Makes Perfect (and Poorer Parents)." *The New York Times,* January 27, p. 11).

Skolnick, Arlene. 1991. *Embattled Paradise: The American Family in an Age of Uncertainty*. New York: Basic Books.

Tatum, Beverly Daniel. 1997. *Why Are All the Black Kids Sitting Together in the Cafeteria? And Other Conversations about Race*. New York: Basic Books.

Thompson, Shona M. 1999. *Mother's Taxi: Sport and Women's Labor*. Albany, NY: SUNY Press.

Thorne, Barrie. 2001. "Growing Up in Oakland: Orbits of Class, 'Race,' and Culture." Paper presented at the annual meeting of the American Sociological Association, August 19, Anaheim, CA.

Van Ausdale, Debra and Joe R. Feagin. 1996. "Using Racial and Ethnic Concepts: The Critical Case of Very Young Children." *American Sociological Review* 61:779–93.

Waksler, Frances. 1991. *Studying the Social Worlds of Children*. Bristol, England: Falmer.

Waters, Mary. 1999. *Black Identities: West Indian Immigrant Dreams and American Realities*. New York: Russell Sage Foundation.

Wright, Erik Olin. 1997. *Class Counts: Comparative Studies in Class Analysis*. Cambridge, England: Cambridge University Press.

Wrigley, Julia. 1989. "Do Young Children Need Intellectual Stimulation? Experts' Advice to Parents, 1900–1985." *History of Education* 29:41–75.

Zelizer, Vivianna. 1985. *Pricing the Priceless Child: The Changing Social Value of Children*. New York: Basic Books.

Zick, Cathleen D. and W. Keith Bryant. 1996. "A New Look at Parents' Time Spent in Child Care: Primary and Secondary Time Use." *Social Science Research* 25:260–80.

Direct correspondence to Annette Lareau, Department of Sociology, 756 Gladfelter Hall, Temple University, Philadelphia, PA 19122 (annette.lareau@temple.edu). An early version of this article was issued as a working paper by the Center for Working Families, University of California, Berkeley. I benefited from audience comments on earlier drafts presented at the American Sociological Association annual meeting in 2000, the University of California (Berkeley, Davis, and San Diego), University of Chicago, University of Pennsylvania, and Temple University. Patricia Berhau, Anita Garey, Karen Hanson, Erin McNamara Horvat, Sam Kaplan, Michele Lamont, Karen Shirley, Barrie Thorne, Elliot Weininger, and Julia Wrigley made helpful suggestions, as did the ASR reviewers. For funding, I thank the Spencer Foundation, Sloan Foundation, ASA/NSF Grants for the Discipline, Temple Grant-in-Aid, and Southern Illinois University. I am indebted to the project's research assistants, particularly Wendi Starr Brown, Gillian Johns, Caitlin Howley-Rowe, Greg Seaton, and Mary Woods, all of whose field notes appear in the article. I thank Nikki Johnson who assisted in production of the manuscript, and M. Katherine Mooney for editorial assistance. Errors are my responsibility.

NOTES

1. In a study of mothers' beliefs about childrearing, Hays (1996) found variations in how working-class and middle-class mothers sorted information, but she concluded that a pattern of "intensive mothering" was present across social classes. My study of behavior found class differences but, as I discuss below, in some instances working-class and poor

parents expressed a desire to enroll their children in organized activities.

2. Some significant differences between the study's working-class and poor families (e.g., only the poor children experienced food shortages) are not highlighted here because, on the dimensions discussed in this paper, the biggest differences were between middle-class and nonmiddle-class families. See Lareau (forthcoming) for a more elaborate discussion as well as Lamont (2000) for distinctions working-class families draw between themselves and the poor; see McLanahan and Sandefur (1994) regarding family structure and children's lives.

3. Case studies of nonrandom samples, such as this one, have the limitation that findings cannot be generalized beyond the cases reported. These examples serve to illustrate conceptual points (Burawoy et al. 1991) rather than to describe representative patterns of behavior. A further limitation of this study is that the data were collected and analyzed over an extended period of time. (see the "Methodology" section).

4. All names of people and places are pseudonyms. The Lawrenceville school was in a white suburban neighborhood in a university community a few hours from a metropolitan area. The student population was about half white and half black; the (disproportionately poor) black children were bused from other neighborhoods.

5. Over three-quarters of the students at Lower Richmond qualified for free lunch; by contrast, Swan did not have a free lunch program.

6. At both sites, we attended school events and observed many parent-teacher conferences. Also, I interviewed the classroom teachers and adults involved in the children's organized activities. These interview data are not presented here.

7. Both schools had computer labs, art programs, and music programs, but Swan had many more resources and much higher average achievement scores. Graffiti and physical confrontations between students were common only at Lower Richmond. At these two sites and in Lawrenceville, white faculty predominated.

8. I located the black middle-class parents through social networks; the white poor families were located through flyers left at welfare offices and social service programs, and posted on telephone poles. Ten white poor families (only) were paid $25 per interview.

9. Of 19 families asked to participate in the intensive study, 7 declined (a response rate of 63 percent). I tried to balance the observational phase sample by gender, race, and class, and to "mix and match" the children on other characteristics, such as their behavior with peers, their relationships with extended family, and their parents' level of involvement in their education. The aim was to lessen the chance that observed differences in behavior would reflect unknown variables (e.g., church attendance, or parents' participation at school). Last, I deliberately included two families (Irwins, Greeleys) who had some "middle-class" traits but who lived in a working-class and poor area, respectively. Including these unusual families seemed conceptually important for disentangling the influences of social class and environment (neighborhood).

10. I analyzed the data for the study as a whole in two ways. I coded themes from the interviews and used Folio Views software to help establish patterns. I also relied on reading the field notes, thinking about similarities and differences across families, searching for disconfirming evidence, and re-reading the field notes.

11. Recruitment to complete the sample was difficult as children needed to be a specific age, race, and class, and to be part of families who were willing to be observed. The white poor boy was recommended by a social service program manager; the black middle-class children were located through extended social networks of mine.

12. We did 12 to 14 observations of the Handlon and Carroll families before settling on the 20-visit pattern. In Alexander Williams's case, the visits occurred over a year. To observe unusual events (e.g., a family reunion), we sometimes went back after formal observations had ended.

13. Families developed preferences, favoring one fieldworker in a team over another. But these preferences were not stable across families, and the field notes did not differ dramatically between fieldworkers. Notes were much more similar than they were different.

14. Wright (1997) uses 12 categories in his neoMarxist approach. Goldthorpe, a neo-Weberian, operationalizes his class schema at levels of aggregation

ranging from 3 to 11 categories (Erikson and Goldthorpe 1993:38–39).

15. Here "poor" refers to the source of income (i.e., government assistance versus labor market) rather than the amount of income. Although lower class is more accurate than poor, it is widely perceived as pejorative. I might have used "underclass," but the literature has defined this term in racialized ways.

16. Dollar figures are from 1994–1995, unless otherwise noted. Income was not used to define class membership, but these data are available from the author.

17. Mr. and Ms. Williams disagreed about the value of their home; the figure here averages what each reported in 1995. Housing prices in their region were lower—and continue to be lower today—than in many other parts of the country. Their property is now worth an estimated $175,000 to $200,000.

18. Alexander's mother goes by Christina Nile at work, but Mrs. Williams at church. Some other mothers' last names also differ from their children's. Here I assign all mothers the same last names as their children.

19. I contacted the Williams family through social networks after I was unable to recruit the black middle-class families who had participated in the classroom observation and interview phase. As a result, I do not have data from classroom observations or parent-teacher conferences for Alexander.

20. The Suzuki method is labor intensive. Students are required to listen to music about one hour per day. Also, both child and parent(s) are expected to practice daily and to attend every lesson together.

21. Hart and Risley (1995) reported a similar difference in speech patterns. In their sample, by about age three, children of professionals had larger vocabularies and spoke more utterances per hour than the *parents* of similarly aged children on welfare.

22. This section focuses primarily on the concerns of black parents. Whites, of course, also benefited from race relations, notably in the scattering of poor white families in working-class neighborhoods rather than being concentrated in dense settings with other poor families (Massey and Denton 1993).

23. Activities coded as "organized" are Scouts/Brownies, music lessons, any type of sports lesson (e.g., gymnastics, karate), any type of league-organized sports (e.g., Little League), dance lessons, choir, religious classes (excluding religious primary school), arts and crafts classes, and any classes held at a recreation center.

24. As other studies have found, the mothers in my sample were far more knowledgeable than the fathers about their children's daily lives and spent more time caring for children (Crouter et. al. 1999; Thompson 1999). Family observations showed fathers playing a very important role in family dynamics, however, especially by contributing laughter and humor (Laresu 2000b).

25. Some data are missing. The list of activities was so long we sometimes shortened it to conserve time (we always asked respondents, however, whether there were any activities their children had experienced that were not covered in the list). On average, middle-class parents were not queried concerning 2.5 of the approximately 20 items on the list; working-class parents were not asked about 3.0 items; and poor parents were not asked about 2.0 items. Since the sample is nonrandom, inferential procedures are not applicable. At a reviewer's request, I carried out a Scheffe post hoc test of group differences and found significant differences (at the $p < .001$ level) between the middle-class children and the working-class and poor children. The difference between working-class and poor children is nonsignificant (at the $p < .05$ level). Statistically significant differences do not occur across racial groups or by gender; nor are there significant interactions between race or gender and class.

26. Recent time-diary data suggest that middle-class parents' reports of how much time their children spend watching television are significantly lower than their children's actual viewing time (Hofferth 1999). There is no comparable gap shown in national data for less educated parents.

27. During an interview, Ms. Yanelli estimated that during the previous two weeks, she had used the belt twice, but she noted that her use varied widely. Not all working-class and poor parents in the study used physical punishment, but the great majority did rely heavily on directives.

28. Interviews were open-ended; respondents' varied answers preclude summarizing the data in a single

scale that would accurately measure differences in kinship ties by class. For details regarding social class and kin group contact, see Fischer (1982).

29. The overall sample included 36 middle-class, 26 working-class, and 26 poor families. For the question on teachers, there were responses from 31 middle-class parents, 21 working-class parents, and 25 poor parents. For the question on doctors, the responses by class numbered 26, 21, and 22. Similar results were found for knowing a psychologist, family counselor, or lawyer (data available from the author). Race did not influence the results.

30. How misguided parents' suspicions might be is hard to assess. The counselor at Lower Richmond, who regularly reported children to the Department of Human Services as victims of neglect, maintained that she did so only in the gravest cases and only after repeated interventions had failed. The working-class and poor parents, however, generally saw "the school's actions" as swift, capricious, and arbitrary.

31. Not all professionals accommodated children's participation. Regardless of these adults' overt attitudes, though, we routinely observed that middle-class mothers monitor and intervene in their children's interactions with professionals.

32. Ms. McAllister told me about this visit; we did not observe it. It is striking that she perceived only the black male fieldworker as being at risk.

33. Middle-class parents sometimes appeared slightly anxious during parent-teacher conferences, but overall, they spoke more and asked educators more questions than did working-class and poor parents.

34. The higher levels of institutional reports of child neglect, child abuse, and other family difficulties among poor families may reflect this group's greater vulnerability to institutional intervention (e.g., see L. Gordon 1989).

35. In 2002, a single sport could cost as much as $5,000 annually. Yearly league fees for ice hockey run to $2,700; equipment costs are high as well (Halbfinger 2002).

36. Middle-class adults do not live problem-free lives, but compared with the working class and poor, they have more varied occupational experiences and greater access to jobs with higher economic returns.

37. Many middle-class parents remarked that forcing a child to take piano lessons was wrong. Nevertheless, they continued to stress the importance of "exposure."

38. Similarly, whether concerted cultivation and the accomplishment of natural growth are new historical developments rather than modifications of earlier forms of childrearing cannot be determined from the study's findings. The "institutionalization of children's leisure" seems to be increasing (Corsaro 1997). Hays (1996) argues that families increasingly are "invaded" by the "logic of impersonal, competitive, contractual, commodified, efficient, profit-maximizing, self-interested relations" (p. 11). In addition to evidence of a new increase in children's organized activities (Sandberg and Hofferth 2001), none of the middle-class parents in the study reported having childhood schedules comparable to their children's. Change over time in parents' intervention in education and in the amount of reasoning in middle-class families also are difficult to determine accurately. Kohn and Schooler's (1983) study suggests little change with regard to reasoning, but other commentators insist there has been a rise in the amount of negotiating between parents and children (Chidekel 2002; Kropp 2001). Such debates can not be resolved without additional careful historical research.

39. The time-use differences we observed were part of the taken-for-granted aspects of daily life; they were generally unnoticed by family members. For example, the working-class Yanellis considered themselves "really busy" if they had one baseball game on Saturday and an extended family gathering on Sunday. The Tallingers and other middle-class families would have considered this a slow weekend.

40. These findings are compatible with others showing children as aware of race at relatively early ages (Van Ausdale and Feagin 1996). At the two sites, girls often played in racially segregated groups during recess; boys tended to play in racially integrated groups.

"Bring Me Home a Black Girl"

Audrey Edwards

The first time I saw my stepson, Ugo, make a move on a girl, he was about 7, and so was she—a dark-skinned little cutie standing at the jukebox in a Brooklyn family diner looking for a song to play. In a flash, Ugo was at her side, shy but bold at the same time. He pretended to be looking for a song, too, but he was mainly just looking at her, instantly in puppy love. "That's right," I said to him, fairly loudly and pointedly. "When it's time to get married, I want you to bring me home a girl just like that—a Black girl." The girl's parents, sitting at a table nearby, looked at me in surprise and then suddenly beamed. Ugo's father, sitting with me, just nodded and grinned.

"Bring me home a Black girl." It's one of those commandments Ugo has heard from me most of his life, right up there with "Don't do drugs," "Finish school" and "Use a condom." Over the years he has rolled his eyes, sighed in exasperation, muttered that I was racist or been mortified whenever I'd blurt out things like "Dark, light, shades in between—it don't matter to me as long as she's Black." But Ugo has also grown up to be very clear about what that edict really means: Don't even think about marrying a White girl.

I myself became clear about this—or clear about a mother's role in imparting to male children what's expected when it comes to marriage—when I interviewed the son of a Black magazine publisher ten years ago. The publisher had three sons and a Black wife who had made it clear to her boys that they were not to bring home any White girls. "We could have them as friends," the eldest son recalled, "but we were definitely not to marry them."

In all the grousing and hand wringing we do over brothers' marrying outside the race, it had never occurred to me that the issue might be addressed by something as simple and basic as child rearing. We tell our sons almost every day what we expect when it comes to their behavior, but we seldom, if ever, tell them what we expect when it comes to that most serious of decisions: choosing a partner. Oh, we may ask vague, cursory questions about the women they bring home: Can she cook? What work does she do? Who are her people? But rarely do we come right out and make the case for marrying Black. Truth be told, we're much more likely to make the case for marrying "light" or marrying someone with "good hair" so we can have "pretty grandbabies." Or we might argue, shouldn't people be allowed to marry whomever they want? Wasn't that one of the goals of integration?

If we were playing on an equal field, yes, we'd all be free to marry anyone. But the fact is, we're not. For Black women, one of the inequities on the current playing field has been the rate at which Black men are marrying outside the race. While most Black men still marry Black women, according to a joint survey by the

U.S. Census Bureau and the Bureau of Labor Statistics, the number of Black men marrying White women has increased tenfold in the last 40 years, up from 25,000 in 1960 to 268,000 today. That's more than double the number of Black women who marry White men.

Where Black people are concerned, the increasing numbers of interracial unions could eventually lead to what sex therapist Gwendolyn Goldsby Grant, Ed.D., calls annihilation through integration, a weakening of the culture and economic resources of the Black community. So the question becomes, How do we ensure our cultural and economic survival as a people? One way is to start early and plainly telling our boys to marry Black girls. We need to put the emphasis on our boys because they are more likely than our girls to choose a White partner. Add to that the fact that men still take the lead when it comes to choosing a marriage partner, and it becomes obvious that molding our boys' attitudes is critical.

Of course, we may first have to get past what we think telling Black boys to marry Black means. "Somehow Black people are taught that to be ethnocentric is to be racist," says Grant. "But to want to be with people who share your values, religion and culture is very normal. It is not anti-anybody else."

Indeed, it seems almost anti-self to want to mate with someone from a culture that has historically denigrated, despised and oppressed you—and continues to do so. "People don't consciously say, 'I don't value myself, so I'm going to seek an image outside my culture,' but the choices you make reflect what you believe," Grant explains. "This is why images are so important. Our children must see themselves positively reflected in the world, and if they don't, they start valuing the dominant culture. And when you worship the dominant culture and pay no attention to your own, you're not making choices for your highest good. You're confused."

As Maxwell C. Manning, an assistant professor of social work at Howard University, points out, "If you look at strong cultures, like the Jews, you'll find they have a high rate of marrying within their group. That's how they remain strong." Manning, who says he would be surprised if his own 21-year-old son "walked in the door with a White woman," notes that when as a young man he dated several White women, his parents were very upset. "That told me I should never think about marrying White," he recalls.

"I really wanted to be connected to my community," he continues. "Carrying the name and the culture is so important, and I think that would have been more difficult had I married a White woman." The expectations of Manning's parents no doubt influenced his choosing a Black woman when it came time to marry, just as his expectations for his son may well lead him to choose a Black woman as his wife.

How parents communicate to their children the importance of marrying within the group will vary, whether it's an in-your-face admonishment like the kind I've always given my stepson, or simply letting your child know, as Manning's parents did, that you're not pleased when he dates White girls. What's most important, says Manning, "is that we communicate to children what our values are. And one of the values should be to marry within the race to further our heritage and our culture."

But culture and heritage are only two factors in a complicated race equation. For me it's just as important that Ugo affirm the beauty and desirability of Black women by choosing to marry one. When he zeroed in on that little Black girl at the jukebox many years ago, he was displaying what I thought was natural—an instinctive attraction to someone who looked like him. But according to experts, by age 7, Black children have already been bombarded by media images that can negatively shape how they view themselves and the partners you'd think they would naturally be drawn to.

That's why it's so important that we constantly affirm our children, helping them to appreciate their own intelligence, beauty and strength. Whether it's in the artwork on your walls, the posters in your child's room or the books and magazines lying around the house, positive Black media images should be as integral a part of a Black child's life as the images coming in through television, videos and other media.

Fortunately for Ugo, his African grandmother and mother and his Afrocentric Black American father have all contributed to his being grounded in a strong Black identity. But that doesn't mean he hasn't also been shaped by seeing his two handsome Black male cousins have relationships and children with White women. So I try to be as relentless in countering the White-is-right images he's assaulted with as our society has been in perpetuating them.

Clearly, one of the most insistent images going is that White women are the most beautiful and therefore should be the most desired. If you buy into this notion, then Black women can never be fully prized—and this is the message we get every time a brother dates or marries a woman who is not Black. Maybe we shouldn't take such behavior personally, but it's damn hard not to. Black women are more likely than women of any other race to remain without a partner. So when Black men marry out of the race, it not only further diminishes the number of brothers available to Black women, but it also undermines our very confidence as desirable women. I don't want this to be a message Ugo ever sends out. He knows that if he wants to keep Mommy Audrey happy, he will bring me home a Black girl.

This is the message senior marketing executive Valerie Williams has also given her 15-year-old son. "I tell him I want to have grandchil-dren who look like me," says Williams, who is frank on racial matters. "I don't want to be sitting around the dinner table at Thanksgiving feeling I have to bite my tongue." Nor does Williams think it's possible to escape issues of race and White supremacy in interracial unions, no matter how great the love may be. "I don't care what anybody says," she argues, "there's not a White person in America who doesn't feel superior to a former slave. Why would I want my son to marry someone who will probably always subconsciously feel she's better than him just because she's White?"

We often forget that relationships are also built on economic foundations and that Black-earned money leaves the community whenever a Black man marries out of the race. This is what rankles whenever we see wealthy Black athletes, entertainers or CEOs of Fortune 500 companies choose to lay their riches at the feet of White women by marrying them. So I have no doubt what motivated the Black publisher's wife to insist all those years ago that her three sons never think about marrying out of the race. Her husband had spent half his life building a multimillion-dollar business, and she did not want the wealth he would leave to his sons to pass out of Black hands. The publisher's wife was very clear about that. And her sons all married beautiful Black women and gave her beautiful Black grandchildren who look like her and will keep the money where it should be—in the Black family. In the Black community.

Last spring, while touring with Ugo the predominantly White college he would attend in the fall, I felt a moment of panic. Too many of the White girls, it seemed, were grinning in his direction. He is 19 now, strapping, handsome and a magnet for women of other races who find Black men as irresistible as we do. "Ugo," I instinctively blurted out, clutching his arm. "Please. Bring me home—" "Don't worry," he interrupted, putting his arm around me with calm reassurance. "I will."

Interracial Intimacy: Sex, Marriage, Identity, and Adoption

Randall Kennedy

BLACK-POWER BACKLASH

By and large, African Americans fall into three camps with respect to white-black interracial marriage. One camp views it as a positive good that decreases social segregation; encourages racial open-mindedness; increases blacks' access to enriching social networks; elevates their status; and empowers black women in their interactions with black men.

A second camp is agnostic, seeing interracial marriage simply as a private choice that individuals should have the right to make. Professor Cornel West, for example, after noting that "more and more white Americans are willing to interact sexually with black Americans *on an equal basis,*" has maintained that he himself "view[s] this [development] as neither cause for celebration nor reason for lament."[1] This is probably the predominant view among blacks. It allows those who espouse it simultaneously to oppose antimiscegenation laws and to disclaim any personal desire to marry across racial lines. Many African Americans are attracted to this position because, among other things, it helps to refute a not infrequent assumption among whites that is deeply annoying to blacks: the notion that blacks, particularly those who are accomplished, attractive, and ambitious, would like nothing better than to be intimate with whites, or even, if it were possible, to *become* white themselves. The pressure of this

assumption prompted a writer who called himself Mordechai to declare in 1827, in the pages of *Freedom's Journal,* the nation's first black newspaper, "I am not covetous of sitting at the table of [the white man], to hold him by his arm in the streets—to marry his daughter…nor to sleep in his bed—neither should I think myself honoured in the possession of all these favours." A hundred and thirty-seven years later, Charles H. King restated the point in the *Negro Digest.* Asserting that "'Miss Anne' [a generic white woman] does not fall into the category of our present needs," King insisted (and entitled his essay), "I Don't Want to Marry Your Daughter."

A third camp repudiates interracial marriage on the ground that black participation in it constitutes an expression of racial disloyalty; implies disapproval of fellow blacks; impedes the perpetuation of black culture; weakens the African American marriage market; and fuels racist mythologies, especially the fiction that blacks lack pride of race. While black opposition to intermarriage has always been a powerful and constant undercurrent, it was largely suppressed prior to the mid-1960s in order to accentuate protest against antimiscegenation laws, which most black enemies of mixed marriage also opposed. Periodically, however, blacks' latent objections did erupt. In 1949, after Walter White, the Negro secretary of the NAACP, divorced his black wife (the mother of his two children) and married a white woman from South Africa, the *Norfolk* [Virginia] *Journal and Guide* spoke for many blacks in suggesting that a "prompt and official announcement that [White] will not return to his post…is in order."[2] Much of the anger over this obviously very personal decision stemmed from fear that segregationists would seize on the marriage as "proof" that what Negro civil rights activists really wanted was not mere "equality" but sex with white women. Also contributing to the anger was the widespread sense that White's actions sent the message that in his eyes, at least, no Negro woman was good enough for him.[3]

By the late 1960s, with the burden of de jure racial stigmatization having been considerably lightened, increasing numbers of blacks felt emboldened to air their disapproval of mixed marriages. As "We Shall Overcome" gave way to "Black Power," the rejection of interracial intimacy gained in prestige and prominence. Concern with improving the image of blacks in the minds of whites yielded to the cultivation of a deeper allegiance to racial solidarity—an allegiance that many blacks perceived as being incompatible with interracial intimacy.[4] Thus, even while the African American social reformer George Wiley dedicated himself to the struggle for racial justice as a leading figure in the Congress for Racial Equality (CORE) and the founder of the National Welfare Rights Organization (NWRO), his marriage to a white woman earned him the scorn of many black activists. In 1972, when he addressed a rally in Washington, D.C., on African Liberation Day, a group of black women heckled him with the taunting chant "Where's your white wife? Where's your white wife?" When he attempted to focus his remarks specifically on the situation of black women, the heckling continued unabated, though the chant changed to "Talking black and sleeping white."[5] Other politically active blacks with white spouses faced similar pres-

sures; among their number were James Farmer, a founder of CORE, and the tenacious activist Julius Hobson. Julius Lester was a longtime member of the Student Non-violent Coordinating Committee (SNCC) and the author of one of the most arrestingly entitled books of that flamboyant era, *Look Out Whitey! Black Power's Gon' Get Your Mama* (1968). For many black activists, however, Lester's writings and ideas were decidedly less significant a measure of his commitment to the cause of African American advancement than was his choice of a white woman to be his wife. To them his marriage bespoke hypocrisy. Ridiculing Lester, a black woman wrote in a letter to the editor of *Ebony* that only a fool would regard him as a trustworthy leader. After all, she charged, he could not even "crawl out of bed" with whites.

The "sleeping white" critique embarrassed a wide variety of individuals, as distinctions between the personal and the political evaporated. At many colleges and universities, black students ostracized other blacks who dated (much less married!) whites. A black student who wanted to walk around "with a blonde draped on his arm" could certainly do so, a student leader at the University of Washington told St. Clair Drake; "All we say," the student continued, "is don't try to join the black studies association." Drake, a leading African American sociologist, himself ran up against this bias: by his account, when he revisited his old high school in 1968, the black student union refused to have anything to do with him because he was involved in an interracial relationship. Likewise shunned, and for the same reason, was Drake's classmate Charles V. Hamilton, the coauthor, with Stokely Carmichael, of *Black Power: The Politics of Liberation in America* (1967).

In some instances, black opposition played a role in the dissolution of interracial marriages. One dramatic example was the breakup of Everett LeRoi Jones (now known as Imamu

Amiri Baraka) and Hettie Jones. LeRoi Jones was born to middle-class black parents in Newark, New Jersey, in 1934. For two years he attended Howard University, which he detested. After serving in the air force for three years, he moved to New York in 1957 and joined the Beat community in Greenwich Village. He worked for *Record Changer* magazine and launched his literary career as a coeditor of *Yugen,* an avant-garde journal that published work by William Burroughs, Gregory Corso, Allen Ginsberg, Jack Kerouac, Charles Olson, and Jones himself. His coeditor was his future wife, Hettie Cohen, a woman of Jewish parentage who had grown up in suburban New York and attended Mary Washington, the women's college of the University of Virginia. Jones and Cohen were married in 1958. His parents accepted the marriage easily, while hers were so horrified by it that they broke off all contact with their daughter.

For a time, the marriage was, according to Hettie Jones, a happy and loving one. But eventually the pressures of bohemian penury, the demands of two children, and infidelities by both husband and wife (including a relationship in which LeRoi Jones had a baby by another woman, who also happened to be white) began to take their toll. Also burdening the marriage were Jones's political activities and ambitions: as the black protest movement gathered steam in the early 1960s, he aimed to become an important figure in it. At the same time, his career as a writer was blossoming. He wrote well-regarded poetry, social and political essays, and an important book, *Blues People* (1963), on the history of African American music. What made LeRoi Jones a celebrity, however, and ensured him a niche in American literary history, was his two-act play *The Dutchman,* which premiered in New York City on March 24, 1964.

In *The Dutchman,* a reticent, bookish, middle-class black man named Clay meets a white temptress named Lula in a New York subway car. The play consists mainly of their verbal combat. Angered by Clay's refusal to dance with her, Lula taunts him:

> Come on, Clay. Let's rub bellies on the train....Forget your social-working mother for a few seconds and let's knock stomachs. Clay, you liver-lipped white man. You would-be Christian. You ain't no nigger, you're just a dirty white man.

And Clay responds in kind:

> Tallulah Bankhead!...Don't you tell me anything! If I'm a middle-class fake white man...let me be....Let me be who I feel like being. Uncle Tom. Thomas. Whoever. It's none of your business....I sit here, in this buttoned-up suit, to keep myself from cutting all your throats....You great liberated whore! You fuck some black man, and right away you're an expert on black people. What a lotta shit that is.

But Lula has the last word, so to speak, when she suddenly stabs Clay to death. Her fellow passengers throw his body out of the subway car and disappear. Alone, Lula takes her seat again. When another Negro man enters the car, she begins anew her lethal routine.

Although Jones was situated in a predominantly white, bohemian milieu when he wrote *The Dutchman,* he had already begun to embrace the idea that it was primarily blacks—indeed, exclusively blacks—to whom he should be addressing his art. Increasingly successful, he was also becoming increasingly radical in his condemnation of white American society. Asked on one occasion by a white woman what whites could do to help solve the race problem, Jones replied, "You can help by dying. You are a cancer. You can help the world's people with your death." Outrageous as this statement would have been coming from anyone, it was even more startling in being directed at a white woman by an African American who was himself married to a white woman. Jones, though, was by no means alone in living within this particular paradox. He noted in his autobiography that at one point he and some other black intellectuals had objected to the presence of white radicals in an organization they were trying to establish. "What was so wild," he recalled, "was that some of us were talking about how we didn't want white people on the committee...but we were all hooked up to white women....Such were the contradictions of that period of political organization." The more prominent Jones became, the more he was accused of hypocrisy. The cultural critic Stanley Kauffmann, for example, asserted that he was an exemplary figure in "the tradition of the fake." Stung by such charges, infatuated by black nationalist rhetoric, inspired by the prospect of re-creating himself, and bored by a disappointing marriage, LeRoi Jones in 1965 divorced his wife, Hettie, in preparation for waging war on behalf of the Black Nation.[6]

Throughout the Black Power era, substantial numbers of African Americans loudly condemned black participation in interracial marriage, especially with whites, deeming it to be racial betrayal. Joyce Blake searingly articulated this sentiment in a 1968 letter to the editor of the *Village Voice:*

> It really hurts and baffles me and many other black sisters to see our black brothers(?) coming down the streets in their African garbs with a white woman on their arms. It is fast becoming a standard joke among the white girls that they can get our men still—African styles and all....
>
> It certainly seems to many black sisters that the Movement is just another subterfuge to aid the Negro male in procuring a white woman. If this be so, then the black sisters don't need it, for surely we have suffered enough humiliation from both white and black men in America.

The argument that intermarriage is destructive of racial solidarity has been, as we have seen, the principal basis of black opposition over the years. Another objection is that it robs black women of black men who should be their "natural" partners, thus weakening the position of black women in the marriage market. Lula Miles advanced this idea in an August 1969 letter to the editor of *Ebony.* Responding to a white woman who had expressed bewilderment at black women's anger, Ms. Miles wrote, "Non-sister wonders why the sight of a black man with a white woman is revolting to a black woman....The name of the game is 'competition.' Non-sister, you are trespassing!" Miraonda J. Stevens reinforced the point the following month in a letter of her own, predicting that "in the future there aren't going to be enough nice black men around for us [black women] to marry."

The "market" critique of interracial marriage has had along history. In 1929 Palestine Wells, a black columnist for the *Baltimore Afro-American,* wrote, "I have a sneaking suspicion that national intermarriage will make it harder to get husbands. A girl has a hard time enough getting a husband, but methinks 'twill be worse. Think how, awful it would be if all the ofay girls with a secret hankering for brown skin men could openly compete with us." Forty-three years later, Katrina Williams echoed Wells's remarks. "The white man is marrying the white woman," she noted. "The black man is marrying the white woman. [W]ho's gonna marry me?" Behind Pickens's anxious question resided more than demographic facts regarding the pool of black men available for marriage. There was, too, the perception (or the fear) that many African American men believed, first, that white women were relatively more desirable than black women, and second, that black women themselves were downright *un*attractive. Again the pages of *Ebony* offered vivid testimony: "Let's just lay all phony excuses aside and get down to the true nitty, nitty, NITTY-GRITTY and tell it like it really is," Mary A. Dowdell wrote in 1969. "Black males hate black women just because they are black. The whole so-called Civil Rights Act was really this: 'I want a white woman because she's white and I not only hate but don't want a black woman because she's black.'...The whole world knows this."

Decades later, African American hostility to interracial intimacy would remain widespread and influential. Three examples are revealing. The first is *Jungle Fever* (1991). Directed by Spike Lee and set in New York City in the early 1990s, the movie focuses on an unhappy interracial affair. Flipper Purify is an ambitious, college-educated black architect who lives in Harlem with his colored wife and their young daughter. Angle Tucci, a young white woman, works for Purify as a secretary. Educated only through high school, she lives in Bensonhurst with her father and brothers, all of whom are outspoken racists. One evening when Purify and Tucci stay late at the office, business concerns are superseded by erotic longings tinged with racial curiosity. He has never been sexually intimate with a white woman, and she has never been sexually intimate with a black man. They bridge that gap in their experience by sexually exploring each other right then and there on a chair and drafting table. Afterward, they both stupidly confide in indiscreet friends who carelessly reveal their secret. Angie Tucci's father throws her out of the family home after viciously beating her for "fucking a nigger." Flipper Purify's wife, Drew, kicks him out, too. Purify and Tucci move into an apartment together, but the arrangement quickly falls apart under the pressure of their own feelings of guilt and uncertainty and the strong disapproval they encounter from blacks and whites alike.

A second expression of contemporary black opposition to interracial intimacy is Lawrence Otis Graham's 1995 essay "I Never Dated a White Girl." Himself educated at Princeton University and Harvard Law School in the 1980s, Graham sought to explain why "black middle class kids...[who are] raised in integrated or mostly white neighborhoods, [and] told to befriend white neighbors, socialize and study with white classmates, join white social and professional organizations and go to work for mostly white employers," are also warned by their parents and friends, "Oh, and by the way, don't ever forget that you are black, and that you should never get so close to whites that you happen to fall in love with them."[7] Graham did more than merely describe this reaction, however; he also justified it, in a candid polemic that might as well have been entitled "Why I Am *Proud* That I Never Dated a White Girl."

A third example is "Black Men, White Women: A Sister Relinquishes Her Anger," an essay by the novelist Bebe Moore Campbell. Recounting the moment when she and her girlfriends spied a handsome black celebrity escorting a white woman at a trendy Beverly Hills restaurant, Campbell reminisced:

> In unison, we moaned, we groaned, we rolled our eyes heavenward. We gnashed our teeth in harmony and made ugly faces. We sang "Unmph! Unpph! Umph!" a capella style, then shook our heads as we lamented for the ten thousandth time the perfidy of black men and cursed trespassing white women who dared to "take our men."...Before lunch was over I had a headache, indigestion, and probably elevated blood pressure.[8]

In each of these works, three themes recur. The first is the burden of the past—the feeling that certain brutal facts of history should dissuade African American men and women from entering into intimate relations with whites.[9] For some black women, the key inhibiting collective memory is of white men raping their kind with impumty.[10] For some black males, the painful counterpoint is the image of the lynchings inflicted on African American men accused of sexual misconduct with white women—another subject we will deal with at length later.[11] Explaining why he had never dated a white girl, Graham cited as a primary reason "the ghost of Emmitt Till," the black youngster from Chicago who was murdered in Mississippi in 1955 for whistling at a white woman.[12] Graham was aware that, fortunately, black men of his generation were much less vulnerable than their predecessors. But partly in homage to those who had gone before him, Graham himself consciously declined to cross racial boundaries that would have been physically hazardous for his forebears to traverse.

A second recurrent idea is that racial pride and loyalty demand that blacks, especially the more successful among them, marry other blacks. Of particular significance in *Jungle Fever* is that the protagonist is an *affluent* and *highly educated* black man. It is precisely because he has "made it" that other black characters in the film—to the approbation of many black filmgoers—are so caustic in condemning his interracial affair. This argument holds that, having been assisted by the communal efforts of African Americans, successful blacks must, in all fairness, "give back" to that community. And one crucial way for them to do that is to make themselves available personally, as spouses, to other blacks. Given the plummeting marriage rate within African American communities, some even contend that this is an essential act of solidarity.[13] Relating how he and his friends regularly engage in "race checking," Graham confided:

> We flip through glowing profiles [about successful blacks] in *People, Ebony,* or *Business Week* quietly praising the latest black trailblazer and role model. Then we look for what we consider the final determinant of this person's black identity— that thing that will allow us to bestow our unqualified appreciation. We look for the

litmus test of loyalty to the race: the photo of the person's spouse or significant other.[14]

Many black critics of interracial marriage see it as a diversion that siphons off valuable human resources that black communities can ill afford to lose. Only a small percentage of the black men who marry do so interracially; in 1999 just 7 percent of married black men had non-black wives. But given the relative paucity of marriageable black men as a consequence of poverty, imprisonment, and other factors, a substantial number of black women feel acutely this loss of potential black mates. In 1992, researchers found that for every three black unmarried women in their twenties, there was only one unmarried black man whose earnings rose above the poverty level. In view of the realities facing black women, resentful disparagement of interracial marriage should come as no surprise. "In a drought," Bebe Moore Campbell wrote, "even one drop of water is missed." Moreover, "for many African American women," she continues, "the thought of black men, particularly those who are successful, dating or marrying white women is like being passed over for the prom by the boy of their dreams, causing them pain, rage, and an overwhelming sense of betrayal and personal rejection."[15] Compiling a roster of prominent blacks either married to or otherwise romantically involved with whites— Clarence Thomas (justice of the Supreme Court of the United States), Henry Louis Gates (chairman of Afro-American Studies at Harvard University), Quincy Jones (stellar musician), Franklin A. Thomas (former president of the Ford Foundation), John Edgar Wideman (prominent novelist), Orlando Patterson (professor of sociology at Harvard University), and Wilbert Tatus (editor of the *Amsterdam News*)[16] —Graham voiced disappointment that so many of "our most talented role models" had made choices that were, or could be plausibly interpreted as, "a means to dissociate…from the black race." When a prominent black person "turns out to be married to a white mate," Graham averred, "our children say, 'Well, if it's so good to be black, why do all my role models date and marry whites?'…As a child growing up in the 'black is beautiful' 1970s," he declared, "I remember asking these questions."

Anticipating the objection that his championing of race matching within marriage constituted a sort of "reverse racism" that was itself no less evil than antiblack bigotry, Graham noted that his beliefs were aimed neither at keeping the races separate nor at assigning a status of superiority to one group over another. Rather, it was his desire, he said, to develop "solutions for the loss of black mentors and role models at a time when the black community is overrun with crime, drug use, a high dropout rate, and a sense that any black who hopes to find…career success must necessarily disassociate himself from his people with the assistance of a white spouse." Seeking to spotlight the systematic consequences of decisions typically defended as innocent assertions of individual autonomy, Graham maintained:

> It's not the discrete decision of any one of these individuals that makes black America stand up and take notice. It is the cumulative effect of each of these personal decisions that bespeaks a frightening pattern for an increasingly impoverished and wayward black community. The cumulative effect is that the very blacks who are potential mentors and supporters of a financially and psychologically depressed black community are increasingly deserting the black community en masse, both physically and emotionally.

A third theme here is that blacks involved in interracial relationships generally suffer from a noxious combination of self-centeredness and self-denigration. The self-centeredness manifests itself in what might be described as con-spicuous consumption of whiteness. In *Jungle Fever,* on-screen critics of Flipper Purify say mockingly that blacks like him are no longer satisfied with obtaining light-skinned colored women as their trophies; nowadays, these critics aver, the Flipper Purifys of Afro-America demand "the real thang"—"Miss Anne," a white female trophy—as the emblematic signature of their prowess.[17] The self-denigration is revealed, so the theory goes, in a yearning for whiteness that necessarily implies a belittling of blackness. Graham, for one, pushed this point hard, asserting that there existed, in many highly visible interracial relationships between black men and white women, a notable asymmetry in which the men were outstanding and the women mediocre. He was frustrated, he wrote, at seeing accomplished blacks aggressively pursuing unaccomplished whites.[18] Various characters in *Jungle Fever* make similar observations. Drew Purify's black girlfriends, commiserating with her, note that it is all too typical that her husband would fall for a white secretary who has not even been to college—in contrast to his wife, a sophisticated, college-educated manager. Purify's brother, Gator, says much the same thing, but with a comedic spin that compares the physical attributes of certain categories of black and white women. Upon meeting Angie, Gator pulls his brother aside and compliments him on his lover's attractiveness. In that sense alone, she is unusual, he says, because while the black women who go out with white men are almost always "slammin'," the white women whom black men date are usually homely—not Penthouse Pets, Gator complains, but outhouse pets.[19]

THE NEW AMALGAMATIONISM

Despite continued opposition to interracial marriage from various quarters, the general situation for people involved in interracial intimacies has never been better. For the most part, the law prohibits officials from taking race into account in licensing marriages, making child-custody decisions, and arranging adoptions.[20] Moreover, across the country, public opinion now permits interracial intimacies to be pursued and enjoyed with unparalleled levels of freedom, security, and support. This trend will almost certainly continue; polling data and common observation indicate that younger people tend to be more liberal on these matters than their elders. Thus, despite the black-power backlash and the remnants of white hostility to "race mixing," the most salient fact about interracial intimacies today is that those involved in them have never been in a stronger position, or one in which optimism regarding the future was more realistic.

Dramatic evidence of this is offered by the career of one of the most controversial figures in recent American history: Justice Clarence Thomas, the ultraconservative black jurist whom President George Bush nominated in 1991 to fill the Supreme Court seat being vacated by Thurgood Marshall.[21] Extraordinary conflict surrounded both the senatorial hearings on his confirmation—during which Thomas's professional and personal suitability for the post was sharply challenged—and the close vote that ultimately put him on the Court. Little negative comment surfaced publicly, however, regarding the nominee's marriage to a white woman, Virginia Lamp.[22] Notable, too, was that among Thomas's most fervent backers were former segregationists and their ideological descendants. Among these, the most evocative and prominent was Strom Thurmond. A founder of the influential Dixiecrat movement, a proponent of massive resistance to *Brown v. Board of Education,* and an opponent of the nomination of Thurgood Marshall, Thurmond had once fought desegregation at every turn.[23] Yet he and many of his fellow conservatives now enthusiastically supported Clarence Thomas. Given the intensity with which such racial traditionalists had always resisted interracial intimacy, their

endorsement of a black Supreme Court nominee who was married to a white woman constituted a significant landmark in American race relations.

Two dissenting opinions have been advanced here. The first holds that white conservatives' acceptance of Thomas was an anomaly, based narrowly on his open dissociation from the mainstream of black politics, and as such reflected no substantive change in that group's racial sentiments. Proponents of this argument contend that Thomas is seen by many conservative whites as an "honorary white" and thus no real challenge to white racial hegemony. They further argue that white racism has not so much diminished as become more sophisticated, eschewing the primitive one-drop rule and embracing instead a subtle situational concept of race that employs factors other than skin color and ancestry as guides to ascription. According to this view, many of Thomas's white supporters consciously or unconsciously "whiten" him because of his ultraconservative political opinions. The second dissent asserts that little can be made of the conservative embrace of Thomas because the social meaning of racial intermarriage has itself been transformed. No longer seen as a threat to the established racial order, such marriages have become acceptable, comforting, and even attractive to dominant elites insofar as they camouflage what remains in essence a white-supremacist pigmentocracy. Those who take this view maintain that in the eyes of many whites, the white wife on the arm of a Negro husband is a sign that the man is safe and wants to assimilate. There is some evidentiary basis for this speculation. For instance, when asked how she had felt about the marriage of her niece to Clarence Thomas, one of Virginia Lamp's aunts responded, "He was so nice, we forgot he was black." Thomas treated her niece so well, this aunt continued, that "all of his other qualities made up for his being black."

Nevertheless, considering the vehemence with which, until recently, most whites have disparaged interracial intimacies, and particularly mixed marriage, even mere tolerance is a notably historic departure. The Thomas-Lamp union was one of a total of approximately 177,000 black-white marriages in America in 1987.[24] In 1960 there were about 51,000 black-white married couples in the United States; in 1970, 65,000; in 1980, 121,000; in 1991, 213,000; and in 1998, 330,000. In other words, between 1960 and 2000, black-white mixed marriages increased more than sixfold. But not only are mixed marriages becoming more numerous; they are also becoming more common among people who are younger and more fertile. Previously, participants in such marriages tended to be older than other brides and grooms. Frequently they were veterans of divorce, embarking on second or third marriages. In recent years, though, interracial couples have been marrying at younger ages than their pioneering predecessors, and have shown a greater inclination to raise children and pursue all of the other "normal" activities that married life offers.

Given the low historical baselines against which trends today are measured, it is easy to exaggerate the scope of black-white marital integration. It should therefore be stressed that mixed marriages remain remarkably rare, comprising a mere .6 percent of the total marriages in 1998, for instance, when 330,000 couples out of 55,305,000 overall had one black and one white partner. Moreover, blacks' racial isolation on the marriage market appears to eclipse that of other people of color. The percentages of Native Americans and Asian Americans marrying whites are much larger than the percentage of blacks doing the same.[25] Professor Nathan Glazer is correct, then, in stating that "blacks stand out uniquely among the array of ethnic and racial groups in the degree to which marriage remains within the group." Among the complex reasons for this

social isolation are aggregate subjective evaluations of marriageability, beauty, personality, comfort, compatibility, and prestige that favor certain groups over others. At the dawn of the twenty-first century, a wide array of social pressures continue to make white-black marital crossings more difficult, more costly, and thus less frequent than other types of interethnic or interracial crossings.

Still, even taking into account the peculiar persistence of the black-white racial divide, the trajectory of this form of miscegenation is clear: through turbulent times and in the face of considerable opposition, the number of black-white marriages has been increasing consistently (albeit slowly) for at least forty years. Reinforcing this growth is the fact that interracial marriage has become compatible with lofty ambitions across a variety of fields—not only entertainment but government service, scholarship, the philanthropic sector, business, and the professions. The Thomas-Lamp marriage is indicative of this trend. So, too, are the unions of William Cohen (former senator from Maine and secretary of defense in the Clinton administration) and his black wife; Peter Norton (inventor of widely used computer software) and his black wife;[26] and Franklin Raines (former director of the Office of Management and Budget and chief executive officer of Fannie Mae) and his white wife. Furthermore, despite the substantial influence of the black-power backlash, some African Americans whose positions make them directly dependent upon black public opinion have managed to marry whites without losing their footing. A good example is Julian Bond, the chairman of the board of directors of the NAACP, whose wife is white.

There are other signs, too, that black-white interracial romance has become more broadly accepted and even, in certain contexts, quite fashionable. One such indicator is advertising. Advertisers seek to persuade people to buy goods and services by increasing awareness of them and associating them with imagined pleasures. In the past, advertisers targeting general audiences with the lure of romance have typically—indeed, overwhelmingly—used couples of the same race. But these days, at least occasionally, interracial couples are being deployed as enticements to shop at Nordstrom's, Club Monaco, or Wal-Mart, or to purchase furniture from IKEA, jeans from Guess, sweaters from Tommy Hilfiger, cologne from Calvin Klein, shampoo from Procter & Gamble, or watches from Gucci.

Television programming also signals important changes in sexual attitudes. Prior to the 1960s, portrayals or even insinuations of black-white interracial romance were virtually nonexistent on TV. The November 22, 1968, episode of the popular science-fiction series *Star Trek* marked a breakthrough in showing a kiss shared by the legendary (white) Captain James T. Kirk and (black) Lieutenant Uhura. Remarkably, however, the characters were not portrayed as actively *wanting* to kiss each other; instead they were *forced* to do so by a villain who captured Kirk's vessel, the starship *Enterprise,* and usurped the will of its crew. Not until 1975 did network television portray a married black-white couple, Tom and Helen Willis, who occupied a prominent place on the popular sitcom *The Jeffersons.* The show, a spinoff of Norman Lear's *All in the Family,* was about an eponymous black family whose patriarch, the hardworking but obnoxious George Jefferson, was obsessed with upward mobility, or what the theme song referred to as "movin' on up." The Willises lived in the same expensive apartment building as the Jeffersons. Although George constantly taunted the couple, calling them zebras, the families ultimately merged when the Jeffersons' son married the Willises' daughter.[27] Since the 1970s, depictions of interracial intimacies have remained rare on commercial television, though they do surface occasionally. In 1989 the short-lived *Robert Guillaume Show* pre-

sented viewers with a romance between a divorced black marriage counselor and his white secretary. The following year, the upstart Fox television network reluctantly aired *True Colors,* a situation comedy centered on the marriage of a black dentist (with two teenage sons) and a white schoolteacher (with a live-in mother and a teenage daughter). According to the show's creator, executives at the three older networks (ABC, CBS, and NBC) expressly stated that they were afraid the interracial marriage would alienate potential advertisers and dissuade at least some local affiliates from broadcasting the program. Notwithstanding cold feet at the top, writers have in the last decade or so succeeded in convincing television executives to air more entertainment fare featuring, or at least noting the existence of, interracial intimacy. Indeed, several of the most popular and influential shows of the 1990s portrayed transracial romances. Sometimes the racial aspect of the relationship was highlighted, as in *L.A. Law*'s dramatization of a black lawyer feeling that he must choose between his white lover and his job as an elected representative of a mainly black constituency. Sometimes it was ignored, as on *Ally McBeal,* where race matters seldom if ever arose in conversations between the white woman attorney and the black male physician with whom she was infatuated. On occasion, on-screen interracial relationships failed. The producers of *ER,* for example, terminated a romance between a black male doctor and a white colleague, not in deference to viewer opposition but because the black actor involved objected. He complained that whereas his character had always been obnoxious in his dealings with black women, he was now being shown as sympathetic in his treatment of the white woman. On other programs, interracial romance was permitted to blossom. In 1994, for example, on *In the Heat of the Night,* the white sheriff of a town in the Deep South married a black woman on-screen,[28] and in 1997, a network production of *Cinderella* paired a black actress in the title role with a Filipino Prince Charming, to great popular acclaim.[29]

In some venues, nonfictional portrayals of interracial intimacy have been sensationally negative, as on confessional talk shows that, for a while, at least, uniformly depicted transracial relationships as troubled, weird, or pathological.[30] In other contexts, however, television programs have acknowledged the gamut of personalities and emotions to be found among those who happen to be involved in interracial intimacies. In the fall of 1999, the Public Broadcasting System (PBS) aired *An American Love Story,* a ten-hour documentary film by Jennifer Fox that chronicled the lives of an interracial family: Bill Sims, a black man, Karen Wilson, a white woman, and their two daughters, Cecily and Chaney. Wilson and Sims first met in 1967, at a resort where he was playing piano in a rhythm-and-blues band and she was vacationing with her parents. He was the son of a cleaning woman and a steelworker who was also a Baptist minister; her father was a machinist, and her mother was a grocery clerk. When their courtship began, Bill was eighteen and Karen seventeen. Neither set of parents objected to the relationship, and both urged the couple to marry after Wilson got pregnant (though they in fact did not do so until the child was six years old).

Whites in Wilson's hometown of Prospect, Ohio, strongly condemned her romance with Sims. Her supposed friends ostracized the couple, and the local sheriff jailed Sims on several occasions for no other reason than to harass him. In 1972 they moved with their baby daughter to Columbus, but even in this larger, less isolated locale, they encountered overt hostility. They suspected bigots of killing their dog and setting their car afire in a successful campaign to frighten them away. They moved again, this time to Flushing, New York, where they hoped to find a more open-minded community.

Over the years, the Wilson-Sims family subsisted largely on Karen's reliable earnings as a manager, supplemented by Bill's spotty wages as, among other things, a carpenter, mail carrier, and musician. At the price of some tedium, *An American Love Story* shows its subjects engaged in all the quotidian tasks of daily life—cooking, cleaning, resting, seeking comfort, venting frustration—that have little or nothing to do with racial differences. It also shows them facing various nonracial crises, including Karen's hysterectomy and Bill's alcoholism. Almost inevitably, though, racial difficulties surface to menace the couple and their children. Among the most poignant segments of the series are wrenching scenes from Cecily's years as an undergraduate at Colgate College, where tyrannical black classmates tell her, essentially, that if she wants to be their friend, she must refuse to join a predominantly white sorority and, more generally, defer to their black-separatist sensibilities. She declines their terms, and they retaliate; she is hurt. Throughout, the television audience is privy to the conflict.[31]

The creators of *An American Love Story* wanted to document an interracial marriage that spanned the final decades of the twentieth century. Its subjects, for their part, wanted to change perceptions through education; this ambition constituted the principal explanation offered by the Sims-Wilson clan for permitting their family life to be examined in such a public manner. Education was also the primary aim cited by the program's director, Jennifer Fox, a white woman who credited her own love affair with a black man with opening her eyes to important areas of American life to which she had previously been blind.[32]

On the big screen, too, recent years have seen an increase in both the number and the quality of depictions of interracial intimacy. There was a time, not so long ago, when the scarcity of such portrayals made keeping track of them easy; now, because of their increasing numbers and variety, that task is much more difficult. True, the fear of an adverse audience response can still cause cautious film producers to suppress interracial romance, not only through their choice of projects but even in their handling of plot points. In John Grisham's novel *The Pelican Brief* (1992), for instance, the protagonists become lovers, but in the screen version (1993), there is no romance; the relationship remains resolutely platonic. The reason for this alteration is obvious: the male lead is played by a black actor (Denzel Washington), and the female lead by a white actress (Julia Roberts). There are, moreover, scores of other examples of black actors apparently being singled out for Hollywood's cold-shower treatment lest they mirror real-life interracial erotic excitement. Prominent among these desexualized roles are Will Smith's character in *Men in Black* (1997) and Wesley Snipes's in *Murder at 1600* (1997). This approach led one wag to remark, in reference to *The Bone Collector* (1999), that the only way Denzel Washington would ever be shown "getting the girl" was if he played a man paralyzed from the waist down. That being said, a number of major motion pictures released in the past decade have followed actors and actresses of all complexions in their pursuit of sexual pleasures across color lines, and have done so with a boldness that probably would not have been tolerated in the environment that generated *Guess Who's Coming to Dinner?* Examples include the explicit erotic grapplings of Lawrence Fishburne and Ellen Barkin in *Bad Company* (1995), Wesley Snipes and Natassia Kinski in *One Night Stand* (1997), Reese Witherspoon and Bookeem Woodbine in *Freeway* (1996), Warren Beatty and Halle Berry in *Bulworth* (1998), Tom Cruise and Thandie Newton in *Mission Impossible 2* (2000), Julia Stiles and Sean Patrick Thomas in *Save the Last Dance* (2000), and Halle Berry and Billy Bob Thornton in *Monster's Ball* (2001).[33] In increasing numbers of films, moreover, interracial intimacy has been emerging as simply one part of a larger story in which racial difference is of little or no significance. This is an important development because presuming the normalcy of interracial intimacy—treating it as "no big deal"—may be more subversive of traditional norms than stressing the racial heterodoxy of such relationships. Although examples of this presumption can be found in several films (e.g., *Pulp Fiction* [1994], Cruel Intentions [1999], and *Mystery Men* [1999]), the most significant was the blockbuster *The Bodyguard* (1992), which starred Kevin Costner and Whitney Houston.

Literature comprises yet another forum in which negative depictions of interracial intimacies are being supplemented by positive portrayals, though the former continue to dwarf the latter. White racist writers have long condemned miscegenation as both unnatural and disgusting. Writing under the pseudonym Oliver Bolokitten, Jerome B. Holgate authored *A Sojourn in the City of Amalgamation, in the Year of Our Lord, 19—* (1835), a novel that envisions a future in which intermarriage is rife. In Holgate's dystopia, white abolitionists associate on intimate terms with blacks, even though their very senses alert them to the danger of their doing so, causing them to retch constantly in reaction to the supposedly foul odors given off by the Negroes. Disregarding their physical repulsion, the white amalgamationists not only persist in their own interracial socializing but also force their children to associate with blacks, even to the extent of drugging resistant daughters. Following in Holgate's footsteps have come many other opponents of miscegenation, similarly racist and similarly mediocre as literary artists. One of these was Gertrude Atherton, author of *Senator North* (1900), a novel in which a white man commits suicide upon learning that the woman he has married is distantly related to African Americans. Another was William Pierce, author of *The Turner Diaries* (1978), an apocalyptic vision of a future in which

Christian white supremacists prevail over their enemies, including blacks, Jews, Latinos, and other whites who have disgraced themselves by associating with their racial inferiors. Pierce enthusiastically depicts the murder of white women who are killed on account of their sexual intimacy with black men.

Black writers, too, have used literature to attack miscegenation. We have already noted the work of LeRoi Jones in this context.[34] There are others as well. In 'Sippi (1967), John Oliver Killens portrays interracial intimacy as an infantile phase that many black men go through before taking on the serious responsibilities of racial loyalty and leadership. Rejecting a white woman who expects him to marry her, the hero of 'Sippi declares that "marrying the white man's daughter is not a part of the Black Power program"—a jilting that the narrator approvingly describes as "sweet revenge."[35] Cecil Brown's *The Life and Loves of Mr. Jiveass Nigger* (1969) offers plenty of interracial sex but no interracial love. "It is a tragedy," the novel's protagonist asserts, "if a black man lets himself love something in a white woman, just as it is if a man lets himself get fucked by another man." Set in Copenhagen, Denmark, in the 1960s, Brown's novel chronicles the shenanigans of a group of black gigolos who service white women. The main character, George Washington, has fled to Scandinavia in order "to get the White Bitch out of his system by wallowing in whiteness until he could live without it." One of the white women he encounters there is the American consul, who pays Washington and other black men for their sexual attention and is so badly beaten by one of them that she is rendered sterile.

Writers of all hues have turned to depictions of interracial romance to highlight the depth and persistence and perniciousness of racism. Although some of these authors may have had no objection themselves to interracial intimacy, they nonetheless portrayed it in ways likely to be viewed by most readers as frightening.

In the novels and stories (*Light in August* [1932]; *Absalom, Absalom!* [1936]; *Go Down, Moses* [1942]) of William Faulkner, for example, interracial intimacy emerges repeatedly as a problem—a problem, moreover, surrounded by shame, misery, ostracism, violence, and death. Other novelists (most of them considerably less skilled than Faulkner) have also highlighted trouble and tragedy in interracial intimacies. Thus, in Anna Dickenson's *What Answer?* (1868), the white English wife of a Negro man dies in childbirth after a race riot drives them from their home in Philadelphia. Years later, the couple's daughter marries a white man, only to be murdered with him in the New York draft riots of 1863. In Albion Tourgee's *Toinette* (1874), a former slave master is struck blind when he decides to propose to the woman who was once his slave mistress. In Lillian Smith's *Strange Fruit* (1944), a black woman's brother kills her white lover, an act that provokes a white mob to murder a wholly innocent African American bystander. In Chester Himes's *The Primitive* (1953), a black man and a white woman become intimate not because they feel a healthy attraction to each other but because they are driven by pathological expediency. He is impelled, like an addict, to sleep with a white woman; as for her, "only when sleeping with a Negro could she feel secure in the knowledge that she wasn't dirt." To add to the misery, the man senselessly kills the woman.[36] In James Baldwin's *Another Country* (1962), a white woman who has become sexually involved with a black man has a nervous breakdown; her black lover commits suicide. In Ann Fairbairn's *Five Smooth Stones* (1966), the hero, a black lawyer-activist, marries his white girlfriend and is almost immediately done in by a vengeful bigot.[37] In *I Want a Black Doll* (1967), Frank Hercules's principal characters have deep feelings of affection for each other but still fail to surmount the racial difficulties that divide them: "They knew ecstasy but never achieved union; never became one, were always straining towards but never really touching each other, were always a Negro man and a white woman." Buffeted by doubts within and hostility without, their life together falls apart. He poisons their relationship with mistaken suspicions that she is seeing another man—a white man. She tries to abort their baby and dies in the process. In Ernest Gaines's *The Autobiography of Miss Jane Pittman* (1971), a white man kills himself because the colored woman he loves refuses, for racial reasons, to marry him. In Calvin Hernton's *Scarecrow* (1974), the black protagonist kills his white wife. In sum, for many writers miscegenation has been the harbinger of mayhem, misery, and death—the very symbol of destructive intimacy.

Distinctly undeveloped is the literary tradition that portrays interracial relationships that are at least potentially rewarding. Pioneering contributions to this tradition include Lydia Maria Child's *A Romance of the Republic* (1867), William Dean Howells's *An Imperative Duty* (1892), Sinclair Lewis's *Kingsblood Royal* (1947), and Willard Savoy's *Alien Land* (1949). In spite of their more benevolent attitude, however, these novels share a striking feature: they all involve "black" figures who look "white," a characteristic that attenuates the challenge posed by their marriages. In *A Romance of the Republic,* the colored women who wed across the race line can and do pass as white for much of their lives. Similarly, the putatively colored man who marries white is actually white himself, having been raised as a slave by mistake. *An Imperative Duty* centers on a woman who was raised as white and learned about her colored ancestry only as an adult. While the white man who becomes her husband is aware of her racial heritage, she continues to hold herself out as white to everyone else. In *Alien Land,* the colored protagonist looks white and passes for white after his marriage. In *Kingsblood Royal,* the central character, who used to be a white racist, publicly identifies himself as colored, transforms his thinking, and becomes a champion of the rights of colored people—as does his white wife, who has herself been a complacent bigot. Still, his situation is hardly that of an ordinary black man: of one thirty-second colored ancestry, he is very much a voluntary Negro.

The attempt to compile a list of novels, stories, or plays in which interracial romance or marriage is portrayed in a positive light, and whose characters are explicitly perceived as colored, makes for an instructive exercise. The rarity of such writings underlines the degree to which miscegenation and its representations have been discouraged. In *Subdued Southern Nobility* (1882), an anonymous novelist crafted a story featuring a Negro woman who happily marries a northern white man, and in *Hearts of Gold* (1896), J. McHenry Jones brought to life a wealthy, educated white woman who happily marries a black man. Then, in the late 1960s, Frank Yerby eschewed the black-power backlash at that time in vogue. *In Speak Now* (1969), he created an interracial couple who, for once, did not have to endure the horrible scourges imposed upon so many of their literary predecessors traversing the color bar. Nor are their racial identities ambiguous, or their characterizations too angelic to credit. The white woman protagonist is initially a bigot, but she evolves. Her affair with the black man whom she grows to love corrects her racist upbringing. Just as she rejects the racial chauvinism of disapproving whites, so, too, does her husband reject that of disapproving blacks. Asked tauntingly whether he has any race pride, Yerby's protagonist answers in the negative. Maintaining that "a biological accident is hardly sufficient motive for self-congratulation," he declares that the only race in which he takes pride "is the human race." Yerby chose to situate his couple outside of the United States, setting their story in France—suggesting, perhaps, that in the late 1960s, at least, America was still too toxic to permit the healthy growth of an interracial affair. That affair does grow, and bloom; it promises the couple a future, as the novel ends on a determinedly optimistic note:

> Quite suddenly they both knew it was going to work. To go on. In spite of everything. That even after it did go flat, become routine, descended to the level of boredom all marriages get to, sooner or later, even if it went bad in any of the ten thousand different ways most legally sanctioned matings do, they'd hold on, endure, cling to one another.…They would be very careful of each other, until that care became a condition of living, and…a means of preserving the tenderness they now felt.

Since the publication of *Speak Now,* a tiny procession of black writers has also approvingly depicted interracial love stories. Barbara Chase-Riboud (*Sally Hemings* [1979]) and Charles Johnson (*The Ox-herding Tale* [1982]) did so in innovative novels that envision loving interracial relationships in the era of slavery—thereby rejecting the dogma that bondage rendered impossible authentic love between masters and slaves.[38] Probing but ultimately approving portraits of interracial relationships set in more recent times include Dorothy West's *The Wedding* (1995) and Stanley Crouch's *Don't the Moon Look Lonesome* (2000).

Sandra Kitt has written a series of novels notable for their tender portrayal of people whose search for companionship takes them across racial lines. In Kitt's *The Color of Love* (1995) and *Close Encounters* (2000), black women fall in love with white policemen. In Eric Jerome Dickey's *Milk in My Coffee* (1998), a young black man whose office is adorned with a photograph of Malcolm X becomes joyfully involved with a white woman he meets during a shared cab ride. The work of both Kitt and Dickey has been categorized as "popular fiction" as opposed to "serious literature"—a label that has limited these writers' artistic and intellectual influence, insofar as their efforts have been largely ignored by academics, intellectuals, and the major book reviews. Nevertheless, the fact that their books have been widely disseminated on the mass market indicates some confidence on the part of profit-minded publishers that a broad audience is open to enjoying interracial love stories.

One of the most memorable of the novels championing interracial relationships is also one of the most neglected. Ann Allen Shockley's *Loving Her* (1974) is the story of Renay Lee, a black woman who flees her abusive black husband, Jerome. Jerome raped Renay on a date when they were both college students; impregnated by the assault, she married him out of fear, ignorance, and desperation. After several years of an increasingly hellish existence punctuated by her husband's cruel sale of her treasured piano, Renay, young daughter in tow, leaves her marriage and moves in with Terry, a white woman with whom she proceeds to fall in love. The escape revives Renay; suddenly "there was life in life now, and love in its moments." But tragedy awaits her: Jerome abducts their daughter, gets drunk, and crashes his car, killing the child. Distraught, Renay leaves Terry, then quickly returns to forge a union that Shockley unabashedly embraces: "Two as one, one as two, waiting for the morning, which promised to be even better than the night."

Shockley audaciously challenges the black-power backlash by treating with respect both the interracial and the lesbian aspects of the Renay-Terry relationship. Many black opponents of interracial intimacy have also been critics of gay and lesbian sexuality.[39] Some have even gone so far as to claim that gay-lesbian sexuality is foreign to authentic black culture, and that black gays and lesbians have merely succumbed to white sexual degeneracy. Shockley's counter-attack on such views is

71

unsparing. She searingly debunks patriarchal black nationalism by picturing Renay as Jerome's slave. Even more provocatively, she imagines a black woman who finds greater sexual pleasure with her white female lover than with her black male husband. Shockley thus simultaneously subverts marriage, the presumed superiority of heterosexuality, the supposed primacy of black male sexual prowess, and the taboo against interracial sex. In college bull sessions, Renay's black friends "would wonder how Lena Horne and Pearl Bailey could wake up in the morning to white faces beside them. But now she knew: you can't confine love to color."[40]

Perhaps the most potent influence in creating new possibilities for interracial intimacy is that wielded by individuals engaged in (or born of) transracial dating, marriage, and parenting. This population, numbering in the hundreds of thousands, exhibits tremendous variety. One generalization that can properly be made about it, however, is that it is becoming increasingly vocal. There was a time, not so long ago, when the vast majority within this group sought invisibility; now, by contrast, many of its members seek recognition and are establishing or joining advocacy organizations devoted to publicizing their views and institutionalizing their presence. Announcing the formation of the Association of Multi-Ethnic Americans (AMEA) in November 1988, Carlos Fernandez declared:

> We who embody the melting pot...stand up, not merely as neutrals in interethnic conflicts, but as intolerant participants against racism from whatever quarter it may come.... We are the faces of the future. Against the travails of regressive interethnic division and strife, we can be a solid core of unity bonding the peoples of all cultures together in the common course of human progress.

People involved in interracial intimacies used to voice quiet requests for simple protection against intimidation and violence. Now their demands are becoming more ambitious. One of these has to do with racial labeling. Many interracial couples object to standardized forms that compel them to designate their children either merely "black" or merely "white." Similarly, many who identify themselves as "mixed"—or "mulatto" or "half-and-half" or "multiracial"—bridle at classificatory regimes that impose singular racial identifications, as if everyone must be *only* white *or* black *or* Latino *or* Asian (etc., etc.). Prior to the census of 2000, the United States Census Bureau counted individuals according to that assumption. But after a good deal of prodding by AMEA and similar groups, the bureau decided to broaden the menu boxes available for indicating racial affiliation. Rather than being limited to only one box, respondents are now authorized to check whatever boxes they deem applicable, though the census bureau continues to decline to offer a separate "multiracial" box.[41] One complaint leveled against the traditional "check one box" regime is that it fosters confusion and inaccuracy—describing as "black," for example, people who are also partly white or partly Native American or partly Asian. Susan Graham, the (white) founder of Project RACE (Reclassify All Children Equally) notes that her "child has been white on the U.S. Census, black at school, and multiracial at home, all at the same time." Beyond the issue of statistical inaccuracy, the system has more personal ramifications, in that it compels mixed individuals to select for recognition only one aspect of their composite background, and thereby subordinate all the other aspects.

The census bureau's multiple-box-checking initiative addresses some but by no means all of the objections raised by critics.[42] Some contend that even the option of checking several boxes indicates, in effect, that multiracial individuals are only parts of other communities, rather than constituent members of a distinct multiracial community of their own. Some observers protest, moreover, the continuation of *any* racial scheme of classification, however it may be supplemented or repackaged. Whatever one may think of the ideas propounded by these various dissidents, it is clear that they are flexing their political muscles as never before and affecting hearts and minds in fundamental ways. They are not content to accept inherited conventions but insist instead on adding their own preferences to America's cultural mix. Professor Maria P. P. Root has demanded a Bill of Rights for racially mixed people, which would include the rights to identify one's race differently in different situations, to change one's racial identity over a lifetime (and more than once), to have loyalties to and identifications with more than one racial group, and to be able freely to choose whom to befriend and love. The winner of the 1995 Miss USA beauty pageant objected to being pegged as "black." "If people are going to know me," Chelsi Smith explained, "it's important for them to know that I'm black and white and that it hasn't been a disadvantage." Tiger Woods likewise does not enjoy being referred to as the first "black" or "African American" golf superstar, believing that those labels obscure other aspects of his ancestry that are just as important to him. He has therefore coined the term "'Cablinasian'-[for] Caucasian, Black, Indian, Asian"—to describe himself.[43] The coinage has proved controversial.[44] Many people, mainly blacks, have accused him of wanting to flee an African American identity that whites will impose upon him regardless of his preferences. ("When the black truck comes around," one observer quipped, "they're gonna haul his ass on it.") Such reactions notwithstanding, the real point here is that Root, Smith, Woods, and tens of thousands more like them have felt sufficiently self-assured to speak up, and have received substantial support in doing so. Their

conduct mirrors and strengthens a new force in America: the will of people engaged in or born of multiracial relationships, who have begun to insist upon public recognition of the full complexity of their lives.

Across the country, scores of interracial support groups have sprung up, among them MOSAIC (Multiethnics of Southern Arizona in Celebration), A Place for Us (North Little Rock, Arkansas), I-Pride (Interracial Intercultural Pride, Berkeley, California), MASC (Multiracial Americans of Southern California, Los Angeles, California), F .C. (Families of Color) Communique (Fort Collins, Colorado), Interracial Family Alliance (Augusta, Georgia), Society for Interracial Families (Troy, Michigan), 4c (Cross Cultural Couples & Children, Plainsboro, New Jersey), the Interracial Club of Buffalo, the Interracial Family Circle of Washington, D.C., and HONEY (Honor Our New Ethnic Youth, Eugene, Oregon). On college campuses, students can join organizations such as FUSION (Wellesley), Kaleidoscope (University of Virginia), Students of Mixed Heritage and Culture (SMHAC, Amherst), Half 'n' Half (Bryn Mawr), and Mixed Plate (Grinnell). These groups offer forums in which people can meet others in their situation, disseminate relevant information, debate, and organize. Although most of these organizations lack deep roots, many display a vigor and resourcefulness that suggest they will survive into the foreseeable future. They stem from and represent a community in the making. It is a community united by a common demand that the larger society respect and be attentive to people who either by descent or by choice fall outside the conventional racial groupings—people who are partners in interracial couples, parents of children whose race is different from their own, and children whose race differs from their parents'. The members of this community want whites to cease viewing them as products or agents of an alarming mongrelization. They want blacks to stop regarding them as inauthentic and unstable in-betweeners. They want security amid the established communities from which they have migrated. They want to emerge from what the writer Lise Funderberg has aptly called the "racial netherworld." They want to enjoy interaction with others without regret or fear, defensiveness or embarrassment. They want respect.

The community arising from interracial intimacies is rent by all manner of divisions. While some of its partisans trumpet pride in their identity,[45] others urge the dampening of such sentiments, fearful that pride will inevitably degenerate into chauvinism—especially in a society in which lighter-skinned hybrids have often been seen as superior to their darker-skinned relatives. Where some voice unequivocally a desire to inculcate a strong sense of multiracial peoplehood, others question the wisdom of creating new racial groups. The most salient feature of this nascent and fractious community, however, is a new sense of assertive self-confidence—a heady feeling that transracial affiliations are, for the first time in American history, being rightly appreciated as valuable resources. An editorial in the spring 2000 issue of *Mavin,* a magazine of "the mixed race experience," is indicative of this spirit. The 2000 census, wrote *Mavin*'s editor in chief, Matt Kelley, is finally granting the mixed race community "institutional recognition":

> Up until now we have been a one- or two-generation-only community....But now, having gained some form of institutional legitimacy, we may perpetuate [ourselves]....We have an opportunity to take advantage of our collective resources and improve discourse both within and outside our fledgling community. That is a social and political cause worth organizing for.

Among the publications supported by and aimed at the emerging community of politically self-conscious multiracial people—particu-

larly those whose affiliations bridge the black-white racial divide—one of the most informative was *Interrace.* Candace Mills, a black woman, and Gabe Grosz, her white husband, started the magazine in 1989. According to them, *Interrace*

> proudly celebrates racial diversity and colorblind love. We celebrate the interracial family, the interracial child and adult, and the interracial couple. We celebrate freedom. Freedom of the pursuit of happiness as every individual sees it, not as society as a whole sees it....*Interrace Magazine* is not a white only, black only, hispanic only, or asian only magazine. *Interrace Magazine* is a people magazine. A magazine for all people involved in interracial relationships and for the beautiful off-spring they create![46]

A low-budget *Ebony* for the multiracial community, *Interrace* was an irregular quarterly that performed a variety of functions. First of all, it served as a mirror, feeding the hunger of multiracial individuals and families to see themselves as part of the social landscape. Accordingly, many of the magazine's pages were given over to photographs of interracial couples, mixed-race children, and multiracial family gatherings.[47] Second, it offered a sounding board for those who wished to relate experiences stemming from their interracial relationships. A 1994 article entitled "When Your In-Laws Drive You Crazy!," by Henry Rubin, described numerous instances of in-laws objecting to marriages on racial grounds. In one particularly sad case history, a black man noted that members of his white fiancée's family had shot at him, beaten him, poured sugar into his gas tank, and slashed his tires. Rubin's own experience with the subject came through his white Jewish mother's disapproval of his marriage to a (presumably Christian) Puerto Rican. Like many features in *Interrace,* the piece ended by emphasizing the potential of bigotry to give way to enlightenment, and injustice to redemption. "With a little patience and a lot of understanding," Rubin promised, "many in-law problems can be handled successfully." His mother, for example, overcame much of her prejudiced disapproval of his wife, managing a transformation that undoubtedly encouraged his conclusion that "if you are persistent and are committed to your interracial relationship then the rewards will surely come your way." *Interrace* constantly served a cheerleading function, self-consciously striving to boost the morale of its constituency. Seeking to rebut the suspicion that interracial intimacies produce misfits and attract mainly weirdos, the magazine highlighted likable people of accomplishment, including Dan O'Brien (an Olympic track and field star and the biracial adopted son of a white couple), Eartha Kitt (a biracial entertainer who has been romantically involved with a number of white men), Peggy Lipton (a white actress, best known for her role on the television series *The Mod Squad,* who was married to the black musical impresario Quincy Jones), and Marian Wright Edelman (the black founder of the Children's Defense Fund who married a white man in Virginia soon after the *Loving* decision).

In an effort to refute still-prevalent beliefs that interracial intimacies are doomed to unhappiness and failure, *Interrace* profiled smiling, vigorous, enraptured couples who had managed to stay together for substantial periods of time. In 1993, for instance, it introduced readers to Charlene McGrady (black), Doug Fearn (white), and Hannon Fearn (mixed) of West Chester, Pennsylvania. Describing their experience, McGrady commented, "We've never felt any overt condemnation....We think this is because we don't walk around with a defensive posture....We know we belong together and act it!...Our marriage is happy, secure and thriving, and not all that different from any other marriage with children." To drive the point home, McGrady concluded her testimony, "I didn't know I could be so happy."

Later that same year, *Interrace* ran another "Success Story," this one about the China family: William China, a black man from South Carolina; Mary China, a white woman from New Jersey; William's child from a previous marriage (to a black woman); and the two children William and Mary had together. The interracial character of the Chinas' marriage had drawn some unwanted attention—opposition to it, for example, had probably prompted one employer to wrongly fire Mary—but by and large the Chinas expressed satisfaction with their lot and high hopes for their future. Believing that "true love *really* is color blind!," Mary China delightedly celebrated the love she felt for her husband and the love he felt for her.

In 1994 *Interrace* profiled the Smith family: a black man, a white woman, and their three highly accomplished children. In 1992 one of the Smith children had received a bachelor of arts degree, the second her degree in medicine, and the third a degree in law. With a measure of both pride and resentment, Maurice Smith contended that "there will be no made-for-TV movie about my family nor will you see us center-stage on a talk show." Keen to counter endlessly repeated tales of woe, Smith noted that he and his wife had been married for twenty-nine years, and that both sets of in-laws had embraced the marriage from the start.

Steve and Ruth White (he is white and she is black) had a harder time of it than the Smiths. When they first contemplated getting married, in 1980, the minister of their church was opposed on racial grounds, as were Steve's parents.[48] Steve White recalls his father declaring, "You really must have hated us to do this. Birds can fall in love with fish but not get married to them." His mother cried and reminded him, among other things, that her best friend had been robbed by a black person. Steve and Ruth got married anyway and went on to create an apparently happy home, write a self-published book about their experience (*Free*

Indeed: An Autobiography of an Interracial Couple), and found an interracial support group, A Place for Us.

Insisting that "dreams can come true and that people can be different and yet still be the same," Darryl Anderson, a white man, informed the *Interrace* community in 1994 that he and his black wife had gotten their start as a married couple at a small-town Wisconsin wedding that was well attended by contingents from both families. He recounted how "the reception turned into a big party and a true mixture of two cultures....Everyone, both young and old, had the time of their lives, dancing Polkas and Waltzes and finishing the evening with the Electric Slide."

Interrace also advertised dating services and cruises and ran personals intended to facilitate interracial romance.[49] Here it reached beyond the mere defense of the right to choose, and supported individuals who expressed a *preference* for men or women of a different race from themselves. Responding retrospectively to a black professor who had asserted offhandedly that black men typically dated or married the uneducated or unattractive white women whom white men passed over, Nicole Bouchet adopted the risky strategy of using herself as a rebuttal witness. Maintaining that she was well educated, at least moderately attractive, and representative of a substantial cadre of white women, Bouchet testified:

> For the past six years, I have been in an interracial relationship with a black man. For as long as I can remember, I have more readily preferred black men. There is nothing pathological about this attraction. All people have preferences. Some people prefer blondes or redheads, larger women—I prefer black men. It's as simple as that. If it is not pathological for white men to prefer white women with bronzed skin and long blond hair, then why can't I prefer black

men? Why does something have to be wrong with me?

Finally, *Interrace* assumed an advisory role, publishing articles intended to help with some of the recurrent difficulties that bedevil those involved in transracial relationships. In 1991, for instance, Sarah Farmer offered advice on dealing; with racists. Her article chronicled how she, a white adoptive mother of a black girl, had gradually learned to control her anger when confronting, people who referred to her as a "nigger lover." Initially, Farmer recalled, her outrage would overcome her ability to respond coherently, but crucial assistance from her daughter had enabled her to take a more reasoned approach. "Now when I am called a nigger-lover," she wrote, "I simply reply, 'No, I am not a nigger-lover, I am a mother. And by the way her name is Jessy. And you can call me Ms. Farmer.' Then I flash an ear-to-ear smile and walk away....No more ranting or raving. Just the simple facts."

Pepper Fisher, a white man, recommended a strategy that he and his black wife used: they bent over backward, he explained, to give the benefit of the doubt to those around them. To illustrate what he saw as the virtue of this strategy, he described two episodes. In the first, he and his wife and their son stopped at a fried-chicken restaurant near their small town, fifty miles from Seattle, Washington. (His in-laws were probably the only black family in the town, he noted in an aside.) When Fisher entered the restaurant with his family, he noticed a woman staring at them. He disregarded her:

> Nothing unusual about it, I told myself. Here we are, Black woman, White man, beautiful kid, small town, bound to happen. Her curiosity is natural, and I learned years ago that a little extra attention from people is just one of the things that come with the interracial territory. Besides, it rarely lasts long because good manners

usually kick in and people soon realize that overt rubbernecking is a little invasive.

On this occasion, though, the woman kept staring, and her mouth dropped open. Offended, Fisher stepped over to her and scolded peremptorily, "Don't stare." He immediately regretted his action, however, realizing that

> there were no winners, only losers. My wife [let] out a groan, which made me feel even worse, and before the girl behind the counter could say "ISTHATFORHERE-ORTOGO," I was sorry I had opened my big mouth.

Later that evening, his wife told him she had been embarrassed by his pettiness, adding "that if the woman was behaving rudely [he] should have just turned away and gone about [his] business." He agreed. After all, he reasoned, the woman might just have been preoccupied with difficulties of her own and gazing blankly into space. And in any event, even if she had been disturbed by his family's presence, he "shouldn't have made her problem into our problem. The world is full of bad attitudes. It's pointless and self-destructive to go head to head with everyone you run into."

To reinforce this conclusion, Fisher related a second story. Years earlier, during a dinner at another restaurant, an elderly white woman seated at the next table had stared at him and his wife. They were just about to confront the woman "when the old gal reached out and touched my wife gently on the arm and said, 'I just want to tell you that you are so beautiful.'" The two women chatted for a few minutes, during which time the elderly woman implicitly communicated that she was "quietly pulling for [them]." The lesson to be learned, Fisher averred, echoing his wife, was that mixed couples simply had to be patient, diplomatic, and willing to assume good motives on the part of others. Interracial couples "can't go around conking people over the head to get their respect. We have to earn that over time,

through the example set by ourselves and our children....We're like ambassadors from the tiny nation of interracial love."

This patient, conciliatory, almost self-abnegating approach was by no means the only or even the dominant one touted in *Interrace*. More typical was advice to be vocal, direct, militant. "Interracial couples and families," Sandy Carillo maintained in 1992, "should no longer feel and carry on as if discretion is the key to survival in a racist society. If we don't make ourselves seen and heard, then how can we really expect for others to learn to accept us and our choices as normal and as natural as theirs?"

People involved in interracial relationships have lately begun to produce a burgeoning body of memoir literature detailing their experiences, ideas, and sentiments.[50] These works reflect a new self-confidence and security, a belief on the part of their authors that they have something unusual and uplifting to share with the world, a sense that many existing understandings of interracial intimacies are mired in misleading and derogatory stereotypes, and a conviction that the old imagery of interracial intimacy is unlikely to change absent determined intervention. Lamenting "the virtual absence...of a written tradition from and about people who have crossed the color line," Maureen T. Reddy wrote in *Crossing the Color Line* (1994) that

> interracial couples begin not as inheritors of a tradition, but as pioneers. Each of us begins at the very beginning, with few but negative guides. If we go looking for information...we find mainly cautionary tales of tragedy and loss, written from a perspective we cannot share. Portrayed mostly from the outside, by both black and white observers, we find our relationships treated as sick manifestations of deep-seated racial myths or rebellions against our families, backgrounds, cultures: the black

partner is in flight from blackness, a victim of internalized racism[, while the] white partner is running from banality, in search of the exotic. These stereotypes are so ingrained in all of us in the United States that, for *both* blacks and whites, there is an automatic presumption of underlying pathology in interracial relationships.

In retracing what she saw as her "journey towards an internalized understanding of race and racism as the white wife of a black husband and the white mother of black children," Reddy emphasized the positive aspects of her unusual racial position. To her, racial difference enriched much more than it burdened her marriage. Describing her partnership with her husband, Doug, Reddy noted that

> contrary to what one might expect from the received wisdom, none of the very few problems Doug and I have had in our marriage have been caused by a racial gap between us. In fact, I think we have had fewer misunderstandings of any kind than do most couples, because from the beginning we knew that the external pressures on us would be enormous and that we would have to keep the inner strength to deal with them together. In other words, inside our marriage, racial differences have worked *for* us.

Even more than marrying across racial lines, interracial parenting reportedly brought Reddy extraordinary joy and enlightenment. Raising a black son, she wrote with an air of gratitude and exhilaration, "awakened me from…a delusion of colorlessness." She acknowledged encountering difficulties: bigoted landlords, insulting motel clerks, spurious "friends." But her book's central message is overwhelmingly upbeat: "Living as a racial bridge," Reddy claimed, could be "wonderfully freeing and endlessly instructive."

Love in Black and White: The Triumph of Love over Prejudice and Taboo (1992), a memoir by Gail and Mark Mathabane, also offers important documentation of the emergent assertiveness of individuals involved in interracial relationships. Gail Mathabane is a white American from a comfortably middle-class family. Her husband is a black South African who was born into poverty during the apartheid era but escaped it by dint of luck, hard work, unusual talent (as a student and as a tennis player), and the generosity of the American tennis star Stan Smith, who, during a tour of South Africa, recognized and nurtured Mark's potential. Gail and Mark met in 1984 in New York City, where both were attending the Columbia Graduate School of Journalism. Their book details the challenges they faced in marrying across the race line, and expresses their shared sense that ultimately they made the right decision. Gail first had to overcome a residue of prejudice and fear left over from her upbringing. In that context, one incident from her childhood outside Austin, Texas, constituted a defining moment: a black boy forcibly kissed her, and when she told a girlfriend about it, the friend responded with horror, "You let that nigger *kiss* you?" Within days, Gail was being called a "nigger lover," despite her insistence that she had neither invited nor welcomed the black boy's attention.[51] Not long after that, Gail's family moved to a suburb of Minneapolis, Minnesota, where, notwithstanding the relative scarcity of blacks, she developed an acute wariness of black men. Seeking to explain the source of this anxiety, her memoir mentions, among other things, two experiences that left a lasting impression on her. One was hearing stories about Negro pimps who lured white girls from their homes and turned them into prostitutes. The other was attending a concert given by the rock musician Prince. She was shocked by his aggressive sexuality and by the appreciation shown him by the predominantly black audience. Frightened, she concluded that blacks possessed a dangerous sexual energy and that "any white girl who dated a black boy was throwing herself away."

After all, she wondered, "who, in her right mind, would give up all her white friends and the love of her family for a black boy?"

A stint at Brown University in the early 1980s helped Gail become more independent and cosmopolitan. Important influences on her thinking during this period were some people of color with whom she became friendly and a Lebanese girlfriend whose preference in male companionship ran strongly to blacks. Gail's maturation, however, by no means precluded the emergence of some significant anxieties when she became seriously involved with Mark. Anticipating resistance from her father, Gail avoided telling him about their relationship for a long while. At one point, her fear that her continued association with Mark might alienate her permanently from her family, friends, and professional ambitions caused her to suspend their romance for about five months. But more than her relatives, it was her own doubts that held her back and kept her from committing to a love that would jeopardize deeply entrenched assumptions. She confessed, for example, that during a weekend visit with an interracial couple on Long Island, New York, she was overcome one evening by a realization that was like "a stab in [her] heart." She had realized, she recalled, "that I wanted a baby with pink cheeks and blue eyes....I wanted what many of us want: a child that reminds us of ourselves as we once were."

The Mathabanes' memoir suggests that initially, Mark faced fewer internal and external obstacles than Gail in pursuing their romance. It was he who pushed them toward marriage. After they married, however, Mark consciously distanced himself from Gail, at least in public. His autobiography *Kaffir Boy* (1986) had become a best-seller and catapulted him into prominence; aware that many blacks in America and elsewhere would react with disappointment and anger to his interracial marriage, he tried to keep it as inconspicuous as possible. For a time, he discouraged Gail from attending his lectures, particularly the ones he gave before black audiences. Once, when she did come to a lecture, he became angry with her. By his account,

> She was the only white at the table of black students who treated me to dinner....Their faces did not conceal their shock on hearing me introduce her as my wife. There were awkward silences, gaps in the conversation, and I could tell many of the students were offended and wondered how she could possibly relate to the issues of race they were discussing.

Afterward, he told Gail that she had exhibited an embarrassing ignorance of African American history and would never understand how it felt to be permanently victimized by racial discrimination. He even questioned whether he had done the right thing in marrying her, given the feelings of so many within the black community.

Despite the various challenges that confronted them, Mark and Gail Mathabane succeeded in marrying, staying together, and creating a family that was soon supplemented by two children, whom they smilingly clutch in the photo that graces the cover of their book. Breaking free of the tethers that constrained them required firm action: Gail had to inform her father that he must accept her love for Mark or risk losing her affection, and Mark had to stop attempting to mollify his readers who opposed interracial marriage. Declining any longer to relegate Gail to the shadows, he "came out" regarding their relationship by placing their wedding photo in a prominent spot in his book *Kaffir Boy in America* (1989). As he later explained, "I was fed up with playing games with my emotions [and] with hurting a woman whose love for me was unqualified." Speaking on their own behalf and on behalf of other interracial couples, Gail and Mark Mathabane have asserted proudly that they are "living proof that blacks and whites do not have to hate each other," "that racial harmony can become a reality," and that all the many things that separate blacks and whites "can be replaced by trust, cooperation, mutual respect, and even love.

As a rule, amalgamationists do not restrict their claims for interracial intimacy's benefits merely to the individuals involved; they also declare, more broadly, that black-white interracial intimacy can be an engine of positive social transformation. The idea of deploying intermarriage programatically is by no means novel. Thomas Jefferson, Patrick Henry, and other white American statesmen proposed that intermarriage between whites and Indians be encouraged as a way of peacefully appropriating the Indians' land and humanely civilizing "the noble savages." These proposals envisioned, at base, the whitening of the red people as a "solution" to the "Indian problem." A few commentators have advanced a similar strategy for "curing" the "Negro problem." Franz Boas suggested in 1921, for example, that

> the greatest hope for the immediate future lies in a lessening of the contrast between negroes and whites....Intermixture will decrease the contrast between extreme racial forms....In a race of octoroons, living among whites, the color question would probably disappear....It would seem, therefore, to be in the interest of society to permit rather than restrain marriages between white men and negro women. It would be futile to expect that our people [white] would tolerate intermarriages in the opposite direction.

Forty years later, Norman Podhoretz would remark that "the wholesale merger of the two races is the most desirable alternative for everyone concerned....The Negro problem can be solved in this country in no other way." Boas and Podhoretz were both considered racial liberals—indeed, racial radicals—when they wrote the statements quoted above. At the same time, they were also pessimistic accommodationists insofar as they believed that white racism could never be comprehensively transformed without a prior whitening of the black population.

Such proposals have received little attention. They would, if noticed, offend simultaneously those whites who loathe the prospect of race mixing and those blacks who despise the idea of "whitening" themselves and their descendants through intermarriage in order to avoid or accommodate antiblack prejudice. Refusing to see blackness as a taint, the latter reject any policy or theory premised on the necessity of systematic racial bleaching.[52]

Another brand of amalgamationism encourages interracial intimacy as a bilateral as opposed to a unilateral process. Its proponents urge a mutual blending rather than a mere extinguishment of blackness, and regard interracial intimacy as a positive good for whites as well as blacks. Among the leading partisans of this approach is Michael Lind. Proclaiming with approval that "a mongrelized population will eventually complement our already-mongrelized culture—and not a moment too soon," Lind argues that removing the race line in intimate affairs is an essential precursor to erasing it everywhere else:

> If people discriminate on the basis of physical race when it comes to the most fundamental matters—sex and reproduction—they can hardly be expected to overlook physical race in a thousand lesser areas of social life. They will not forget they are white or black when it comes to voting or hiring, only to suddenly remember they are white or black when it comes to sex and marriage. Race-consciousness cannot be turned on and off....Either it is very strong, or it is very attenuated, with respect to *all* matters, intimate and public, profound and trivial.

An outspoken and distinguished African American amalgamationist is Professor

Orlando Patterson.[53] A champion of transracial free trade in intimacy in general, Patterson lauds the benefits of interracial marriage in particular. He maintains that interracial marriage typically makes accessible to those involved valuable new sources of "cultural capital," including advice, know-how, and social networks. "When we marry," he has written, "we engage in an exchange of social and cultural dowries potentially far more valuable than gold-rimmed china."[54] In making his case, Patterson points to the upward mobility of Jews and Japanese Americans (both groups with much higher levels of intermarriage than blacks) and to the remarkable success of certain black men who have ignored racial custom by enjoying white paramours.[55] He maintains that there are at least two lessons to be drawn from the evidence: "If you want in, you marry in. And if you are from a group with impoverished social networks, you have even more reason to do so." He claims that the dissolution of the informal racial boundaries that divide the marriage market would redound especially to the benefit of black women, by alleviating, to an appreciable extent, the marriage squeeze that afflicts them with special force due to the paucity of marriageable black men. Patterson envisions large numbers of white men who will increasingly become open to the possibility of marrying black women—if such women will simply give them a chance. He observes, moreover, that even a relatively small incursion by black women into the ranks of marriageable white men would substantially enlarge that former group's marital options. After all, if just one in five of the nonblack male population came a-courting, black women would see an immediate doubling of the potential pool of spouses available to them. According to Patterson, this would be a good thing not only because it would make marriage more accessible to those black women desirous of it, but also because the presence of larger numbers of white (and other) suitors would strengthen the hand of black women in their dealings with black men. As Patterson sees it, by forswearing nonblack suitors, many black women have senselessly put themselves at the mercy of black men, who have exploited their market position by declining to be as accommodating as they might have to be in the face of greater competition.

Finally, Patterson argues that widespread intermarriage is necessary to the full integration of blacks into American life. He agrees with Calvin Hernton's assertion that intermarriage is "the crucial test in determining when a people have completely won their way into the mainstream of any given society." He therefore urges blacks, particularly African American women, to renounce doctrines that militate against interracial intimacy. Higher rates of intermarriage, he counsels, "will complete the process of total integration as [blacks] become to other Americans not only full members of the political and moral community, but also people whom 'we' marry. When that happens," he avers, "the goal of integration will have been fully achieved."

Some may question whether higher rates of interracial marriage will do and signify as much as Patterson and other amalgamationists contend. The history of race relations in racially divided societies elsewhere offers ample evidence that racial hierarchy can coexist alongside high rates of miscegenation and even intermarriage. In considering "the uncertain legacy of miscegenation," Professor Anthony W Marx has noted that despite considerable race mixing and a formal repudiation of racism, Brazil nonetheless constructed and retains "an informal racial order that [discriminates] against blacks and browns." Contrary to optimistic projections, miscegenation did not so much ensure upward mobility for dark Brazilians as reinforce a myth of mobility. That myth has undergirded a pigmentocracy that continues to privilege whiteness. A similar outcome is possible in the United States. Various peoples of color—Latinos, Asians,

Native Americans, and light-skinned Negroes—could well intermarry with whites in increasingly large numbers and join with them in a de facto alliance *against* darker-skinned Negroes, who would thus remain racial outcasts even in a more racially mixed society. We cannot merely assume that increased rates of interracial marriage will propel the society beyond the grip of racial conflict.[56] Historically, though, at least in the United States, openness to interracial marriage has been a good barometer of racial enlightenment in thought and practice. As a general rule, those persons, institutions, and communities that have been most welcoming of interracial marriage (and other intimate interracial associations) are also those that have most determinedly embraced racial justice, a healthy respect for diverse desires, and a belief in the essential oneness of humanity.

NOTES

1. West proceeds, however, to soften his expressed indifference somewhat by rhapsodizing that "anytime two human beings find genuine pleasure, joy, and love, the stars smile and the universe is enriched" (*Race Matters* [1993; reprint, 1994], 122).

2. For more on Walter White, see pages 287–89.

3. Although White escaped ouster, he lost influence within the NAACP in part as a consequence of the controversy over his second marriage. See Nathan Patrick Tillman Jr., "Walter Francis White: A Study in Interest Group Leadership" (Ph.D. diss., University of Wisconsin, 1961), 141–70.

4. In the early 1970s, opposition to interracial intimacy also manifested itself in denunciations of interracial adoption. For a discussion of this topic, see pages 393–98; 402–46.

5. In the poem "Niggers Are Scared of Revolution," the black nationalist group the Last Poets scoffed at fellow blacks whom they perceived as insufficiently committed to challenging the white establishment. A repeated target of the Last Poets' ire were "niggers [who] shoot sharp glances at white women," and "niggers" who sighed, "Oooooh

white thighs. Oooh white thighs." See Abiodur Oyewole, Umer Bin Hassan, with Kim Greene, *On a Mission: Selected Poems and History of the Last Poets* (1996), 61–64.

6. In 1970, having changed his name to Imamu Amiri Baraka, the former LeRoi Jones wrote:

   The Leftists have reintroduced the white woman for the precise purpose of stunting the [black] nation....Must it be our fate to be the police dogs of "revolutionary white boys," egged on by Sheena...the blond jungle queen[?]...As long as any *thing* separates the black man and the black woman from moving together, being together, being absolutely in tune, each doing what they are supposed to do, then the nation will never re-emerge. [Imamu Amiri Baraka, *Raise Race Rays Raze: Essays Since 1965* (1971), 153.]

7. In a memoir about his struggles with interracial intimacy, Brent Staples recalled his grandmother telling him, "Boy, you bet' not bring me no white girl, you hear?" ("The White Girl Problem," *New York Woman,* March 1989). Likewise, Diane Weathers reported that on the day she left home for college, her grandmother admonished her, "Don't come back to this house with a white man" ("White Boys," *Essence,* April 1990).

8. Surveying women's perceptions of stressful phenomena, a psychologist at the University of Michigan found in the late 1990s that among her black respondents, the sight of black-white interracial couples constituted the second most often cited source of anxiety, ahead of economic worries but behind a perceived deficiency of personal time. According to the researcher, many black women "see an increase in interracial couples as a decrease in their chances of finding a partner" (quoted in Richard Morin, "Unconventional Wisdom: New Facts and Hot Stars from the Social Sciences," *Washington Post,* June 29, 1997).

9. Melba Pattillo Beals recalled that when she informed her mother she had married a white man, the immediate response was "How can you marry a white man after all the pain white folks have caused you?" (*White Is a State of Mind: A Memoir* [1999], 159).

10. See pages 162–69.

11. See pages 192–99.

12. For more on Till, see pages 203–5.

   In *Jungle Fever,* when Flipper Purify brings his white lover home to meet his parents, his elderly father is far from approving. A retired minister from Georgia, he lectures the couple on the exploitation of enslaved women by white masters who grabbed "every piece of black poontang [they] could lay [their] hands on." He then regales them with images of lynchings passively observed by white women standing on racial pedestals, who dreamed of what it would be like to have "one of them big black bucks that their husbands were so desperately afraid of."

13. According to Professor Halford Fairchild, "For black men to date and marry white women in the face of our lingering debt to each other is irresponsible. The brother who dates or marries interracially has sold out. We have a responsibility to each other. We are under siege. We are at war. To sleep with the enemy is treason, racial treason" (quoted in Lynn Norment, "Black Men/White Women: What's Behind the Furor," *Ebony* Nov. 1994, p. 50).

14. The "litmus test" employed by Graham and his friends is widespread and intergenerational. Writer Jake Lamar noted that his mother "kept a mental shit list of black celebrities who had white wives or girlfriends" (*Bourgeois Blues: An American Memoir* [1991], 156).

15. As Denan Miller and Nick Chiles explain it,

   Any brother who shows up to the ball with someone who looks like the original Cinderella is gonna get called out by the sistahs—or at least talked about after the party's over. And that goes for every sistah, from the one who's physically repulsed by the sight of a white girl wrapped around a brother to those of us who are down with the "Color Doesn't Matter Committee." No matter how repressed or progressive we are when it comes to matters of the heart, we all think the same thing when we see her and him together: Either brotherman has that self-hating identity complex thing happening, or he thinks black girls are somehow inferior to Cindy. [*What Brothers Think, What Sistahs Know: The Real Deal on Love and Relationships* (1999), 83.]

See also Aliona L. Gibson, *Nappy: Growing Up Black and Female in America* (2000), 104–17. Gibson's discussion of interracial relationships is contained in a chapter entitled "Ultimate Insult."

16. This list could be supplemented by the addition of James Baldwin, Harry Belafonte, Kobe Bryant, Benny Carter, Diahann Carroll, Ward Connerly, Michael Jackson, James Earl Jones, Martin Kilson, Jamaica Kincaid, Audre Lorde, Thurgood Marshall Jr., Michael K. Powell, Richard Pryor, Paul Robeson, Paul Robeson Jr., Diana Ross, Shelby Steele, and William Julius Wilson.

17. An arresting articulation of the idea of the white woman as trophy was offered by Frantz Fanon, a black Martinican anticolonialist theoretician. Fanon, who himself married a white woman, declared that when his "restless hands caress…white breasts, they grasp white civilization and dignity and make them [his]" (*Black Skin, White Masks* [1967], 63; see also David Macey, *Frantz Fanon: A Biography* [2001]).

18. The notion that in interracial marriages, black men may in fact trade superior educational or economic attainments for the racial prestige provided even by less accomplished white women was posited as a plausible hypothesis by the distinguished sociologist Robert K. Merton. We should expect, Merton maintained, the pairing of lower-class white women with upper-class Negro men in situations in which "the Negro male exchanges his higher economic position for the white female's higher caste status." See "Intermarriage and the Social Structure: Fact and Theory," in Milton L. Barron, ed., *The Blending American: Patterns of Intermarriage* (1972), 28. See also Kingsley Davis, "Intermarriage in Caste Societies," *American Anthropologist* 43 (1941): 388. Merton's hypothesis is probably the single most fervently discussed theoretical contribution to the sociology of intermarriage. See, e.g., Zhenchao Quien, "Breaking the Racial Barriers: Variations in Interracial Marriage Between 1980 and 1990," *Demography* 34 (1997): 263, 273 (presenting data consistent with the hypothesis); Ernest Porterfield, *Black and White Mixed Marriages* (1978), 86–97 (suggesting that the data do not support Merton's hypothesis); Thomas P. Monahan, "The Occupational Clan of Couples Entering into Interracial Marriages," *Journal of Comparative Family Studies* 7 (1976): 175 (also disputing Merton's conclusions).

19. Nicole Bouchet recounts that in the 1990s, in a college class on feminist theory, an African American woman professor proffered the following impression of the sort of white women whom black men usually dated or married: "uneducated, unattractive, trailer-park trash that white men don't want anyway" ("On the Contrary," *Interrace,* no. 43 [1998])

In the first novel written by an African American woman, Harriet E. Wilson's *Our Nig; or, Sketches from the Life of a Free Black* (1859), a pathetic black man, Jim, desires to marry an ill-educated, impoverished, unattractive woman whose principal appeal for him resides in her whiteness. While wooing this woman, Jim says, revealingly, "I's black outside, I know, but I's got a white heart inside" (*Our Nig; or Sketches from the Life of a Free Black* [1859; reprint, 1983]).

20. An important exception is the Indian Child Welfare Act. For more on this, see pages 480–518.

21. Thurgood Marshall, the first black Supreme Court justice, could himself be said to have entered into an interracial marriage when he wed his second wife, Celia Suyat, a Hawaiian of Filipino ancestry. (His first wife, an African American, died in 1954.) At the time of his remarriage, Marshall was the legendary director of litigation for the NAACP, whose leadership worried about the potential fallout. In fact, there was none. (See Juan Williams, *Thurgood Marshall: American Revolutionary* [1998], 243–44.) The relatively uncontroversial nature of the Marshall-Suyat marriage may reflect the sense of many onlookers that it was not really cross-racial, as the new Mrs. Marshall was sufficiently colored to count as a Negro.

22. The negative comments that did surface tended to come from blacks. Professor Russell Adams of the Howard University Department of Afro-American Studies, for example, was quoted as remarking that Thomas's "marrying of a white woman is a sign of his rejection of the black community." Likewise, Barbara Reynolds, a black columnist for *USA Today,* noted of Thomas, "Here's a man who's going to decide crucial issues for the country and he has already said no to blacks; he has already said if he can't paint himself white he'll think white and marry a white woman." See Laura Blumenfeld, "The Nominee's Soul Mate; Clarence Thomas's Wife Shares His Ideas. She's No Stranger to Controversy. And She's Adding to His," *Washington Post,* September 10, 1991.

23. For Thurmond's own experience with interracial intimacy and the difficulties encountered in obtaining such information, see page 57.

24. In one sense, the Thomas-Lamp alliance followed the pattern of most black-white interracial marriages: 121,000—or 68 percent—were between black men and white women. Similarly, of the 330,000 such marriages in 1998, 210,000—or 64 percent—involved black husbands and white wives (U.S. Bureau of the Census, 1999). The striking gender differential in blacks' involvement in interracial marriage dates back at least to the 1950s. See Porterfield, *Black and White Mixed Marriages,* 85–98; David M. Heer, "The Prevalence of Black-White Marriage in the United States, 1960 and 1970," *Journal of Marriage and the Family* 36 (1974): 246. Lately, however, an increasing number of black women have also begun to marry across racial lines. In 1980, of 121,000 black-white marriages, 27,000 were between white males and black females; in 1991 the figure was 75,000 out of 231,000. In 1998, in 330,000 black-white couples, there were 120,000 black wives (United States Census Bureau, "MS-3 Interracial Married Couples: 1760 to Present," January 7, 1999). See also Maria P. P. Root, *Love's Revolution: Interracial Marriage* (2001), 179–88. For journalistic explorations of this phenomenon, see Pamela Johnson, "The Color of Love," *Essence,* July 2002; Laura B. Randolph, "Black Woman/White Man: What's Goin' On?," *Ebony,* March 1989; Dorothy Tucker, "Guess Who's Coming to Dinner *Now?*," *Essence,* April 1987; Shawn D. Lewis, "Black Woman/White Man: The 'Other' Mixed Marriage," *Ebony* January 1978.

25. "Over 93 percent of whites and of blacks marry within their own groups, in contrast to about 70 percent of Asians and of Hispanics and less than one-third of American Indians." Roderick J. Harrison and Claudette E. Bennett, "Racial and Ethnic Diversity," in Reynolds Farley, ed., *State of the Union: America in the 1990s—Vol. Two: Social Trends* (1995), 165.

When people of Latino and Asian ancestry marry exogamously, "their spouses are very likely to be white; interracial marriages in the United States [have seldom] involved the mixing of two minority groups" (Ibid.).

26. Reflecting on his marriage, Peter Norton once mused, "Other than sex itself, why do you want to spend your life in the company of a woman as

opposed to a best male friend? Part of the answer has to do with the wonderful, bizarre, inexplicable differences between male psychology and female psychology. Well, in the same vein, why would you want to spend your life with a person from the same ethnic background? You miss the frisson" (quoted in David Owen, "The Straddler," *The New Yorker,* January 30, 1995).

27. Roxie Roker, the black actress who played Helen Willis, was herself married to a white man. The popular musician Lenny Kravitz is their son. See Lynn Norment, "Am I Black, White, or in Between?," Ebony August 1995; "Roxie Roker, 66, Who Broke Barrier in Her Marriage on TV's *Jeffersons,*" New York Times, December 6, 1995

28. Denise Nicholas, who played the character whom the sheriff married, actively shaped the public image of her role, particularly with respect to the interracial relationship. Nicholas felt that the characters "should either break [the relationship] off or get married because oftentimes, historically, interracial relationships were back-alley affairs, hidden and lied about, particularly in the South. It became really important to me that the [characters] do something dignified; I didn't want my character to be cheap" ("Denise Nicholas and Carroll O'Connor Wed on TV Drama 'In the Heat of the Night,'" *Jet,* May 9, 1994). It should be recalled that the basis for the television series was the film of the same name (1967), which featured a thoroughly bigoted white sheriff (played by Rod Steiger, in an Academy Award-winning performance).

29. ABC's hugely successful musical production starred Brandy as Cinderella and Paolo Montalban as the prince. Taking the role of Prince Charming's mother, the queen, was a black actress, Whoopi Goldberg, while the king was played by a white actor, Victor Garber. See Veronica Chambers, "The Myth of Cinderella," *Newsweek,* November 3, 1997; "Cinderella TV Music Special Produces Spectacular Rating for ABC," *Jet,* November 24, 1997.

30. Such depictions were no accident. When television producers sought guests for these programs, they advertised for people who had had *bad* experiences in or on account of interracial relationships. It was this bias that gave rise to episodes such as "Woman Disowned by Her Family for Dating a Black Man" on *Jenny Jones* and "Blacks and Blondes: White Girls Dating Black Guys for Sex, Style, and Status" on *Geraldo.*

31. Several months after *An American Love Story* aired, Cecily Wilson married a white union organizer whom she had met on a blind date. See "Weddings: Cecily Wilson, Gregory Speller," *New York Times,* May 7, 2000.

32. Fox has stated that she was surprised by some of her relatives' negative reactions to her interracial relationship, and surprised, too, by the regularity of the racial mistreatment her black lover suffered. In retrospect, she observes, "it was almost like I was deluded or something; I thought I was living in a different world than I was living in" (quoted in Paula Span, "Modern Family Life in Black and White: PBS Documentary Chronicles an Interracial Marriage," *Washington Post,* September 9, 1999).

33. Two excellent coming-of-age films that evoke the hazards and rewards of teenage interracial dating in the 1950s are Robert De Niro's *A Bronx Tale* (1993) and Barry Levinson's *Liberty Heights* (2000).

34. See pages 113–14.

35. The jilted white woman is a racist unaware of her prejudice. "I gave you my pure white body," she fumes at her former beau, "and you're entirely ungrateful about it. I mean, I even overlooked the fact that you were black" (John Oliver Killens, *'Sippi* [1967], 341).

36. Chester Himes once pronounced interracial sexual relationships "battlefields of racial antagonism" (quoted in Jonathan Little, "Definition Through Difference: The Tradition of Black-White Miscegenation in American Fiction" [Ph.D. diss., University of Wisconsin-Madison, 1988], 254). His novels offered dismaying reports from that front; see, e.g., *If He Hollers Let Him Go* (1943), *Lonely Crusade* (1947), *The Third Generation* (1954), and *Pinktoes* (1961).

37. Further illustrating the doom that supposedly shadows interracial marriages is an anguished alcoholic character in *Five Smooth Stones,* who passes for white for a time at Vassar College before dropping out. She is the daughter of a frightfully unhappy interracial couple who either committed suicide together or killed each other. For an account of a real episode of passing at Vassar, see pages 294–95. Of the novels mentioned here, Fairbairn's was one of the most popular in its day, though now it has been largely forgotten. A Book-of-the-Month Club selection, it sold more than a million copies and went through ten printings. Its author wrote under a

pseudonym; her real name was Dorothy Tate. See Marcia Press, "That Black Man—White Woman Thing: Images of an American Taboo" (Ph.D. diss., Indiana University, 1989), 141.

38. See pages 41–49.

39. Recalling his struggle to come out to his black family, activist-intellectual Keith Boykin wrote:

> Over the phone, I told my sister I was gay and she accepted it very supportively. Her most intrusive question about my boyfriend was predictable. "Is he black or white?" she asked. "White," I sheepishly responded. That simple question led me to examine whether my family would react more favorably to my being involved with a black man than with a white woman. Homosexual and interracial relationships raise many of the same concerns to black families, including continuation of the family, humiliation of the family, and commitment to the race. A black man who dates only men raises the specter of the extinction of the family name, potentially causes embarrassment to the family and often suggests an irresponsible disregard for the need to create strong black families. Dating a white woman raises similar concerns, compromising the racial purity of the family and the couple's offspring. black homosexuals dating each other raises concerns too, but at least [it] suggest[s] some appreciation of the beauty within the race; it does not seem as much an abandonment of blackness as does interracial dating. The shared racial identity develops a much stronger family bond than any presumed identity based on sexual orientation. I never polled my family members, but ultimately I decided that some would be more disturbed by my dating a white woman, while others would be more upset by my dating a black man. This confusion helped me realize that I had to live my life for myself, not for my family. [*One More River to Cross: Black and Gay in America* (1996), 22–23]

40. Other fictional explorations of interracial same-sex romance include Timothy Murphy, *Getting Off Clean* (1997), Steven Corbin, *Fragments That Remain* (1993), and Wallace Thurman, *Infants of the Spring* (1932).

41. Although they failed to persuade the United States Census Bureau to offer the "multiracial" box for the 2000 census, multiracialist reformers have succeeded in convincing a number of state governments—including those of Georgia, Illinois, Florida, Indiana, Michigan, and Ohio—to require that such a box be provided on state forms that collect racial data. They have also managed to convince several important private institutions, among them Harvard University, to add a "multiracial" category alongside the other, more familiar and established, choices. See Tanya Kateri Hernandez, "'Multiracial' Discourse: Racial Classifications in an Era of Color-Blind Jurisprudence," *Maryland Law Review* 57 (1998): 97, 98 n. 4.

42. When the racial-classification issue was decided for the 2000 census, the person in charge of the supervisory agency was Franklin Raines, a black man married to a white woman. Franklin and Wendy Raines had two children who themselves faced this classification dilemma. See Julia Malone, "Facing the Racial Question: More Categories in the Census," *The Atlanta Journal and Constitution,* October 15, 1997.

43. Woods made his views known on Oprah Winfrey's television show soon after he won the prestigious Masters golf tournament. See Greg Couch, "Woods: I'm More Than Black," *Chicago Sun-Times,* April 22, 1997, p, 1.

44. In a satirical essay entitled "The Mulatto Millennium," Danzy Senna facetiously defined "Cablinasian" thus:

> A rare exotic breed found mostly in California. This is the mother of all mixtures….A show mulatto, with great performance skills, the Cablinasian will be whoever the crowd wants him to be, and can switch at the drop of a dime. Does not, however, answer to the name Black….Note: If you spot a Cablinasian, please contact the Benetton Promotions Bureau. [In Claudine Chiawei O'Hearn, ed., *Half and Half: Writers on Growing Up Biracial and Bicultural* (1998), 26.]

For a powerful defense of Woods's position, see Gary Kamiya, "Cablinasian like Me," Salon.com, April 1997. For a critique, see Leonard Pitts, "Is There Room in This Sweet Land of Liberty for Such a Thing as 'Cablinasian'? Face It, Tiger: If

They Say You're Black, Then You're Black," *Baltimore Sun,* April 29, 1997.

45. A letter published in *Spectrum,* the newsletter of the Multiracial American, of Southern California (MASC), flatly stated, "Like it or not, racially mixed people are the most beautiful people of all." See Lisa Jones, *Bulletproof Diva: Tales of Race. Sex and Hair* (1994), 59. Similarly prideful is Carlos A. Fernandez's remark that the multiracial community "is uniquely situated to confront racial and interethnic issues because of the special experiences and understanding we acquire in the intimacy of our families and our personalities" ("Testimony of the Association of Multi-ethnic Americans Before the Subcommittee on Census, Statistics, and Postal Personnel of the U.S. House of Representatives," in Naomi Zack, ed., *American Mixed Race: The Culture of Microdiversity* [1995]).

46. Mills and Grosz met in 1980, when she was a fifteen-year-old student and track star at a public high school in Los Angeles, and he was a twenty-eight-year-old teacher and track coach. Two years later, they became sexually intimate. Her parents found out and pressed for a criminal prosecution. Grosz was convicted of illegal sexual intercourse with a minor, put on three years' probation, and ordered to stay away from Mills until she was eighteen. Two weeks after Mills graduated from high school, she and Grosz were married; eventually they became parents. See *Interrace,* November/December 1989, pp. 15–20; November/December 1992, p. 2; July/August 1990, pp. 9–10.

Mills was clearly the dominant figure in running the magazine. (Grosz's name appeared on the masthead for several years but dropped off it as of the May 2000 issue.) Explaining why she started *Interrace* at a time when she had little money and no publishing experience, Mills states, "[I] wanted my biracial daughter (then 5 years old) to have a magazine of her own, one that would positively and truthfully explore interracial relationships and multiracial identity....I was young and ambitious and obsessed with my desire to make a difference" (*Interrace,* spring 2000, p. 2). It seems, sadly, that Interrace has ceased publication.

47. Seeking material and an audience for a book of photographs and stories, *Interrace* maintained in an advertisement that "you and your spouse can be included in...*The Greatest Love: A Celebration of Interracial Marriage,* which will portray the beauty and joy of interracial marriage. Please send us one or two wedding photos that best capture the joy of the moment." See back cover of *Interrace* 46 (1999).

48. There were other, nonracial factors that might have justified parental caution or skepticism, notably the fact that Ruth already had three children by previous unstable relationships. But those did not comprise the primary basis for the opposition voiced by Steve's parents; racial difference did. See Tia L. Daniel, "An Overview of Historical Amalgamationists and the Modern Amalgamationist Impulse" (third-year paper, Harvard Law School, 1998), 40 (on file at Harvard Law School Library, in the Interracial Intimacies Collection).

49. The following are representative of the personals that appeared in Interrace:

SBM, 34, in-shape, educated, professional, financially secure with a sense of humor. Seeks honest, sincere, affectionate woman of any race who desires meaningful relationship.

Are you the right woman for me? Blue-collar SWM, honest down-to-earth. Enjoys day trips, walks on the beach and movies. Seeks same in Caribbean, African, or black American woman.

Classy 44-year-old SWF looking to have fun with a tall, handsome, romantic African American gentleman.

Attractive SBF, 28 y/o, ISO honest, open-minded, down-to-earth single Latino or white male for LTR leading to marriage.

See *Interrace Singles,* no. 3 (1999), pp. 35, 37.

50. See, e.g., Rebecca Walker, *Black, White Jewish: Autobiography of a Shifting Self* (2001); Jane Lazarre, *Beyond the Whiteness of Whiteness: Memoir of a White Mother of Black Sons* (1997); James McBride, *The Color of Water: A Black Man's Tribute to His White Mother* (1997); Gregory Howard Williams, *Life on the Color Line* (1995); Lise Funderburg, *Black, White, Other: Biracial Americans Talk About Race and Identity* (1994); Walt Harrington, *Crossings: A White Man's Journey into Black America* (1992); Hettie Jones, *How I Became Hettie Jones* (1990); Patrick Huber, *Two Races Beyond the Altar* (1976).

51. According to Gail, while "dating Mexicans was fine, even 'cool'...if a white girl did so much as speak for more than five minutes with a black boy

she was labeled an NL (nigger lover). Blacks and whites never touched each other, never danced together, never came in close contact with each other except through sports, like football and wrestling" (Mark Mathabane and Gail Mathabane, *Love in Black and White: The Triumph of Love over Prejudice and Taboo* [1992], 30).

52. For a satirical critique of plans to address racism by getting rid of blackness, see George Schuyler's *Black No More* (1931), discussed on pages 344–51

53. Another noteworthy African American amalgamationist, Joseph R. Washington Jr. maintained:

> We can and we must create conditions whereby every American home anticipates with high expectations the possibility of welcoming into the family a black or white sister, brother, daughter, or son, though this may be a reality for only a precious few. It is sheer rhetoric to proclaim the American dream and espouse the American creed without at the same time affirming the goodness and desiring the possibility of brotherhood and sisterhood in black and white within the immediate or very near family. [Marriage in Black and White (1972; 1993), 326.]

54. According to Patterson:

> When one marries into another ethnic group, one greatly expands one's social network. Every spouse brings a cultural dowry of social networks and cultural capital in the form of childrearing patterns, and it is to reap this rich harvest of social and cultural capital that Americans [other than black Americans] are busily intermarrying with each other, fully exploring....their "ethnic" options. [Orlando Patterson, *The Ordeal of Integration: Progress and Resentment in America's "Racial" Crisis* (1997), 195.]

55. Patterson writes that "Afro-American men have disproportionately relied on Euro-American lovers to provide them with a link to networks and cultural information that are critical for their success. This pattern goes all the way back to Booker T. Washington and Frederick Douglass" (*Ordeal of Integration,* 197). Furthermore, he claims that "the recent expose of the late Ron Brown's complicated love affair with [a Euro-American] on whom he depended heavily for counsel, funds, and contacts, is merely the tip of a long, historical iceberg" (ibid.).

That Douglass and Brown both engaged in interracial love affairs is clear. (For information on Douglass, see pages 72–75; for information on Brown, see Steven Holmes, *Ron Brown: An Uncommon Life* [2000], and Peter J. Boyer, "Ron Brown's Secrets," The New Yorker, June 9, 1997.) Patterson probably errs, however, with respect to Washington. He offers no source for his comment, and Louis R. Harlan's comprehensive biography of Washington contains no reference to any interracial liaisons (*Booker T. Washington: The Making of a Black Leader, 1856–1901* [1972]; *Booker T. Washington: The Wizard of Tuskegee, 1901–1915* [1983]). In 1911 a white woman in New York City caused a furor by accusing Washington of addressing her in a familiar fashion ("Hello, sweetheart" was the alleged salutation). There is good reason, however, to doubt her word (see Harlan, *Wizard of Tuskegee,* 379–404).

56. Michael Lind warns, for example, that "shifting patterns of racial intermarriage suggest that the [coming years] may see the replacement of the historic white-black dichotomy in America with a troubling new division, one between beige and black" ("The Beige and the Black," *New York Times Magazine,* August 16, 1998). See also Roger Sanjek, "Intermarriage and the Future of Races in the United States," in Steven Gregory and Roger Sanjek, eds., *Race* (1994).

Part 2: Education

Does Multicultural Education Warrant Reconstruction for the 21st Century?

Charles C. Jackson

INTRODUCTION

The specter of introducing the type of multicultural education for the 21st century that is advocated by many educators is a most foreboding thought. While well intentioned, they have gravitated to a position that emphasizes the **infusion** of multiculturalism throughout the curriculum (Spring, 2000). Although this appears to be a worthwhile endeavor and worthy of support even from those who stand on the fringe of the multicultural ideal, when examined more critically, there appears to be considerably more to the notion of **infusion.** First, multiculturalism is a process—a continuous process—and not something that one does necessarily once or even twice. Second, it involves components that may make even the heartiest enthusiast question whether it is a serious educational panacea. And third, it has the potential of actually revolutionizing the curriculum in ways that were perhaps never intended.

BRIEF HISTORICAL OVERVIEW

In a very real sense, multicultural education can be conceived of as an extension of the civil rights movement. As African Americans struggled over the years to expand their civil rights, they were joined by other oppressed groups, and the focus broadened inevitably to include education. In this context, the issue of the elimination of discrimination in schools was not just a push for the right for black youth to attend school with (and sit next to) white youth, it was part of a broader struggle for equity and the pursuit of equality of opportunity. The effort to desegregate the public schools was tactical in the sense that it only began with the push for school integration. Initially, this involved breaking down the barriers that prevented black and white children from attending the same schools. But, at the heart of the effort was a concern for quality education for African American youth. The next step was the push for more black and brown teachers and administrative staffs in public schools. While positive responses to these quests have proven to be difficult, it has not impeded the next step in the desegregation struggle—reform of the curricula to more realistically reflect the historical experiences and voices of oppressed groups. This struggle has moved from the streets to the school boardrooms (especially in urban areas) and even into the boardrooms of the textbook industry and into the hallowed halls of state legislatures.

Some multiculturalists have argued forcefully for black studies, especially on predominantly white college campuses, as part of the multicultural education movement. In some cases, they have gone so far as to advocate the separation of minority students from the dominant group and the implementation of pedagogies that counteract the omissions and distortions of minority groups in the traditional Eurocentric curriculum (Grant and Gomez, 1996).

WHAT IS MULTICULTURAL EDUCATION?

There are many advocates for multiculturalism who have generated a number of conceptions regarding its nature. Consequently, it is not simple to define. Perhaps, it is better understood in terms of what it attempts to do (i.e., its goals), rather than as a list of descriptive features. Banks (1999) has identified five broad goals that speak to the nature of multicultural education. **One is to provide the student with viable cultural and ethnic alternatives.** Systematically, the traditional Eurocentric curriculum has omitted and distorted the historical realities of people of color (e.g., African Americans, Mexican Americans, and Native Americans). Equally important, it has denied European American students the richness and the contributions of "other" cultures. This amounts to a type of "miseducation" for all students.

A second goal is to help all students gain a better understanding of themselves and their culture, and of other cultures and peoples as well. They should develop the ability to perceive the world from multiple perspectives. This aspect of the traditional Eurocentric curriculum has been quite conspicuous by its absence. In fact, a number of educators contend that the expressed purpose of the public schools, historically, was to reshape the immigrants into "Americans." This involved teaching them to discard their original cultures and adopt those beliefs, values, and customs that were thought to typify America.

Ellwood P. Cubberley, one of the country's most respected educators, believed that (early in the eighteen hundreds) the patterns of national life already had been established along the lines of an English-speaking and English-behaving society. The task that Cubberley gave to the country's educators was one of assimilating the immigrants into a monolithic version of American life (Gutek 1997, 300).

A third goal is to help students develop the skills, attitudes, and necessary knowledge for not only meeting the challenges of their own cultures, but also for interacting effectively with other cultures. The focus here is not only on students of color, but on European American students as well. They, too, must develop a sophisticated understanding and appreciation of other cultures (especially the cultures of oppressed groups).

A fourth goal is to help eliminate discrimination. Particular attention is given to racism, sexism, and social class biases. While seeking to eliminate discrimination, it also encourages members of oppressed groups to embrace their own heritage. The celebration of one's own cultural heritage does not warrant the denigration of other cultures. Embracing one's culture holds special significance for many people of color who have encountered distortions and omissions of their lived experiences in the traditional curriculum.

A final goal is to help students achieve academic success. It asserts that important skills—reading, writing, social, communication, computer, and computation—are achieved through the use of an effective multicultural education program. Curricular content that is relevant and based on the lives of students has proven to be highly motivating and effective (Graff 1992).

Almost without exception, texts that advocate and discuss the goals (purposes) of multicultural education tend to stress a number of common emphases. First, they propose that it is designed to help maximize the potential of all students. Next, they suggest that it is a type of education reform that will change the curriculum structurally. Third, it will help foster better understanding, tolerance, and appreciation of other cultures. Fourth, it is a reform movement that may never be achieved fully, because it is not something that is accomplished in one course or one weekend training session. Bennett (1999, 11) suggests that "multicultural education is comprised of four interactive dimensions: 1) the movement toward equity; 2) curriculum reform; 3) the process of becoming interculturally competent; and 4) the commitment to combat prejudice and discrimination, especially racism." Banks and Banks (1989) propose a similar construction of multicultural education by isolating at least three dimensions. First, it is an *idea* or *concept* that proposes that all students, regardless of status or background, should have equal opportunities to learn. It also supports the notion that the manner in which schools are structured currently provides some groups with greater opportunities to succeed than others. Second, as a *reform movement,* multicultural education attempts to restructure the educational enterprise, from the public school to the university, to enhance the opportunities of all students. This entails eliminating the barriers that are based on race, social class, gender, exceptionality, and cultural heritage. The restructuring is not restricted to superficial curricula changes, but involves structural changes across the board—from the manner in which teachers are trained to teach, to the selection of materials, to the affirmation of each and every child. Third, multicultural education is an on-going *process*. It is not necessarily something that is accomplished through a single multicultural education course, in-service workshop, or training session. In fact, it is a **set** of initiatives that are designed to improve academic achievement for all students.

Spring (2000) suggests that there are four important goals of multicultural education: 1) to develop and build tolerance of other cultures; 2) to eliminate racism; 3) to **infuse** the content of different cultural groups; and 4) to teach students to view the world from multiple perspectives. Spring indicates that accomplishing these goals will contribute to the reduction of racial and ethnic tensions across cultures. Sleeter and Grant (1999) suggest that multicultural education is both ideology and theory. Ideology is prescriptive and indicates "what ought to be," while theory explains "how social systems actually work." While both aspects of multicultural education are important, most multiculturalists tend to focus more on ""what ought to be." Given the current state of the public school curriculum, perhaps more attention should be given to ideology.

Multicultural education rests on two ideologies—cultural pluralism and equal opportunity. Cultural pluralism embodies the acceptance of diversity, the respect for differences, and the right of the individual to participate actively in all aspects of society without having to give up his/her unique identity (Sleeter and Grant 1999, 152). Equal opportunity, being grounded in law (eg., *Brown v. Board of Education,* 1954) means, according to Spring (1999), that all members of society will be afforded an equal chance to enter any occupation or social class. The Supreme Court (in *Brown*) tied dialectically the idea of equality of opportunity in general to equal educational opportunity. Consequently, it would be difficult to obtain equality of opportunity in general without first having experienced equality of educational opportunity. This implies that practices that interfere with equality of educational opportunity (e.g., racist educational practices and patterns) constitute, not only a breach of law, but a denial equal opportunity also.

Grant and Gomez (1996) established five broad approaches to multicultural education that tend to account for its different perspectives: *Teaching the Exceptional and Culturally Different; Human Relations; Single-Group Studies; Multicultural Education; and Education that is Multicultural and Social*

Reconstructionist. The Teaching the Exceptional and Culturally Different approach is grounded in the notion of helping the "other" to adjust to the traditional curriculum. In fact, some multiculturalists refer to this perspective as the add-on approach. While a few modifications are made to accommodate the particular needs of some students, no major structural changes occur: most of the effort involves trying to help students fit into the existing structure.

The *Human Relations* approach attempts to "assimilate" all students into the dominant practices of the classroom and school. Essentially, it has two major foci: 1) to introduce lessons on stereotyping, discrimination, and cultural differences (much of which occurs in collaborative and cooperative groupings); and 2) to develop and maintain harmony among students with the explicit purpose of developing positive regard for everyone (a logical corollary outcome is positive **self** concepts also). *Single-Group Studies* attempt to promote social structural equality and to raise the level of consciousness of a particular group. Since it has been assailed by opponents of multiculturalism as being divisive (Schlesinger, 1992; Ravitch, 1991/1992), it is quite controversial among the five approaches. Typically, it is based in ethnic studies or studies that focus on oppressed groups. While exclusivity is not mandatory, the approach does focus on the culture, history, heroes, heroines, and contributions of the target group, and it suggests that such study might be conducted more effectively away from the traditional course of study. It is assumed that such a setting would allow for more in-depth coverage and discussion.

Multicultural Education is grounded in attempts to achieve structural changes in education. It attempts to promote both social equality and cultural pluralism. It goes beyond merely changing the curriculum and accommodating individual student differences, it advocates a "re-socialization" of the teacher

and structural changes in the entire educational enterprise—from elementary school to higher education. Education that is *Multicultural and Social Reconstroctionist* is the most radical (and controversial) of the approaches. Grant and Gomez (1996) state that:

> (I)t extends the previous approaches and supports education for everyone. It promotes social and structural equality and cultural pluralism. It provides a climate in which students can work toward structural equality, accept lifestyles different from their own, and understand the importance of equal opportunity for all people. The curriculum is organized around social issues involving race, class, gender, disability, and sexual orientation. It also involves the history and lives of many United States peoples and uses the lives of students in the classroom as the starting point for analyzing oppression, teaching critical thinking skills, and developing social action and empowerment skills" (p.10).

Banks and Banks (1993) suggest that multicultural education is not only an idea, but that it is also an educational reform movement and a process. As a reform movement, it challenges the type and nature of reform that has occurred traditionally in this country. It does not merely advocate the addition or deletion of certain courses, but it challenges the very nature of the curriculum itself. Herein lies much of the debate over multicultural education, for when it is implemented, long-standing distortions about European American tradition and culture are exposed and opened for criticism. While there is much that America can take pride in, there is much that is reprehensible and perverse. For the most part, the traditional approach has glossed over the latter, distorted it; or mitigated its severity. For example, slavery is rarely, if ever, portrayed in most U.S. history books with anything that approaches the reality of its inhumanity. Instead, it has been referred to as the "peculiar institution, " or as an unfortunate part of U.S. history (1). Equally evasive has been the discussions of the treatment of Native Americans, Asian Americans, Mexicans/ Mexican Americans (and other Spanish speaking people) in U. S. history.

> Our country's history on race relations has been mired in tragedy, including the enslavement of Africans, the murder of Native Americans, and the seizing of two-thirds of Mexico's arable land in addition to all of Puerto Rico and Hawaii, making these people domestic, conquered, minority groups (2).

As a process, multicultural education is continually evolving—addressing the needs of an ever-changing student population. Banks and Banks suggest that multicultural education, as a process:

> will never be realized fully. Educational equality, like liberty and justice, are ideals toward which human beings work but never fully attain. Racism, sexism, and discrimination against people with disabilities will exist to some extent no matter how hard we work to eliminate these problems. Because the goals of multicultural education can never be attained fully, we work continually to increase educational equality for all students (3).

Spring (1996) gives further credence to the position taken by Banks and Banks. He starts by indicating, in *American Education,* that whereas the dominant culture in the United States was European initially; it was transplanted during the early colonial period; and through social and political conditions, it was modified into a European-American culture. Today, it is the culture that dominates the public schools (4). Campbell adds to this discussion by suggesting that:

> The dominant worldview in U.S. society and, therefore, U.S. schools, has been defined by the values, attitudes, beliefs, and

folkways of the European American majority. [Their] patterns of communication and life are used as criteria by which to judge right and wrong behavior. In the classroom, this cultural domination is reinforced by the preponderance of middle class, European American teachers who unconsciously use their cultural values to judge their students' work and behavior (5).

It is unfortunate that, for the vast majority of majority-group teachers, this is an unconscious posture (one that, because of their socialization, they believe to be correct). But it is downright ironic and disturbing that many African American teachers are products of the Eurocentric educational system and, therefore, subscribe wholeheartedly to the same cultural values. Put another way, the ethnocentric baggage that they carry into the classroom clouds their perceptions of the legitimacy of alternative ways of perceiving, valuing, and behaving. Typically, students from ethnic cultures are accepted and respected only to the extent that they demonstrate middle class mannerism (i.e., language, values, and behaviors). Campbell suggests that "teachers need to understand how their own cultures affect their lives, their teaching strategies, and the lives of their students" (6).

THE INFUSION OF MULTIPLE CULTURES INTO THE CURRICULUM

Much of what is being discussed regarding multicultural education is the **infusion** of content concerning other cultures into the public school curriculum. The idea is to cease being exclusively Eurocentric and begin including the contributions of art, literature, science, and motifs from other cultures, especially those that have been marginalized in the traditional public school curriculum. Quite a few questions have been raised concerning the nature of this inclusion, especially inquiries about whether the content of the proposed material merits inclusion. Many have argued that the contributions of people of color and women, for the most part, have been minimal at best. In fact, the argument continues with the assertion that the curriculum has to be distorted severely in order to include these groups. Questions such as, "What have persons of color or women contributed to the founding of this nation?" "Which persons of color or women have held positions of influence in politics, business, religion, or industry that have been pivotal in the growth and development of this country?" "Where are their contributions in literature, music, and art?" In fact, "What are their contributions to the grand march of Western civilization?" It is precisely these types of questions that have hastened the push for multicultural education, because much of what has been taught in the curriculum of the West, according to advocates like Molefi Asante, has been either a distortion or a lie regarding people of color (and women). And most of this can be traced directly to the paradigm of Eurosupremacy.

THE MULTICULTURAL DEBATE

Why does the prospect of multicultural education hold such trepidation for some people? Clearly, if the concept were implemented fully, it would do nothing less than revolutionize the curriculum. It would foreshadow an eventual re-shuffling of the status quo. Greater equality of opportunity would, in fact, become a reality. People of color, women, and even working class and poor whites, would begin to gain greater shares of the political and economic wealth of the nation. In light of these hypotheticals, it becomes clear why there is opposition to multicultural education, and the source of the opposition becomes clear also.

Until the present time, much of the opposition has come from the intellectual right. However, this does not imply that the liberal-minded educational establishment is all that comfortable with the prospect of a truly multicultural curriculum. Critics like Diane Savitch and Arthur Schlesinger, Jr. have gone so far as to say that multicultural education will "disunite" America. At the heart of this repudiation is the contention that, first, America already has a well-defined culture; and second, that the "cult of ethnicity" exaggerates differences, intensifies resentments and antagonisms, and drives ever deeper the awful wedges between races and nationalities (7). Schlesinger is one of those who perceives multiculturalism as a "cult of ethnicity" that exaggerates, rather than minimizes, differences. This is perhaps the most puzzling attack on multiculturalism to date, for it attempts to shift the blame for societal fragmentation on to multiculturalism. Obviously, Schlesinger has chosen to ignore the entire history of the United States. From the segregation of blacks and whites during the period of enslavement; to the separation of the Chinese during the building of the railroads; to the separation of Mexicans during the western and southwestern period of expansion (manifest destiny); to the legal period of segregation of African Americans for fifty-eight years (following the *Plessy* decision); to the exiguous enforcement of desegregation mandates (following the *Brown* decision) throughout the 1960s and 1970s; to the half-hearted implementation of affirmation action; and even to the requirement by the federal government (along with most other institutions) that citizens identify themselves racially or ethnically, Schlesinger's position could be viewed as totally outlandish, even absurd.

Historically, it has been the marginalized groups who have fought for inclusion. In fact, African Americans have embraced integration and fought more for the unification of society than any other group in the history of this nation. Multicultural education does not advocate separatism but is, in fact, based on a premise of universal inclusion. In this context, inclusion means without regard to culture, ethnicity, race, nationality, religion, sex, handicap, or sexual orientation. Opponents of multicultural education, like Savitch and Schlesinger, do not (and perhaps cannot) see how pervasive racism and sexism are throughout the curriculum. Perhaps since it is a curriculum that validates their culture (the Eurocentric culture), they are too close.

Perhaps a simple example will illustrate the fact that proximity to the curriculum blinds many Eurocentric scholars from seeing their own cultural biases. What color was Jesus of Nazareth? He has been portrayed as white through much of the media, and throughout the existence of this country. This is contrary to the description presented in revelations in *The Holy Bible.* Consider this: Joseph took Mary and Jesus to Egypt to escape the proclamation by Herod that all boys who were two years of age and younger were to be put to death, in an attempt to circumvent the prophesy concerning the Christ. It is recorded in Halley's Handbook of *The Holy Bible* (and almost every version of "The New Testament") that Joseph, along with Mary and Jesus, stayed in Egypt for a period of one to two years. In other words, they hid from Herod during this period. What enabled them to blend in with the population in Egypt and go unnoticed?

The Arab invasion of Egypt took place in 641 AD (8), meaning that the Arab population took control of Egypt 641 years after the death of Christ. Prior to that time, Egypt was inhabited and ruled by black folk. Even today, the majority of the inhabitants of Egypt are black. This is the setting that allowed Joseph, Mary, and the infant Jesus, who must have been as black as the slaves in the old South in America, to become lost among the many black faces in Egypt. The facts are there, yet, this distortion has never been corrected in the curriculum, or in the Church.

In comparing the two settings (old Egypt and the old South in America), it was much easier for fugitive blacks to avoid detection in Egypt during that time than it was for black run-away slaves to avoid detection in pre-Civil War America. This is true because most of the population of America, at that time, either looked like Caucasians, Mexicans, or Indians (the portion of the U.S. population that resides currently on reservations in the western and southwestern regions of the United States). At least, it is clear that slaves were not white, neither did they look like the current majority population. This made it relatively simple for slave owners in the antebellum South to locate their run-away slaves. Unlike the indentured servants from Europe (who constituted a large proportion of the first long-term workers in colonial America), they could not just run away to another colony and disappear among the populace.

These distortions are allowed to stand for Cleopatra, Rameses, Moses, Hannibal, and a whole host of other historical figures. Even Crispus Attucks, a black man, the first person to die in the Boston Massacre leading up to the Revolutionary War, has been changed from a free black man to a Nantuckett Indian in some textbooks. Granville Woods, Benjamin Banneker, and Frederick M. Jones are almost never mentioned in our history textbooks. Granville Woods was one of the most prolific inventors of the 19th century. According to Leonard Jeffries, Woods took Thomas Edison to court on two separate occasions for attempting to steal his inventions; and he won! Benjamin Banneker, not only published a yearly Almanac, like the other Benjamin of his time, but he conceptualized and developed the blueprint for the nation's capital—Washington, DC—after the French engineers left unexpectedly.

CONCLUSION

Typically, the term "black" has had a pejorative connotation for many people in our society—not only for European Americans, but also for many black folk. We speak of the black lie versus the white lie, black heart versus (the pure) white heart, black magic versus white magic, black sheep versus white sheep, black cat versus (the) white cat. Even in the game of checkers, the black pieces move last. Many things in this society are designated as either black or white, with black more often representing what is bad, while white tends to represent what is perceived as good. This notion has been transferred to people: white is better than black; and light is better than dark. If you're white, you're all right; if you're brown, stick around; and if you're black, get back (9). Unfortunately, many of us still inhere these ridiculous notions, and this is pure unadulterated racism. It has distorted and corrupted the curriculum in the West and, particularly, in the United States. Consequently, the **infusion** of multiculturalism into the curriculum is not enough if it does nothing to cleanse it of the lies, distortions, and deliberate omissions. Recently, Molefi Asante indicated, in a personal conversation, that the entire school curriculum in the U.S. needs to be cleansed of its lies and distortions, but more importantly of its inherent racism (10).

As one begins to examine critically the idea of a multicultural curriculum, its powerful possibilities become clear, especially if it were implemented in the manner in which its advocates suggest. The concern that some European Americans have regarding multiculturalism is that it will somehow tarnish the American ideal and severely circumscribe the options for others. Nothing could be further from the truth. Multiculturalism has the potential of greater empowerment for all Americans. Truth and knowledge are the most powerful tools any citizen can possess in a democracy. It is not just an innovation for marginalized groups. All of society would benefit from the long-term changes it would evoke. Therefore, as Banks and Banks (1993) indicate: "The challenge to multicultural educators, in both theory and practice, is how to increase equity for one particular victimized group without limiting the opportunities of another."

REFERENCES

Asante, Molefi K., *Afrocentricity,* African World Press, Inc., Trenton, New Jersey. 1988.

Asante, Molefi K., *Historical and Cultural Atlas of African Americans,* New York: Macmillan Publishing Co. 1991.

Banks, James A. *An Introduction to Multicultural Education,* (2nd Ed), Boston: Allyn and Bacon, 1999.

Banks, James A. and Cherry A. M. Banks (ed.), *Multicultural Education: Issues and Perspectives* 2nd 1993. Boston: Allyn and Bacon.

Bennett, Christine, I. *Comprehensive Multicultural Education: Theory and Practice,* Boston: Allyn & Bacon, 1999.

Bernal, Martin, *Black Athena: The Afroasian Roots of Classical Civilization,* New Brunswick: Rutgers University Press, 1987-1991.

Campbell, Duane E., *Choosing Democracy: A Practical Guide to Multicultural Education,* Englewood Cliffs, New Jersey: Merrill/Prentice Hall. p.57. 1996.

Grant, Carl A. "Challenging the Myths About Multicultural Education, " *Education 97/98: Annual Editions,* editor, Fred Shultz, Article 31, pp. 185-189. Reprinted from *Multicultural Education,* Winter 1994, pp. 4–9.

Grant, Carl A and Mary L. Gomez, *Making Schooling Multicultural: Campus and Classroom,* 1996, Englewood Cliffs, New Jersey: Prentice Hall.

Graff, G. *Beyond the cultural Wars: How Teaching the Conflicts Can Revitalize American Education.* New York: Norton, 1992.

Gutek, Gerald L., *Historical and Philosophical Foundations of Education: A Biographical Introduction.* 2nd ed. Upper Saddle River, NJ: Merrilll/Prentice Hall, 1997, 300.

Rouser, Neil O. "Multicultural Education for the Dominant Culture: Toward the Development of a

Multicultural Sense of Self, *Urban Education,* Vol. 31, No .2, pp. 125–148. May, 1996.

James, George G. M., *Stolen Legacy: Greek Philosophy is Stolen Egyptian Philosophy,* African World Press, Inc., Trenton, New Jersey. 1992.

Jones, Rhett S. "Black Studies' Failures and 'First Negroes," *Black Issues in Higher Education,* October 20, 1994. p. 128. Vol. 11, No.17.

Kaltsounis, Theodore, "Multicultural Education and Citizenship Education at a j Crossroads: Searching for Common Ground," *Social Studies.* Vol. .88, No.1, pp. 18–22, January, 1997.

Ladson-Billings, Gloria, "What We Can Learn from Multicultural Education Research." *Education 97/98: Annual Editions,* editor, Fred Shultz, Article 30, pp. 181–184. Reprinted from *Educational Leadership,* May 1994, pp. 22–26.

Lefkowitz, Mary, K., *Not Out of Africa: How Afrocentrism Became an Excuse to Teach Myth as History.* New York: Basic Books/Harper Collins (1997).

Robertson, Ian, *Sociology.* 3rd ed. New York: Worth Publishers, Inc. 1987. p. 305

Schlessinger, Arthur Jr., *The Disuniting of America: Reflection on a Multicultural Society.* New York: Norton, 1992.

Sleeter, Christine E. and Carl A. Grant. *Making Choices for Multicultural Education: Five Approaches to Race,. Class, and Gender.* Columbus, Ohio: Merrilll/Prentice Hall. 1999.

Spring, Joel, *American Education* (7th ed). New York: McGraw/Hill, 1996.

Spring, Joel. *American Education.* Boston Burr Ridge, Illinois: McGraw/Hill, 2000.

Timm, Joan T. *Four Perspectives in Multicultural Education.* Belmont: Wadsworth Publishing Co., 1996.

NOTES

1. Duane E. Campbell in *Choosing Democracy: A Practical Guide to Multicultural Education* states: "An accurate inclusion of the African American contribution to U.S. history provides a substantial alternative interpretation of much of the United States' past. In other words, when the African American perspective is added, familiar historical events may be subject to different interpretations." p.57.

2. Campbell, *Ibid.,* p. 51.

3. James A. Banks and Cherry A. McGee Banks, *Ibid.,* p. 4.1993.

4. Joel Spring, *Ibid* (1996).

5. Campbell, *Ibid.,* p .30.

6. Campbell, *Ibid.,* p. 30. I would argue that those members of ethnic groups who have learned to "code switch" and adopt middle class Eurocentric behavior patterns have a greater likelihood of succeeding in school.

7. Arthur Schlesinger Jr. *The Disuniting of America, Whittle* Direct Books, p. 58, 1991.

8. See the *New American Desk Encyclopedia,* p. 399.

9. A historical phrase that appears to have originated in the early Jim Crow era. It has even been translated into several songs during that period.

10. In a personal conversation with Molefi Asante (1994), he indicated that multiculturalism is a good start in cleaning up the curriculum, but if it does not seek to eliminate racism from the curriculum, it is a deficient concept.

Policy as the Transformation of Intentions: Making Multicultural Education Policy

Margaret Placier, Peter M. Hall, S. Benson McKendall, and Karen S. Cockrell

This qualitative policy study applies an interactionist famework, for policy analysis, especially the concept of intentions, to an examination of the construction of multicultural education policy in a midwestern U.S. school district. Intentions—purposes and goals meant to shape the behavior of actors in the future and at other sites—motivate actors to act in the policy arena, to use policy as a vehicle for realizing their purposes. Initiated in response to a racial conflict in a high school, the policy process entailed the school board's creation of a committee including many African American community members to generate recommendations for improving race relations. During the process, the school board's intentions, and those of many community members, were transformed due to the administration's reinforcement of district conventions and power structures. Race relations became multicultural issues. Community members who misconstrued the process as granting them real policy-making authority were most disappointed with the outcomes.

This Study applies an interactionist framework designed to capture the complexity of policy processes (Hall, 1995; Hall & McGinty, 1997) to construction of multicultural education policy in a school district. We will focus on one key concept in the framework: intentions. Policies convey intentions, and policy making cannot be understood without understanding actors' intentions. Policy is not a concrete text to be implemented but a transformation of intentions in which content, practices, and consequences are generated in the dynamics.

The study responds to the need to augment the limited knowledge base in the area of multicultural education policy (Grant & Millar, 1992; Persell, Dougherty, & Wenglinsky, 1993). More precisely, Cornbleth and Waugh (1993) call for a kind of multicultural policy study paying "systematic attention to the politics of policy-in-the-making" (p. 36) in contrasting settings with different dynamics. The capacity to capture these dynamics is the focus of the framework and methods we employ. We assume that policy making is adapted to the particular organizational culture and structure in which it unfolds. However, micro-level, contextualized studies of policy processes need not be atheoretical (Hall, 1995). Our study portrays a process in the context of a specific school district, and it exemplifies ways of thinking that multicultural theorists have identified (Banks, 1994; Hoffman, 1997; Sleeter & Grant, 1994) and researchers have observed in other contexts (Borman, Timm, Al-amin, & Winston, 1992; Cockrell, 1996; Combleth & Waugh, 1995; Foster, 1990).

THEORETICAL FRAMEWORK: INTENTIONS AND THEIR TRANSFORMATION

Policy, as we see it, is a process. Typical policy discourse bifurcates that process into stages called policy making and policy implementation, implying that policy is a concrete thing made in one place or time and then transmitted elsewhere to be practiced. Rather, policy is constituted when actors representing multiple interests and roles interact in conditions of uncertainty and ambiguity (Estes & Edmonds, 1981).

We conceptualize policy as a transformation of intentions, an ambiguous, multifaceted, interactive process. *Intentions*—purposes and goals meant to shape the behavior of actors in the future and at other sites—motivate actors to act in the policy arena, to use policy as a vehicle for realizing their purposes. The transformation of intentions in a conventional sense occurs when actors aim specific actions at a problem for announced purposes. For example, legislators may transform their intention to equalize school funding into a finance plan. Intentions may, on the other hand, be implicit or unannounced, but their symbolic representations can be seen in the form, content, and consequences of policy processes. The transformation of intentions can convey an even more flexible and less linear process, whereby actors with divergent or conflicting intentions enter the process at different points and adjust to one another within and across sites to construct policy. Transformation can be a double entendre in which some actors' subtexts seek to subvert or resist others' intentions. There may be unanticipated contingencies and unintended consequences. The transformation of intentions can also bring attention to the emergence of new or previously unrecognized intentions. Finally, the transformation of intentions recognizes that actors have uses for policy other than the substantive resolution of problems. They may intend to advance their careers, reputations, or influence through policy efforts.

Two dimensions enhance understanding of intentions: process/ content and consensual/ plural. Process intentions are concerned with advancing the process or getting the job done, whereas content intentions refer to the product: what is included and what is given priority. Consensual intentions refer to recognition of a collective interest in certain actions, the degree to which common intentions can be realized through group consensus and coordination. Plural intentions refer to divergent group or individual interests and the degree to which intentions are realized through conflict, resistance, and mobilizing resources to support different policy agendas.

So far, we have emphasized contingency and ambiguity, but the policy process also occurs in an organizational context entailing the following:

Structural linkages. The process stretches temporally through phases and spatially across linked sites. Policy can be analyzed as a conditional matrix—a web of interrelated conditions, action/interaction, and consequences—in which the consequences of one context become conditions for the next (Curry, 1997; Datnow, Hubbard, & Mehan, 1998; Strauss & Corbin, 1990). Policy initiators, dependent on those who follow to fulfill their intentions, set conditions that both limit and facilitate later action. Conditional effects vary due to tight or loose linkages between phases/sites and between initiators and those to whom they delegate responsibility. Policy initiators may intentionally grant delegates a level of autonomy, but, whether intended or not, delegates will have at least some discretion. If decisions set unclear conditions, if communication is poor, or if linkages are weak, they may have more. Even the strongest linkages are not automatic and must be enacted to have effects.

Institutional conventions. Conventions are taken-for-granted ways of understanding, communicating, and doing for accomplishing collective activity that act as hedges against contingency, conflict, and resistance in the process. They make cooperation and coordination simpler, quicker, and more efficient, but they also constrain alternatives and may privilege some interests over others (Becker, 1982). Moreover, conventions may be counterproductive in certain cases, subverting the intentions of policy initiators.

Distribution of power. Power tips the scales in favor of some actors' intentions. Those who dominate the organization and have greater access to resources can shape the context in which subordinates act, a form of metapower (Baumgartner, Buckley, Burns, & Schuster, 1976; Hall, 1997). The organizational culture and its conventions are resources for leaders (Clegg, 1989; Sewell, 1992). However, as noted earlier, they must delegate responsibility to fulfill their intentions, which introduces discretion and interpretation. Thus, despite leaders' advantages, contingency, conflict, and resistance are possible, and initial intentions are inevitably somewhat transformed.

Two previous case studies of district multicultural education policy illustrate these points. A state department of education hired Borman et al. (1992) to assess a district's racial environment after African Americans[1] reported concerns about an interracial high school fight. African Americans saw the fight not as an isolated incident but as a symptom of deep problems in district-community and teacher-student relations. State officials' response, funding a university research team to study the problem, transformed African Americans' intentions to mobilize state power over the district into research. The researchers found that European Americans and African Americans had very different images of the district. To bridge this gap, they recommended comprehensive integration of multicultural education.

However, they doubted this would occur due to educators' racial attitudes, assimilationist ideology, and bias for piecemeal solutions, along with unclear administrative support. The researchers had no authority, and their intentions were blocked by district conventions and power dynamics.

A study of multicultural education policy in a local educational authority (LEA) in England (Foster, 1990) found that a human relations approach stressing positive cross-cultural interactions failed to ameliorate low achievement and disruptive behavior among Afro-Caribbean students. Administrators reidentified the problem as racism. The chief education officer directed all head teachers to report racial incidents and all schools to develop antiracist policies. However, this was not strictly a top-down process. At least one school was consistently ahead of LEA policies because of a cadre of progressive teachers and parental pressure. LEA policies were not specific enough to give clear direction to schools that were not committed to or informed about antiracist education. Policy ambiguity and loose LEA-school linkages allowed wide variation in interpretation by school-level delegates.

As these studies illustrate, analyses of district policy processes must consider how linkages with national or state policy may affect local action. When federal or state initiatives are weak, ambiguous, or absent, as has been the case with multicultural education in the United States (Cornbleth & Waugh, 1995; Golinick, 1995; Greene & Heflin, 1992; Stevenson & Gonzalez, 1992), local district actors are free to reject multicultural education or to construct its meanings very differently in response to local beliefs and conditions. Urban districts are most likely to face school board, state, or federal court mandates for implementation (Stevenson & Gonzalez, 1992).

METHOD

Our study combined qualitative data collection strategies to triangulate among sources in order to construct a more complex and trustworthy analysis. One author was a participant observer at meetings of a district's Committee on Multicultural Issues, which is the focus of our study, and was in fact appointed chair of a subcommittee of this group. His inside perspective was invaluable, but for balance, another researcher served as a non-participant observer during meetings, keeping detailed field notes. Another data source was 12 interviews with a sample of 14 committee members (2 couples elected to be interviewed jointly), conducted by researchers who were not involved in the process.[2] Interviewees included the committee chair (a district administrator), 2 other district administrators, chairs and members from two subcommittees, and 2 school board members who sponsored the committee's formation. Of the interviewees, 8 were African American, 4 were European American, and 2 were Middle Eastern first-generation immigrants;[3] 5 were men and 9 were women. The audiotaped interviews, which followed a semi-structured protocol and ranged from 40 to 90 minutes in length, elicited an understanding of the interviewees' intentions and whether they perceived these intentions as being fulfilled through the policy process. An extensive file of documents and news reports provided additional data.

The author who participated on the committee originated the theoretical framework, and other researchers did the data analysis and writing. A previous report (Placier, Hall, & Davis, 1997) concentrated on observation and document data to describe the process. This study, in contrast, uses the observations and documents as context and concentrates on the interviews. By coding and sorting the data with Qualpro software, we identified participants' process and content intentions, as well as their perceptions of what occurred. A limitation is that the interviews came several months after committee meetings ended. Participants' retrospective reports of their intentions may reflect post hoc reconstructions or rationalizations of their actions.

THE CONTEXT

Policy studies should look at how the "particular locality influences investigation, interpretation and action" (Combleth & Waugh, 1995, p. 29). Our setting is Westwood, a midsized city with an economy dominated by higher education, health care, insurance, and light industry. At the time, the district's growing student population of 14,500 was 80% European American, 15% African American, 4% Asian, and 1% Other. Some schools had significant numbers of immigrant or refugee students from more than 20 nations.

Westwood School District has few external incentives for implementing multicultural education. The district is not affected by federal desegregation or civil rights court orders, and the state has not actively promoted this reform (Gollnick, 1995). A state school improvement program begun during the 1980s' excellence period requires district reviews every 5 years. One standard is, "Multicultural and gender-fair concepts and practice are infused in curriculum, instructional programs and all other school activities." This is strong language, but the state has not sanctioned noncomplying districts, which are in the vast majority.

The district administration's most strenuous efforts have gone toward maintaining a reputation for high academic achievement. At the time of our study, the same European American male superintendent had led the district for 17 years and had set the tone for district culture. He generally acted in a low-key, behind-the-scenes style, controlling how issues reached the board and rarely taking strong public positions on controversial issues.

Public comment and debate at board meetings were limited, and administrators tried to minimize negative press coverage. Occasionally, the board and/or administration appointed community committees to study problems and make recommendations, but their actions were carefully managed, and the administration put the final spin on all recommendations (Glazier, 1994).[4]

Racial issues were not new to the district's policy agenda. Before the 1954 *Brown* decision, students and teachers were segregated by race. As desegregation occurred during the following decade, there were protests over low African American participation in extracurricular activities at the high school and teacher-parent tensions over what teachers considered discipline problems with African American elementary students. Negotiations with school administrators led to creation of new extracurricular groups; Black studies courses; and a program, Home-School Links, a liaison between African American parents and the schools.

In the early 1990s, the district adopted outcome-based education (OBE), with some outcomes relating to cultural diversity, for example, "Describe and address the challenges of a multicultural society and world." Curricula were supposed to align with these outcomes, but, in the face of political criticism, the district was downplaying OBE. The district had also adopted site-based management, allowing principals and teachers a degree of autonomy. Some schools, particularly schools with African American and recent immigrant or refugee students, had initiated multicultural activities. At schools in mostly European American neighborhoods, however, educators remarked that because they did not have much diversity, multiculturalism was not a priority. Teacher autonomy was also a district value, and a norm was that teachers could not be required to do anything. Some teachers had developed multicultural curricula; others

showed little interest. The staff development program offered teachers a menu of choices. If a session on multicultural education were offered, a teacher might or might not choose to attend.

These aspects of the district context had important effects on the making of multicultural education policy. Based on district outcomes as well as efforts of some schools and teachers, some district personnel perceived that they had already made strides toward multicultural education. This was in contrast to the perception of community critics, particularly African Americans, that the district was doing very little to address their concerns.

THE POLICY PROCESS

Catalyst for action. The timeline in Table 1 summarizes the process in our study. The interviewees attributed formation of the Committee on Multicultural Issues to one event: a speech by an African American professor at a high school's Black History Month assembly. Invited to speak about contributions of African Americans, the speaker said he overheard European American students complaining about the assembly and decided to deliver a critique of racism in schools. Some European American students took offense, and some African American students voiced agreement. Fights broke out and were reported as anything from a riot to minor shoves. Some school staff responded defensively to the speaker's critique. Counselors spent hours calming students down. The speaker received death threats. The media gave the incident extensive coverage, but district administrators tried to minimize its seriousness and emphasized that it would not undermine progress in race relations.

The Westwood school board had six members, five European American and one African American, although the latter was absent during the following events. At the March board meeting, one member, a European American male, proposed forming a Committee on Race Relations. He said he had heard of four racial incidents, and although he knew the district was making efforts, this latest one suggested it was time to evaluate those efforts and (as paraphrased in the minutes), "begin to talk to one another in serious face-to-face discussions, to teach our children through our actions." After some discussion, the vote on the motion was unanimous. The same board member wrote the Committee's *charge,* or assignment of respon-

sibility: to investigate what the district was currently doing about race relations, to identify areas of deficiency, and to recommend specific improvements along with cost estimates. This established the committee as a board committee, and board members emphasized that it was their initiative. However, in line with district conventions, they delegated the process to the administration.

The superintendent appointed a central office administrator, an African American woman of long experience in the district, to be the com-

Table 1: Timeline of Committee Process	
February	Black History Month high school speaker, student conflicts
	Media coverage
March	School board votes to establish Committee on Race Relations
	Membership and management of committee delegated to administration
March through June	Superintendent appoints district administrator as committee chair
	Call for volunteers in the media, recruitment of other members
	Negotiation between board and administration over membership
	Administration changes name to Committee on Multicultural Issues
	Administration assigns members to subcommittees and appoints subchairs
June 30	Kickoff meeting of the committee
	Charges distributed to subcommittees
	Speeches from board president and consultant
July through mid-August	Subcommittee meetings
	Members strategize to fulfill their process and content intentions
	Media coverage of some members' criticisms of district control
August	Subcommittees give committee chair their recommendations
September	Committee meets for public presentation of subcommittee recommendations
	Committee dissolved
October	Committee chair develops report to the board
	Negotiation with committee members over including all recommendations
November	Committee chair submits report to the board, prioritizing certain recommendations for funding
	Board accepts report and chair's recommendations for funding
December	Superintendent brings specific funding proposals to the board

mittee chair. She was in a difficult, cross-pressured position. African Americans would expect her backing, and the administration would expect efficient, conflict-free management. The superintendent and other administrators would offer her little public support. She announced in the media that anyone interested in serving on the committee should call her office. She also drafted a list of members to be recruited, primarily people who had previously worked on district committees and/or were well known in the community, as well as district staff. The committee chair said that she tried to balance membership to include district staff and community members, racial and cultural groups, men and women. When the board saw the list, however, some wanted to nominate people they saw as excluded because of their critical perspectives or who had contacted them rather than the administration. Because of this negotiation, the list was not finalized until June. Summer meetings meant that some prominent members would attend rarely (if at all), which had undeterminable effects.[5] Meanwhile, the administration changed the committee's name to the Committee on Multicultural Issues. The committee chair said the change was intended to prevent the committee from falling into a blame game of complaints about racism she had seen before. She wanted a positive, action-oriented approach. Transformation of the board's intentions had begun.

The committee chair assigned members—again trying to balance race, gender, district, and community—to four subcommittees: Curriculum, Cultural Awareness and Tolerance, Extracurricular Activities, and Minority Recruitment. She also appointed the subchairs, respectively: a European American male university professor, a Middle Eastern first-generation immigrant male university administrator, an African American female parent volunteer, and an African American female assistant principal. The subcommittees

were given 6 weeks to generate recommendations to the board. The entire committee met only twice, for a kickoff meeting and at the end to report on recommendations. At the kickoff meeting, the committee chair distributed to each subcommittee specific charges, or lists of responsibilities, which were written with the board member who had initiated the process. However, there was no explanation of the respective roles of the board, administration, and committee for the benefit of community members who were new to such involvement. A consultant from a federally funded agency spoke, expressing a social reconstructionist view of multicultural education that some participants thought conveyed the administration's intentions.[6] The board president spoke about the damaging effects of racism. The meeting left the impression that Westwood's racial tensions were finally to be addressed.

Despite this hopeful beginning, in the aftermath of the process, we knew from conversations that some community members were disappointed. Our data analysis found that their complaints could be understood by contrasting their intentions for participating ("what I wanted to happen or believed should have happened") with their descriptions of what did occur. Process intentions described the means, and content intentions described the ends or outcomes of participation. Most of the community members' talk concerned their specific subcommittees, of which we focused on two: (a) Curriculum and (b) Cultural Awareness and Tolerance (abbreviated hereafter as Cultural Awareness). The other two, Extracurricular Activities and Minority Hiring, had more narrowly defined tasks and proceeded in a straightforward way to generate recommendations.[7] For our two focus subcommittees, we analyzed intentions and descriptions of the subchairs and most active (in terms of attendance and participation) community members. See Table 2 for profiles of the community interviewees.

Process intentions versus descriptions of what happened. Interviewees' talk about the process showed differences among board members, administrators, and community members.

Board members. In meetings, speeches, and interviews, board members emphasized responding to community concerns about racial incidents. Their process intentions were expressed in the committee charge to investigate and make recommendations. Board members also wanted the process to be inclusive and were not as concerned as the administration that including members who were critical and/or new to district involvement might be disruptive. In terms of describing the process, once they had negotiated membership and delegated management to the administration, they observed a few meetings but did not have detailed knowledge of what occurred. They did not seem too concerned with the process as long as it was perceived as open and reasonable and generated supportable recommendations. They did not mention that given time constraints, the committee could not have investigated the district in any meaningful way.

Administrators. The administration intended the process to be a small window of openness to community input, during which the committee would generate recommendations in a quick, businesslike way. They described the process as choosing a balanced membership and keeping the members on task to meet the timeline. As the committee chair put it, "We did not want that committee to be a troubleshooting committee [or] an oversight committee for the whole year. We wanted it to come in and look at its charge, to make recommendations and move away." The process had to be managed well to arrive at recommendations in line with district conventions. The committee chair feared the committee might fall into the pitfalls and landmines she had observed on other race relations groups:

I was worried....If we had been stuck on race relations and the blame game, we could have taken...years just talking and getting every bit of injustice that has ever been heaped on anyone out into the open, and maybe we could have embarrassed a few people.

In her view, making "stakeholders" angry was always unproductive. Some members upset the balance or timeline by switching subcommittees or dwelling on their problems with the schools, "venting" their emotions, as one administrator called it. Some community members, another noted, simply did not understand how the district works or what committees are supposed to do. Nevertheless, in the end, the committee chair reflected, "I credit the people in this community, the way we handled it....We tried to structure it as a centrist point of view." One administrator defined the process primarily as a way to show the community what the district was already doing, to correct misperceptions rather than to propose a change in direction.

Curriculum subcommittee. This subcommittee's specific charge was to address the following questions: "How are the different cultural backgrounds of Westwood students represented in the curriculum?" and "What special programs promote academic excellence among minority group students? Attempt to prevent dropping out?" The first question concerned content integration, and the second addressed equalizing outcomes for all student populations (Banks, 1994). The meetings of this group were intense but not contentious, which the members attributed to the subchair's facilitation.[8] The subchair said, "My stance since the 1960s has been to work the limits of the system, on the boundaries, from the outside, but to be responsible—not a bomb-thrower." His process intentions were to value the views of African Americans, to be a source of information on multicultural education, and to expand the charge beyond "restricted, conventional notions of 'curriculum,' to include the social context of schooling." He took the charge to investigate the problem seriously, intending to request district data to substantiate whether practices such as tracking and discipline had disproportionate effects on African American students, as anecdotal reports suggested. However, this intention was blocked when the district would not provide such data. Yet, he felt that his subcommittee process went relatively well. In fact, compared to his prior experience on district committees, this one was more inclusive and less "managed." He had hoped the committee would continue, to accomplish more, but discerned that this was not the administration's intention. His prior experience allowed him to understand how the district worked, and although disappointed, he was "not surprised it happened that way."

The most active members of this subcommittee were three African American men. A working-class father of three Westwood students, Member C1 had called the central office to express concerns about the high school incident and was invited to join the committee. His perception, however, was that most committee members were selected because they were "figures in the community." As a high school graduate of the 1970s, he said,

> It astonished me that racial relations had broken down as badly as they had. My memory...was I thought it was an exceptional atmosphere because not only were there no racial boundaries drawn...there weren't any type of social status boundaries.

He and his wife, who attended some meetings, wanted to open the schools to community participation and to improve schooling for African American children. He realized the group had to stay on task but wished they had had more time to "reach the goal." Although everyone "spoke their minds" in the subcommittee and their report was based on "consensus," he

guessed that the committee chair and subchairs decided what to bring to the board, and "that process I wasn't in on." As for the board, "there probably were some meetings that were held, really closed meetings, to deal with the issue. The school board does that quite often [laughs]." His participation had not changed his feeling of being a district outsider.

Member C2, a doctoral candidate at the university, was more positive about the process. He heard about the committee after membership was decided but asked the committee chair if he could sit in, and she approved. His wife, a district employee, sat in on another subcommittee. Like Member C1, he thought membership was biased against "troublesome" people and in favor of those with "stature." He did not trust the administration's intentions and thought most educators were "defensive and antagonistic" in the face of criticism. However, he believed he could counter district intentions by mobilizing his resources of advanced education, writing and speaking skills, and media contacts. He portrayed himself and his wife as having the cultural capital needed in this context, by being "fairly organized, articulate, and committed...not just a noisome bunch....Our comments and observations were substantive rather than argumentative." He "read voraciously" between meetings so that he could "make a lot of intelligent noise." Media scrutiny, he argued, made the process fair even if the district did not intend it. He also developed a positive relationship with the chair of the Curriculum subcommittee, whom he described as a fair, "firm-willed," "benevolent dictator" who kept the group on task, "enlightened" his views, and evaluated ideas based on "merit." Like Member C1, he suspected that the committee chair and subchairs met "away from us rabble rousers, where they talked about...what they wanted to do and how they wanted to do it." The subcommittee structure, he felt, was intended to avoid large, "raucous" meetings. Although he

Table 2: Profiles of Community Interviewees

Identity	Selection	Process Intention	Content Intention
Curriculum subcommittee Subchair European American male University professor Parent District involvement	Recruited, appointed chair	Value African American views Provide information Expand charge and collect data on structural issues	Implement a complex approach to multicultural education Address structural issues
Member C1 African American male Government employee Parent Active in community	Called chair to volunteer	Open, inclusive Advocate for African American children Stay on task, hope for more time	Consistent district policy Required staff training Curriculum integration Vocational opportunities
Member C2 African American male Ph.D. candidate Parent District employee spouse	Asked chair to sit in	Be articulate, effective Represent African Americans	Required staff training Curriculum integration
Member C3 Immigrant female Business owner Parent District involvement	Recruited	Participate actively Achieve narrowly defined goals, given timeline	Required staff training Specialized language and culture courses Parent involvement
Cultural Awareness subcommittee Subchair Immigrant male University administrator Parent District involvement	Recruited, appointed chair	Reach consensus Balanced, inclusive discussion Continue committee	Staff training Hire specialists Parent involvement and education
Member A1 African American female Social services Parent	Volunteered through chair	Participate actively Advocate for African American parents and children Inclusive, not district control Survey community opinion Continue committee, monitor	Required staff training Minority teachers Hire specialist Reform home-school links
Member A2 European American female Parent District involvement	Called board member to volunteer	Inclusive, not district control Clear decision-making process Survey community opinion Continue committee, monitor	Staff training Address issues behind racial incident Minority teachers Parent education
Member A3 African American male Retired professional Religious leader Elected to board	Recruited	Include all members' ideas Continue committee, monitor	Staff training Representation of African Americans in activities Hire specialist Curriculum change District accountability

was skeptical of the district, he believed he played a major role: "I flatter myself to think that some things might not have happened but for my presence."

The third African American man, a working-class, Islamic[9] community activist, was appointed to the committee after a board member's insistence. Appointed to Minority Hiring, he switched himself to the Curriculum subcommittee at the first meeting. He was so dissatisfied with the process that he declined to be interviewed for our study. His intention as expressed in meetings and to the media was to exert outside pressure on a district he saw as closed and elitist. He used radio and newspaper contacts to draw attention, much of it critical, to the process. In fact, a board member speculated that this man's charges that the committee was too "conservative" may have kept right-wing opposition to multicultural education from surfacing in Westwood.

Member C3, a business owner, had actively promoted cross-cultural understanding in her children's schools and was eager to participate on the committee. Because of her role as a parent volunteer, she had concrete knowledge of what the district was already doing related to cultural diversity. Whereas her impressions were generally positive and she did not express mistrust toward the district, she did feel that they could do much more. She described the process positively: "We did not negate any suggestions, basically. When any committee member gave us any ideas or suggestions, they were put on paper, discussed, and then refined." She was disappointed that some people selected for membership were basically "nonexistent," but pleased that volunteers such as Member C2 were fully included. Her major concern was that the task was too extensive for the time provided: that the committee could be just a "starting point." Her expectations were not as high as those of Member C1, who seemed subsequently more disappointed.

Cultural Awareness subcommittee. This subcommittee's specific charge was to address the following questions: "What components of the Westwood Public School curriculum teach tolerance, appreciation, and acceptance or racial and cultural diversity?" "What staff development programs does the district employ to promote cultural awareness and sensitivity among faculty, staff, and administration?" "What programs are meant to facilitate positive communication and cooperation between teachers, parents, and students from different racial and cultural backgrounds?" These questions defined the policy issue as improving human relations (Sleeter & Grant, 1994) or prejudice reduction (Banks, 1994) and reflected the board and administration's analysis of the causes of the Black History Month conflict. Ironically, given their charge, this group was very conflictual and became a source of administrator concerns about venting and the blame game. The Cultural Awareness subchair administered a university program that provided services to the schools. From his experience in this role and as a parent, he deemed the district could do more to instill cultural knowledge. His process intention was to develop common understandings, but he was faced with plural, conflicting intentions and had to act as a "mediator" during "heated discussions" among "strong-willed people." For example, Members A1 and A2 wanted to conduct a survey on school-community relations, which he argued was impossible. He said, "There was no way in such a short time we could have come up with the requirements or the requests that were made of us." Moreover, "momentum" was lost when the committee was abruptly disbanded after generating recommendations. By the end, he seemed frustrated and cynical.

Members A1 and A2 became allies during the meetings. Member A1 called the central office to volunteer, motivated by problems in the treatment of her sons and other low-income, particularly African American, children. Her intention was

> to get in there and try to see if any other Black parents were having the problems that I had, and how many other Black parents I could help that were afraid to speak out or didn't have the common knowledge to know that they have rights.

In press coverage of the committee, she was very vocal. Member A2, a middle-class woman with a doctoral degree, also volunteered but was not selected until she pressured a school board member she knew: "I just kept it up and I wouldn't let them not listen to me. I really wanted to be on the committee." In common with Member A1, her process intentions were for the committee to be inclusive and community focused, not district dominated. She was appointed to Minority Hiring but also attended the Cultural Awareness subcommittee on her own initiative because she believed she had more "expertise" in this area.

Like Members C1 and C2, Members A1 and A2 criticized the district's membership selection, arguing that district personnel on subcommittees constrained discussion. Member A1 said,

> You have parents here that are not going to voice what they have complaints about with the school system when you have an administrative person sitting here, that you would think they would retaliate because your children are in the school system.

According to these two, the decision-making process was rushed and arbitrary, and a working definition of multicultural education was neither provided nor developed. They felt that their efforts were not appreciated; for example, Member A2 completed research that was not used, and the subchair blocked their intention to do a community survey. Member A2 described the subchair as "extremely democratic" at the start but said her impression

changed when he did not take her seriously. Member A1 believed the subchair did not respect women. Moreover, the district would not provide them with data, and the committee chair (a "dictator," said Member A2) deleted their ideas from the final report. Member A1 said,

> We thought we would get to stay as a committee until all our things were put in place, and that we would still have something to say…[but] we were told when we went to that final board meeting, "Thank you for your help."

Member A2 blamed this "termination" on the committee chair: "She wanted the subcommittee meetings to be stopped before they did, and then she just said, 'This is the deadline, this is it,' and it was cut off."

Member A3 had been recruited because of his reputation as a community leader. He noted that each subcommittee member had an "agenda," and "There were times when we had to…take a break, to try to get some order back." But, in general, the subcommittee process was "excellent" because "you could bring up your idea, present it, discuss the pros and cons about it.…It went very well." His process intention, that every member's ideas be included in the recommendations, had been met. If not, he said, members had ample opportunity to express their objections to the board. In fact, shortly after the process ended, Member A3 was elected to the board, and this role clearly influenced his interview responses. He said that as a board member, his biggest regret about the process (in common with Members A1 and A2) was that the committee did not become a standing committee, because

> Once you have a group of people that you have gone through this in depth, you want to make sure that same group can get together and look at the program at year end or have a report generated for all the

committee members saying, "Here's what we've done."

It was significant that even as a board member, he felt he had little power to enforce the recommendations. Instead, he hoped the community would "hold our feet to the fire."

In summary, in terms of process intentions, board members wanted to respond to community concerns by setting up a visible structure for community participation and focusing the process minimally with a general, open-ended charge. However, the time frame was hardly conducive to this kind of loosely structured process. In line with district conventions, the board entrusted management of the process to the administration, whose process intentions were characterized by bureaucratic efficiency and administrative control of district operations. The chair intended to meet the deadline by controlling subcommittee assignments, keeping people on task, and limiting unproductive complaining. Community members took the charge to investigate the issues seriously, but the district's timeline and restrictions on access to data made this impossible. Some newcomers to district involvement also seemed to believe that the committee had been given real, lasting authority, which the committee chair then withdrew, even though the charge asked only for recommendations to the board.

Before reporting findings on content intentions, we must describe the process of generating the committee's recommendations to the board. Each subcommittee developed a long list of recommendations that included most individual members' ideas. The committee chair developed these into a report that was fairly detailed but did leave out some recommendations important to specific individuals (e.g., the Islamic member's recommendation of Arabic as a foreign language). Several members called her and the press to protest these omissions. In response, the chair included all of the original recommendations in an

appendix to the report. When she presented the report to the board, however, she read some highlights and urged the board to read the entire report including the appendices. Then she said that "we" (the administration) recommended budgeting for a multi-cultural coordinator, establishing district and building multicultural task forces, expanding an existing minority intern program to attract young people into teaching, budgeting funds for curriculum materials and staff development, and appointing someone to work on access to extracurricular activities. The specificity of the subcommittees' recommendations (members' content intentions) was lost. The board voted unanimously to accept the report but funded only the administration's list. For many community members, this revealed heretofore implicit power relations among the board, administration, and committee.

Content intentions versus descriptions of outcomes. What did interviewees want the process to accomplish? What did they think it had accomplished? The board's charge to the committee did not specify any desired outcomes. The district also did not specify a definition of multicultural education, which made the goals ambiguous and open to social construction.[10] As previously mentioned, at the kickoff meeting, an outside consultant made a strong argument for social reconstruction, and the board president spoke against racism, but charges distributed to the two subcommittees in this study emphasized curriculum changes and human relations. The consultant was supposed to meet with the committee during the process, but a family emergency interfered. We can only speculate whether she might have tipped the balance of power in the process. At the last subcommittee meetings, the committee chair abruptly circulated a very simplistic definition of multicultural education that she said should guide the recommendations: "Multicultural education: Understanding and appreciating differences, as it relates to race, gender, national origin, exceptionality, religion and age." By that time, each subcommittee had coped with the ambiguity by developing their own ideas about what the process was to accomplish.

Board members. Consistent with their charge, board members said that they intended to receive an analysis of the district's practices and recommendations for improvements. They emphasized addressing the causes of the Black History Month conflict, which they saw as lack of tolerance or understanding among different groups. They also related the dearth of minority teachers and the need for training of existing teachers to this problem. One said she had hoped the committee would take a strong stand against racism, although the board had not specified this in any subcommittee's charge. In terms of whether their intentions had been fulfilled, board members had guardedly positive reactions. They had not been actively involved in committee meetings, having delegated this to the administration, and they saw in the report and the administration's subsequent actions how their intentions had been transformed. One noted that the report had no information on estimated costs, as requested in the charge, but admitted that providing estimated costs would have been difficult for community members. Board members also knew that all the recommendations could not be funded and relied on the administration to prioritize. The board member who had initiated the process was pleased that the board succeeded in adopting a "progressive" report without a conservative backlash. When the board accepted the report, he read a letter to the committee thanking them for trying to do something "real hard" and saying, "I hope someday you can say your committee was the fulcrum on which the lever turned." But, by the time of his interview, he wished that there had been more "momentum from the administration

and the board to keep this moving forward" and questioned if they had accomplished enough. The member who intended a direct approach to racism felt the report needed a little more emphasis on the idea of racism and what the causes were, its existence, how people can learn to respond appropriately....I really didn't think that was stated explicitly....I felt very strongly that we as a district needed to be very clear...that we simply were not going to tolerate any sort of actions, comments, or attitudes that were racist from anyone.

She mailed the committee members a letter to this effect; however, for some reason, she did not express this concern publicly in board meetings.

Administrators. The committee chair, of course, had hoped the committee would not focus on racism, and her intention prevailed. She said that she had simply hoped to "start a conversation" about "everyone feeling comfortable" in the schools. Although she wanted infusion of content about cultural groups, she did not want to "rewrite history." All administrators mentioned improved minority hiring and teacher training. They also said they had hoped the committee would recommend creation of an organizational base for implementation, that is, a new staff position. This may have been an example of post hoc reconstruction of intentions because there was no indication at the start that anyone foresaw creation of a multicultural coordinator position.

In explaining her prioritization process, the committee chair stressed the different roles of the administration and community in policy making:

I believe in input, and I believe in empowering teachers, and I believe in participatory management...because that works in a building, [but] what community people sometimes don't see, if I say, "Gee, I want all of your input," and I remember I had this teacher who said, "You're always asking for input and I told you what I wanted and you didn't do it," and it's almost like "input" means "I tell you to do this and you ought to do it" and not that you ought not to weigh that with everything else that you're doing.

She said that although she had a "great deal of respect for [committee members] and their energy," an administrator has to

look at this long list of things, and if we gave the board a hundred things we wanted done right away, somebody's going to have to boil it down to, "Where do we start?"…If you give somebody five things, they'll get started on them.

Administrators' portrayals of the outcomes reflected confidence in the district. Low turnout at a committee follow-up meeting indicated to them that the former members were busy and had moved on to other issues ("The public is fickle," one noted) or simply trusted the district. The committee chair said,

It could be that they have found a forum in their schools and in their school families to address some of the things they were worried about that they hadn't before. So they are feeling empowered. In fact, I had about ten members tell me that "I'm feeling empowered a little bit now."

The committee chair saw community involvement as most appropriate in the new building-level multicultural committees. She knew that some members were critical because they wanted top—down control: "They wanted the board to say 'Thou shalt not' and 'Thou shall' and police the schools to make sure it happened." But, from her perspective, "outside" people "mandating" what school people should do would not work.

Curriculum subcommittee. A supporter of school restructuring, the Curriculum subchair wanted the district to adopt a complex approach to multicultural education, modeled on James Banks's work, that included "structural issues, beyond the cosmetic, beyond food and festivals." As mentioned earlier, he had hoped to substantiate this through data on tracking and discipline procedures aggregated by race, which were not provided. Therefore, he opened his subcommittee report with "Structure and Process" as the first category of recommendations: "The district should develop, gather and analyze data on student performance by backgrounds, assess whether relationships exist with particular school practices and curricula, and develop alternative modes where necessary and feasible." He reflected that although the district was unlikely to do this, "I felt we had gotten more than we expected, had opened up the possibilities." He had also "done more than the board expected, by putting the ideas of [African American members] on the table." He supported creation of a multicultural coordinator position. Finally, he mused, "You can look at it this way: Is the glass one quarter full or three-quarters empty?" If the administration had foregone their conventional patterns of control, more might have been accomplished, but that would require a change in district culture.

There was consensus among the other members that one outcome should have been required training in cultural differences for district staff and students. Member C1 stressed that he wanted district-wide consistency in the meaning of *multicultural* and "uniform" implementation: "The school system should have set a standard that said, 'Look, this is what we expect to be accomplished'" rather than leaving it up to individual teachers. Other intentions for curriculum change varied in ways that seemed related to identity and self-interest. Member C1 was the only interviewee to propose vocational opportunities for non-college-bound students. He observed that the district boasted "how proud they were of sending off 60% of their students to college. Okay, what about the other 40%?…How are we satisfying every student's needs?" The contrast with Members C2 and C3, who emphasized more advanced "academic" knowledge and college-prep courses, may reflect differences in education and social class. Member C2 was worried that teachers treated middle-class children such as his the same way they treated low-income children, as if they were "ineducable." Member C3, the immigrant, stressed improvement of foreign language and international education, whereas the African Americans stressed infusion of content on African Americans. The Islamic member proposed Arabic language courses. Member C3, the parent volunteer, stressed parent involvement and education.

As for descriptions of the outcomes, Member C1 was the most negative and claimed that his view represented many in the community who felt "betrayed when the final outcomes were reported to the public because nothing in general was going to change." One of his greatest disappointments was that there would be no mandatory teacher training and no common district standards for multicultural education. He could not fathom the district's reluctance to "force" teachers to change: "In my field I do what I'm told....You're expected to accomplish the goals the employer sets....Teachers are employees just like everyone else in this society." He concluded that educators would defend the "status quo" until parents mobilized. "A neglected people are an unhappy people," he argued,

> and I think that's what's happened in this community and in our society....No longer is a large portion of our society still uneducated. We're aware of issues, and I think that when people become dissatisfied, you will have an upheaval.

Member C2's mixed reactions to the outcomes related to his role in the process. He was successful in writing the outcomes he favored into the report and said, "I'm pretty satisfied with

what happened, especially the things I was involved with." By a quirk that illustrates the uncertainties of policy processes, he also influenced the outcomes of the Cultural Awareness subcommittee, which his wife attended. As they told the story, when her subchair could not attend the last meeting, she facilitated development of the recommendations and took the draft home to edit. Her husband, meanwhile, was working on his list of recommendations for the last Curriculum subcommittee meeting. Taking advantage of his writing skills, they collaborated to create two similar lists, making it appear that the two groups independently reached nearly the same conclusions. He said, "I've always got a kind of laugh out of this [because] I jury rigged the whole thing." Similarity in the two lists added strength to those recommendations and helped them survive the committee chair's cut. When the report was presented to the board, only the Curriculum subchair realized what had happened, and he "turned to me in a kind of wry way as was his wont and said, I guess you feel pretty influential right about now." Seeing his words in the final report made Member C2 feel he had outwitted those in power. In contrast, others perceived that more powerful people blocked their intentions. Member C2 believed that the university and the influence of "eggheads" such as his subchair made Westwood receptive to new ideas. However, district implementation was wanting: "I left [the follow-up meeting] thinking that the most we had gotten was a nice little list of things the district had done, had already put into place."

Member C3 had not expected dramatic change because "nothing was cut and dry in terms of being implemented immediately." She realized the recommendations would take time. By the time of her interview, however, she did not see much movement past the "starting point" the committee had set, which was disappointing.

Cultural Awareness subcommittee. Despite the divisiveness of their process, these interviewees had similar content intentions. They proposed activities to improve cross-cultural or interracial understanding, such as required training in cultural differences and communication for district staff, conducted by persons with specialized expertise. They wanted to prevent incidents similar to the Black History Month conflict, involving tension among students or between school personnel and parents. All noted the importance of involving parents and improving home-school communication. The one notable conflict in content intentions related to ethnic differences. The subchair wanted to focus on multiple, international cultures but said that from some members, "I certainly learned very fast…and very harshly that in fact there was the greater issue of race between what is African American and White."

In terms of their perceptions of the outcomes, there was a level of consensus: None were enthusiastic. Asked what the committee had accomplished, the subchair responded, "Not much, I think. Maybe that's a little harsh." The only "good thing" he identified was the relative consensus across subcommittees on certain recommendations. A source of contention, he said, was that he had "streamlined" his subcommittee members' recommendations to eliminate repetition as well as ideas he considered "divergent from the mission" or "unrealistic." He doubted the likelihood of district action on those recommendations once community involvement ended. Member A1 said, "Maybe the school system would like to believe that we accomplished something, but I'd have to say that I took a lot of time out, volunteering, going to meetings, and I feel like nothing was accomplished." Moreover, she was struck that the district had not budgeted any funds to implement the recommendations. "I'm embarrassed by the total report," Member A2 remarked. Taking the "glass half full" approach, however, she did feel that by "stirring up trouble" the committee forced the district to do more than they would have other-

wise. The new school board member, Member A3, was pleased that the board had adopted the report but concerned that it did not address district accountability for implementation. Without that, the recommendations were moot; the committee had raised "awareness" but little more. As a board member, he said, he intended to ask, "Are we where we anticipated we would be?" Like Member C1, these members were disappointed that the district did not adopt required staff training. Member A1 said that making training voluntary meant that a "child is still going to have a bad day if they run into one [school person] that doesn't have that training or understanding."

In summary, although the process intentions of the administration and community participants clashed, in most cases, their content intentions were similar, focused on curriculum changes and improvements in human relations. The tension we observed did not as much reflect differences in conceptions of multicultural education as differences between administrators and community members over community power in policy making—who would decide which content intentions would survive. Community members' dissatisfaction emerged from their negative perceptions of district leaders' mobilization of power and district conventions. They also disagreed with the administration over another process issue, the means by which to achieve the outcomes—requiring educators to change and monitoring their progress versus school-level control. The board, caught in the middle, seemed relatively passive or ineffectual.

CONCLUSIONS

What we learned about the participants. Intentions of board members and administrators in this study parallel perspectives on policy in LaRocque's (1986) study of a Canadian school district. Board members took a classical or technological perspective, focusing on generating a policy document in response to community concerns, expecting that educators would implement what was written. They had little knowledge of the processes of constructing or implementing the recommendations. Administrators took a political perspective, focusing on negotiating and managing potential conflicts with community members and the board. They hoped to survive a short episode of community participation without public relations disasters—restoring order, control, and public trust. They did not oppose multicultural education, at least in a human relations sense; the issue was who should determine, implement, and evaluate multicultural policy. In LaRocque's study, teachers and principals took a cultural or evolutionary perspective, focusing on how policy would affect relationships and procedures in the school. In this case, community participants, especially parents, adopted the perspective that policy should improve everyday interactions among educators, children, and parents. This was the source of their demands for required staff training and community monitoring of implementation.

Another finding was that shared racial identity did not always signify consensual intentions. African American interviewees' intentions seemed to be related to education, social class, gender, and positions as district insiders or outsiders. The committee chair especially was in a cross-pressured position because of the complexity of her identity as a middle-class, African American, female administrator. A nonsynchronous theory of race relations in which racial groups are not treated as monolithic entities seems consistent with our interactionist framework and more helpful in understanding participation in policy processes (McCarthy, 1988).

What we learned about the process. How did the process transform participants' intentions? Our study is limited because we did not collect data on intentions at the start of the process. There is a possibility that in retrospect, the participants could not recall their initial inten-

tions. From observations of the meetings, it seemed that some intentions remained consistent, and others evolved or were reconstructed over time. The first significant transformation occurred when the committee chair decided to shift the focus from race relations, which the board first identified as the cause of the Black History Month incident, to multicultural issues. Troyna and Hatcher (1991) argue that experience with multicultural policy in Britain shows that multiculturalism, defined as a "celebration of ethnic lifestyles" and an "endorsement of rationalism" in response to racial prejudice, is an inadequate response to racist incidents in schools. They advocate a "flashpoint" model entailing a complex, multileveled approach to explaining and responding to such incidents. Policy making in this case became only loosely related to the situation that originally confronted the board. Although administrators did not ignore or deny the incident, a common response according to Troyna and Hatcher, they deflected attention from it with their unfocused approach. One board member recognized this too late.

Community members also perceived a transformation of intentions during the committee chair's editing of their recommendation lists, reflecting her construal of the structural linkage between community input and board adoption of policy, with administrative prioritization as a mediating step. Administrators argued that some community members' ideas were impractical, meaning inconsistent with district conventions. Another case study (Scheurich & Imber, 1991) similarly describes the Johnsonville school board's appointment of a "pluralistic constituency committee" to give voice to a representative group of parents. Parents with more knowledge, power, and resources had more influence on the committee both because they were more likely to be selected in the first place and because of their adeptness at promoting their intentions in meetings. Low-income Black parents' preferences were not seriously considered by the educational or community elite. These authors argue that whereas "culturalist" school leaders are preferable to functionalists,

> if school reform is to become a truly democratic enterprise…the pluralism advocated by the culturalists must become a critical pluralism, one that is highly attentive to the significant differences in knowledge, power and resources of various community constituencies and to the ways in which these differences affect school policy and decision making. (Scheurich & Imber, 1991, p. 317)

Parents who become involved in such processes are often viewed by school officials as representing merely private interests in their children (e.g., venting), as opposed to the broader public interest served by professionals or elite policy makers (Fine, 1997).

As Hoffman (1997) notes, "the voices of those who are best qualified to reflect on diversity are in effect outside, simply because they are, ironically, too different or unconnected to the mainstream" (p. 388). Historical and social frameworks lying "beneath the surface layer of cultural difference," Cockrell (1996) observes, inform parent-school interactions, and conditions constraining interactions "lie squarely within the contested bounds of politics, economics, and social circumstances" (p. 394). The process in our study manifested real divisions between the district and community, with the committee chair acting as boundary manager. Some community members' criticisms showed that they misconstrued the process as crossing the boundary, acquiring actual long-term policy-making authority through which to change the practices of resistant educators. However, the board and administration did not delegate them this authority. These participants were more discouraged than those who construed the process as a temporary boundary opening that they could strategically exploit. The latter felt that they were more successful than expected in

fulfilling their intentions. However, they still had little influence over implementation after the boundary closed. Administrators argued that outside community members must learn how schools work if they want to influence practices on the inside. From their espoused site-based management position, top-down mandates or community monitoring of school people's actions would not work. They saw the school as the appropriate site where community members could cross the boundary to work in collaboration with school people.

Another thing learned about the process was that new issues quickly took precedence on the district's agenda. The board was soon embroiled in hiring a new superintendent, solving budget problems, finding space for a mushrooming student population, and confronting a long-overdue redistricting issue charged with racial and social class implications. Multicultural education faded to the background as a relatively innocuous series of cultural activities not connected (as it could have been, as a structural equity issue) with redistricting. When a new state requirement that districts release achievement scores by race revealed significant differences between Westwood's African American and European American students, the board member who had initiated the multicultural effort explained in a newspaper column that the differences were a matter of social class, not race or culture. A long-range planning report showed that the board was divided on whether multicultural education was among its top priorities.

Contributions to theory building. This study enlarges the usefulness of the transformation of intentions framework for policy analysis (Hall, 1995; Hall & McGinty, 1997). The interview methods provided a way to identify intentions. The study also clarified how intentions frame the process but are also refrained by it. In this ongoing dialectic, the predetermined structure of the process both constrains and facilitates intentions. As Borman et al.

(1992) found, organizational leaders are likely to try to use their greater control to block intentions that run counter to institutional conventions and power relations unless those intentions are backed by external and/or internal political support. Adept participants figure out how to work any looseness in the structure, taking advantage of ambiguity. It helps if they also have resources or capital (material, cultural, or social) to advance their intentions, if they use the media well, and if they act collectively rather than as isolated individuals. But, even then, they may not influence the behavior of those who come after them in the process, those to whom implementation is delegated.

Two issues plague multicultural education policy: difficulties in defining multicultural (Hoffman, 1996, 1997; Lee & Saini, 1996; Mattai, 1992; Troyna, 1987; Watson, 1988) and political conflicts (Cornbleth & Waugh, 1995; Howe, 1992; Kohl, 1991; Washburn, 1994). Engaging in processes that surface and address these issues requires time. The emphasis in this case was on doing something quickly in response to the board and the media, which meant suppressing or cutting short potentially volatile discussions. Although the committee chair argued that too much time could be spent mired in such discussions and although, for administrators, the period of intense media scrutiny may have seemed excruciatingly long, without sufficient time, the process resulted in a list of recommendations that did not constitute a coherent policy statement offering clear direction to school-level delegates or the new multicultural coordinator, whose position was only half time and devoid of authority. The result, we know from subsequent study, was a jumble of cultural activities rather than a well-considered strategy for addressing the causes of racial conflicts, limited parent involvement, and disparities in achievement.

Applications to practice: what might have been. Our view of the policy process as ambiguous and contingent seems to preclude offering rules for practice, but hindsight suggests conditions that might have improved the outcomes. First, the participants required greater clarity about district conventions with regard to the respective roles of advisory committees, the administration, and the board. If the roles of the board, administration, school personnel, and community participants in policy making are fundamentally different, this must be mutually understood at the outset, but the possibility of more democratic ways of structuring participation should also be considered (Fine, 1997; Scheurich & Imber, 1991). Second, despite their dread of conflict and negative media coverage, the administration should have listened more openly to community members' perspectives and provided time and facilitation (perhaps by an experienced facilitator or mediator) for consensus building around the causes of and responses to the Black History Month conflict. We do not take a Pollyanna position that dialogue alone would lead to a positive outcome in a community with long-standing racial conflicts (Scheurich & Imber, 1991); however, the hurried and unfocused process in this case only exacerbated these conflicts. Third, the district should have been open to investigating factors related to the high school incident. Foster (1990) argues that effective multicultural policies are based on evidence of actual school conditions and practices, not vague rhetoric. The administration did not allow the committee to collect data on such conditions and practices, which led some community members to suspect that the district had some thing to hide and was rushing the process to keep them from discovering it.

Thus, this case demonstrates the strength of the boundary between public schools and the public, reinforced by professional administrators. Renegotiating that boundary is one of the major challenges facing U.S. public schools in the 21st century if they are to develop and survive as multicultural, democratic institutions.

NOTES

1. We will use *African American and European American* except to accurately reflect the usages of other authors, our interviewees, or district documents.

2. We conducted 17 interviews, but two interviewees withdrew, and we did not use 1 interview once we decided to focus on only two subcommittees.

3. These two members are identified as Middle Eastern because to specify their countries of origin would identify them individually, which we promised not to do.

4. The author who was a member of the committee had served on other district committees and had firsthand knowledge of how they were conducted.

5. For example, the local and state National Association for the Advance of Colored People president, a strong advocate, as well as some prominent community and university leaders with expertise in multicultural education could not attend many or all meetings.

6. The speaker was recommended by the district's English as a second language (ESL) coordinator; it was our impression that the administration did not know she would present a radical, political perspective.

7. The other subchairs were allies of the committee chair, part of a network of educated African American women. This pattern of delegating multicultural issues to African American women needs exploration. Appointment of the district personnel director to Minority Hiring led Member A2 to complain that he stifled criticism of the district.

8. Keep in mind that they knew their subchair was a researcher on this project.

9. He was not a Black Muslim but attended a mosque with a multinational membership.

10. We thought that interviewees might have competing definitions of multicultural education, but this was not the case. All were clear that multicultural education went beyond a shallow food-and-festivals or a negative cultural deficit approach. When we categorized responses on this topic, most fit Banks's (1994) "curriculum infusion" and "prejudice reduction" categories, but very few fit Sleeter and Grant's (1994) "social reconstructionist" or Banks's (1994) "social action" positions.

REFERENCES

Banks, J. A. (1994). *Multiethnic education: Theory and practice* (3rd ed.). New York: Allyn & Bacon.

Baumgartner, K., Buckley, W., Burns, T., & Schuster, P. (1976). Meta-power and the structuring of social hierarchy. In T. Burns & W. Buckley (Eds.), *Social structures and their transformation* (pp. 215–288). Beverly Hills, CA: Sage.

Becker, H. (1982). *Art worlds.* Berkeley: University of California Press.

Borman, K., Timm, P., Al-amin, Z., & Winston, M. (1992). Using multiple strategies to assess multicultural education in a school district. In C. Grant (Ed.), *Research and multicultural education: From the margins to the mainstream* (pp. 71–88). London: Falmer

Clegg, S. (1989). *Frameworks of power:* London: Sage.

Cockrell, K. S. (1996). Communication gatekeeping: A response to mediating conditions in American Indian and school personnel interactions. *Journal of School Leadership, 6,* 368–398.

Combleth, C., & Waugh, D. (1993). The great speckled bird: Education policy-in-the-making. *Educational Researcher, 11*(7), 31-37.

Combleth, C., & Waugh, D. (1995). *The great speckled bird: Multicultural politics and education.* New York: St. Martin's.

Curry, B. K. (1997). Continuity and reform: A new discourse for discussion of change in schools. *Educational Planning, 11*(1), 21–30.

Estes, C., & Edmonds, B. (1981). Symbolic interaction and social policy analysis. *Symbolic Interaction, 4*(1), 75–86.

Fine, M. (1997). [Ap]parent involvement: Reflections on parents, power and urban public schools. In A. Halsey, H. Lauder, P. Brown, & A. S. Wells (Eds.), *Education: Culture, economy, society* (pp. 460–475). New York: Oxford University Press.

Foster, P. (1990). *Policy and practices in multicultural and anti-racist education.* London: Routledge.

Glazier, J. D. (1994). *Career ladder policy, formation and implementation: A symbolic interactionist approach to local policy practices.* Unpublished doctoral thesis, University of Missouri, Columbia.

Gollnick, D. M. (1995). National and state initiatives for multicultural education in the United States. In J. A. Banks & C.A.M. Banks (Eds.), *Handbook of research on multicultural education* (pp. 44–64). New York: Simon & Schuster MacMillan.

Grant, C., & Millar, S. (1992). Research and multicultural education: Barriers, needs and boundaries. In C. Grant (Ed.), *Research and multicultural education* (pp. 7–18). London: Falmer.

Greene, T. G., & Heflin, J. F. (1992). State governments and multicultural education policy. *Equity and Excellence*, 25(2–4), 145–150.

Hall, P. M. (1995). The consequences of qualitative analysis for sociological theory: Beyond the micro level. *Sociological Quarterly*, 36, 397–423.

Hall, P. M. (1997). Meta-power, social organization and the shaping of social action. *Symbolic Interaction*, 20, 397–418.

Hall, P. M., & McGinty, P. J. (1997). Policy as the transformation of intentions: Producing program from statute. *Sociological Quarterly*, 38, 439–467.

Hoffman, D. M. (1996). Culture and self in multicultural education: Reflections on discourse, text and practice. *American Educational Research Journal*, 33, 545–569.

Hoffman, D. M. (1997). Diversity in practice: Perspectives on concept, context, and policy. *Educational Policy*, 11, 375–392.

Howe, K. R. (1992). Liberal democracy, equal educational opportunity, and the challenge of multiculturalism. *American Educational Research Journal*, 19, 445–470.

Kohl, H. (1991). The politically correct bypass: Multiculturalism and the public schools. *Social Policy*, 22 (l), 33–40.

LaRocque, L. (1986). Policy implementation in a school district: A multiperspective approach. *Canadian Journal of Education*, 11, 486–508.

Lee, D., & Saini, S. (1996). Antiracist multicultural education: From policy to planned implementation. *Multicultural Teaching*, 14(3), 21–25.

Mattai, P. R. (1992). Rethinking the nature of multicultural education: Has it lost its focus or is it being misused? *Journal of Negro Education*, 61(1), 65–77.

McCarthy, C. (1988). Rethinking liberal and radical perspectives on racial inequality in schooling: Making the case for nonsynchrony. *Harvard Education Review*, 58, 265–279.

Persell, C., Dougherty, K., & Wenglinsky, H. (1993, October). *Equity and diversity in American education* (Unpublished Report of Round Table #1). OERI Conference on Equity and Excellence in Education: The Policy Uses of Sociology, Washington, DC.

Placier, M., Hall, P. M., & Davis, B. (1997). Making multicultural education policy: The transformation of intentions. In P. Hall (Ed.), *Race, ethnicity and multicultural education: Vol. 1. Missouri symposium on research in educational policy* (pp. 169–201). New York: Garland.

Scheurich, J. J., & Imber, M. (1991). Educational reforms can reproduce societal inequities: A case study. *Educational Administration Quarterly*, 27, 297–320.

Sewell, W. (1992). A theory of structure: Duality, agency and transformation. *American Journal of Sociology*, 98(l), 1–29.

Sleeter, C., & Grant, C. (1994). *Making choices for multicultural education* (2nd ed.). New York: MacMillan.

Stevenson, Z., & Gonzalez, L. (1992). Contemporary practices in multicultural approaches to education among the largest American school districts. *Journal of Negro Education*, 61, 356–369.

Strauss, A., & Corbin, J. (1990). *Basics of qualitative research: Grounded theory procedures and techniques.* Newbury Park, CA: Sage.

Troyna, B. (1987). Beyond multiculturalism: Towards the enactment of anti-racist education in policy, provision and pedagogy. *Oxford Review of Education*, 13, 307–320.

Troyna, B., & Hatcher, R. (1991). Racist incidents in schools: A framework for analysis. *Journal of Educational Policy*, 6(1), 17–31.

Washburn, D. E. (1994). Let's take a hard look at multicultural education. *Multicultural Education*, 2(2), 20–23.

Watson, J. (1988). From assimilation to anti-racism: Changing educational policies in England and Wales. *Journal of Multilingual and Multicultural Development*, 9, 531–552.

African American Men and Women in Higher Education: "Filling the Glass" in the New Millennium

Kimberly Edelin-Freeman

African Americans have made significant progress in post-secondary enrollment and degree completions during the past two decades. Indeed, in African-American higher education, the glass is "half full." But serious challenges remain. While the number of African Americans enrolling in higher education institutions and earning degrees has increased over the last two decades, they continue to lag behind among undergraduate, graduate, or professional students compared to their percentage of the traditional student-age population. In addition, African-American women have made far greater strides in higher education than African-American men at every level.

Thus, in the 21st century—when a college degree will more than ever be a virtual prerequisite for a good job and a decent income—a primary challenge for African Americans is to significantly increase the numbers of young black men and women who go to college and then on to graduate or professional schools.

Although this essay examines the status of African Americans in higher education, I will focus on the dynamics of their enrollment and degree completions at all levels and at different types of colleges and universities during the past two decades, and then, suggest policies and programs for sustaining and increas-ing the progress of African-American men and women in higher education. In this essay, I will leave several other important topics in African-American higher education, including affirmative action, financial aid, teacher preparation, and the status and progress of African Americans in such academic disciplines as education, science, and engineering for other scholars and other essays.

AFRICAN-AMERICAN ENROLLMENT AT AMERICA'S COLLEGES AND UNIVERSITIES

In 1997, African Americans constituted 10.7 percent of all students at America's colleges and universities, according to *Two Decades of Progress: African Americans Moving Forward in Higher Education* (1999), by the Frederick D. Patterson Research Institute of the UNCF/College Fund (Table 1). African Americans comprised 11.2 percent of all undergraduates, 7.5 percent of all graduate students, and 7.1 percent of all first-professional students. In 1997, there were more than 1.5 million African Americans enrolled in higher education, compared to just over 1 million in 1978. Ninety percent were enrolled as undergraduates. As the number of African-American undergraduates has increased by 43 percent since the 1970s, the number of African-

American women undergraduates has far surpassed the number of black undergraduate men.

Further, research done for the *African-American Education Data Book* (1997), also published by the Patterson Institute, found that there are more than twice as many African-American women among graduate students as African-American men. However, the ratio between the genders at the first-professional level is relatively equal, although there is increasing concern about the declining number of African-American men enrolling in and completing medical school. The October 1999 report of the American Association of Medical Colleges on medical school applicants and matriculating students found that, amidst a general decline of male applicants to medical schools, the number of African-American male applicants fell by 15 percent from 1998. In addition, the number of African-American men entering medical schools declined by 16 percent to 383—the lowest in the decade. The report also indicated that the number of minority applicants of all groups fell almost 7 percent between 1998 and 1999.

The numerical status of African-American men in higher education is a cause for concern. However, it is also important to recognize that African-American men have increased their enrollment over the past twenty years at the undergraduate, graduate, and first-professional levels (see Table 2). It's just that that increase has been overshadowed by the spectacular progress of African-American women, which in percentage terms has been greater than that of white women and white men as well (Table 2). Nonetheless, African-American women are still underrepresented in higher education relative to their percentage of the population.

ENROLLMENT OF AFRICAN AMERICANS AT TWO-YEAR VERSUS FOUR-YEAR COLLEGES AND UNIVERSITIES

There are more African-American students at both two-year and four-year institutions than ever. The number of African-American first-time full-time freshmen increased at four-year colleges and universities by 15 percent over the past two decades (Table 3). Enrollment of first-time full-time freshmen is one indicator of access to postsecondary education, and for African Americans, that access has increased by 27 percent during the last ten years. The progress of African-American undergraduates at four-year colleges and universities follows a similar trend and shows greater growth than African-American first-time full-time freshmen. While the majority (54 percent) of African-American undergraduates are enrolled in four-year colleges and universities, close to half, 46 percent, are in two-year colleges. (A larger share of Hispanic [61 percent] and Native American [53 percent] undergraduates enroll in two-year institutions than four-year institutions, compared with 42 percent of white and 46 percent of Asian undergraduates enrolled in two-year colleges.)

Limited information exists thus far about African-American undergraduates at two-year institutions and the effectiveness of these institutions. One thing is certain: the benefit of attending a two-year college is greatest if a students goes on to earn a bachelor's degree. However, research by the UNCF/College Fund found evidence that suggests that only 15 percent of African-American two-year public college students transferred to a four-year college or university within five years, compared with 22 percent of whites. Far more research on African-American community college students is warranted and vital in order that they and Black America as a whole benefit as fully as possible from their matriculation.

Table 1: Enrollment Distribution at All Colleges and Universities and Historically Black Colleges and Universities
By Race, Sex, and Level of Study: Fall 1997

ALL COLLEGES AND UNIVERSITIES	TOTAL			AFRICAN AMERICAN			WHITE		
	TOTAL	MEN	WOMEN	TOTAL	MEN	WOMEN	TOTAL	MEN	WOMEN
Total Enrollment	14,345,416	6,329,960	8,015,456	1,532,755	572,538	960,217	10,160,933	4,504,812	5,656,121
Row %	100.0%	44.1%	55.9%	10.7%	4.0%	6.7%	70.8%	31.4%	39.4%
Column %	100.0%	100.0%	100.0%	100.0%	100.0%	100.0%	100.0%	100.0%	100.0%
Undergraduates	12,298,256	5,405,394	6,892,862	1,379,917	520,590	859,327	8,681,801	3,857,320	4,824,481
Row %	100.0%	44.0%	56.0%	11.2%	4.2%	7.0%	70.6%	31.4%	39.2%
Column %	85.7%	85.4%	86.0%	90.0%	90.9%	89.5%	85.4%	85.6%	85.3%
Graduate	1,750,628	756,134	994,494	131,650	42,809	88,841	1,260,190	519,475	740,715
Row %	100.0%	43.2%	56.8%	7.5%	2.4%	5.1%	72.0%	29.7%	42.3%
Column %	12.2%	11.9%	12.4%	8.6%	7.5%	9.3%	12.4%	11.5%	13.1%
First Professional	296,532	168,432	128,100	21,188	9,139	12,049	218,942	128,017	90,925
Row %	100.0%	56.8%	43.2%	7.1%	3.1%	4.1%	73.8%	43.2%	30.7%
Column %	2.1%	2.7%	1.6%	1.4%	1.6%	1.3%	2.2%	2.8%	1.6%

HISTORICALLY BLACK COLLEGES AND UNIVERSITIES	TOTAL			AFRICAN AMERICAN			WHITE		
	TOTAL	MEN	WOMEN	TOTAL	MEN	WOMEN	TOTAL	MEN	WOMEN
Total Enrollment	265,858	105,649	160,209	219,684	85,679	134,005	31,883	12,667	19,216
Row %	100.0%	39.7%	60.3%	82.6%	32.2%	50.4%	12.0%	4.8%	7.2%
Column %	100.0%	100.0%	100.0%	100.0%	100.0%	100.0%	100.0%	100.0%	100.0%
Undergraduates	234,052	94,688	139,364	197,407	78,487	118,920	25,232	10,430	14,802
Row %	100.0%	40.5%	59.5%	84.3%	33.5%	50.8%	10.8%	4.5%	6.3%
Column %	88.0%	89.6%	87.0%	89.9%	91.6%	88.7%	79.1%	82.3%	77.0%
Graduate	27,481	8,883	18,598	19,164	5,775	13,389	6,046	1,907	4,139
Row %	100.0%	32.3%	67.7%	69.7%	21.0%	48.7%	22.0%	6.9%	15.1%
Column %	10.3%	8.4%	11.6%	8.7%	6.7%	10.0%	19.0%	15.1%	21.5%
First Professional	4,325	2,078	2,247	3,113	1,417	1,696	605	330	275
Row %	100.0%	48.0%	52.0%	72.0%	32.8%	39.2%	14.0%	7.6%	6.4%
Column %	1.6%	2.0%	1.4%	1.4%	1.7%	1.3%	1.9%	2.6%	1.4%

Source: Analysis of Integrated Postsecondary Education Data System

Table 1: Enrollment Distribution at All Colleges and Universities and Historically Black Colleges and Universities (continued)
By Race, Sex, and Level of Study: Fall 1997

	HISPANIC			ASIAN			NATIVE AMERICAN		
	TOTAL	MEN	WOMEN	TOTAL	MEN	WOMEN	TOTAL	MEN	WOMEN
ALL COLLEGES AND UNIVERSITIES									
Total Enrollment	1,200,106	518,078	682,028	851,487	414,048	437,439	138,835	57,567	81,268
Row %	8.4%	3.6%	4.8%	5.9%	2.9%	3.0%	1.0%	0.4%	0.6%
Column %	100.0%	100.0%	100.0%	100.0%	100.0%	100.0%	100.0%	100.0%	100.0%
Undergraduates	1,107,807	479,132	628,675	736,561	356,069	380,492	127,183	52,648	74,535
Row %	9.0%	3.9%	5.1%	6.0%	2.9%	3.1%	1.0%	0.4%	0.6%
Column %	92.3%	92.5%	92.2%	86.5%	86.0%	87.0%	91.6%	91.5%	91.7%
Graduate	78,448	31,319	47,129	82,116	40,421	41,695	9,377	3,696	5,681
Row %	4.5%	1.8%	2.7%	4.7%	2.3%	2.4%	0.5%	0.2%	0.3%
Column %	6.5%	6.0%	6.9%	9.6%	9.8%	9.5%	6.8%	6.4%	7.0%
First Professional	13,851	7,627	6,224	32,810	17,558	15,252	2,275	1,223	1,052
Row %	4.7%	2.6%	2.1%	11.1%	5.9%	5.1%	0.8%	0.4%	0.4%
Column %	1.2%	1.5%	0.9%	3.9%	4.2%	3.5%	1.6%	2.1%	1.3%
HISTORICALLY BLACK COLLEGES AND UNIVERSITIES									
Total Enrollment	5,605	2,682	2,923	2,208	1,088	1,120	747	303	444
Row %	2.1%	1.0	1.1%	0.8%	0.4%	0.4%	0.3%	0.1%	0.2%
Column %	100.0%	100.0%	100.0%	100.0%	100.0%	100.0%	100.0%	100.0%	100.0%
Undergraduates	5,147	2,467	2,680	1,426	701	725	595	239	356
Row %	2.2%	1.1%	1.1%	0.6%	0.3%	0.3%	0.3%	0.1%	0.2%
Column %	91.81%	922.0%	91.77%	64.6%	64.4%	64.7%	79.7%	78.9%	80.2%
Graduate	349	149	200	558	269	289	136	54	82
Row %	1.3%	0.5%	0.7%	2.0%	1.0%	1.1%	0.5%	0.2%	0.3%
Column %	6.2%	5.6%	6.8%	25.3%	24.7%	25.8%	18.2%	17.8%	18.5%
First Profession	109	66	43	224	118	106	16	10	6
Row %	2.5%	1.5%	1.0%	5.2%	2.7%	2.5%	0.4%	0.2%	0.1%
Column %	1.9%	2.5%	1.5%	10.1%	10.8%	9.5%	2.1%	3.3%	1.4%

Source: Analysis of Integrated Postsecondary Education Data System

Table 2: Increase in Number of Students Enrolled
By Race, Sex, and Level of Study: 1976 to 1997

DEGREE LEVEL	AFRICAN AMERICAN WOMEN	AFRICAN-AMERICAN MEN	WHITE WOMEN	WHITE MEN
Undergraduate	68%	21%	31%	–5%
Graduate	91%	34%	41%	–12%
First Professional	209%	27%	91%	–26%

Source: Analysis of Integrated Postsecondary Education Data System

Figure No. 1: Percent of Students Who First Enrolled in a Public Two-Year College Who Transferred to a Four-Year College or University Within Five Years

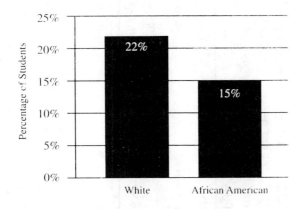

Source: Two Decades of Progress: African Americans Moving Forward in Higher Education, Frederick D. Patterson Research Institute, 1999.

THE REPRESENTATION OF AFRICAN-AMERICAN MEN AND WOMEN AMONG DEGREE RECIPIENTS

Associate degree recipients make up the largest cohort of African-American degree recipients, as they do for Hispanic Americans and Native Americans (Table 4). Conversely, African Americans are most severely underrepresented among doctoral degree recipients, at 3.9 percent. The greatest representation of whites is among bachelor's degree (74.9 percent) and first-professional degree recipients

(74.9 percent). For Asians, their greatest representation is among first-professional degree recipients (9.2 percent).

In 1997, African-American women earned almost twice as many bachelor's degrees, and more than double the number of master's degrees as African-American men. The disparity is smaller at the first-professional and doctoral levels. (Table 5).

THE ROLE AND PROMINENCE OF HISTORICALLY BLACK COLLEGES AND UNIVERSITIES

Any discussion of African-American higher education must have as a central component the role and importance of Historically Black Colleges and Universities, which were established in the era of legal segregation by churches, freedmen's societies, religious groups, and philanthropists (Hill, 1985). Since their inception, HBCUs have used a steadfast commitment to effectively utilize scarce resources in providing African Americans access to a high-quality college education. Historically and currently, they produce the majority of African-American teachers and substantial numbers of activists, scholars, physicians, attorneys, and corporate executives. HBCUs are perennially the top producers of African-American degree recipients in many academic disciplines.

Table 3: Undergraduate Enrollment at Two-Year Colleges and Four-Year Colleges and Universities

By Race, Sex, and Level of Study: Fall 1997 (Number of students in parentheses)

LEVEL	TOTAL			AFRICAN AMERICAN			WHITE		
	TOTAL	MEN	WOMEN	TOTAL	MEN	WOMEN	TOTAL	MEN	WOMEN
Total*	100.0%	100.0%	100.0%	100.0%	100.0%	100.0%	100.0%	100.0%	100.0%
	12,298,256	5,405,394	6,892,862	1,379,917	520,590	859,327	8,681,801	3,857,320	4,824,481
Two-Year College	44.5%	43.2%	45.5%	46.2%	45.9%	46.4%	42.4%	41.0%	43.4%
	5,468,761	2,334,882	3,133,879	637,316	238,866	398,450	3,677,077	1,581,469	2,095,608
Four-Year College	55.5%	56.8%	54.5%	53.8%	54.1%	53.6%	57.6%	59.0%	56.5%
	6,827,516	3,069,650	3,757,866	742,048	281,488	460,560	5,003,607	2,275,383	2,728,224

LEVEL	HISPANIC			ASIAN			NATIVE AMERICAN		
	TOTAL	MEN	WOMEN	TOTAL	MEN	WOMEN	TOTAL	MEN	WOMEN
Total*	100.0%	100.0%	100.0%	100.0%	100.0%	100.0%	100.0%	100.0%	100.0%
	1,107,807	479,132	628,675	736,561	356,069	380,492	127,183	52,648	74,535
Two-Year College	60.6%	60.3%	60.9%	45.5%	45.3%	45.7%	53.1%	52.1%	53.8%
	671,881	288,713	383,168	335,048	161,225	173,823	67,513	27,424	40,089
Four-Year College	39.3%	39.7%	39.0%	54.5%	54.7%	54.3%	46.9%	47.9%	46.2%
	435,687	190,299	245,388	401,461	194,811	206,650	59,654	25,220	34,434

Source: Analysis of Integrated Postsecondary Education Data System

*Total undergraduate enrollment includes enrollment at less than two-year institutions

Table 4: Number and Percent of Degrees Awarded
By Level of Study, Race, Sex, and Type of Institution: 1997

	TOTAL			AFRICAN AMERICAN			WHITE		
ALL COLLEGES AND UNIVERSITIES	TOTAL	MEN	WOMEN	TOTAL	MEN	WOMEN	TOTAL	MEN	WOMEN
Associate's Degrees	541,970	211,511	330,459	51,527	17,534	33,993	400,300	156,614	243,686
Row %	100.0%	39.0%	61.0%	9.5%	3.2%	6.3%	73.9%	28.9%	45.0%
Bachelor's Degrees	1,171,901	520,161	651,740	91,915	32,697	59,218	877,735	392,533	485,202
Row %	100.0%	44.4%	55.6%	7.8%	2.8%	5.1%	74.9%	33.5%	41.4%
Master's Degrees	419,056	180,801	238,255	26,907	8,435	18,472	288,327	117,932	170,395
Row %	100.0%	43.1%	56.9%	6.4%	2.0%	4.4%	68.8%	28.1%	40.7%
Doctorate Degrees	45,589	26,929	18,660	1,794	765	1,029	27,199	14,685	12,514
Row %	100.0%	59.1%	40.9%	3.9%	1.7%	2.3%	59.7%	32.2%	27.4%
Professional Degrees	78,498	45,420	33,078	5,153	2,139	3,014	58,767	35,076	23,691
Row %	100.0%	57.9%	42.1 %	6.6%	2.7%	3.8%	74.9%	44.7%	30.2%
HISTORICALLY BLACK COLLEGES AND UNIVERSITIES	TOTAL	MEN	WOMEN	TOTAL	MEN	WOMEN	TOTAL	MEN	WOMEN
Associate's Degrees	2,847	989	1,858	1,430	428	1,002	1,098	403	695
Row %	100.0%	34.7%	65.3%	50.2%	15.0%	35.2%	38.6%	14.2%	24.4%
Bachelor's Degrees	29,300	10,675	18,625	25,063	8,904	16,159	2,994	1,150	1,844
Row %	100.0%	36.4%	63.6%	85.5%	30.4%	55.2%	10.2%	3.9%	6.3%
Master's Degrees	6,389	1,940	4,449	4,179	1,156	3,023	1,613	463	1,150
Row %	100.0%	30.4%	69.6%	65.4%	18.1%	47.3%	25.2%	7.2%	18.0%
Doctorate Degrees	239	111	128	155	69	86	33	14	19
Row %	100.0%	46.4%	53.6%	64.9%	28.9%	36.0%	13.8%	5.9%	7.9%
Professional Degrees	1,274	584	690	853	356	497	212	132	80
Row %	100.0%	45.8%	54.2%	67.0%	27.9%	39.0%	16.6%	10.4%	6.3%

Source: Analysis of Integrated Postsecondary Education Data System

continued

Table 4: Number and Percent of Degrees Awarded (continued)
By Level of Study, Race, Sex, and Type of Institution: 1997

	HISPANIC			ASIAN			NATIVE AMERICAN		
ALL COLLEGES AND UNIVERSITIES	TOTAL	MEN	WOMEN	TOTAL	MEN	WOMEN	TOTAL	MEN	WOMEN
Associate's Degrees	39,287	15,997	23,290	23,431	10,111	13,320	5,520	1,870	3,650
Row %	7.2%	3.0%	4.3%	4.3%	1.9%	2.5%	1.0%	0.3%	0.7%
Bachelor's Degrees	60,846	25,602	35,244	67,004	31,615	35,389	7,237	2,914	4,323
Row %	5.2%	2.2%	3.0%	5.7%	2.7%	3.0%	0.6%	0.2%	0.4%
Master's Degrees	14,572	5,847	8,725	17,875	8,569	9,306	1,844	697	1,147
Row %	3.5%	1.4%	2.1%	4.3%	2.0%	2.2%	0.4%	0.2%	0.3%
Doctorate Degrees	1,064	557	507	2,341	1,415	926	169	84	85
Row %	2.3%	1.2%	1.1%	5.1%	3.1%	2.0%	0.4%	0.2%	0.2%
Professional Degrees	3,525	1,933	1,592	7,232	3,886	3,346	501	282	219
Row %	4.5%	2.5%	2.0%	9.2%	5.0%	4.3%	0.6%	0.4%	0.3%
HISTORICALLY BLACK COLLEGES AND UNIVERSITIES	TOTAL	MEN	WOMEN	TOTAL	MEN	WOMEN	TOTAL	MEN	WOMEN
Associate's Degrees	211	107	104	37	14	23	4	2	2
Row %	7.4%	3.8%	3.7%	1.3%	0.5%	0.8%	0.1%	0.1%	0.1%
Bachelor's Degrees	187	81	106	190	100	90	55	15	40
Row %	0.6%	0.3%	0.4%	0.6%	0.3%	0.3%	0.2%	0.1%	0.1%
Master's Degrees	64	22	42	124	68	56	12	3	9
Row %	1.0%	0.3%	0.7%	1.9%	1.1%	0.9%	0.2%	0.0%	0.1%
Doctorate Degrees	3	0	3	6	4	2	1	1	0
Row %	1.3%	0.0%	1.3%	2.5%	1.7%	0.8%	0.4%	0.4%	0.0%
Professional Degrees	72	41	31	70	33	37	2	1	1
Row %	5.7%	3.2%	2.4%	5.5%	2.6%	2.9%	0.2%	0.1%	0.1%

Source: Analysis of Integrated Postsecondary Education Data System

Table 5: Increase in Number of Degrees Awarded
By Race, Sex, and Level of Study: 1977 to 1997

DEGREE LEVEL	AFRICAN AMERICAN WOMEN	AFRICAN-AMERICAN MEN	WHITE WOMEN	WHITE MEN
Undergraduate	68%	21%	31%	–5%
Associate's	91%	14%	49%	–12%
Bachelor's	77%	30%	31%	–10%
Master's	39%	8%	34%	–15%
Doctorate	111%	–.1%	84%	–27%
First Professional	288%	22%	123%	–27%

Source: Analysis of Integrated Postsecondary Education Data System

Table 6 shows that HBCUs account for 14.3 percent of both African-American total enrollment in higher education and African-American undergraduate enrollment. African-American graduate students at HBCUs make up 14.6 percent of all African-American graduate students, and African-American first-professional students enrolled at HBCUs make up 14.7 percent of all African-American first-professional students. More than one-quarter of African-American undergraduates at four-year institutions are enrolled at four-year HBCUs, compared with only 1.6 percent of African-American undergraduates at two-year colleges. Similarly, 27.3 percent of all African-American bachelor's degree recipients come from HBCUs, as do 15.5 percent of all African-American master's degree recipients, 8.6 percent of all African-American doctorate recipients, and 16.6 percent of all African-American first-professional degree recipients.

African Americans are the largest cohort of bachelor's degree recipients at HBCUs (Table 4), and the largest cohort of all associate's degree recipients. As with higher education in general, at HBCUs African-American women are a substantial presence They comprise just over 55 percent of all bachelor's degree recipients at HBCUs, compared with 30.4 percent for African-American men. Similarly, African-American women comprise 36 percent and 39 percent of all doctoral and first-professional degree recipients at HBCUs, compared to just under 29 percent and 28 percent, respectively, for African-American men.

One of the most compelling pieces of evidence of the significance of HBCUs in African-American postsecondary education is the proportion of African-American college graduates being produced by HBCUs. HBCUs constitute only 3 percent of all four-year colleges and universities but graduate more than one-fourth of all African-American bachelor's degree recipients. That proportion is even greater in the Southern states, where the majority of HBCUs are located. In Alabama, Virginia, Mississippi, North Carolina, Louisiana, and Washington, D.C., one-half to three-quarters of all African-American college graduates are produced by HBCUs (Table 7). These findings are extraordinary because in each of these states, HBCUs constitute less than 30 percent of all four-year colleges and universities. In Washington D.C., where the greatest proportion of African-American college graduates come from two HBCUs, there are twelve other institutions of higher education.

Table 6: Number and Representation of African Americans at HBCUs: 1997

	TOTAL		AFRICAN AMERICAN		WHITE		HISPANIC		ASIAN		NATIVE AMERICAN	
	Number	%	Number	%	Number	%	Number	%	Number	%	Number	%
Total Enrollment	14,345,416	100.0%	1,532,755	100.0%	10,160,933	100.0%	1,200,106	100.0%	851,487	100.0%	138,835	100.0%
HBCU Total Enrollment	265,858	1.9%	219,684	14.3%	31,883	0.3%	5,605	0.5%	2,208	0.3%	747	0.5%
Total Undergraduate Enrollment	12,298,256	100.0%	1,379,917	100.0%	8,681,801	100.0%	1,107,807	100.0%	736,561	100.0%	127,183	100.0%
HBCU Undergraduate Enrollment	234,052	1.9%	197,407	14.3%	25,232	0.3%	5,147	0.5%	1,426	0.2%	595	0.5%
Total Graduate Enrollment	1,750,628	100.0%	131,650	100.0%	1,260,190	100.0%	78,448	100.0%	82,116	100.0%	9,377	100.0%
HBCU Graduate Enrollment	27,481	1.6%	19,164	14.6%	6,046	0.5%	349	0.4%	558	0.7%	136	1.5%
Total First-Professional Enrollment	296,532	100.0%	21,188	100.0%	218,942	100.0%	13,851	100.0%	32,810	100.0%	2,275	100.0%
HBCU First-Professional Enrollment	4,325	1.5%	3,113	14.7%	605	0.3%	109	0.8%	224	0.7%	16	0.7%
Total Four-Year Undergraduate Enrollment	6,827,516	100.0%	742,048	100.0%	5,003,607	100.0%	435,687	100.0%	401,461	100.0%	59,654	100.0%
HBCU Four-Year Undergraduate Enrollment	247,090	3.6%	209,342	28.2%	27,357	0.5%	2,014	0.5%	2,026	0.5%	678	1.1%
Total Two-Year Undergraduate Enrollment	5,468,761	100.0%	637,316	100.0%	3,677,077	100.0%	671,881	100.0%	335,048	100.0%	67,513	100.0%
HBCU Two-Year Undergraduate Enrollment	18,768	0.3%	10,342	1.6%	4,526	0.1%	3,591	0.5%	182	0.1%	69	0.1%
Total Associate's Degrees	541,970	100.0%	51,527	100.0%	400,300	100.0%	39,287	100.0%	23,431	100.0%	5,520	100.0%
HBCU Associate's Degrees	2,847	0.5%	1,430	2.8%	1,098	0.3%	211	0.5%	37	0.2%	4	0.1%
Total Bachelor's Degrees	1,171,901	100.0%	91,915	100.0%	877,735	100.0%	60,846	100.0%	67,004	100.0%	7,237	100.0%
HBCU Bachelors Degrees	29,300	2.5%	25,063	27.3%	2,994	0.3%	187	0.3%	190	0.3%	55	0.8%
Total Master's Degrees	419,056	100.0%	26,907	100.0%	288,327	100.0%	14,572	100.0%	17,875	100.0%	1,844	100.0%
HBCU Master's Degrees	6,389	1.5%	4,179	15.5%	1,613	0.6%	64	0.4%	124	0.7%	12	0.7%
Total Doctorate Degrees	45,589	100.0%	1,794	100.0%	27,199	100.0%	1,064	100.0%	2,341	100.0%	169	100.0%
HBCU Doctorate Degrees	239	0.5%	155	8.6%	83	0.1%	3	0.3%	6	0.3%	1	0.6%
Total First-Professional Degrees	78,498	100.0%	5,153	100.0%	58,767	100.0%	3,525	100.0%	7,232	100.0%	501	100.0%
HBCU First-Professional Degrees	1,274	1.6%	853	16.6%	212	0.4%	72	2.0%	70	1.0%	2	0.4%

Source: Analysis of Integrated Postsecondary Education Data System

Table 7: Number and Percent of African-American Bachelor's Degree Recipients
By Type of Institution, Sex, and Southern State: 1997

SOUTHERN STATE	ALL COLLEGES AND UNIVERSITIES						HBCUs					
	TOTAL	%	MEN	%	WOMEN	%	TOTAL	%	MEN	%	WOMEN	%
Washington, DC	2,020	100.0%	705	34.9%	1,315	65.1%	1,515	75.0%	549	77.9%	966	73.5%
Louisiana	4,145	100.0%	1,395	33.7%	2,750	66.3%	2,760	66.6%	932	66.8%	1,828	66.5%
North Carolina	5,797	100.0%	1,966	33.9%	3,831	66.1%	3,562	61.4%	1,230	62.6%	2,332	60.9%
Mississippi	2,669	100.0%	941	35.3%	1,728	64.7%	1,606	60.2%	614	65.2%	992	57.4%
Virginia	4,182	100.0%	1,522	36.4%	2,660	63.6%	2,157	51.6%	775	50.9%	1,382	52.0%
Alabama	3,978	100.0%	1,391	35.0%	2,587	65.0%	2,041	51.3%	766	55.1%	1,275	49.3%
Georgia	5,442	100.0%	1,914	35.2%	3,528	64.8%	2,484	45.6%	968	5_0.6%	1,516	43.0%
Arkansas	981	100.0%	332	33.8%	649	66.2%	445	45.4%	159	47.9%	286	44.1%
Maryland	3,682	100.0%	1,233	33.5%	2,449	66.5%	1,595	43.3%	505	41.0%	1,090	44.5%
South Carolina	2,823	100.0%	936	33.2%	1,887	66.8%	1,153	40.8%	408	43.6%	745	39.5%
Tennessee	2,421	100.0%	863	35.6%	1,558	64.4%	917	37.9%	305	35.3%	612	39.3%
Florida	5,296	100.0%	1,818	34.3%	3,478	65.7%	1,703	32.2%	583	32.1%	1,120	32.2%
Texas	5,230	100.0%	1,866	35.7%	3,364	64.3%	1,511	28.9%	528	28.3%	983	29.2%
Oklahoma	873	100.0%	356	40.8%	517	59.2%	240	27.5%	81	22.8%	159	30.8%
West Virginia	278	100.0%	139	50.0%	139	50.0%	67	24.1%	31	22.3%	36	25.9%
Kentucky	758	100.0%	319	42.1%	439	57.9%	113	14.9%	46	14.4%	67	15.3%

Source: Analysis of Integrated Postsecondary Education Data System

Figure No. 2: Percent of 1992–93 African-American Bachelor's Degree Recipients Who Attended Graduate School in 1993–94

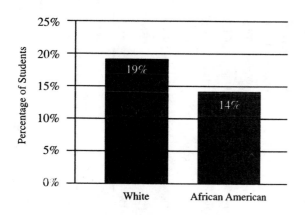

Source: Two Decades of Progress: African Americans Moving Forward in Higher Education, Frederick D. Patterson Research Institute, 1999.

The strength of HBCUs has been their legacy of producing black graduates at a far greater rate than white institutions, and this quality of HBCUs is as true today as it was over 100 years ago when most of these institutions were created. Constantine (1995, 1999) has shown that African-American HBCU graduates earn higher wages than African-American non-HBCU graduates. There is also evidence to suggest that African-American graduates of HBCUs are more likely to attend graduate school than African-American graduates of predominately white institutions. The report *Two Decades of Progress: African Americans Moving Forward in Higher Education,* shows that African-American HBCU bachelor's degree recipients in 1993 were more likely to be enrolled in graduate and professional schools the year after receiving their bachelor's degree than African Americans who did not attend an HBCU. Figure 2 shows that 19 percent of African-American HBCU graduates were enrolled in graduate or professional schools, compared with only 14 percent of African-American non-HBCU graduates.

CONCLUSIONS AND IMPLICATIONS

African Americans have made significant strides in higher education over the past two decades. But if that progress is to continue—at a much keener pace than at present, three important areas of the construct of the education of African American must draw our concern: African Americans in community colleges; the role and future of HBCUs; and the elementary and secondary schooling of African Americans.

AFRICAN AMERICANS IN COMMUNITY COLLEGES

A significant portion of African-American students in higher education are in community colleges. Many of these students do not go on to four-year institutions to earn bachelor's degrees, which limits their economic and employment potential. Community colleges offer an inexpensive alternative to higher education and can provide students with similar marketable skills as four-year students *if* they continue their education at a four-year college and eventually earn their bachelor's degrees (Coley, 1999). Given that some 45 percent of all black undergraduates attend community colleges, enhancing the quality of education at two-year colleges and the rate of transfer to four-year institutions is critical for African-American higher education.

Coley (1999) and Garibaldi (1999) suggest that redefining articulation agreements between two-year and four-year institutions—smoothing the process of transferring a student's community-college credits to a four-year institution—is critical to increasing the number of community college students that eventually earn their bachelor's degrees. Historically Black Colleges and Universities ought to consider themselves prime places to develop models of articulation agreements between two-year colleges and four-year colleges and universities since community colleges and HBCUs share the mission of providing students who otherwise might not have had the opportunity with access to higher education. Such a partnership between community colleges and HBCUs already exists. In 1999, City College of San Francisco announced an articulation agreement with 15 HBCUs, including Howard University, Spelman College, Florida A & M University, Morehouse College, and Morris Brown College. This historic program can provide a gateway to HBCUs that many African-American youngsters might otherwise have missed.

THE ROLE AND FUTURE OF HISTORICALLY BLACK COLLEGES AND UNIVERSITIES

HBCUs continue to play a vital role in African American higher education. But they are in a struggle for survival. State-mandated desegregation has transformed the student populations of several public HBCUs from predominantly black to predominantly white.

But, even as they face these challenges, it is that the focus of HBCUs shift from survival to prosperity. They must enhance the quality of their academic programs, their facilities, and their revenues and endowments. These institutions have provided undeniable evidence of their effectiveness. Now they must more intensively "sell" themselves—that is, what they can offer African-American and other post-secondary students.

HBCUs should also be rewarded with increased funding and development opportunities from federal and state governments, businesses, and foundations, for their significant and disproportionate contribution to the degree attainment of African Americans. Such increased resources will allow HBCUs to more

effectively create their "market niche" and attract the best and the brightest faculty and students. (For example, Xavier University, has established itself as the leader in sending the greatest number of African Americans to medical school every year.)

The alumni of HBCUs have a significant part to play in the growth of these institutions, too. Endowments of the 39 UNCF member institutions combined total only about $704 million, compared with Harvard University's $13 billion endowment, $800 million each for Smith College and Wellesley Colleges, and $4.00 million each at Bowdoin College and Oberlin College (*The Chronicle of Higher Education Almanac 1999–2000*, 1999). Only about 11 percent of HBCU alumni contribute to their alma maters, compared with a national average of 30 percent. It is time for HBCU alumni to give to their alma maters in far greater numbers.

Historically Black colleges and universities can garner greater resources and enhance their faculty and facilities through several mechanisms, including partnerships, capital campaigns, and increased research activities. They can establish partnerships with other higher education institutions as well as local businesses that would increase course and program offerings, provide students with employment and additional educational opportunities, enhance research capabilities and activities, and enhance community relations. Of course, some HBCUs have followed this path for many years; but the partnership model must become more common among HBCUs and be pursued with greater intensity in order to leverage the resources and increase productivity of the institutions.

Albeit acknowledging that the majority of HBCUs are small liberal arts colleges, it is critical that they, individually and as a group, increase their research capacity and productivity. HBCUs are largely being left out of the research industry and the development of new knowledge. Only Howard University, among the 105 HBCUs, is a Research I institution (Black Issues in Higher Education, 1998).[1] HBCUs must find ways to include themselves in the knowledge-building industry, for research activities provide institutions with more funds and greater resources. It also enables students to gain invaluable research experiences and skills, which increases their competitiveness for graduate school and in the labor market.

Initiatives have been established recently to increase the research capacity of HBCUs and the research productivity of HBCU faculty. The Research Partnerships Program of the Pennsylvania State University Center for Human Development and Family Research in Diverse Contexts headed by Dr. Linda Burton is one example. The purpose of this program is to develop research on family studies among faculty members at HBCUs and other minority-serving institutions. The National Institutes of Health launched a program under its National Institute of General Medical Sciences, Division of Minority Opportunities in Research. Special initiatives of the division include meetings and other activities that build networks among individuals and educational institutions to promote minority participation in sponsored biomedical research.

ELEMENTARY AND SECONDARY SCHOOLING OF AFRICAN AMERICANS

Numerous studies provide evidence that academic preparation in high school is the most important determinant of success in higher education (i.e., Adelman, 1999; Perna, 2000). When students take college preparatory classes in high school (i.e., they are enrolled in the academic track), they are more likely to enroll in a four-year college or university (Perna, 2000), and to attain a bachelor's degree (Adelman, 1999). Moreover, the quality of the

secondary school curriculum is especially important for college success for African-American students. In his study of bachelor's degree attainment, Adelman (2000) found that academic resources (high school curriculum, test scores, and class rank) were more important predictors of bachelor's degree attainment than socioeconomic status, continuous enrollment in college, and college grades. He also found that the impact of high school academic resources was more pronounced for African Americans and Hispanics than whites.

These findings are encouraging and disheartening. On the one hand, policymakers and practitioners can direct their efforts toward ensuring that students from all backgrounds are encouraged and prepared to enroll in the academic track in high school. High school counselors and administrators should strongly advise African-American and other minority students to take college preparatory classes and to participate in Advance Placement courses (The College Board, 1999). On the other hand, schools attended mostly by African Americans are more likely than schools with fewer African-American students to offer remedial courses, be high-poverty schools, have teacher vacancies, and to employ teachers who are not certified in the subjects they are teaching (Darling-Hammond, 1997; Nettles and Perna, 19976; U.S. Department of Education, 1997). Nettles and Perna (1997b) showed that the percentage of students participating in both remedial English and math in public elementary and secondary schools increases with the concentration of African-American students. It is troubling that so many African-American elementary and secondary students are not receiving the quality-education they deserve and that will prepare them for higher education.

In their recent report on minority high achievement, The College Board provides examples of elementary and secondary schools that are providing minority students with good quality curricula and achieving success. The report indicates that one source of success is a demanding curriculum and associated teaching strategies. Another key to success is the attention given to professional development and support of teachers to implement the curriculum and use prescribed instructional strategies. In elementary and high school, administrators and teachers must hold the highest expectation for African-American students and provide them with the most challenging and interesting curricula. It is critical also that teachers are trained in the fields they are teaching and that they are given in-service support and continuous opportunities for further development.

It is at the elementary and secondary levels that the issue of the African-American male in higher education should be addressed. While it remains true that African-American men often find work more viable and necessary than higher education, and that African-American men earn higher wages than African-American women at the same educational level (U.S. Census Bureau), the lower number and progress of African-American men in higher education is alarming. Watson (1999) states that the disparity in higher education among African-American men and women is a long-term problem that begins in junior high schools. He attributes the relative failure of black males to several reasons, including teachers finding it easier to work with girls; the streets appearing to be an attractive alternative; insufficient supplementary educational activities after school, on weekends, and during the summer; and absent fathers and positive role models.

From my own research and experiences, I have heard the despair of many white female teachers that they are not "reaching" their black male students and that they do not know how to repair the incongruity. Given that 87 percent of teachers are white and more than one-third of all public school students are nonwhite, familiarizing white teachers with students from various cultures, backgrounds, and even genders should be a priority of pre-service and in-service teacher education and training as a core component. It is also critical that greater effort and resources be targeted toward recruiting teachers of color.

In conclusion, the glass is "half-full" in African-American higher education. Nonetheless, there is still significant work to do in order to continue the progress and rectify remaining disparities. It is necessary that both African-American men and women break ground in higher education and attain the highest levels of achievement. With what the future holds, and the defining role of higher education, we can ill-afford to have only "half" of our population progressing and succeeding—African-American men and women must advance together in the new millennium, charting new pathways and changing the course of history.

REFERENCES

Adelman, C. (1999). *Answers in the tool box: Academic intensity, attendance patterns, and bachelor's degree attainment.* Jessup, MD: Education Publications Center, U.S. Department of Education.

Black Issues in Higher Education. (March, 1998). Charting a black research agenda. *Black Issues in Higher Education, 15,* 24–27.

Coley R. J. (2000). *The American community college turns 100: A look at its students, programs, and prospects.* NJ: Educational Testing Service, Policy Information Center. Princeton

Constantine, J. M. (1995). The effect of attending historically black colleges and universities on future wages of black students. *Industrial and Labor Relations Review, 48,* 531–546.

Constantine, J. M. (1999). Black colleges and beyond: An analysis of labor market experiences of black college students. *Review of African American Education, 1,* 83–102.

Darling-Hammond, L. (1997). *Doing what matters most: Investing in quality teaching.* New York: National Commission on Teaching and America's Future.

Garibaldi, A (1999). Bridging the great divide between two-year and four-year college enrollments of African Americans & other minority students. *Just the Facts,* 1, 8–12.

Hill, S. T (1985). *The traditionally black institutions of higher education: 1860 to 1982.* Washington, D.C.: National Center for Education Statistics, U.S. Department of Education.

Nettles, M. T, and L. W Pema,(1997a). *TheAfrican American education data book, volume I: Postsecondary education.* Fairfax, VA: Frederick D. Patterson Research Institute.

Nettles, M. T, and L. W. Perna,(l997b). *The African American education data book, volume II: Preschool through high school education.* Fairfax, VA: Frederick D. Patterson Research Institute.

Nettles, M. T, L. W Perna, and K. E. Freeman (1999). *Two decades of progress: African Americans moving forward in higher education.* Fairfax, VA: Frederick D. Patterson Research Institute.

Perna, L. W. (2000). Differences in the decision to attend college among African Americans, Hispanics, and whites. *The Journal of Higher Education,* 71, 117–141.

The Chronicle of Higher Education 1999–2000 Almanac Issue. Washington, D.C.: *The Chronicle of Higher Education.*

The College Board. (1999). *A report of the national task force on minority high achievement.* New York: The College Board.

United States Census Bureau. (1998). *Educational attainment in the United States: March 1997.* Washington, D.C.: U.S. Census Bureau.

United States Department of Education, National Center for Education Statistics. (1997). *America's teachers: Profile of a profession, 1993–1994.* Washington, D.C.: U.S. Department of Education.

Watson, B. (1999). African American higher education: Differences between men and women. *Just the Facts,* 1, 19–22.

NOTES

1. The Carnegie Foundation for the Advancement of Teaching classifies Research I institutions as those that offer a range of baccalaureate programs, are committed to graduate education through the doctorate, and give high priority to research. They award 50 or more doctoral degrees each year. In addition, they receive $40 million or more annually in federal support for research.

Voice of Dissent

Pamela Burdman

Berkeley professor and author of the controversial book Losing the Race, *Dr. John McWhorter speaks to* Black Issues *about leaving the African American Studies Department, being a Black professor and his intense media coverage.*

Dr. John McWhorter was little known outside the field of linguistics until the Oakland school board passed its controversial proposal on ebonies in late 1996. One of a handful of Black linguists, and the only one openly critical of the Oakland plan, McWhorter was for days a regular feature on network news shows. In his latest book, Losing the Race: Self-Sabotage in Black America, *McWhorter continues to be a voice of dissent among Black intellectuals. Since the cancer (racism) is basically eradicated, he says, African Americans should drop the chemotherapy—like policies of affirmative action that taint their achievements, though he supports affirmative action in some arenas. He urges Black people to stop seeing themselves as victims, stop espousing separatist visions and stop seeing intellectual achievement as the province of White people.*

McWhorter's academic specialty is language change and language contact, with a concentration on pidgin and Creole languages. He has written two books on Creoles and one on ebonies. His next book, The Power of Babel, *will appear later this year.*

BI: You have said some Black people agree with your ideas, but they don't think these things should be aired publicly? Why do you think it's important to bring these ideas into public discussion?

JM: Residual racism is not an obstacle to success as much as we've all been told. We need to start discussing this openly, because these days the overt message we tend to send to new generations of Black students is Whitey's out to get you and this is something that's going to check your progress. The covert feeling that more and more African Americans have is that this isn't really true. Unfortunately, if the overt message is what young people, in particular, Black college students, tend to hear, then I think we end up

stanching our potential. And I also think, frankly, that we end up perpetuating racism as White people watch this kind of debate and become more and more disenchanted with the civil rights revolution.

BI: Yet, in analyzing the three "cults" you discuss in the book: "victimology," separatism and anti-intellectualism,, you call them products of history, a seeming point of agreement with some of your detractors. Why didn't you emphasize that point more?

JM: A great many people have traced the roots of these things. This is not a book of scholarship. I have written several scholarly books. This is an informed editorial. There is a sense that many African Americans have taken too much to heart, that history is destiny, which is a tic that I see in a great many very smart and concerned African Americans. The statement is assumed to be that "this is because of sharecropping and segregation," rather than "this is because of segregation and sharecropping, and here's what we're going to do to get beyond it." It's that second part that interests me more than the first part in the year 2001.

BI: But didn't you ever feel the instinct to dwell on the first part?

JM: Well, if you're a Black teenager who grew up with a social worker mother who did not like White people very much, then naturally you're going to start falling for that line. What made me feel differently was simply the empirical evidence. You live a life, you watch White people, you see the things that happen to you, you read your history, and you realize there is something very different about the world I live in than the world people were living in even 30 years ago.

There are mainstream things in life that I love very, very much just as themselves. One of them is foreign languages. I love old movies. The Black ones are nice, but really what first hooked me was Fred and Ginger. I have loved dinosaurs since I was a child. There's nothing Black about that. Developing that oppositional Black identity means that you have to give those things up, and I couldn't do that. I'm too much of a nerd.

BI: You say Black students consider school a "White thing," to the extent that you have never had a student who wasn't African American "disappear without explanation or turn in a test that made me wonder how she could have attended class and done so badly." I know some professors at Berkeley dispute that experience. How have students reacted?

JM: Since I left the African American Studies Department, I don't have as many Black students as I used to have. A couple of Black students have approached me on campus dis-

mayed. A couple have approached me agreeing with me. I hear there are students who despise what I have written. I am working now, rather closely, with three Black students here, and as far as they're concerned, it's not really an issue. They are pretty much exceptions to what I talk about; I hate to say it, partly because we no longer have racial preferences here, and so the Black students are here for the very same reason everybody else is.

The professors who say they've never seen this, with only one exception, are professors who are teaching what you might call "Black courses" or courses whose subjects are particularly directed toward the victim culture. My thumbnail hypothesis is that African American students might tend to devote themselves more wholeheartedly to courses like this, that would speak to them spiritually in this way. What you don't hear is that there's a kind of a silent, I can't say majority, but a great many Berkeley professors, very concerned, enlightened, thinking White people, who agree completely with the things I have said. Now they're not going to write an op-ed…No White person wants to seem like they're a racist.

BI: You have written about UC President Richard Atkinson's proposal to scrap the SAT, and it sounds like you don't believe him when he says it's not about race.

JM: Of course not. It's about race, and I accept his concern and his pity. It's clear why he can't admit it. Richard Atkinson is very understandably operating under the impression that a White man of his generation would—that it's simply impossible for Black and Latino kids to do well on an abstract standardized test, because society keeps them from doing well. But he's not thinking about the fact that there are a great many Black and Latino students who are not poor. As far as I'm concerned, any Black education solution that doesn't set standards as high for us as for everyone else is an insult.

BI: When did you leave African American Studies and what prompted that?

JM: I left African American Studies in the spring of 1998 for the simple reason that it was a department that was very unfriendly to me. Ebonics was not a big deal to them. Ebonics was more of interest in linguistics departments than it was to the African American Studies Department. It wasn't that. But I guess I didn't walk the walk or talk the talk enough for them. I wasn't Black enough for them. I was faintly disliked, and I found it extremely uncomfortable. I think that the department does not challenge its students and that it was a den of mediocrity with the exception of two or three people.

BI: I couldn't help but wonder, reading the book,, about (African American Studies professor) June Jordan. She comes up often, in veer negative terms. Were there personal conflicts?

JM: I don't bear any animus toward her. I don't like her ideology. The reason that I quoted her by name, whereas many people I just said a professor or person, was that we did an ebonics debate in early 1997, where she basically verbally jumped me and made fun of me in a forum in which I couldn't defend myself. We were supposed to be colleagues in the same department, and she strayed from what academics are supposed to do and just did a backyard, ghetto catfight sort of thing. After what she did to me that day, why should I keep her name out of it? I needed a few names. I needed it to be clear that I was talking about real people. I could not have written this book if I was still in the African American Studies Department, but when I left the African American Studies Department, I had no idea I was going to write this book.

BI: You received tenure in early 1999, a year before the book came out. Would you have published this book before having tenure?

JM: Certainly. Think about it: Is UC Berkeley going to fire a young Black professor for

expressing views that are against the mainstream? The irony would be rich. Even before I had tenure, they couldn't fire me. Not to mention that I had been almost overly diligent in my academic work. I have a CV a mile long.

BI: If you weren't Black enough for the African American, Studies professors, wouldn't Black students respond that way, too?

JM: As I say in the book, the Black students tended to be my favorites. If anything, I think some of them were kind of playing me to an extent, because we got along so well. But the sort of things I saw went beyond even what would explain that. It was hard to write that section, because I like these kids. A lot of people think I don't like Black people. No, I know that I'm doing well for the race. We need the honesty first. I have a stack of old exams from that time sitting over there, and every six months, I go through it to make sure that I'm not crazy. This needed to be written about.

BI: You've written a lot for a 35-year-old professor. Is that in any way related to the feeling you describe in the book of somehow being diminished by having been a beneficiary of affirmative action? It is a way of proving yourself?

JM: No, it isn't, although that's a very apt question. I do it because I love it. I love writing more than anything. I'm not trying to prove anything. And to be honest, the sad and simple fact is no matter how much I write, it's not considered the same as if I were White. There is always a sense that it's a Black professor who has done these things and I think there's always a suspicion that the things I wrote were not as scientifically rigorous.

For example, there's one professor in this department—it's clear he doesn't think I speak French. Time and time again, he has seen me speaking French. He has read my CV. He has seen a whole paper that I wrote in

French. He still has the assumption that I don't speak the language.

BI: **And that's not racism?**

JM: No. He can't quite process it, but he's not a racist. But it's the sort of thing that I'm talking about: There is a sense that I'm a bit of a performing monkey, and there always will be. I was meant to be a scholar. I think both Whites and Blacks see that as something that a Black person only does to study themselves and not solely to do head work. I can't change that in my lifetime, but that is my tiny burden to bear. And frankly I think that's a darn sight better than where I would have been 50 years ago.

BI: **Having; left African American Studies, what are your thoughts about ethnic studies as a discipline?**

JM: It varies from department to department. A major in Blackness and being Black and what it used to be like to be Black, unfortunately in practice has a way of teaching Black kids the extent to which they are victims even if they didn't know it before. It teaches Black kids about literature that people of their own ethnicity wrote, and that means that that's a course they're not taking about literature of the world. In an ideal world, I would like to see there be advanced degrees in those things. But for undergraduates, I would have it be just a minor. However, I don't think of ethnic studies departments as a scourge. It gives many Black students a great sense of belonging to be in those departments.

BI: **You voted for Ralph Nader, you think Mumia Abu-Jamal was wrongly imprisoned, yet you've been contacted, I assume warmly, by Ward Connerly and Clarence Thomas. You wrote that Black people should be open-minded about George Bush. You've been described as a conservative. How do you describe yourself politically?**

JM: I'm a centrist. "Black conservative" is a very sloppy label, because it means only one thing: a Black person who doesn't agree with racial preferences. That's it. One litmus test that you see is that Orlando Patterson, who wrote a very widely reviewed and very readable book called The Ordeal of Integration, says a lot of the things I say and is just as snippy in his tone sometimes as I am, but who decides that affirmative action ought to be continued. As such, somehow he keeps his good Black person's stripes. I'm the other litmus test. Because I don't believe in affirmative action, suddenly I am allied with Clarence Thomas. I can't fix that. The more you rail against a label, the more it's going to stick.

BI: **Have any of these experiences changed your views or made you more open to conservative points of view?**

JM: I would say that the experiences I've had since this book has come out have probably moved me a little bit to the right than I was before in terms of how I see a race getting ahead. I'm appalled at everything I see going on in the Bush administration, except for what relates to race. For me, it's becoming a wedge issue like abortion for some women. I'm not a Republican. This administration keeps reminding me I will never be a conservative. It's really how I feel about how a race moves up, and the idea that self-help or government-assisted self-help is a conservative position to take shows that our sense of what liberal and conservative is getting extremely confused these days. My commitment is to raising a previously oppressed group upward that I belong to, and yet I'm a conservative? No. Clearly, that makes no sense. As time goes by, that label will lose its sting, as it becomes clear that we quote—unquote Black conservatives are the vanguard.

BI: **What are the signs that Black conservatives are the vanguard?**

JM: For example, there's a movement among Black ministers to develop closer relationships with Republicans, the idea being to solicit funds for churches to help inner-city communities. These ministers are not leftists in the sense of thinking that community pathology is OK because the White man won't cough up. But it's a more centrist Democratic than your Ishmael Reed would want. Here's another example: Shelby Steele 11 years ago caught holy hell with his book. I'm not catching as much. I have 1,100 pieces of mail, and of them, probably 400 of them are from Black people. And almost all of it is in praise. They're ordinary Black people who have stopped seeing themselves in the Black radical message of, say, the Congressional Black Caucus. There is a gestural lag, which is that Black people once they're in the voting booth, seem to think that the only party they should vote for is Democratic, but if you look at polls of how most Black people seem to feel about many things, we're not really a very Democratic race anymore, and that will start to show.

BI: **Before this article, you complained to me about articles you felt were taking pot shots at you, and yet, I think a lot of professors would envy the amount of coverage you've gotten.**

JM: Not this kind of coverage. One thing nobody ever believes is that I really didn't know this book was going to be so successful. I wrote the book as just my 2 cents. This book was a very hard sell. It went through four proposals. The advance was quite moderate. I really expected to spend last fall semester sitting in my study, and then all of a sudden, I'm on TV every week. It's a chore frankly. Most Black interviewers think you're a freak. The White interviewers are a little too enthusiastic. You're on the line every time. Nothing is funnier to me than reading the occasional person saying I love seeing my face on TV.

BI: **Does that mean you'll avoid writing these kinds of things in the future to avoid the glare?**

JM: There will never be another book where I spend 300 pages criticizing Black people. Publishers in New York would love for me to write that book, and I've told them no. There will be a book that treats race, but it's going to surround race with a whole bunch of other topics. It's going to be a more philosophical book. The limelight is exhausting, and if there is more limelight, I would like it to be as something other than being a critic of Black people. I can't get my message out without ever going on TV. But it's not fun.

BI: **Do you think your message is getting out?**

JM: I do. I did an appearance on "Fox News Sunday." It shot my book up to No. 1 on Amazon for three days.

BI: **How many copies have you sold?**

JM: Approaching 44,000.

BI: **You mentioned to me that you may have children some day. Given what you've written in the book,, how would you feel about being, a parent to a Black child growing up in the early part of the 21st century?**

JM: No child of mine could possibly take on those attitudes. My little girl will not be swayed by what Black kids tell her. I will exert too much of an influence on her. I just know that in my heart. By the time I have kids, it's going to be a rather different world. My children will grow up in a pretty interracial environment.

Book Review:
Losing the Race
by John McWhorter

Darren Rhym

Before reading Losing the Race, I was unaware of who John McWhorter was. After reading the book, I think McWhorter raises some of the most important questions facing African Americans today. The questions are complex and often difficult to listen to. They are even painful at times but very necessary, in my opinion, because black Americans need to come to terms with the reality of where black Americans are as a people and where they are going.

The front and back covers of this Perennial paperback quote reviews from the Washington Post and the Wall Street Journal. The quotes, written upon the unfocused face of a young black man, use pathos to draw the reader in—to get him or her riled up—in an attempt to sell the text to the reader. The back cover asks, "Why do so many African Americans—even comfortably middle class ones—continue to see racism as a defining factor in their lives?" Another passage seeks to categorize McWhorter, by comparing him to Shelby Steele and Stanley Crouch. Other quotes refer to McWhorter as explosive and his book as a must read. I agree. Having taught composition for more than a decade, I recognize a good argument when I see one. However, since reading the text my most prevalent question is, is anyone willing to listen to McWhorter's argument? McWhorter forces blacks and whites to question whether racism is holding blacks back or whether blacks are destroying themselves with their own culture.

In the preface, McWhorter explains that his text seeks to "show that black America is currently caught in certain ideological holding patterns that are today much more serious barriers to black well-being than is white racism, and constitute nothing less than a continuous, self-sustaining act of self-sabotage" (x). McWhorter's statement is but one of the colors in a book that constructs an intellectual Rubik's Cube. After reading the text, it was my hope that the book would elicit dialogue from all Americans, black and white, rich and poor, intellectual and anti-intellectual, but apparently America has not yet progressed beyond the same problems that plagued the country 100 years ago. Many black people that I spoke to about the text were defensive and ever ready to revert to the anti-intellectual "truisms" that McWhorter writes about in the text. The comfort of these truisms makes it difficult for black people who embrace anti-intellectualism to accept the challenge of thinking outside of the box and utilizing deductive or inductive reasoning to solve problems, instead of blaming others and feeling victimized. Dependence upon truisms prohibit believers from even entertaining the idea that something other than racism may be contributing to problems that black people face in this country. Hence, it appears that Americans are more apt to be haunted by the race issues that W. E. B. Du Bois called the problem of the twentieth century than to look inward to find solutions to problems.

In Shelby Steele's book, The Content of Our Character, he talks about innocence and how the conflict concerning race in America can almost be summed up in the concept that both sides, black and white, are trying to claim innocence. I find that McWhorter's thematic theories of Victimology, Separatism, and Anti-intellectualism are thought provoking and interesting enough to be given consideration. I think intellectualism demands that these thoughts be heard, internalized, and evaluated, but they most certainly must not be dismissed without consideration. This very act would do nothing more than support McWhorter's theories.

Black people are not monolithic. There is no singular black experience, and this makes the discussion of problems that black people face a complex undertaking. This undertaking is made even more difficult by what McWhorter defines as Anti-intellectualism. The black intellectual, particularly the black male intellectual, has always taken a back seat to the jock, the entertainer, and/or "the player." Likewise, it is common for black students to terrorize and/or ostracize "smart kids." Historically, black students have adopted a survival tactic from slavery and feigned ignorance in an attempt to gain acceptance from peers. Thus, it is not at all difficult to find examples for any of McWhorter's thematic theories. Yet, for some reason that I cannot

explain, many black readers find it difficult to accept blame for the condition of present day African Americans and are still convinced that black people fail because of racism.

McWhorter's mission is to persuade his readers that black people too often act like victims, seek to separate themselves from other groups, and then insist upon being judged or dealt with by separate standards, and also are guilty of being anti-intellect and anti-education. I find his text persuasive, although at times McWhorter's tone creates distance. I find that this distance can be misconstrued as blaming or finger pointing and those who do not consider themselves intellectuals resent this.

I was so inspired by McWhorter's handling of the issues that black Americans face today that I required my students to read his book. I was curious to how they would react. At first they, like I, were offended and defensive, and then the more they read, the more they thought, the more complex and difficult the experience and the assignments became. The power of McWhorter's text lies in its potential and its possibilities. In reading the text there is the possibility that fewer black people will perceive themselves as victims. There is the possibility that separatist notions will no longer be seen as viable options or solutions. And, there is the possibility that intellectualism will be viewed as cool by all students. When this happens student's potential will increase. I do not believe that Losing the Race is necessarily a book with any answers, but it takes a step in the right direction by asking the right questions.

Darren Rhym
Morehouse College

Part 3: Economics

The Decline of the Black Athlete: An Online Exclusive: Extended Interview with Harry Edwards

David Leonard

Harry Edwards says the golden age of black athleticism is over. Is he serious? ColorLines staffer David Leonard does the asking.

After three decades years in the spotlight, as sociology professor at the University of California, and as a consultant to the San Francisco 49ers, Dr. Harry Edwards remains one of the premier activists in sports. ColorLines *last spoke to Dr. Edwards on his role in organizing the "Revolt of the Black Athlete" at the Mexico City Olympics in 1968 (*ColorLines, *Vol. 1, No. 1).*

On October 26, 1999, I sat down with Dr. Edwards at his Berkeley office. Dr. Edwards is a professor of sociology at the University of California, Berkeley, and a consultant for the San Francisco 49ers, who has written extensively on issues of sports and society.

More than that, Edwards continues to be an activist within the sports world. And his role as a teacher is not limited to the classroom. After along day of teaching, Edwards took the time, before our late interview, to counsel a player about his future in sports.

Lately, Dr. Edwards has been engaging another heated debate over the role of athletics in the black community. While black athletes have never been more visible or more culturally influential, Edwards now advances the provocative thesis that the "golden age" of black athletes is over. ColorLines *recently asked Edwards exactly what he means. Is he out of touch or on point? You decide.*

CL: In the last year many people have spoke about America's love affair with the women's world cup team as an example of America's, and the sports world's, advancement in terms of gender issues. How much progress do you see?

HE: Progress is a very, very difficult concept to quantify. It is very difficult to measure qualitatively, in terms of the reception that a team, such as the women's soccer team got. In examining progress you realize how complex the entity really is. I think that one needs to look beyond the sited reception to other things to get some indication.

So when we look at the women's soccer team, we, first of all, see that the team was projected as an all-American, family-oriented team, which was a sideways suggestion that the team was not about those lesbians. It was also projected as a substantially "white-girl-next-door" team, which was again, as one person stated outright, to provide an example to counter the bad behavior of men in men's sports, which is to say black men in particular. They are looking at the Lawrence Phillips', Dennis Rodmans', O.J. Simpsons', Jim Browns' and quote countering that image. Neither the all-American girl team,

149

nor the "white-girl-next-door" has anything to do with women's sports.

In other words, the reception at those levels was not a reception for the women's soccer team, but a reception revolving around the utility of the women's soccer team by those who would keep things pretty much the way they are. And of course this is evidenced in the kinds of endorsements some members of the team received following the World Cup. You had, for example, soccer Barbie, which is one of the most sexist images in American society. The soccer Barbie thing was indicative of the utility of the women's world cup team for conservative propaganda interests. Then, of course, the athletic bra endorsement that Brandi Chastain got was again indicative of the maintenance of traditional images of women. It would be the equivalent of giving Sammy Sosa or Mark McGwire the Jockey jock strap endorsement, indicative of masculine and masculine sexual focus. The athletic bra endorsement was again about keeping women essentially subjugated.

CL: A student of mine wrote a paper in which he juxtaposed the image of Tommie Smith and John Carlos in 1968 versus that of Charles Barkley and Michael Jordan during the 1992 Olympics—the raised black fist compared to a draping America flag strategically placed to cover up a Reebok label on their sweatsuits. What do these opposing images say about the last thirty years of black sports participation?

HE: It says that black athletes have become sufficiently integrated into the sports system. They have a stake in all of the business dimensions of that system. Thirty years ago there would not have been any issue of them covering the Reebok slogan because they would not have had the Nike contract that was in conflict with it. That would have gone to a white athlete. So what this change tells me is that black athletes are sufficiently integrated into the business matrix of sports. That there is something there, a business interest, which they feel obliged to protect. Thirty

years ago that was not the case. We are talking about different times.

CL: In a number of spaces you have argued that we are currently witnessing the end of the "golden age of black sports participation." Why the "golden era" in sports for black athletic participation coming to an end?

HE: By the time we finish looking at the last thirty years, through societal processes, through institutional erosion, through the degradation of the black athletic pool, through disqualification, judicial procedures and deaths, we have so emaciated the talent pool, that we are beginning to see a dropoff in performance at every level, in all sports where blacks participate in numbers. We are simply disqualifying, jailing, burying, and leaving behind our black athletes, right along with our potential black doctors, black lawyers, and so forth.

So as we look at high school sports, an increasing number of high schools cannot even field a team. Last year in San Francisco there were three high schools that could not field a football team. A number of years ago, Richmond High, which was one of the great schools to produce athletes out of the bay area, had five people try out for the football team. Even if they have enough players, they often times cannot afford to put a team on the field.

You look at boxing and the same things are happening. I remember when you had Ali, Frazier, Ernie Shavers, Ernie Terrell, George Foreman, Floyd Patterson, Buster Mathis, and Sonny Liston. These were just the people who were the acknowledged contenders. Now, you have Evander Holyfield, basically a puffed-up cruiser weight, and Mike Tyson, who spends more time in trouble out of the ring, when he is not getting in trouble in the ring. Where are the boxers? The boxers are in the cemetery, the boxers are in jail, the boxers are in gangs, and the boxers are on the street. That is where the potential football, basketball, and baseball players are as well.

The talent pool in the black community has been so eroded that when you have a sport that is eighty percent black, like the NFL, or eighty-eight percent, like the NBA, the fallout is going to show up. If you look at the basketball this situation becomes crystal clear. In 1990 twenty-seven out of twenty-nine teams averaged over one hundred points. In 1997 only four teams averaged more than 100 points, and last year only team, the Sacramento Kings, was able to average this amount. Every statistic is down. You look at the collegiate level and you will see the same statistical decline. In every statistical category the performance standards are down: freethrow average, points per game, rebound average, assist average.

Why? You just don't have as great an athlete today. We are jailing, burying and disqualifying our potential point guards, wide-receivers, running backs, power forwards, centers, and so forth, at a very early age. If we look at it historically, literally from 1947, when Jackie Robinson broke into the major leagues, to 1997, fifty years marked the golden age of the black athlete, the age of sports participation. Blacks dominated boxing, basketball, football, track, and even baseball; all sports they participated in high numbers. Now we are seeing a precipitous dropoff and the reasons are not inside sport, but the reasons in society, which are ultimately reflective in sport.

CL: So what will the next thirty years look like?

HE: I think over the next thirty years we are going to continue to see a decline of black athletic participation. I think we are also going to see more importantly a phenomenal split within the black community, as a consequence of that. The black middle-class moving on to become doctors, lawyers, and engineers. The black masses, in traditional black communities, not moving at all. Being left behind and increasingly in the twenty-first century living an early twentieth century existence. That is going to be a particularly explosive situation.

The overwhelming majority of black athletes come out of the lower echelons of black society. I don't think it is accidental when you look at the inordinate number of blacks in jail and the proportionate number of blacks not on athletic teams. You are essentially looking at the same guy. They both have numbers; they are both in uniforms, and they both belong to gangs. They only call one the Crips, or the Bloods, while they call the other team the 49ers, Warriors, As, or the Giants. They are all in pursuit of respect. They all, at one level or another, keep score. The parallels are all there. It is the same guy.

But I think what you are looking at over the next thirty years is that the guy in the jail uniform is going to outstrip, in both numbers and impact, the guy in the athletic uniform. I think the next thirty years is going to see that kind of transformation. We are going to be looking at the same guy, but only increasingly he is going to be wearing a jailhouse number, a jailhouse uniform, instead of a sports team number, and an athletic uniform.

CL: So might the twenty-first century be the "Golden Age" of white athletics or the "Golden Age" of Latino athletics?

HE: I think that ultimately the twenty-first century will be a global sports age. The world is so small and sports is so international that I think you are going to see the same thing in American sports that you see in basketball and baseball today, with some differences. Basketball is increasingly recruiting from overseas. So you look at people coming from Eastern Europe, Africa and other parts of the world, you see the future of sports. Right now, forty percent of major league baseball players are foreign born. We are going to see more and more of that. Whites are not just going to fill slots because blacks are not there. So, overwhelmingly, you are going to be looking at American sports that are inordinately participated in by foreign-born athletes.

More generally, I believe sports are going to change. They are going to take on the hype of wrestling to cover the lack of quality of performance. I think you are going to get sports hyped more and more as a business, and less and less as a performance craft. So you will have lesser athletes in there, along with a few rules changes to keep scoring up, but you won't see the caliber of players you saw in the past. You will still have the hitting, the dunks, but most importantly you will have the games being hyped, rules being changed, so that points keep going up, and the fans keep watching the games, and the money keeps rolling in.

CL: Last year, Sports Illustrated featured a cover story of "What Ever Happened to the White Athlete?" Do you know what has happened to the white athlete?

HE: Well, the white athlete over the last fifty years has simply been displaced by a pool of largely untapped athletic talent, generated by a lack of alternative high-prestige occupational opportunities for masses of young black males, and increasing females. I think that once this untapped pool of talent had access to three or four sports it was inevitable that ultimately blacks would end up representing disproportionately high numbers. That is what happen to the white athlete in basketball, football, track, not field, boxing and to a certain extent in baseball.

But in ninety-five percent of American sports the white athlete is there in numbers and dominant. The white athlete is there in swimming. The white athlete is there in diving. The white athlete is there in water polo. The white athlete is there in golf. The white athlete is there in tennis. The white athlete is there in badminton. The white athlete is there in auto racing. The white athlete is there in horse racing. The white athlete is there in soccer, walking, gymnastics, and all the winter sports in dominant numbers. What happened to the white athlete? The white athlete is there, except in those three, four, or five sports where blacks have had access.

The other thing that has happened is that blacks have changed the nature of some sports. Black culture, isolated from white society, from slavery right up to integration, developed styles of playing basketball, football, baseball, and boxing, that whites had to learn to accommodate to or get out of the sport. So if you'd brought in a point guard, who dribbled the ball through his legs, and passed the ball behind this back, you better have a guy to guard him. Otherwise you were at a severe disadvantage. What this generally meant was going into the black community to get someone who had played that kind of ball. Finally, whites have access to the full spectrum of sports, and the full spectrum of high-prestige occupational positions. They are not channeled into sports in disproportionately high numbers, and that white talent for sports is spread out across all occupations, and across all sports. Well, blacks don't typically have those same opportunities.

CL: Several years ago you argued that the black community's "singled-minded pursuit of sports" represented a severe problem within the black community. Looking back on this argument, do you still maintain this position, or have you changed your views on black athletic participation?

HE: There is still, thank God, a disproportionately high emphasis on sports achievement in black society, relative to other high-prestige occupational career aspirations. Given what is happening to young black people, who have essentially disconnected from virtually every institutional structure in society, sports may be our last hook and handle. They are unemployed, in disproportionately high numbers, and increasingly they are unemployable. They dropout of school in disproportionately high numbers, and now they are not just uneducated and miseducated, but often times diseducated. They have disengaged even from the black church. They are affiliated with the gangs, not the church. The street is their temple; the gang leader is their pastor. They don't seek the respect of anybody but each other. But they still want to "be like Mike."

That sports emphasis gives us a hook and a handle on them. Through midnight basketball, through Saturday football, or recreational facilities, we can put them back in contact with the clergy, mentors, health workers, counselors, government workers, with people from the economic and corporate sector. Without that we have no way of getting them at all, except through police and judicial action.

I still maintain that there is a high and inordinate emphasis on sports in the black community. That emphasis has been transmuted, however, by the processes of the "end of the golden age of black athletics" from a liability to a virtue, in a sense that it may provide us with the last hook and handle that we have on a substantial proportion of this generation of young black people.

CL: So you disagree with John Hoberman, who in his book *Darwin's Athletes,* argues that blacks should get out of sports, because such a singled-minded pursuit of sports has historically hurt the black community, while fueling societal racism?

HE: Yes! *Darwin's Athletes* is the classic case of intellectually picking up the ball and running the wrong way. You can not look at sport, where a certain level of opportunity has been opened up, and say that because of the racist spin that white society, and white culture, puts on achievement in that arena, that blacks should desist, not just from valuing that sports participation, from idealizing the people who participate in sports, but that we should get out of it all together. To say that blacks should not be involved in the numbers that we are, and put that emphasis on sports that we have, because of a racist interpretation that whites have put on that, is like saying, A, whites have cancer, therefore, let's, treat, B, black folks. The emphasis should be upon why it is that white society has to put that racist emphasis upon black sports achievement, and secondly why is the achievement limited to sports in disproportionately high numbers, and not at least representative across the full spectrum of high-prestige occupational categories. These are the issues that Hoberman should have been dealing with.

CL: As we approach the twenty-first century, what do you think will be the greatest challenge in sports over the next hundred years?

HE: Sports always recapitulates society, in terms of its character, dynamics, and the structure of human relations. Just as I believe emphatically that the challenge of the twenty-first century will be diversity in all of its guises, the challenge in sports in the twenty-first century is going to be diversity. We are going to be looking at circumstances where we cannot separate out race, from class, gender, sexuality, techno-class status or age.

I worry about what is going to happen to this society. We are already in a situation where we are expecting children to play games that they cannot afford to watch. They, especially the classes that generate the athletes, can't afford the ticket to get into the stadium; they can't afford money for the pay-per-view. And who are the people that are the driving forces behind the teams: the children of the sixties. They are the ones who own the teams, who run the media, who establish the standards of what is going to cost what. Even as we attack them, we continue to expect them to be the athletes on our teams. Even as we jail them, even as we disqualify them from schools, even as we revoke the social services that support them, even as we eliminate the affirmative action that brings them to college campuses, we still want them to be on our teams. So as we look at the situation it becomes very, very clear that we are headed for a set of crises, all of which revolve around diversity in sports, just as in society.

Historically Black Colleges and Universities (HBCUs) as Agents of Change for the Development of Minority Businesses

Arinola O. Adebayo, Adeyemi A. Adekoya,
and O. Felix Ayadi

This article attempts to make a wake-up call to Historically Black Colleges and Universities (HBCUs) to respond to the plight of minority business owners while also fulfilling their role of educating students. Although the state of minority businesses was much better than what the public is made to believe, however, these businesses continue to face challenges. Aside from the traditional problem of limited capital resources many challenges have ensued from the economic, social, and political changes in our society today. As long as the current political and economic climates persist, leading to a negative impact on the economies of minority population, institutions of higher learning, particularly HBCUs, have a unique opportunity to be the catalyst of change in the development and promotion of minority businesses.

The leadership role historically Black colleges and universities (HBCUs) have played and continue to play in the overall growth and development of minorities in general and African Americans in particular has never been in question. What is not clear is whether these institutions can also serve as necessary incubators and as agents of change for laying a firm foundation in the development of minority businesses. This article focuses on the challenges and problems plaguing minority businesses in today's economy, and some possible solutions to the identified problems are explored.

Recent trade developments across the globe and growth opportunities for minority-owned businesses suggest the potential role HBCUs can play in bringing about a positive change to the development of minority businesses

(Boston, 1995). A minority business is a business enterprise that is owned and operated by one or more socially or economically disadvantaged persons, where such disadvantage arises from cultural, racial, or severe economic circumstances.

The persistent resentment from the majority population of the society toward affirmative action and other ancillary government programs in recent years and the wave of workforce downsizing in both government and private industries have increasingly forced minorities to espouse the concept of entrepreneurship: hence, a rapid growth in the creation of minority businesses. In fact, current U.S. Census Bureau's estimates show that minority businesses show one of the fastest growth rates in the overall U.S. economy. As long as the current political and economic climates leading to a negative impact on the economies of minority population persist, institutions of higher learning, particularly HBCUs, have a unique opportunity to be the catalyst of change in the development and promotion of minority businesses.

PROBLEMS FACING MINORITY BUSINESSES

According to the U.S. Census Bureau's 1992 survey of minority-owned enterprises, there was a significant increase in the number of business start-ups as well as in sales revenues. Although the state of minority businesses was much better than what was reported by the U.S. Census Bureau, these businesses continue to face challenges (Butler, 1995/1996; Allen, 1990). Aside from the traditional problem of limited capital resources, many challenges have ensued from the economic, social, and political changes in our society today.

LIMITED ACCESS TO CAPITAL

A limited access to capital is still a major challenge despite loan programs such as Small Administration's 7(a) Guaranteed Business Loan Program. It has been reported that minority businesses received a significantly small portion of the loans awarded each year to small businesses; and this significantly small portion decreases every year. According to Beech (1997), "Some black business owners say persistent loan discrimination is making fair access to capital difficult." In addition, the volume of paperwork required to obtain the 7(a) loan has discouraged many minority business owners from applying for this loan, although some attempts have been made to reduce the application paperwork required through the "LowDoc" Program. The shortage of capital seems to be one of the critical problems that minority businesses face.

RESENTMENT TOWARD AFFIRMATIVE ACTION PROGRAMS

The persistent resentment from the society toward affirmative action programs has exacerbated the difficulty of minority businesses in getting government contracts. For example, the California's Proposition 209, the California Civil Rights Initiative, prohibits consideration of race, gender, or ethnicity in all areas of the state's system of public contracting, employment, and education. In addition, the effect of *Adarand Construction v. Pena* case restricted the use of race as a consideration in awarding federal contracts. The anti-affirmative action sentiments also led to the proposal to revise the Small Business Administration's 8(a) program, a program designed to promote fair competition among small firms or organizations. These anti-affirmative action policies have set the clock back for minority businesses, which have always been competitively disadvantaged. The erosion of minority set-aside program has created the need for minority entrepreneurs to formulate new strategies for doing business today. The wave of business mergers among majority businesses (the top *Fortune* 500 companies) has made it difficult for minority businesses to compete for profitable business.

CHALLENGES OF TECHNOLOGY

Technology is yet another challenge that minority businesses face in today's economy. The use of technology in minority businesses is minimal. Minority business owners or their employees either lack the technological knowledge and skills or they cannot afford the cost of technology. Access to market and business information is now available and fairly inexpensive. The type of information necessary in the operation of a business can be readily accessed via the Internet or through the use of computer technology. Accounting functions can be performed by using the available inexpensive computer software. However, minority businesses often do not capitalize on these resources; hence, high operating costs put them out of competition. Another challenge in this area is the fact that technology changes at such a rapid pace that it is impossible for minority businesses to keep up with the changes. Minority businesses just do not have adequate financial and, often-times, human resources to keep up with technology. In the face of a budget crunch, staff training becomes a low priority.

LACK OF PLANNING AND FORESIGHT

Inadequate preparation on the part of the business owners has caused many businesses to fail. Most business owners start their businesses having only the skill required to operate the business but fail to prepare for the other crucial factors necessary to run the business. They often do not have a business plan or financial projection; are not cognizant of the legal, environmental, or social requirements as well as government regulations that relate to the business; and most important, have no provision for appropriate bookkeeping and accounting functions. Beech (1997) reported that Frank R. Gittens, a business financial consultant at Arizona's Bank One, observed that "African-American business owners call daily, but they really don't have a clue as to how much money they want to borrow. They don't have a business plan or financial projections." Furthermore, minority businesses fall victim to IRS and other tax agencies' scrutiny due to lack of adequate documentation, so that in most cases, businesses are forced to liquidate. If business owners are aware of related legal, environmental, or social requirements at the start of the business, they usually can make adequate provisions to comply with these requirements. Sadly, most failed businesses learned the harsh lessons of the costly devastation of ignorance too late.

The main focus of this article is to explore the possible roles of the HBCUs in bringing about solutions rather than to catalog the problems facing minority enterprises; however, we agree with Smith and Moore (1985) that the rate of growth and development of minority enterprises is severely constrained as a result of the concentration of these businesses' market environments that are relatively unstable. Consequently, the businesses face a potential for low growth and its attendant low profitability. Any attempt to reverse the misfortunes for the businesses would require a well-structured approach at the local and regional levels to assist minority entrepreneurs to penetrate high-growth and/or high-profit-oriented industries.

POTENTIAL SOLUTIONS TO THE PROBLEMS OF MINORITY BUSINESSES

There are some possible solutions to combating the challenges facing minority businesses today. First and foremost, minority business owners have to develop strategies for obtaining clients or customers and maintaining them. In the wake of the anti-affirmative action programs, Rooselvet Roby of California-based Reese Network commented, "We have to get off our feet and stop begging for equal opportunity. We just need to lick our wounds, move on and stop asking for special treatment" (Reynolds, 1996). This is the harsh reality of the society in which we live today. As the economic, social, and political climates change at will, the business communities will have to adapt to the changes. Minority business owners cannot expect business to continue as usual. Some of the strategies that minority business owners should consider and possibly embrace are discussed below.

FORMAL BUSINESS KNOWLEDGE

The business owner must be well prepared to face all challenges prior to starting the business. He or she must learn the fundamentals of the business. What this means is that the business owner must be knowledgeable of the social, legal, environmental, and political aspects of the business. There must be a business plan and financial projections that will serve as a guide to operating the business. Identify the potential clients/customers so that the business can focus available resources effectively (Booth et al., 1995; Padgett, 1995; Smith, 1996).

PARTNERING

Minority business owners should explore the idea of partnering. Partnering is a means whereby a minority business enters into a partnership relationship with a majority business. This type of relationship allows the minority business to learn about the operation and needs of the majority business. The goal of the minority business is to look for an opportunity to supply the majority business with its products or services. This relationship gives the majority business the opportunity to support a minority business as well. The minority business benefits tremendously as it avoids fierce competition from other minority and majority businesses.

COOPERATIVE EFFORT BETWEEN HBCUs AND MINORITY BUSINESS OWNERS

Minority businesses should enter into cooperative activities with institutions of higher learning for supply of training and research activities, assistance from business development centers on campuses, supply of human resources through internships, and technological resource and training. Most institutions of higher learning have developed the resources

to promote entrepreneurship in their communities (Anonymous, 1997b). Minority businesses can collaborate with these institutions in solving most of the challenges mentioned above.

MATCHMAKING

The concept of matchmaking is yet another method that can be used to benefit minority businesses. The idea of matchmaking is to increase opportunities for minority businesses to participate in the free enterprise system through the formation, development, and preservation of competitive minority-owned firms (Richardson, 1995). One of the benefits of the Commerce Department's Minority Business Development Agency is its matchmaking activities. Paul R. Weber IV of the Commerce Department's Minority Business Development Agency (MBDA) stated that the agency maintains a database of minority firms and their capabilities, which is used to broker a lot of relationships between those companies and major *Fortune* 1,000 firms that have a need for their product or services (Beech, 1997). In addition, MBDA entered into an agreement with the Commerce Department's International Trade Administration (ITA) to assist U.S. minority-owned companies to overcome exporting hurdles and compete in an international marketplace.

NETWORKING

Last, networking or peer-to-peer networking provides a mechanism for minority businesses to access opportunities beyond the Black community (Beech, 1997). Networking enhances business capability of minority businesses through support and motivation; examples and role models; expert opinion and counseling; and access to opportunities, information, and resources (Gnyawali et al., 1994). Minority businesses should become members of different relevant associations, clubs, and trade fairs.

ROLE OF HBCUS IN GROOMING MINORITY BUSINESSES

In a treatise, Ayadi (1994) proposed a working relationship between the HBCUs and minority enterprises. Such a relationship would benefit both parties given that HBCUs would be more receptive to and understand the problems facing the fledgling minority businesses. Similar calls have been made by other researchers, especially Heyliger (1992); Murphy (1992); Anonymous, 1997a; Barthelemy, 1984; and Buss (1997). The thesis of this article is to examine five different ways through which HBCUs can be used as catalysts for grooming small business with the utmost objective of fulfilling their service obligations to their community. These five initiatives are examined in the following subsections.

ENTREPRENEURSHIP EDUCATION AND CURRICULUM DEVELOPMENT

The literature is not quite categorical about the relationship between educational achievement and success in entrepreneurial venture. However, Bates (1989) remarked that "highly educated owners employing larger financial capital inputs are more likely to create viable, lasting firms than poorly educated cohorts whose financial capital inputs are less bountiful." He argued that among other demographic traits, a potential entrepreneur's level of education is a major determinant of the loan amounts that commercial lenders extend to small business formations.

According to Gorman, Hanlon, and King (1997), personal characteristics do influence a person's inclination toward entrepreneurship. The personal characteristics that can be influenced through a formal program of education include values and attitudes, personal goals, creativity, propensity to take risks, and locus of control. According to Bandura (1986), education has the potential of serving a preparatory

function in relation to new venture initiation. The entrepreneurial learning process can be enhanced in an environment with role models with the aim of strengthening personal networks. The role of educational institutions is to establish an enterprise culture in the educational process that would focus on both pre-start-up and post-start-up management skills. As Knight (1987) articulated, an appropriate framework and methodology for teaching entrepreneurship should incorporate opportunity identification, strategy development, resource acquisition, and implementation.

To foster entrepreneurial growth and development, HBCUs should get out of the traditional method and focus of instruction that assumes that business schools' graduates are prepared to take positions in a large corporation. According to Heyliger (1992), the traditional approach superimposes the functional areas of business on a liberal arts background with the hope that graduates with a broad management education will be able to adapt within a large organizational setup even as the setup adapts to its changing environment. He proposed a dualistic curriculum that has a potential of being cost-effective by linking minority entrepreneurs and students. According to Heyliger, a well-structured program will include hands-on experience in all kinds of businesses but especially budding small businesses. In a recent interview conducted by Black Enterprise, the interviewees (selected HBCU business deans) emphasized the importance of quality business education that emphasizes entrepreneurship. This proposal has the potential of giving students the skills and options to work for a large corporation, work for a small to medium-size firm, or become an entrepreneur on graduation.

ENTREPRENEURIAL DEVELOPMENT CENTERS (EDCs)

HBCUs should strive to establish small business development units whose focus would be completely different from that of the existing government agencies. These new small business centers would assist minority entrepreneurs to conceptualize business plans, evaluate business proposals, assist in the preparation of bank loan applications, or explore other sources of financing and help to establish bookkeeping systems.

In addition to the services identified, the EDCs should be operated as incubation centers with businesses serving as laboratories. HBCUs' faculty should be fully involved in the operation of these centers as consultants or members of advisory councils for the small businesses. The faculty should be a part of the development and implementation of business plans for minority enterprises. On a periodic basis, minority entrepreneurs should be updated through professional development courses on leadership skills. In this spirit, Matthew (1996) argues for a periodic get-together among minority entrepreneurs for the purpose of brainstorming on issues of common concern. Through this initiative, faculty at HBCUs could build a reservoir of business cases that is appropriate for use in their classrooms.

Many business owners mistakenly consider business plans as instruments for borrowing money from financial institutions. The EDCs should help these businesses to follow their road maps as documented in the business plans. Personnel from the EDCs should meet with the management of emerging firms on a periodic basis with the task of reviewing their business plans in light of environmental changes. The key intention is to encourage these entrepreneurs not to abandon their business plans (Lewis, 1993–1994).

An EDC should be a source of nontraditional loans to budding firms that require operating capital. This can be done through a business capital fund that seeks contributions and grants from governments, businesses, and individuals. As a precondition for obtaining a loan from the business capital fund, an entrepreneur should be required to undergo some specified number of hours of management training.

The involvement of students in the operation of the EDCs should also be considered. They are at a great advantage to observe how real businesses are managed. More important, students' skills could be needed in such areas are market studies, quality control, and bookkeeping, including payroll, data processing, and benefit tracking systems. In addition to this, students can secure internship opportunities in these emerging businesses. Murphy (1992) noted that businesses often reap the benefits of special projects and tasks undertaken by interns that are not feasible with the current workforce. Moreover, interns can be used to supplement and complement the existing workforce. An internship program also expands the choices available to students in terms of exploring career fields in different industries. It represents a way students bridge the gap between classroom theories and hands-on experience. The benefits to HBCUs are immeasurable too. An internship program represents an avenue for getting a feedback on the quality of academic programs in terms of curriculum content and the character of their graduates.

MATCHMAKING, NETWORKING AND STRATEGIC ALLIANCES

It has been documented in various related publications that the concept of matchmaking is an emerging technique used today to foster the development and growth of small businesses. The major challenge that business enterprises face is the difficulty in getting bank (financial institution) financing. The other alternative, equity financing, has also proven to be a challenge as well. Brown (1994b) stated that an increasing number of fledgling companies are looking for viable sources of equity, but investors are hard to find. The matchmaking efforts have been focused on financing, that is, making the exercise of finding capital for business ventures a little less painful. The idea of matchmaking focuses on linking businesses up with investors where the goals, objectives, and strategies of the business entities match those of the investors. Although the matchmaking concept has a great potential for success in finding capital, it has even more potential for success in promoting business expansion and growth. Who are these matchmakers? Brown (1994a) identified a handful of business groups and universities as matchmakers that have engaged in the matchmaking process by maintaining computer networks used to match entrepreneurs with private and institutional investors. Brown (1994a) reported Massachusetts Institute of Technology as an institution of higher learning that is a matchmaker.

In light of the potential services that can be provided through matchmaking, it is undoubtedly clear that the HBCUs can play a major role in fostering minority business ventures by taking up the role of a matchmaker. HBCUs can obtain important information such as business plan and objectives, financial projections, products sold and/or services rendered, significant strategies, and any other pertinent information from businesses (majority and minority) and investors to create a database for networking. If the HBCUs can develop and maintain such a database of information, they can become a central source of business assistance to minority businesses. Using the database, HBCUs will be able to link potential investors with businesses that are in need of capital where the profiles of both parties are compatible. Businesses are introduced to potential

investors based on specified criteria maintained in the database, and vice versa. As the matchmaking efforts are successful, minority businesses are relieved of the traditional problem of capital shortage. Several business organizations and governmental agencies are promoting matchmaking efforts. Scott and Brown (1995) have strongly argued in favor of minority businesses' access to the international market. HBCUs should play a role in promoting minority businesses by matching them with compatible international business organizations. The U.S. Commerce Department's MBDA and ITA collaboration is an attempt to assist minority-owned businesses to overcome the problems associated with product exportation to the international marketplace so that they can compete internationally. Such efforts led to a group of business leaders participating in a recent Minority Business Trade and Matchmaker Trade Delegation to Port-au-Prince and Cap Haitien, Haiti (Richardson, 1995).

Through matchmaking, HBCUs can provide networking opportunity, thereby solving another problem that plagues minority businesses. Typically, majority business owners network through membership in social clubs and attendance at social events of the various social organizations, such as country club and golf course activities. At these various events, majority business owners have the opportunity to share business ideas and solicit business relationships. This type of networking has not been, for the most part, a viable option for minority business owners. Hence, the matchmaking concept will serve to provide a means of networking for minority business.

Furthermore, HBCUs can use the information in the database to match a minority enterprise with a majority enterprise where both entities complement each other. This effort can result in the majority entity becoming a customer of the minority business, thereby creating a customer-vendor relationship. These matchmaking efforts are occurring on a local level as well. This is a great time for the institutions of higher learning to play a great part.

The initial capital outlay of the matchmaking effort can be funded through private and public donations, and services fees can be charged to maintain the program. The effort will benefit all parties involved. The minority business will have the convenience of obtaining, at a relatively low cost, pertinent information from a central clearinghouse that is otherwise impossible. Furthermore, minority business entities can avoid the bureaucratic problems and difficulties of obtaining funds through the Small Business Administration 7(a) loan program and the financial institutions. The majority businesses benefit from the effort in the sense that they have the opportunity to participate in the progress of minority business endeavors while their business needs are met by their minority counterpart. On a more important note, majority business entities derive social benefits because the matchmaking effort presents them with the opportunity to improve and maintain positive public image (public relation) and broaden their customer/client bases. The HBCUs benefit as they are perceived as a major force in the promotion of business ventures, particularly those of the minority business entities.

TECHNOLOGY

An important area where HBCUs can contribute to the growth and development of minority businesses is technology. To the extent that in this day and age, known as the information age, the computer and, indeed, information technology (IT) have become the lifeblood and the driving force of most successful businesses, the same is expected to hold true for minority businesses. The unique role HBCUs can play in the development and sustenance of minority businesses through technology assumes dramatic proportions

given that the success of any modern business is inextricably joined to how well technology is applied.

A strategy through which technology-related assistance could be provided to existing and emerging minority businesses is education. The profound, permanent, and pervasive nature of IT and its penetrating impact on modern business demands that business people be information literate. It is therefore imperative that at the most basic level, every minority business owner/entrepreneur should be aware, knowledgeable of, and able to interact effectively with the computer. Education on how to interact with the computer to apply productivity tools in the five major need areas of business—that is, word processing, spreadsheets, database processing, graphics, and electronic communication (e-mail and the Internet)—can be the very first step in the right direction for HBCUs and minority businesses collaboration. Short-term seminars, refresher courses, and hands-on tutorials may be potential candidates for implementing the education initiative, considering the fact these strategies have proven valuable in other situations (Marchand & Horton, 1986; Synnot, 1987).

Beyond being information literate, it is important for minority business leaders to recognize and internalize the philosophy that information now ranks as one of the fundamental cornerstones of a modern business. Like man, money, and market, information should be given the serious attention it deserves. HBCUs' responsibility to minority businesses should, among others, include the provision of necessary education to enable minority entrepreneurs to rethink their businesses in the new information economy. Having understood the real issues surrounding strategic use of information and its associated technologies, minority-business owners should therefore be able to embrace the imperatives of the information economy requiring that (a) information should be treated as a strategic asset and (b) information management should be tied to strategic business planning.

The emerging National Information Infrastructure (NII) or information highway is giving increased access to a vast selection of goods and services. As these electronic markets unfold and as many more businesses become members of the online community at an unprecedented rate, minority businesses cannot afford not to join the bandwagon. HBCUs can play a major role by initiating and nurturing the necessary and desired culture shift expected of minority businesses. The presence of minority businesses on the World Wide Web and the Internet can be made possible by the Web-authoring expertise waiting to be tapped on HBCU campuses.

It is common knowledge that the emergence of the NII offers dramatic new business opportunities as well as new ways to run existing minority businesses. For example, electronic transactions are now commonplace in the business and government environments in the industrialized world. In the United States alone, greater than 60% of all companies are exchanging data electronically while engaging in accounting, controlling, production management, funds transfer, record-keeping, purchasing, and selling activities. Consumers also use various information technologies to browse through electronic catalogs and thereafter to transact business. Again, HBCUs can provide what it takes in terms of education and technical support for minority businesses to become active participants in electronic commerce. There are other avenues where HBCUs technical assistance and support can be invaluable. HBCUs can serve as consultants providing a myriad of services, ranging from technology purchase guidance to troubleshooting.

GLOBALIZATION

Business Week recently conducted a study of midsize U.S. firms to identify the characteris-

tics these businesses adhere to in their successful internationalization programs. Some of these characteristics are maintaining lean headquarters, getting into partnerships, employing foreigners to manage offshore operations with the hope of bringing these managers into senior positions at home, and being customer focused by designing products that meet the expectations of customers. HBCUs have a niche in this area when it comes to helping minority businesses. Through their capability to conduct effective market research, HBCUs can match foreign business operators with compatible minority entrepreneurs at home. Furthermore, the research efforts of HBCUs can be used to identify market characteristics and business culture in several foreign countries to the advantage of emerging minority operations in the United States. This approach has been successfully used at Kennesaw State University (Torkornoo, 1997).

CONCLUSION

The 1992 U.S. Census Bureau's *Survey of Minority-Owned Enterprises* reported a significant increase in the number of business start-ups as well as in sales revenues. Although the state of minority businesses was much better than was reported, these businesses continue to face challenges. Aside from the traditional problem of limited capital resources, many challenges have ensued from the economic, social, and political changes in our society today. As long as the current political and economic climates persist, leading to a negative impact on the economies of minority population, institutions of higher learning, particularly HBCUs, have a unique opportunity to be the catalyst of change in the development and promotion of minority businesses. The attempt in this article has been to make a wake-up call to HBCUs to respond to the plight of minority business owners while also fulfilling their role of educating students.

Five strategic approaches are proposed in this article. They include the revamping of the traditional business curriculum to accommodate students who would graduate to become entrepreneurs, the use of networking and match-making, the establishment of effective entrepreneurial development centers, the use of technology, and helping minority businesses implement their internationalization programs. It is hoped that a careful implementation of these initiatives would yield good fruits for both HBCUs and these budding minority enterprises.

AUTHOR'S NOTE

An earlier version of this article was presented at the 1998 Annual Conference of the National Association of African American Studies in Houston, Texas, February 10–14, 1998. The authors would like to thank those participants who gave us some useful comments.

REFERENCES

Allen, J. E. (1990, October). The Growth and Diversification of Black businesses. *Focus,* pp. 5–7.

Anonymous. (1997a). Preparing Future Business Leaders Today. *Black Enterprise,* 27(7), 92.

Anonymous. (19976). There is Opportunity and there Is Action. *Fortune,* 136(3), 67.

Ayadi, O. F. (1994). The Role of Historically Black Colleges and Universities in a Renewed Black Capitalism. *Business and Economic Review,* 8(1), 1–19.

Bandura, A. & Cervone, D. (1986). Differential Engagement of Self-reactive Influences in Cognitive Motivation. *Organizational Behavior and Human Decision Processes,* 38(1), 92–114.

Barthelemy, S. J. (1984). The Role of Black Colleges in Nurturing Leadership. In A. Garibaldi (Ed.), *Black Colleges and Universities: Challenges for the Future.* New York: Praeger.

Bates, T. (1989, Fall). The Changing Nature of Minority Business: A Comparative Analysis of Asian,

Nonminority, and Black-owned Businesses. *Review of Black Political Economy,* pp. 25–42.

Beech, W. M., (1997). The State of Small Black Business. *Black Enterprise,* 28(4), 65.

Booth, R., Corriher, S. E., & Geurin, V. S. (1995). The Head Rules the Heart in Business Education. *S.A.M. Advanced Management Journal,* 60(3), 40.

Boston, T. D. (1995). Characteristics of Black-owned Corporations in Atlanta: With Comments on the SMOBE Undercount. *Review of Black Political Economy,* 23(4), 85–99.

Brown, C. M. (1994x). Computer-driven Financing. *Black Enterprise,* 24(11), 50.

Brown, C. M. (19946). Match-making for Venture Capital. *Black Enterprise,* 24(11), 48.

Buss, D. D. (1997). Taking Care of Local Business. *Nation's Business,* 85(7), 42.

Butler, J. S. (1995/1996). Entrepreneurship and the Advantages of the Inner City: How to Augment the Porter Thesis. *Review of Black Political Economy,* 24(2/3), 39–49.

Gnyawali, D. R., & Fogel, D. S. (1994). Environments for Entrepreneurship Development: Key Dimension. *Black Enterprise,* 18(4), 43.

Gorman, G., Hanlon, D., & King, W. (1997). Some Research Perspectives on Entrepreneurship Education, Enterprise Education and Education of Small Business Management: A Ten-year Literature Review. *International Small Business Journal,* 15(3), 56–77.

Heyliger, W. E. (1992, June 18–20). *Dualistic Management Programs: A Strategy for Local Economic Development.* Proceedings of the National Economic Summit Conference hosted by NISME, Oklahoma City, OK.

Knight, R. M. (1987). Corporate Innovation and Entrepreneurship: A Canadian Study. *The Journal of Product Innovation Management,* 4(4), 284–298.

Lewis, J. (1993–1994). Six Basic Principles for Successfully Expanding Your Business; Principles #1–#6. *Minorities and Women in Business,* 9(2)–10(1).

Marchand, D. A., & Horton, F. W. (1986). *INFOTRENDS: Profiting from Your Information Resources.* New York: John Wiley.

Matthew, S. (1996). An Annual Summit for Black Entrepreneurs. *Black Enterprise,* 27(4), 69.

Murphy, M. C. (1992, June 18–20). *HBCUs, Minority Business and Internships.* Proceedings of the National Economic Summit Conference hosted by NISME, Oklahoma City, OK.

Padgett, T (1995). Venturing into Business. *Black Enterprise, 25*(9), 38.

Reynolds, R. (1996). Creating a New Business Agenda. *Black Enterprise, 26*(6), 76.

Richardson, L. L. (1995). Minority Business Development Agency Hhelps Minority-owned Firms Overcome Export Hurdles and Compete in the Iinternational Mmarketplace. *Business America, 116*(9), 25.

Scott, M. S., & Brown, C. M. (1995). The State of Black Business. *Black Enterprise, 26*(4), 74.

Smith, E. L. (1996). Is Black Business Paving the Way? *Black Enterprise, 26*(11), 194.

Smith, W A., & Moore, J. V. (1985). East-West Differences in Black Economic Development. *Journal of Black Studies, 76,* 131–154.

Synnot, W. R.(1987). *The Information Weapon, Winning Customers and Markets with Technology.* New York: John Wiley.

Torkomoo, H. K. (1997, November 21–23). *Internationalizing Small and Medium Size Businesses: A Model of University/Business Project.* Proceedings of the 1997 Annual Conference of the Association for Global Business, Washington, DC.

U.S. Census Bureau. (1992). *Survey of Minority-owned Enterprises.* Washington, DC: Author.

Arinola O. Adebayo is a Certified Public Accountant. She earned a B.S. in Accounting from Arkansas State University and an M.B.A. from Radford University. Ms. Adebayo, a KPMG Scholar, is currently pursuing a PhD in Accounting with a minor in Information Systems at Virginia Commonwealth University. Ms. Adebayo has taught Accounting for over ten years. Her areas of teaching are Managerial Accounting and Auditing.

Adeyemi A. Adekoya is an associate professor of information systems, at Virginia State University. Petersburg, VA. He received his Ph.D. in information systems from Syracuse University, Syracuse, NY His research interests include system design and implementation methodologies, as well as technology transfer and capacity building.

O. Felix Ayadi is a professor of finance at Texas Southern University, Houston, TX. He received his Ph. D. in finance from The University of Mississippi, Oxford, MS. His research interests include international finance, market efficiency issues, small business finance and pedagogy issues. He has published over forty refereed articles.

Media Meltdown: With Urban Marketing So Hot, Black-owned Ad Agencies Are Prime Targets for Acquisitions and Mergers

Cassandra Hayes

In the 1970s they were brand-new, in the '80s they were novel, by the '90s they had forged a niche and come into their own. Now, in 2000, they're being snatched up like gold: they're America's black-owned advertising agencies.

"There's no 'irrational exuberance' to be found among those aggressively pursuing African American ad agencies and the consumers they represent'; says Ken Smikle, president of Chicago-based Target Market News, a marketing research firm that tracks the trends of black consumers, in quoting Federal Reserve Chairman Alan Greenspan. "The trends of 1998 have continued, and the landscape, while it hasn't grown much in acreage, has certainly gotten a lot greener."

Like a Siren at sea, the urban market lured marketers with the thumping sound and in-your-face attitude of hip-hop culture. This phenomenon changed the face of mainstream advertising, having a major influence not only on the youth market but also on society as a whole. General-market agencies now sought to capture this business by aligning with black-owned agencies with their fingers on this pulse. And last year proved to be the year of the alliance, with the top three African American-owned agencies talking merger with the behemoth general-market firms. Two of them actually aligned.

Overall, business was good for the industry. Chalk that up to a bullish economy that continues to foster an increase in all advertising, especially on the Internet. Total U.S. advertising revenues for 1999 were $215.2 billion, according to Robert J. Coen, senior vice president and forecasting director at Universal McCann in New York, the media arm of McCann-Erickson Worldwide—a 6.8% increase over 1998's $201.6 billion. Of that, $1.1 billion was targeted to the African American market, with some 30% pocketed by black-owned ad agencies, according to Target Market News. Last year, billings of the 20 black-owned ad agencies on the **BE ADVERTISING AGENCIES** list increased 21.3% from 1998.

"It was a spectacular year for both general-market and multicultural agencies, and great work correlates with great years," notes Michael Donahue, executive vice president of member services at the American Association of Advertising Agencies (AAAA) in New York. "Contributing to that growth is the fact that the total dotcom business was so large that it had an impact on the revenue stream of any agency doing dotcom business."

A RUSH FOR BLACK GOLD

There's no mistaking it. In the past, black-owned agencies faced the problem of convincing major advertisers to take the ethnic market seriously. No longer is this the case. With the multibillion-dollar urban market so hard to ignore, mainstream advertising agencies and marketers alike can't harvest the talent and resources required to capitalize on it fast enough. Fashioning their own boutique agencies—specialized smaller agencies within an agency—they still foundered as they tried to keep pace with the market's volume, demand and nuances. Finally, the big boys decided that they needed more than input from the agencies; they needed the agencies themselves.

"Clients realized that there was great opportunity in this market and didn't want to lose the profitability [so they opted to] extend the reach of their marketing dollars," says Greg Head, president of HeadFirst Market Research in Stone Mountain, Georgia. General-market agencies were then challenged to market to this audience, partner with an African American agency or lose this business altogether.

Hence, in 1998, smaller, urban market-focused agencies such as New York's Spike/DDB, headed by movie director Spike Lee, Vigilante and Chicago's Stedman Graham & Partners were formed under the leadership of advertising giants DDB Needham, Leo Burnett and True North Communications, respectively. Not to be outdone, the old guard began making deals of their own.

"I find it interesting that many people in the industry attacked my integrity, calling me a setup guy and saying that the white conglomerate was exploiting me, and that now everyone is collaborating with them," says Lee, president of Spike/DDB (No. 16 on the BE ADVERTISING AGENCIES list, with billings of $9.8 million). Spike/DDB lists the clothing maker Ecko, State Farm Insurance, ABC Television and Jaguar automobiles among its clients.

The first African American agency to bail was Chicago-based Burrell Communications Group (No. 3 on the BE ADVERTISING AGENCIES list with billings of $175.2 millions), whose clients include Coca-Cola, Kellogg, McDonald's, Exxon Mobil, Procter & Gamble and Sears, Roebuck. Last June, Burrell sold a 49% share of its business to the giant French agency Publicis.

Following suit, Southfield, Michigan-based Don Coleman Advertising (DCA) (No. 2 on the BE ADVERTISING AGENCIES list, with $202 million in billings), joined forces with True North Communications Inc. in September. Under the deal, Don Coleman, president of DCA, became CEO and chairman of True North's multicultural marketing division—New American Strategies Group—which also includes ethnic agency Stedman Graham & Partners.

If nothing else, these alliances certainly haven't hurt business. In March, after an extensive, nationwide agency review, the nation's No. 2 commercial air carrier, American Airlines, gave DCA its much-coveted African American business. This made DCA the first African American agency of record for a major airline. With Timerlin McClain—a True North entity—as the airline's general-marketing agency, the alliance has the makings of every mainstream agency's dream: nesting almost all of a client's business under one roof.

Industry insiders say the merger, while good for Coleman, may have sparked the unexpected exit of former DCA partner, executive vice president and ethnic marketing guru Chuck Morrison, who left for UniWorld in January.

The access to resources was also the primary impetus behind the Burrell merger. "The partnership with Publicis offers us several advantages—access to human, financial, and technology resources," says CEO Thomas Burrell. "We are now able to offer clients a broader range of rnarketing communication services.

"Of the partnering choices we had Publicis made the most sense. First, the personal chemistry was great. We shared a common vision for the future; with Publicis just starting to mount a major expansion into the U.S. market, we were able to play a more major role in that development than would be provided by the more 'overcrowded' alternatives.

"Lastly, we were conflict free. As a matter of fact, we already shared a. relationship with the Coca-Cola Co., and have since gained the agency of record assignment of Soft Sheen, a division of Publicis' client, L'Oreal."

Will the tag team effort spell big business for Burrell? Heide Gardner, vice president of diversity and strategic programs at the American Advertising Federation Foundation (AAFF), a national trade organization based in Washington, D.C., predicts high marks, and says, "I expect to see a lot of business from Burrell as it continues to aggressively leverage its relationship with Publicis."

While the terms of these two deals were not disclosed, it is generally believed that agencies can go for 1.5 times their revenue. In Burrell's case, that could amount to $32.7 million, according to *Advertising Age*.

"These mergers are good because they recognize the sweat equity that multicultural agencies have put into the business," says the AAAA's Donahue. Nonetheless, there are still some skeptics. "Despite being minority owned, you certainly cannot deny the fact that the large company is going to influence the culture and take some control out of African American hands," says Gene Morris, president of Chicago-based E. Morris Communications (No. 8 on the BE ADVERTISING AGENCIES list, with billings of $27.1 million), which recently added Ralston Purina to its client list. E. Morris, which also has McDonald's (regional), Wal-mart and Oldsmobile accounts, was scoped out by general-market agencies as well.

PENDING CONFLICTS

Despite the boon for black-owned agencies, a downside hovers: sibling rivalry. "General-market agencies are conglomerates, and there is a threat that conflicts and competition could breed among black agencies under the same corporate umbrella. The question is: will they be seen as separate when they go after business in a category in which their ethnic counterpart already has an account?" warns Smikle, referring to the True North/Coleman/Stedman Graham & Partners marriage. For example, to avoid a conflict of interest, an agency can only have one account in any given category, so if one has a fast-food client, then it can't go after another one. While a strong concern, "these

2000 TOP 20 Black Owned Advertising Agencies	1998	1999	% Change
Number of Employees	779	811	4.11%
Billings*	$886.514	$1075.61	21.33%

*In millions of dollar, to the nearest thousand. As of December 31, 1999. Prepared by B.E. Research. Reviewed by Mitchell & Titus LLP

conflicts are nothing new for the general-market agencies located under one roof that are forced to compete," says Head. "For the holding company it is a way to pitch for all existing soft drink or automobile accounts and, if successful, garnering a larger portion of a category's business in their pocket."

Another thorny issue is the National Minority Supplier Development Council's (NMSDC) move this past February. Under a new guideline, an agency certified as minority controlled can sell up to a 70% ownership stake as long as 51% of voting stock, daily management control and the majority of board seats remain in the hands of minorities.

"To say that 51% of a voting stock will remain with African Americans is not a reality. Why would someone buy 70% of a business and allow it to remain in the hands of 30% of the owners?" notes Morris, who is also chairman of the AAAA. "This will only lead to even more front companies and create an abuse of the system:"

However, adds Gardner, "Advertisers don't want controversy and may want to deal with black-owned agencies where there is a minority interest. This kind of political consideration is definitely going to be a factor. This will be especially true as the federal government looks to open doors for black agencies to compete directly with general-market firms for prime contracts and general-market business."

EVERYBODY GETS TO PLAY

Despite the rumbling at the top, the spoils have not only gone to the larger black agencies. In other deals, Omnicom Group Partners, which has holdings in ad leaders DDB Needham Worldwide and BBDO Worldwide, took a 49% stake in start-up Footsteps, a New York-based black agency. Created in January 2000 with Alvin Gay, a former executive at UniWorld, and Verdia Johnson, formerly with Stedman

Graham & Partners, Footsteps landed Mercedes-Benz as its first and, at press time, only client.

"Marketing has dramatically changed for black advertisers," says Johnson, Footsteps' presiden and a former advertising director at BLACK ENTERPRISE magazine. "In the past, it, wasn't about business. It was about a handout and a way to appease the [minority advertisers] that were calling. Today, it is truly about business. Our account planning is what sets us apart from other black agencies, and African American marketing has not been taken to the extent that we're going to take it" Gay, the agency's managing partner, says that Footsteps will go beyond the traditional consumer barometers of focus groups and surveys, and "talk to people about who they are and what they want to grasp."

Other movers include Russell Simmons of Rush Media, who recently formed a joint venture with West Coast-based Deutsch Inc. to form dRush, an agency that will target urban youth.

SLOW MOVEMENT ON THE WEB

With more than $1.8 billion in Internet advertising in 1999, the field is ripe for ethnic agencies. The Internet promises one-to-one, real-time marketing, but it has yet to really spread its wings. "I see more black agency activity in this area especially with the media mix and a proliferation of Afrocentric dotcoms," says AAFF's Gardner. "However, it is still a challenge to sell to advertisers because of the misconception that black America isn't wired and doesn't have income and education levels that call for dotcom ads."

It's a misconception indeed. In fact, the 4.9 million African Americans surfing the Web are younger, wealthier and more educated than those not currently online, according to a

HOW WE SELECTED THE TOP AGENCIES

We canvassed the *Standard Directory of Advertising Agencies,* combed industry publications and made inquires in the field to compile a list of full-service advertising agencies in the U.S. that are 51% black owned. Surveys were sent to these agencies. Those that responded and met the criteria were placed into our ranking.

To qualify as a full-service advertising agency, the company has to make media placements—that is, purchase time and/or space for its clients' advertising. Companies that only provide consulting services, or only create or produce advertising or only do media placements do not qualify as full-service agencies.

We elected to list only the 20 highest-earning agencies, based on 1999 performance, on the assumption that these firms were most likely to have at least one national account and a minimum of $2 million in billings.

An agency's financial status is measured in terms of billings, monies allocated by an advertiser to its agency to buy time on television and/or radio, or space in publications and other print media. These media outlets then pay a commission back to the agency in the form of a discount in the 15%–22% range, which the agency counts as revenue. Other sources of revenue for an agency include production fees that the agency charges the client to produce the advertising, and fees for adjunct services such as public relations, consulting and promotional work.

Our ranking is based on a combined total of actualized billings plus capitalized billings (where commissions have not yet been paid, but the media buys were completed) and other agency fees reported as revenues, an accepted industry practice for reporting earnings status. In most all cases, this accounts for the differences between *Red Book* figures and agency-reported figures.

recent survey conducted by Cyber Dialogue, a leading Internet customer relationship management company. The survey revealed that nearly half were under age 30, with an average income of $58,000; more than one-third have graduated from college.

"The last three clients who've walked through my door have been dotcom companies," says Charlotte Roy, president of Atlanta-based Roy Communications, which, in March, merged with the Hispanic agency Vargas Flores & Amigos of Atlanta. "Over the years, clients have asked if I could handle the Hispanic market and I never felt comfortable saying yes. I worked with Dan Vargas and Tony Flores for years, and the union just made sense," recalls Roy, whose client list includes Procter & Gamble, Johnson & Johnson and General Mills.

"Dotcom companies want us to help them bring business to their sites, not only through the Web but with traditional media to drive the bulk of the traffic," she adds. The alliance also includes a partnership with Chicago-based Pinnacle Associates Group, headed by Suzanne Fuller, which offers marketing and community-relations expertise. The new company will adopt the Pinnacle name.

GOING IT ALONE

Of the top five, UniWorld, Oakland, California-based Carol H. Williams Advertising (CHWA) (No. 6 on the BE ADVERTISING AGENCIES list) and The Chisholm-Mingo Group Inc. (No. 4 on the BE ADVERTISING AGENCIES list, with billings of more than $100.5 million) of New York are still holding their own, for now absent a deep-pocketed, big brother general-market agency. UniWorld, which boasts AT&T, Burger King and Ford among its clients, had a great year, with billings jumping from $160.4 million in 1998 to $230 million in 1999, putting it in the No. 1 spot on the BE ADVERTISING AGENCIES list.

CHWA, BE's 1999 Advertising Agency of the Year, had a gangbuster year with $61 million in billings, superlative creative for established clients such as Coors and Nissan, and by nabbing new accounts with Silicon Graphics, San Francisco International Airport, Census 2000 and BP Amoco—formerly a Vince Cullers Advertising account (Cullers is No. 15 on the BE ADVERTISING AGENCIES list, with billings of $10 million). Adds Williams, "This niche was created to give African American agencies an opportunity to share in the revenues of this industry and compete without consistently being knocked out by the long arm of big mass-marketing agencies. These acquisitions and alliances are creating a highly different environment, where media-impacted dollars are used to purchase relationships that cannot be forged by agencies like mine. It definitely makes it more difficult."

As the alliance virus continues to spread throughout the industry, the question still lurks: is it opportunistic to remain independent? "If your creative is great and a client sees your dedication to the business, then an agency can stand alone," says Lee. However, Williams, who, in speaking for herself may also express the sentiments of many other minority agencies, says, "Only if you're a real warrior with true grit, [you don't] mind seeing your blood, smelling your sweat and tasting your tears, can you stay."

Part 4:
Government/Politics

Ten Reasons Why Reparations for Slavery Is a Bad Idea for Blacks— and Racists Too

David Horowitz

ONE—THERE IS NO SINGLE GROUP CLEARLY RESPONSIBLE FOR THE CRIME OF SLAVERY: Black Africans and Arabs were responsible for enslaving the ancestors of African-Americans. There were 3,000 black slave-owners in the ante-bellum United States. Are reparations to be paid by their descendants too?

TWO—THERE IS NO ONE GROUP THAT BENEFITED EXCLUSIVELY FROM ITS FRUITS: The claim for reparations is premised on the false assumption that only whites have benefited from slavery. If slave labor created wealth for Americans, then obviously it has created wealth for black Americans as well, including the descendants of slaves. The GNP of black America is so large that it makes the African-American community the 10th most prosperous "nation" in the world. American blacks on average enjoy per capita incomes in the range of twenty to fifty times that of blacks living in any of the African nations from which they were kidnapped.

THREE—ONLY A TINY MINORITY OF WHITE AMERICANS EVER OWNED SLAVES, AND OTHERS GAVE THEIR LIVES TO FREE THEM: Only a tiny minority of Americans ever owned slaves. This is true even for those who lived in the ante-bellum South where only one white in five was a slaveholder. Why should their descendants owe a debt? What about the descendants of the 350,000 Union soldiers who died to free the slaves? They gave their lives. What possible moral principle would ask them to pay (through their descendants) again?

FOUR—AMERICA TODAY IS A MULTI-ETHNIC NATION AND MOST AMERICANS HAVE NO CONNECTION (DIRECT OR INDIRECT) TO SLAVERY: The two great waves of American immigration occurred after 1880 and then after 1960. What rationale would require Vietnamese boat people, Russian refuseniks, Iranian refugees, and Armenian victims of the Turkish persecution, Jews, Mexicans Greeks, or Polish, Hungarian, Cambodian and Korean victims of Communism, to pay reparations to American blacks?

FIVE—THE HISTORICAL PRECEDENTS USED TO JUSTIFY THE REPARATIONS CLAIM DO NOT APPLY, AND THE CLAIM ITSELF IS BASED ON RACE NOT INJURY: The historical precedents generally invoked to justify the reparations claim are payments to Jewish survivors of the Holocaust, Japanese-Americans and African-American victims of racial experiments in Tuskegee, or racial outrages in Rosewood and Oklahoma City. But in each case, the recipients of reparations were the direct victims of the injustice or their immediate families. This would be the only case of reparations to people who were not immediately affected and whose sole qualification to receive reparations would be racial. As has already been pointed out, during the slavery era, many blacks were free men or slave-owners themselves, yet the reparations claimants make no distinction between the roles blacks actually played in the injustice itself. Randall Robinson's book on reparations, The Debt, which is the manifesto of the reparations movement is pointedly sub-titled "What America Owes to Blacks." If this is not racism, what is?

SIX—THE REPARATIONS ARGUMENT IS BASED ON THE UNFOUNDED CLAIM THAT ALL AFRICAN-AMERICAN DESCENDANTS OF SLAVES SUFFER FROM THE ECONOMIC CONSEQUENCES OF SLAVERY AND DISCRIMINATION: No evidence-based attempt has been made to prove that living individuals have been adversely affected by a slave system that was ended over 150 years ago. But there is plenty of evidence the hardships that occurred were hardships that individuals could and did overcome. The black middle-class in America is a prosperous community that is now larger in absolute terms than the black underclass. Does its existence not suggest that economic adversity is the result of failures of individual character rather than the lingering after-effects of racial discrimination and a slave system that ceased to exist well over a century ago? West Indian blacks in America are also descended from slaves but their average incomes are equivalent to the average incomes of whites (and nearly 25% higher than the average incomes of American born blacks). How is it that slavery adversely affected one large group of descendants but not the other? How can government be expected to decide an issue that is so subjective—and yet so critical—to the case?

SEVEN—THE REPARATIONS CLAIM IS ONE MORE ATTEMPT TO TURN AFRICAN-AMERICANS INTO VICTIMS. IT SENDS A DAMAGING MESSAGE TO THE AFRICAN-AMERICAN COMMUNITY: The renewed sense of grievance—which is what the claim for reparations will inevitably create—is neither a constructive nor a helpful message for black leaders to be sending to

their communities and to others. To focus the social passions of African-Americans on what some Americans may have done to their ancestors fifty or a hundred and fifty years ago is to burden them with a crippling sense of victimhood. How are the millions of refugees from tyranny and genocide who are now living in America going to receive these claims, moreover, except as demands for special treatment, an extravagant new handout that is only necessary because some blacks can't seem to locate the ladder of opportunity within reach of others—many less privileged than themselves?

EIGHT—REPARATIONS TO AFRICAN AMERICANS HAVE ALREADY BEEN PAID: Since the passage of the Civil Rights Acts and the advent of the Great Society in 1965, trillions of dollars in transfer payments have been made to African-Americans in the form of welfare benefits and racial preferences (in contracts, job placements and educational admissions)—all under the rationale of redressing historic racial grievances. It is said that reparations are necessary to achieve a healing between African-Americans and other Americans. If trillion dollar restitutions and a wholesale rewriting of American law (in order to accommodate racial preferences) for African-Americans is not enough to achieve a "healing," what will?

NINE—WHAT ABOUT THE DEBT BLACKS OWE TO AMERICA?: Slavery existed for thousands of years before the Atlantic slave trade was born, and in all societies. But in the thousand years of its existence, there never was an anti-slavery movement until white Christians—Englishmen and Americans—created one. If not for the anti-slavery attitudes and military power of white Englishmen and Americans, the slave trade would not have been brought to an end. If not for the sacrifices of white soldiers and a white American president who gave his life to sign the Emancipation Proclamation, blacks in America would still be slaves. If not for the dedication of Americans of all ethnicities and colors to a society based on the principle that all men are created equal, blacks in America would not enjoy the highest standard of living of blacks anywhere in the world, and indeed one of the highest standards of living of any people in the world. They would not enjoy the greatest freedoms and the most thoroughly protected individual rights anywhere. Where is the gratitude of black America and its leaders for those gifts?

TEN—THE REPARATIONS CLAIM IS A SEPARATIST IDEA THAT SETS AFRICAN-AMERICANS AGAINST THE NATION THAT GAVE THEM FREEDOM: Blacks were here before the Mayflower. Who is more American than the descendants of African slaves? For the African-American community to isolate itself even further from America is to embark on a course whose implications are troubling. Yet the African-American community has had a long-running flirtation with separatists, nationalists and the political left, who want African-Americans to be no part of America's social contract. African-Americans should reject this temptation.

For all America's faults, African-Americans have an enormous stake in their country and its heritage. It is this heritage that is really under attack by the reparations movement. The reparations claim is one more assault on America, conducted by racial separatists and the political left. It is an attack not only on white Americans, but on all Americans—especially African-Americans.

America's African-American citizens are the richest and most privileged black people alive—a bounty that is a direct result of the heritage that is under assault. The American idea needs the support of its African-American citizens. But African-Americans also need the support of the American idea. For it is this idea that led to the principles and institutions that have set African-Americans—and all of us—free.

Ten Reasons:
A Response to David Horowitz

Ernest Allen, Jr. and Robert Chrisman

David Horowitz's Article, "Ten Reasons Why Reparations for Slavery is a Bad Idea and Racist Too," recently achieved circulation in a handful of college newspapers throughout the United States as a paid advertisement sponsored by the Center for the Study of Popular Culture. Since then it has appeared in numerous other mainstream publications. While Horowitz's article pretends to address the issues of reparations, it is not about reparations at all. It is, rather, a well-heeled, coordinated attack on Black Americans which is calculated to elicit division and strife. Horowitz reportedly attempted to place his article in some 50 student newspapers at universities and colleges across the country, and was successful in purchasing space in such newspapers at Brown, Duke, Arizona, UC Berkeley UC Davis, University of Chicago, and University of Wisconsin, paying an average of $700 per paper. His campaign has succeeded in fomenting outrage, dissension, and grief wherever it has appeared. Unfortunately, both its supporters and its foes too often have categorized the issue as one centering on "free speech." The sale and purchase of advertising space is not a matter of free speech, however, but involves an exchange of commodities. Professor Lewis Gordon of Brown University put it very well, saying that "what concerned me was that the ad was both hate speech and a solicitation for financial support to develop antiblack ad space. I was concerned that it would embolden white supremacists and antiblack racists." At a March 15 panel held at UC Berkeley, Horowitz also conceded that his paid advertisement did not constitute a free speech issue.

As one examines the text of Horowitz's article, it becomes apparent that it is not a reasoned essay addressed to the topic of reparations: it is, rather, a racist polemic against African-Americans and Africans that is neither responsible nor informed, relying heavily upon sophistry and a Hitlerian "Big Lie" technique. To our knowledge, only one of Horowitz's ten "reasons" has been challenged by a black scholar as to source, accuracy, and validity. It is our intention here to briefly rebut his slanders in order to pave the way for an honest and forthright debate on reparations. In these efforts we focus not just on slavery, but also the legacy of slavery which continues to inform institutional as well as individual behavior in the U.S. to this day. Although we recognize that white America still owes a debt to the descendants of slaves, in addressing Horowitz's distortions of history we do not act as advocates for a specific form of reparations.

1. THERE IS NO SINGLE GROUP CLEARLY RESPONSIBLE FOR THE CRIME OF SLAVERY

Horowitz's first argument, relativist in structure, can only lead to two conclusions: 1) societies are not responsible for their actions and 2) since "everyone" was responsible for slavery, no one was responsible. While diverse groups on different continents certainly participated in the trade, the principal responsibility for internationalization of that trade and the institutionalization of slavery in the so-called New World rests with European and American individuals and institutions. The transatlantic slave trade began with the importation of African slaves into Hispaniola by Spain in the early 1500s. Nationals of France, England, Portugal, and the Netherlands, supported by their respective governments and powerful religious institutions, quickly entered the trade and extracted their pieces of silver as well. By conservative estimates, 14 million enslaved Africans survived the horror of the Middle Passage for the purpose of producing wealth for Europeans and Euro-Americans in the New World.

While there is some evidence of blacks owning slaves for profit purposes—most notably the creole caste in Louisiana—the numbers were small. As historian James Oakes noted, "By 1830 there were some 3,775 free black slaveholders across the South....The evidence is overwhelming that the vast majority of black slaveholders were free men who purchased members of their families or who acted out of benevolence." (Oakes, 47–48.)

2. THERE IS NO SINGLE GROUP THAT BENEFITED EXCLUSIVELY FROM SLAVERY

Horowitz's second point, which is also a relativist one, seeks to dismiss the argument that white Americans benefited as a group from slavery, contending that the material benefits of slavery could not accrue in an exclusive way to a single group. But such sophistry evades the basic issue: who benefited primarily from slavery? Those who were responsible for the institutionalized enslavement of people of African descent also received the primary benefits from such actions. New England slave traders, merchants, bankers, and insurance companies all profited from the slave trade, which required a wide variety of commodities ranging from sails, chandlery, foodstuffs, and guns, to cloth goods and other items for trading purposes. Both prior to and after the American Revolution, slaveholding was a principal path for white upward mobility in the South. The white native-born as well as immigrant groups such as Germans, Scots-Irish, and the like participated. In 1860, cotton was the country's largest single export.

As Eric Williams and C.L.R. James have demonstrated, the free labor provided by slavery was central to the growth of industry in western Europe and the United States; simultaneously, as Walter Rodney has argued, slavery depressed and destabilized the economies of African states. Slaveholders benefited primarily from the institution, of course, and generally in proportion to the number of slaves that they held. But the sharing of the proceeds of slave exploitation spilled across class lines within white communities as well.

As historian John Hope Franklin recently affirmed in a rebuttal to Horowitz's claims:

"All whites and no slaves benefited from American slavery. All blacks had no rights that they could claim as their own. All whites, including the vast majority who had no slaves, were not only encouraged but authorized to exercise dominion over all slaves, thereby adding strength to the system of control.

"If David Horowitz had read James D. DeBow's 'The Interest in Slavery of the Southern Non-slaveholder,' he would not have blundered into the fantasy of claiming that no single group benefited from slavery. Planters did, of course. New York merchants did, of course. Even poor whites benefited from the legal advantage they enjoyed over all blacks as well as from the psychological advantage of having a group beneath them."

The context of the African-American argument for reparations is confined to the practice and consequences of slavery within the United States, from the colonial period on through final abolition and the aftermath, circa 1619–1865. Contrary to Horowitz's assertion, there is no record of institutionalized white enslavement in colonial America. Horowitz is confusing the indenture of white labor, which usually lasted seven years or so during the early colonial period, with enslavement. African slavery was expanded, in fact, to replace the inefficient and unenforceable white indenture system. (Smith)

Seeking to claim that African-Americans, too, have benefited from slavery, Horowitz points to the relative prosperity of African-Americans in comparison to their counterparts on the African continent. However, his argument that, "the GNP of black America makes the African-American community the 10th most prosperous 'nation' in the world" is based upon a false analogy. GNP is defined as "the total market value of all the goods and services produced by a nation during a specified period." Black Americans are not a nation and have no GNP. Horowitz confuses disposable income and "consumer power" with the generation of wealth.

3. ONLY A TINY MINORITY OF WHITE AMERICANS EVER OWNED SLAVES, AND OTHERS GAVE THEIR LIVES TO FREE THEM

Most white Union troops were drafted into the Union army in a war which the federal government initially defined as a "war to preserve the union." In large part because they feared that freed slaves would flee the South and "take their jobs" while they themselves were engaged in warfare with Confederate troops, recently drafted white conscripts in New York City and elsewhere rioted during the summer of 1865, taking a heavy toll on black civilian life and property. Too many instances can be cited where white northern troops plundered the personal property of slaves, appropriating their bedding, chickens, pigs, and foodstuffs as they swept through the South. On the other hand, it is certainly true that there also existed principled white commanders and troops who were committed abolitionists.

However, Horowitz's focus on what he mistakenly considers to be the overriding, benevolent aim of white Union troops in the Civil War obscures the role that blacks themselves played in their own liberation. African-Americans were initially forbidden by the Union to fight in the Civil War, and black leaders such as Frederick Douglass and Martin Delany demanded the right to fight for their freedom. When racist doctrine finally conceded to military necessity, blacks were recruited into the Union Army in 1862 at approximately half the pay of white soldiers—a situation which was partially rectified by an act of Congress in mid-1864. Some 170,000 blacks served in the Civil War, representing nearly one third of the free black population.

By 1860, four million blacks in the U.S. were enslaved; some 500,000 were nominally free. Because of slavery, racist laws, and racist policies, blacks were denied the chance to compete for the opportunities and resources of America that were available to native whites and immigrants: labor opportunities, free enterprise, and land. The promise of "forty acres and a mule" to former slaves was effectively nullified by the actions of President Andrew Johnson. And because the best land offered by the Homestead Act of 1862 and its subsequent revisions quickly fell under the sway of white homesteaders and speculators, most former slaves were unable to take advantage of its provisions.

4. MOST LIVING AMERICANS HAVE NO CONNECTION (DIRECT OR INDIRECT) TO SLAVERY

As Joseph Anderson, member of the National Council of African-American Men, observed, "the arguments for reparations aren't made on the basis of whether every white person directly gained from slavery. The arguments are made on the basis that slavery was institutionalized and protected by law in the United States. As the government is an entity that survives generations, its debts and obligations survive the lifespan of any particular individuals.... Governments make restitution to victims as a group or class." (*San Francisco Chronicle,* March 26, 2001, p. A21.)

Most Americans today were not alive during World War II. Yet reparations to Japanese Americans for their internment in concentration camps during the war was paid out of current government sources contributed to by contemporary Americans. Passage of time does not negate the responsibility of government in crimes against humanity. Similarly, German corporations are not the "same" corporations that supported the Holocaust; their personnel and policies today belong to generations removed from their earlier criminal behavior. Yet, these corporations are being successfully sued by Jews for their past actions. In the same vein, the U.S. government is not the same government as it was in the pre-Civil War era, yet its debts and obligations from the past are no less relevant today.

5. THE HISTORICAL PRECEDENTS USED TO JUSTIFY THE REPARATIONS CLAIM DO NOT APPLY, AND THE CLAIM ITSELF IS BASED ON RACE NOT INJURY

As noted in our repsonse to "Reason 4," the historical precedents for the reparations claims of African-Americans are fully consistent with restitution accorded other historical groups for atrocities committed against them. Second, the injury in question—that of slavery—was inflicted upon a people designated as a race. The descendants of that people—still socially constructed as a race today—continue to suffer the institutional legacies of slavery some one hundred thirty-five years after its demise. To attempt to separate the issue of so-called race from that of injury in this instance is pure sophistry. For example, the criminal (in)justice system today largely continues to operate as it did under slavery—for the protection of white citizens against black "outsiders." Although no longer inscribed in law, this very attitude is implicit to processes of law enforcement, prosecution, and incarceration, guiding the behavior of police, prosecutors, judges, juries, wardens, and parole boards. Hence, African-Americans continue to experience higher rates of incarceration than do whites charged with similar crimes, endure longer sentences for the same classes of crimes perpetrated by whites, and, compared to white inmates, receive far less consideration by parole boards when being considered for release.

Slavery was an institution sanctioned by the highest laws of the land with a degree of support from the Constitution itself. The institution of slavery established the idea and the practice that American democracy was "for whites only." There are many white Americans whose actions (or lack thereof) reveal such sentiments today—witness the response of the media and the general populace to the blatant disfranchisement of African-Americans in Florida during the last presidential election. Would such complacency exist if African-Americans were considered "real citizens"? And despite the dramatic successes of the Civil Rights movement of the 1950s and 60s, the majority of black Americans do not enjoy the same rights as white Americans in the economic sphere. (We continue this argument in the following section.)

6. THE REPARATIONS ARGUMENT IS BASED ON THE UNFOUNDED CLAIM THAT ALL AFRICAN-AMERICAN DESCENDANTS OF SLAVES SUFFER FROM THE ECONOMIC CONSEQUENCES OF SLAVERY AND DISCRIMINATION

Most blacks suffered and continue to suffer the economic consequences of slavery and its aftermath. As of 1998, median white family income in the U.S. was $49,023; median black family income was $29,404, just 60% of white income. (2001 New York Times Almanac, p. 319) Further, the costs of living within the United States far exceed those of African nations. The present poverty level for an American family of four is $17,029. Twenty-three and three-fifths percent (23.6%) of all black families live below the poverty level.

When one examines net financial worth, which reflects, in part, the wealth handed down within families from generation to generation, the figures appear much starker. Recently, sociologists Melvin L. Oliver and Thomas M. Shapiro found that just a little over a decade ago, the net financial worth of white American families with zero or negative net financial worth stood at around 25%; that of Hispanic households at 54%; and that of black American households at almost 61%. (Oliver & Shapiro, p. 87) The inability to accrue net financial worth is also directly related to hiring practices in which black Americans are "last hired" when the economy experiences an upturn, and "first fired" when it falls on hard times.

And as historian John Hope Franklin remarked on the legacy of slavery for black education: "laws enacted by states forbade the teaching of blacks any means of acquiring knowledge— including the alphabet—which is the legacy of disadvantage of educational privatization and discrimination experienced by African-Americans in 2001."

Horowitz's comparison of African-Americans with Jamaicans is a false analogy, ignoring the different historical contexts of the two populations. The British government ended slavery in Jamaica and its other West Indian territories in 1836, paying West Indian slaveholders $20,000,000 pounds ($100,000,000 U.S. dollars) to free the slaves, and leaving the black Jamaicans, who comprised 90% of that island's population, relatively free. Though still facing racist obstacles, Jamaicans come to the U.S. as voluntary immigrants, with greater opportunity to weigh, choose, and develop their options.

7. THE REPARATIONS CLAIM IS ONE MORE ATTEMPT TO TURN AFRICAN-AMERICANS INTO VICTIMS. IT SENDS A DAMAGING MESSAGE TO THE AFRICAN-AMERICAN COMMUNITY

What is a victim? Black people have certainly been victimized, but acknowledgment of that fact is not a case of "playing the victim" but of seeking justice. There is no validity to Horowitz's comparison between black Americans and victims of oppressive regimes who have voluntary immigrated to these shores. Further, many members of those populations, such as Chileans and Salvadorans, direct their energies for redress toward the governments of their own oppressive nations—which is precisely what black Americans are doing. Horowitz's racism is expressed in his contemptuous characterization of reparations as "an extravagant new handout that is only necessary because some blacks can't seem to locate the ladder of opportunity within reach of others, many of whom are less privileged than themselves." What Horowitz fails to acknowledge is that racism continues as an ideology and a material force within the U.S., providing blacks with no ladder that reaches the top. The damage lies in the systematic treatment of black people in the U.S., not their claims against those who initiated this damage and their spiritual descendants who continue its perpetuation.

8. REPARATIONS TO AFRICAN-AMERICANS HAVE ALREADY BEEN PAID

The nearest the U.S. government came to full and permanent restitution of African-Americans was the spontaneous redistribution of land brought about by General William Sherman's Field Order 15 in January, 1865, which empowered Union commanders to make land grants and give other material assistance to newly liberated blacks. But that order was rescinded by President Andrew Johnson later in the year. Efforts by Representative Thaddeus Stevens and other radical Republicans to provide the proverbial "40 acres and a mule" which would have carved up huge plantations of the defeated Confederacy into modest land grants for blacks and poor whites never got out of the House of Representatives. The debt has not been paid.

"Welfare benefits and racial preferences" are not reparations. The welfare system was set in place in the 1930s to alleviate the poverty of the Great Depression, and more whites than blacks received welfare. So-called "racial preferences" come not from benevolence but from lawsuits by blacks against white businesses, government agencies, and municipalities which practice racial discrimination.

9. WHAT ABOUT THE DEBT BLACKS OWE TO AMERICA?

Horowitz's assertion that "in the thousand years of slavery's existence, there never was an anti-slavery movement until white Anglo-Saxon Christians created one," only demonstrates his ignorance concerning the formidable efforts of blacks to free themselves. Led by black Toussaint L'Ouverture, the Haitian revo-

lution of 1793 overthrew the French slave system, created the first black republic in the world, and intensified the activities of black and white anti-slavery movements in the U.S. Slave insurrections and conspiracies such as those of Gabriel (1800), Denmark Vesey (1822), and Nat Turner (1831) were potent sources of black resistance; black abolitionists such as Harriet Tubman, Frederick Douglass, Richard Allen, Sojourner Truth, Martin Delany, David Walker, and Henry Highland Garnet waged an incessant struggle against slavery through agencies such as the press, notably Douglass's North Star and its variants, which ran from 1847 to 1863 (blacks, moreover, constituted some 75% of the subscribers to William Lloyd Garrison's Liberator newspaper in its first four years); the Underground Railroad, the Negro Convention Movement, local, state, and national anti-slavery societies, and the slave narrative. Black Americans were in no ways the passive recipients of freedom from anyone, whether viewed from the perspective of black participation in the abolitionist movement, the flight of slaves from plantations and farms during the Civil War, or the enlistment of black troops in the Union army.

The idea of black debt to U.S. society is a rehash of the Christian missionary argument of the 17th and 18th centuries: because Africans were considered heathens, it was therefore legitimate to enslave them and drag them in chains to a Christian nation. Following their partial conversion, their moral and material lot were improved, for which black folk should be eternally grateful. Slave ideologues John Calhoun and George Fitzhugh updated this idea in the 19th century, arguing that blacks were better off under slavery than whites in the North who received wages, due to the paternalism and benevolence of the plantation system which assured perpetual employment, shelter, and board. Please excuse the analogy, but if someone chops off your fingers and then hands them back to you, should you be "grateful" for having received your mangled fingers, or enraged that they were chopped off in the first place?

10. THE REPARATIONS CLAIM IS A SEPARATIST IDEA THAT SETS AFRICAN AMERICANS AGAINST THE NATION THAT GAVE THEM FREEDOM

Again, Horowitz reverses matters. Blacks are already separated from white America in fundamental matters such as income, family wealth, housing, legal treatment, education, and political representation. Andrew Hacker, for example, has argued the case persuasively in his book Two Nations. To ignore such divisions, and then charge those who raise valid claims against society with promoting divisiveness, offers a classic example of "blaming the victim." And we have already refuted the spurious point that African-Americans were the passive recipients of benevolent white individuals or institutions which "gave" them freedom.

Too many Americans tend to view history as "something that happened in the past," something that is "over and done," and thus has no bearing upon the present. Especially in the case of slavery, nothing could be further from the truth. As historian John Hope Franklin noted in his response to Horowitz:

"Most living Americans do have a connection with slavery. They have inherited the preferential advantage, if they are white, or the loathsome disadvantage, if they are black; and those positions are virtually as alive today as they were in the 19th century. The pattern of housing, the discrimination in employment, the resistance to equal opportunity in education, the racial profiling, the inequities in the administration of justice, the low expectation of blacks in the discharge of duties assigned to them, the widespread belief that blacks have physical prowess but little intellectual capaci-

ties and the widespread opposition to affirmative action, as if that had not been enjoyed by whites for three centuries, all indicate that the vestiges of slavery are still with us.

"And as long as there are pro-slavery protagonists among us, hiding behind such absurdities as 'we are all in this together' or 'it hurts me as much as it hurts you' or 'slavery benefited you as much as it benefited me,' we will suffer from the inability to confront the tragic legacies of slavery and deal with them in a forthright and constructive manner.

"Most important, we must never fall victim to some scheme designed to create a controversy among potential allies in order to divide them and, at the same time, exploit them for its own special purpose."

REFERENCES

2001 New York Times Almanac (New York: Penguin Books, 2000).

America, Richard F., Paying the Social Debt: *What White America Owes Black America* (Westport, CT: Praeger, 1998).

DeBow. J. D. B., "The Interest in Slavery of the Southern Non-Slaveholder," in *Slavery Defended: The Views of the Old South,* ed. Eric L. McKitrick (Englewood Cliffs, NJ: Prentice-Hall, 1963), 169–77.

Berlin, Ira, and others, *Slaves No More: Three Essays on Emancipation and the Civil War* (Cambridge [England]; New York: Cambridge University Press, 1992).

Conley, Dalton, Being Black, *Living in the Red: Race, Wealth, and Social Polity in America* (Berkeley. University of California Press, 1999).

Cox, LaWanda, "The Promise of Land for the Freedmen," *Mississippi Valley Historical Review* 45 (December 1958): 41340.

Cornish, Dudley Taylor, *The Sable Arm: Black Troops in the Union Army 1861–1865* (1956; rpt. Lawrence, KS: University Press of Kansas, 1987).

Foner, Eric, *Free Soil, Free Labor, Free Men: the Ideology of the Republican Party Before the Civil War* (New York: Oxford University Press, 1970).

Franklin John Hope, and Alfred A. Moss, Jr., *From Slavery to Freedom: A History of African Americans,* 7th ed. (New York: McGraw-Hill, 1994).

Hacker, Andrew, *Two Nations: Black and White, Separate, Hostile, Unequal* rev. ed. (New York: Ballantine Books, 1995).

Horton, James Oliver and Lois E. Horton, *In Hope of Liberty: Culture, Community; and Protest Among Northern Free Blacks, 1700–1860* (New York: Oxford University Press, 1997).

Huston, James L., "Property Rights in Slavery and the Coming of the Civil War," *Journal of Southern History* 65 (1999): 249–86.

Oakes, James, *The Ruling Race: A History of American Slaveholders* (New York: Vintage Books, 1989).

Oliver Melvin L., and Thomas M. Shapiro, *Black Wealth/White Wealth: A New Perspective on Racial Inequality* (New York: Routledge, 1995).

Quarles, Benjamin, *Black Abolitionists* (New York: Oxford University Press, 1969).

———, *The Negro in the Civil War* (Boston: Little, Brown, 1959).

Rodney, Walter, *How Europe Underdeveloped Africa,* rev. ed. (Washington, DC: Howard University Press, 1981).

Salzman, Jack, David Lionel Smith, and Cornel West, eds., *Encyclopedia of African-American Culture and History,* 5 vols. (New York: Macmillan Library Reference USA: Simon & Schuster Macmillan; London: Simon & Schuster and Prentice Hall International, 1996).

Schemo, Diana Jean, "An Ad Provokes Campus Protests and Pushes Limits of Expression," *New York Times,* 21 March 2001, pp. Al, A17.

Smith, Abbot Emerson, *Colonists in Bondage, White Servitude and Convict Labor in America, 1607–1776* (Chapel Hill: Pub. for the Institute of Early American History and Culture at Williamsburg, Va., by the University of North Carolina Press, 1947).

Solow Barbara L., and Stanley L. Engerman, eds., *British Capitalism and Caribbean Slavery: The Legacy of Eric Williams* (Cambridge [Cambridgeshire]; New York: Cambridge University Press, 1987).

Williams, Eric, *Capitalism & Slavery* (1944; rpt. New York: Russell & Russell, 1961).

Anti-racism and the Abolition of Whiteness:
Rhetorical Strategies of Domination Among "Race Traitors"

Dreama Moon and Lisa A. Flores

The development of whiteness studies over the last decade has been welcomed by some, and noted with trepidation by others. An outgrowth of the work of race scholars of color, whiteness studies has been the topic of much recent debate. A body of scholarship that takes whiteness as its central focus cannot afford to be ignored by either academics or the lay public. This paper overviews two primary tendencies within whiteness studies, anti-racism and abolitionism, and notes their points of divergence. In particular, the abolition rhetoric of self-proclaimed "race traitors" is interrogated. It is imperative that discourses that are positioned as "oppositional" be monitored for their repressive strains. We suggest that positioning whiteness studies as an intersectional practice may help whiteness scholars avoid some of the conceptual traps in which Race Traitor *finds itself.*

Why talk about whiteness, given the risk that by undertaking intellectual work on whiteness one might contribute to processes of recentering rather than decentering it, as well as reifying the term and its "inhabitants"? (Frankenberg, 1997, p. 1)

In April 1997, the University of California at Berkeley hosted "The Making and Unmaking of Whiteness," the first academic conference in the United States dedicated to "talking about whiteness" (Kaufman, 1996). Organized by a group of Berkeley graduate students, the conference attracted a diverse crowd of Asian/Asian American, African American, Latino/Latino, and white academics and anti-racist activists as well as a fair amount of media attention (Goodman, 1997). Some people expressed concerns, similar to those raised above by Frankenberg, that the conference would turn into a white lovefest, while others assumed that the conference was yet another event in the ongoing backlash against ethnic studies in California (Goodman, 1997).

Conference co-organizer Matt Wray said, "The point of the conference is not to pile on more white guilt nor is it to celebrate whiteness. This is the process of trying to understand whiteness with the belief and hope that it might help us out of our current racial impasse (where) things seem to be so polarized and deadlocked" (Chao, 1997, p. A-7). In identifying this focus, the conference organizers, in accord with other whiteness scholars (see Projansky & Ono, 1999), position whiteness as strategy rather than an identity position. That is, the central concern with whiteness, and within whiteness studies, is not whiteness per se, "but what whiteness is so often used to do" (Projansky & Ono, 1999, p. 171). Thus, the conference organizers emphasized understanding the mechanisms that create whiteness, and its role in holding the current social structure together (Goodman, 1997). In addition, Michael Omi, a Berkeley professor of ethnic studies, said the conference was driven by a "firm anti-racist stance" (Goodman, 1997, p. A16). And yet, the conference and its stated goals raised a degree of skepticism in some quarters. This suspicion seemed to move in one of two directions: fear that already limited attention to, and resources for combating racism might be diverted to the study of whiteness, and doubt that white people could study whiteness in a meaningful manner. In an interview about his perceptions of the conference, Michael Eric Dyson, professor of African-American studies at DePaul University, spoke to the first concern:

> There's a suspicion among African-Americans that whiteness studies is a sneaky form of narcissism. At the very moment when African-American studies and Asian-American studies and so on are really coming into their own, you have whiteness studies shifting the focus and maybe the resources back to white people and their perspective. (Talbot, 1997, p. 116)

Sharon Elise, an African American sociologist interviewed at the conference, spoke to the second concern when she pointed out to an all-white panel, "it concerns me that we have a panel of white scholars using white standards to investigate whiteness. To me, this seems somewhat naive" (as cited in Burdman, 1997, A7).

Dyson's and Elise's comments are not isolated ones in the ongoing discussion about whiteness studies. Considered a subspeciality within ethnic studies, the "new" whiteness studies has been both deeply criticized and heralded as a necessary next step in the struggle against racism, white supremacy, and white privilege within the United States (Frankenberg, 1997;

Giroux, 1997; Jackson, 1999; Kinchloe & Steinberg, 1998). We position the term "new" within quotes to draw attention to the fact that scholars of color have written about whiteness and white privilege for at least 100 years (for example, see Baldwin, 1984; Dubois, 1920; hooks, 1990, 1992a, 1992b; Hughes, 1934; Jacobs, 1861; Morrison, 1992); however, as Peggy McIntosh notes, "it took white people to put (whiteness studies) on the map for white people" (as cited in Haynes, 1998, p. 10B). In other words, what's likely to be "new" about the "new" whiteness studies is that it is white people who are doing it.

The apparent contradictions and perspectival dissension reported at the Berkeley conference between academicians and activists typify the tensions within this fledgling, and often suspect, field of study. In this essay, we lay out some of the tensions within whiteness studies, and argue that the notion of intersectionality could be used by whiteness scholars to avoid some of the conceptual traps in which many find themselves. In the first section, we briefly lay out two central impulses within whiteness studies, anti-racist and abolitionist thought. En route, we unpack a recent critique of whiteness studies leveled by abolitionist whiteness theorists, a group of (mostly) whites calling themselves "race traitors." In the second section, we show how strains of repressive thought manifest throughout abolitionist anti-whiteness rhetoric by examining the ways this discourse reinscribes white privilege. We end by suggesting how K. Crenshaw's (1991, 1992, 1993) notion of intersectionality could be fruitfully utilized by "race traitors" to undercut abolitionists' seeming investment in whiteness, masculinity, and heterosexuality. Our analysis points to the need to monitor resistance discourses for traces of oppressive ideologies and rework them accordingly (Sloop, 1994).

THE STATE OF WHITENESS STUDIES

Whiteness studies emerged in the wake. of political and intellectual challenges made by anti-racists, and out of "critiques of racism and the racial order focused on positions of subordination" levied by scholars of color (Frankenberg, 1997, p. 2). We think the metaphors of "making" and "unmaking" used in the conference title exemplify two central impulses within whiteness studies, anti-racist and abolitionist whiteness scholarship. We first explore whiteness scholarship which wishes to reconfigure whiteness, and then abolitionist discourse that argues for the abolition of whiteness.

MAKING WHITENESS, RENDERING WHITENESS VISIBLE

Although whiteness studies is by no means an intellectually homogeneous body of thought, this work seems to share at least three characteristics. These elements include an impulse to mark and thus, come to understand, whiteness; a commitment to anti-racist or anti-white supremacist politics; and a desire to build emancipatory notions of whiteness (Alcoff, 1998; Bonnett, 1996a, 1996b; Dyer, 1998; Frankenberg, 1993, 1997; Giroux, 1997; Hill, 1997; Johnson, 1999; Kaufman, 1996; Kinchloe & Steinberg, 1998; Lipsitz, 1998; Nakayama & Martin, 1999; Newitz & Wray, 1997; Winant, 1997). We explore these characteristics in more detail below.

Within the current wave of whiteness studies, writers Richard Dyer (1988), Ruth Frankenberg (1993), bell hooks (1990), Toni Morrison (1992), and Mab Segrest (1994a, 1994b) were among the first to argue that an important element of the anti-racist agenda is the need to map the terrain of whiteness. Each in their own way argues that those wanting to preserve white supremacy are likely to insist on whiteness remaining invisible and unmarked. In their groundbreaking 1995 article, Nakayama and Krizek began the process of particularizing white experience and introduced this important political project to the field of communication (for others in communication who have since pursued this work, see C. Crenshaw, 19976; DeLuca, 1999; Jackson, 1999; Lee, 1999; Marty, 1999; Moon, 1999; Nakayama & Martin, 1999; Projansky & Ono, 1999; Shome, 1996, 1999; Steyn, 1999; Supriya, 1999).

Along with Dyer (1988), Nakayama and Krizek argued that once the space of whiteness is exposed, culturally positioned, delimited, rendered visible, and deterritorialized, then, whiteness will lose its power to dominate. C. Crenshaw (1997a) further suggests that the rhetorical silences of whiteness must be overturned if we are to effectively resist racism. As she notes, it is within these silences that the power of whiteness is invoked. By rendering whiteness visible, these scholars believe that whites will come to understand that "their experiences, perceptions, and economic positions have been profoundly affected by being constituted as a white" (Alcoff, 1998, p. 8), and that by getting in touch with whiteness and its attendant privilege, they will identify and reduce/eliminate their racism (Katz, 1978; Marty, 1999; Terry, 1975). For this reason, antiracist politics are a central part of the whiteness studies agenda (Marty, 1999). Frankenberg summarizes this position succinctly when she cautions that:

> Whiteness must be marked, investigated, and understood if whites are to be effective antiracists but unless the political content of that project is kept clear and central, the study of whiteness is likely to become a form of self-help for white people in an identity crisis. (as cited in Kaufman, 1996, p. 200)

In other words, as Projansky and Ono (1999) caution, to study whiteness without a clear mission of unpacking the ways in which whiteness is used to maintain privileged power and to marginalize and disempower "others," is to be complicit with the project of white domination.

While the forging of a white identity that resists white privilege and white supremacy is an ongoing subject of debate among whiteness scholars, it is also one of their strongest points of agreement. Each hopes that, at the end of unpacking whiteness within the context of antiracist politics, progressive and opposition-al forms of whiteness might be articulated. However, a central concern among whiteness scholars is that, to date, a compelling vision of a liberatory whiteness and/or white identity has yet to be articulated (also see, Alcoff, 1998; Bailey, 1998; Giroux, 1997; Kinchloe & Steinberg, 1998; Lipsitz, 1998; Steyn, 1999; Winant, 1997).

UNMAKING WHITENESS THE ABOLITIONIST WAY

Whiteness studies has come under heavy cri-tique from a group of predominantly white people who refer to themselves as the "new abolitionists" (also known as "race traitors"). Abolitionist theorists are particularly critical of the whiteness studies' goals of understand-ing and re-articulating whiteness. They claim that to "study" whiteness offers white people reasons "to glorify whiteness and do nothing to improve our current circumstances" (Large, 1999, p. L1). In fact, Ignatiev (1999) refers to this preference for white re-articulation over white erasure as "a failure of political nerve" (p. 7). He goes on to say that trying to re-artic-ulate whiteness is similar to trying to re-artic-ulate child abuse or rape.

For abolitionists, there is nothing to gain by re-articulating whiteness, and much to be lost. In this view, white identity is positioned as a form of false consciousness that impedes the devel-opment of working class alliances (Bonnet, 1996b; Garvey & Ignatiev, 1997; Ignatiev, 1999; Roediger, 1994). The general assump-tion is that once those who look white refuse to "act white," then social agents will be forced to deal with whites and others on some other basis which, they argue, will be class position (Garvey & Ignatiev, 1997). As this occurs, for-merly white people will realize their class commonalities, unite, and wage class warfare against their common oppressors (i.e., the State and its repressive institutions). In this respect these abolitionist theorists are similar to other Marxist/neo-Marxist race theorists who see whiteness primarily as an impediment to class solidarity (see, for example, Miles, 1989; Solomos, 1986).

Abolitionists also reject antiracism as a foun-dation for anti-white supremacy struggle (for example, see "Editorial," 1993; Niles, 1999). In fact, they see antiracists as part of the prob-lem, rather than the solution. "Race traitors" believe that the primary social problem is not "race" or "racism," but the *white* race. In their view, antiracist rhetoric reinscribes the notion of "race" in its very efforts to resist the *effects* of racism. So, for abolitionist theorists, it is "whitism," not racism, that is at the root of social injustice (Niles, 1999). As Niles (1999) observes, "the signs in the segregated South did not read 'Racists Only,' they read, 'Whites Only' " (p. 4).

For this reason, abolitionists are committed to *abolishing* whiteness—not to "reframing," "redeeming," or "deconstructing" it (Ignatiev, 1999). In fact, they argue that, given the his-torical context out of which white as a social category emerged, there can be no "positive" forms of white identity. In Roediger's (1994) words, "it is not merely that whiteness is oppressive and false, it is *nothing but* oppres-sive and false" (p. 13). For them, retention of *any* form of white identity is problematic as it reinscribes white supremacy and oppressive racial hierarchies (Ignatiev, 1997).

As a result, rather than understand whiteness, abolitionist theorists encourage a general "giving up" of/on whiteness. This is the area in which they are most in disagreement with whiteness scholars who want to retain, or at least, reinvent some liberatory form of whiteness. Abolitionist theorists argue that it is only in the symbolic deaths of whites that they can be resurrected or reborn as workers, youth, women, gays or to any other identity (Ignatiev, 1997). Indeed, as part of their political agenda of "race treason," abolitionists chronicle "Huck Finn moments," acts that signal "individual and collective breaks with white solidarity" (Garvey & Ignatiev, 1997, p. 349). In the next section, we examine this discourse more closely. We focus particularly on the discourse that emerges in the publication *Race Traitor,* which has become a prominent voice in the new abolitionist rhetoric. We will also demonstrate how abolitionist discourse unwittingly reinscribes, and ultimately depends on, white privilege for its articulation and that it treats whiteness in monolithic, unreflexive ways.

RACE TRAITOR AND THE (UN)MAKING OF WHITENESS

In our analysis of abolitionist discourse, we primarily focused on the organizational journal, *Race Traitor: Treason to Whiteness is Loyalty to Humanity* (hereafter referred to as *Race Traitor*) published by New Abolitionists, Inc. In addition to the primary text, we examined information available at their website (www.posffun.com/racetraitor) such as speech transcripts, and their newsletter, *The New Abolitionist,* interviews with the editors published in popular magazines and newspapers, and essays—written by the editors published in academic sources. Lastly, one of the authors engaged in informal discussions with one of the editors of *Race Traitor,* Noel Ignatiev, both over email and face-to-face.

The journal, *Race Traitor,* attracts a fairly wide readership as evidenced by those who write essays and letters to the editor. We have noted academics, grassroots activists, right-wing militia types, prisoners, students, and others. The founding editors of *Race Traitor* are two white men, Noel Ignatiev and John Garvey, both were formerly grassroots activists and are currently academics. Much of our discussion focuses on Ignatiev as he has assumed a much more public role in disseminating the abolitionist agenda than has Garvey.

The opening piece in the first issue of one of the abolitionists' primary rhetorical text, *Race Traitor,* declares that a major goal of this "new" abolitionist movement is to "chronicle and analyze the making, re-making and un-making of whiteness" ("Editorial," 1993, p. 6). Throughout the journal, in contributed essays, writings by the editors, and letters to the editors, readers witness this making, re-making, and un-making process. Contemporary and historical accounts and descriptions of whiteness illustrate its making—or what whiteness is and how it came to be that way. The project of race traitors is to participate in the un-making of whiteness and the remaking of race treason. As we demonstrate below, the abolitionist emphasis on making, re-making, and un-making ultimately recenters whiteness. In "making" whiteness, race traitors rely on a monolithic notion of whiteness that assumes whiteness is the foundational oppression. The "re-making" and "un-making" process furthers the recentering of whiteness in five key ways: by positioning white people as the ultimate agents of change, by ignoring the actions of and lessons learned from Blacks and other people of color who have participated in anti-racist activism, by requiring approval from Blacks for the actions of whites, by appealing to a domination ideology of individuality, and by encouraging a general appropriation of

Blackness by whites (anonymous reviewer, personal communication, November 19, 1999).

MAKING WHITENESS: THE WHITENESS WE LOVE TO HATE

A central task for race traitors is to identify and destroy what they see as the hegemonic white race. Thus, much effort is given to defining and illustrating whiteness so that it may be eradicated. The mission statement, which appears in full as the first piece in the first issue, and then in an abbreviated form on the back cover of every issue of *Race Traitor,* begins by noting that "the white race is a historically constructed social formation." In this, and other similar statements, *Race Traitor* explicitly denounces the long-held notion of "race" as a biological essence. For instance, in "Exchange," Ignatiev, one of the editors, states, "When I speak of 'race' I have in mind not the superficial biological differences among the various branches of humankind…but the social distinctions that attach to racial identification" (1996, p. 28). Likewise, Day (1994) writes, "An elementary principle of race treason is that whiteness is a social construction and not a biological fact" (p. 57), while Boyer (1998) identifies whiteness as an "ideological fabrication" (p. 117).

In their attempts to define whiteness in order to abolish it, race traitors justify its eradication by situating whiteness as quintessentially evil. Whiteness is depicted throughout *Race Traitor* as encompassing all social evils, as both the root and the enactment of evil. This particular framing of whiteness-as-monolithic evil is problematic in view of their previous race-as-social construction position, and plagues their subsequent arguments. This monolithic construction of whiteness comes out most clearly in one letter to the editor which effectively equates whiteness with the Anti-Christ (Salahuddin, 1994). Whites, in effect, are

described as being "tricked by the devil" (Oliver, 1995, p. 117), while in other places, whiteness is a "the quintessential Peculiar institution," "deranged," and "privilege of greed and dominion" (Eakins, 1995, p. 4; "Editorial," 1994, p. 108; Fredrickson, 1994, p. 85). Additionally whiteness is associated with villainous State institutions, such as law-enforcement, media, and social services (Autonomous Zone, 1997; Ervin, 1994; Olson, 1995) and situated as the enactment of privilege (Boyer, 1998; Eakins, 1995; Ignatiev, 1999). In fact, one of the primary goals of *Race Traitor* is to eliminate the State as we know it. Their critique of the State and its institutions also extends to liberal efforts to reform the system which they see as un-reformable. In their view, efforts to eradicate white supremacy that do not include opposition to the State only reinforce the authority of the State, which they position as the most important agency in maintaining racial oppression (Ignatiev, 1997).

Because whiteness is an inherently evil social construction that is enacted through participation in oppressive institutions and practices, such as through policing and the acceptance of white privilege, for race traitors, the logical choice is to opt out of whiteness. To race traitors, this choice is not contingent on skin color, but on choosing to participate in whiteness. As such, race traitors do not define themselves as "white," and distinguish between being of European descent (having white skin) and being white. Sleeter (1995), for example, illustrates this notion of whiteness as distinct from white skin/features: "To break with whiteness, I must first distinguish between being a white person of European ancestry, and one who identifies as 'white'" (p. 21).

Race traitors often opt out of whiteness by associating with people of color. In a letter to the editors, one reader writes "This [rare traitor] is me." Identifying himself as white, he writes:

I will not date whites. It must be a racially mixed relationship for me. I used to be more open-minded and would consider dating all races—however the racist ideology of other whites pushed me to a conclusion of exclusion of the white race for me. I read everything I can on Third World countries, especially Africa and the Caribbean. My ex-wife was Jamaican. So I say my son is Ja-merican. (Demick, 1995, p. 112)

Another letter-writer, Hill (1998) shares her experiences and qualifications as a race traitor, "I feel like a race traitor. My husband is African-American, I consider myself Italian (although born in this country) not white, and I'm much more comfortable in groups with people of color" (p. 109). Similarly, Gilbert (1994) writes about the importance of his relationships with people of color: "For the most part I feel at home with black people. I've got plenty of black inside me. And I think most of the whiteness I grew up with has washed away" (p. 10) (see also Chas, 1997 and K, 1997).

In these and other discussions, *Race Traitor* offers important insights into the historical formation of "white" and "black" as relational racial constructs. When *Race Traitor* defines whiteness as "social evil" and as the enactment of racial privilege, they highlight the historical context of white oppression/black resistance. However, in so doing, they ignore Omi and Winant's (1994) observation that as social practices, such as affirmative action laws, change so do our understandings and enactments of racial categories. Thus, to maintain a notion of whiteness that is defined only in terms of its oppressive roots and practices is to freeze, what race theorists argue, is a fluid sociohistorical process (Clifford, 1988; Omi & Winant, 1993, 1994; Rosaldo, 1993; Volpe, 1996).

In the act of freezing whiteness, race traitors ultimately recenter it. In part, this recentering

occurs through the tendency in *Race Traitor* to position whiteness as the primary or foundational source of oppression. The editors argue, "The key to solving the social problems of our age is to abolish the white race. Until that task is performed, there can be no universal reform, and even partial reform will prove elusive, because white influence permeates every issue in U.S. society, whether domestic or foreign" ("Editorial," 1993, p. 1). The Chicago Surrealists (1998) add, "Everyone knows that white supremacy is the single biggest obstacle to working-class emancipation. It is also the major stumbling-block in the way of women's equality, for white supremacy is inherently androcentric" (p. 4). The primacy of whiteness as the first obstacle to confront emerges in Boyer (1998): "Surely the belief in 'whiteness' is sicker, more dangerous, and deadlier, than any psychosis" (p. 119) (see also, Filemyr, 1999; Fraser, 1993; Ignatiev, 1993; Rawson, 1997).

When whiteness is positioned as the quintessential oppression, whiteness is recentered as the primary social and historical force. Rather than identifying the contributions of white culture in politics, medicine, science, and law as most mainstream American (white) texts are wont to do, race traitors instead foreground the "Great White Evil Man." In other words, rather than representing white culture as the *best* of all that been thought, said, and done, abolitionists render whiteness (and its primary agent, the white man) as the worst of all that has been thought, said, and done. In this way, *Race Traitor* continues the tradition of reifying whiteness and things white. In directing our attention to this reified whiteness, the opportunity for abolitionists to benefit from other discourses of struggle is lost. If whiteness is all, oppresses all, and must be abolished in order to free all, then related and intertwined struggles around other forms of domination (i.e., based on sex, sexual orientation, religion, etc.) are effectively relegated to the margins (once again) of the social arena. This marginalization prevents dialogue and strategizing among anti-whiteness and other liberatory struggles. In addition, our eyes are drawn once more away from the needs and interests of other social groups, and toward the light of whiteness. This inadvertent recentering of whiteness also causes problems for abolitionists' vision of a new type of "white," race traitor. We explore these issues in the next section.

UN-MAKING WHITES, RE-MAKING RACE TRAITORS

As mentioned, the historical construction of whiteness that is identified by race traitors reduces whiteness to an evil, one that must be destroyed. Refusing the reconstructionist approach of anti-racists, race traitors are committed to the abolition of whiteness and the white race. The distinction between the approach of race traitors and that of anti-racists is outlined in the opening editorial of the first issue in which the editors argue, "Advocating the abolition of the white race is distinct from what is called anti-racism" ("Editorial," 1993, p. 1). They further outline the abolitionist approach as against anti-racism when they note, in the same editorial, that they are unlikely to publish articles "promoting inter-racial harmony" ("Editorial," 1993, p. 8). Ignatiev (1999) reinforces this position when he argues, "The abolitionists study whiteness in order to abolish it—not to…'deconstruct' or redeem'… it" (p. 7) (see also "Editors' reply," 1994). The language of abolition appears throughout the writings and from not only the editors, but also from contributors and readers (see, for instance, "Editorial, 1996a; Boyer, 1998; Bragg, 1998; "Editorial," 1994; Epperson, 1997; Ignatiev, 1996, 1999; Kelley et al., 1997; "Renew," 1999; Rosemont, 1998; Rubio, 1994).

The abolition of whiteness creates a space for the remaking process in which "so-called" whites become race traitors (the phrase "so-called" is one of the ways in which race traitors refer to themselves, seemingly in an attempt to call into question, or distance themselves from, their presumed whiteness). The re-making process is largely one of learning from the actions of others about how to participate in race treason. In this emphasis on enacting a new politics of race treason, *Race Traitor* searches U. S. history and literature as well as present-day examples for models of behavior for "race traitors." To actualize their vision, they challenge the traditional discourse of whiteness through revisioning, recovering, and reinterpreting common social myths and narratives. As observed by Hasian and Flores (1997), while myths are often fabrications, "they are nevertheless the substance of identity, the images that mobilize the masses, and transform relationships of power" (p. 96). Myths are central to the process of re-defining white consciousness and moving whites to relinquish whiteness and adopt an identity grounded in race treason.

The process of remaking whiteness is often accomplished through the resurrection of appropriate models of race traitors. The two most commonly evoked heroes are John Brown and Huck Finn. Both choices fit with the agenda of race treason in that both are white males who associated with Blacks and were actively involved in struggles to help Blacks. Thus, *Race Traitor* resurrects white men who have directly taken matters in their own hands. The turn to John Brown and Huck Finn as cultural heroes for race traitors deserves special attention. One issue each is devoted to Brown and Finn (Winter 1999 and Summer 1993), while others mention each often (for other references to John Brown, see "Editorial," 1993; Ignatiev, 1994; Kurnick, 1993. For additional references to Huck Finn, see "Editors' reply," 1998; "Editorial," 1996b; "Editorial," 1994).

The Summer 1993 issue of *Race Traitor* highlights Mark Twain's Huck Finn. Positioning the character Huck Finn as one of the original "race traitors," *Race Traitor* uses this narrative to re-create or re-member an originary white man who breaks from "sivilization" (sic) and "take[s] the steps that will lead to…freedom" ("Huckleberry Finn," 1993, p. 40). Huck Finn is reviewed in several essays, all of which use the narrative to teach "race traitors" how to refuse whiteness. One lesson is illustrated through the equation of Huck Finn with Robin Hood, who promotes social justice with a creative redistribution of wealth (Weiss, 1993, p. 42). The Huck Finn myth also encourages a critique of social institutions such as the legal system by pointing out that some laws are inhumane. In the relationship between Huck and Jim, Huck comes to realize Jim's inherent humanity—a lesson from which all "race traitors" can benefit (D'Andrea, 1993).

The re-membering of this story also challenges the assumption that Western society is civilized while Africa is barbaric. Fritschel (1993) reframes barbarianism by connecting it with the nature of white treatment of Blacks in the United States. Henson (1999) compares two characters in a novel by Russell Banks to Huck and Jim. Not surprisingly, the two characters are a young white boy and an older black man, or as Henson describes them: "A young boy running away from respectability and school—and sexual abuse—and the kindly old man, what a father should be, himself a fugitive, an illegal alien subject to deportation and worse" (p. 79). This emphasis on the story of Huck Finn provides a moral center for "race traitors," suggesting that the development of a new moral consciousness is a key move in relinquishing white privilege.

Race traitors also turn to John Brown, another noteworthy white man who was the leader of the Harper's Ferry rebellion in 1859. Brown represents a man who was willing to risk his life for social justice. He is quoted as saying,

"[I]f we lose our lives it will perhaps do more for the cause [abolition] than our lives could be worth in any other way" (as cited in Karcher, 1993, p. 23). Karcher, in her essay, positions John Brown's raid on Harper's Ferry as the paradigmatic example of race treason, and indeed Brown, a white man murdered at the hands of other white men, serves as a reified example of revolutionary white manhood. Thus, for "race traitors," the John Brown myth stands as a guide for how to organize and carry out the anti-whiteness revolution.

The appeal of John Brown as cultural hero is different than that of Huck and Jim, for John Brown seems to be the adult version of Huck, a man who now knows right from wrong and is willing to risk life, his and others, for his moral goals. Henson (1999) explains that the John Brown story illustrates an important lesson for race traitors, "That race and its consequences are evil and must be destroyed and that this is a mission worthy of dedicating one's life to. He [Brown] alone among the abolitionists of his time believed that the barriers of race could be dissolved and he identified so completely with the slave [note the singular use of the term, and the erasure of all complexity in slavery] as to take his cause as his own" (Henson, 1999, p. 80). The appeal of Brown, for Banks and Henson, it seems is in part the appeal of the "noblest patriarch of all" (Henson, 1999, p. 83). The story of John Brown and the importance of him as hero for race traitors lies in his belief that violence was the only possible way to end the racist system of slavery. Henson (1999) writes, "John Brown has moved inexorably to war through the logic of his own opposition to slavery. 'Slavery is evil: kill it.' No other path was open to Brown" (p. 84).

These mythic heroes provide white people with new forms of subjectivity that serve to displace traditional enactments of whiteness. In John Brown and Huck Finn, whites find an identity in the negation of traditional whiteness. While the mythic heroes Huck and Brown are important models for race traitors, ordinary people can also illustrate the process of race treason. A common approach in race treason is disrupting the category of whiteness by calling into question assumptions that white people will stand together as whites. Olson (1995), for example, illustrates his act of treason. He describes an instance in which he, a so-called white, and a number of others, mainly people of color, witnessed police officers shoot and kill a man. While Olson cannot verify exactly what happened, the end result was that about 12 police officers repeatedly shot a white man who was holding two kitchen knives. In standing with the largely non-white crowd and against the police, who are positioned as white, Olson offers himself as an example of race treason. He argues, "The respect that whites like myself received depended on the extent to which we did not act 'white'—that is, like a cop, a slimy reporter, or a scared moron…we whites in the crowd were outraged at the police with everyone else, and although we were not Black or Chicano we were, for a moment, not really white either" (Olson, 1995, pp. 11–12). Destabilizing whiteness also occurs when individuals explicitly denounce the assumption that they are white. Swayne (1996) describes a time in which a white male attorney assumed her status as white, and she responded, "I believe you are assuming facts not in evidence.…First of all you're assuming I'm white" (p. 96). Dailey (1997) acts similarly by calling into question racial categories and proposing that he was unable to identify his race, while Tenenbaum (1996) describes an instance in which an older white man expressed his hopes that Tenenbaum would "take down the big niggers" and Tenenbaum responds, "Did you know that my father was a Black man?" even though his father was not Black.

Although the aim of *Race Traitor* and abolitionists may be well-intentioned, unfortunately

whiteness emerges as an "omnipresent and all-powerful historical force" (Bonnett, 1996b, p. 153). In their laying out of whiteness as the blame for various social injustices, race traitors inadvertently subject whiteness to a new kind of recentering in which "whiteness, and white people, are turned into the key agents of historical change, the shapers of contemporary America" (Bonnett, 1996b, p. 153). Not only do race traitors do so in their construction of a monolithic evil whiteness and reification of individual acts of white repudiation, but they also insist upon reenvisioning and then, appropriating "blackness." This is perhaps one of the most problematic and critiqued trends in abolitionist discourse (for example, see Bonnett, 1996a, 1996b).

CELEBRATORY ACTS AS PROBLEMATIC

In refocusing our gaze to whiteness, we then are enabled to turn to a sustained celebration of the efforts of race traitors in the abolition of whiteness. As mentioned earlier, this celebration often takes the form of reporting traitorous deeds such as historical examples of race treason, maintenance of interracial relations, and public denials of white identity. These celebratory acts recenter whiteness in at least two problematic ways. First, they trivialize the actions of Blacks and other people of color throughout history against racism. In addition, they require Black adoration.

The emphasis on and celebration of treasonous acts by white race traitors trivialize the efforts of people of color. For example, Peeples (1994) describes his decision to stand with a group of Blacks protesting their forced exclusion from a department store restaurant. He recounts, "Despite the doubt and terror which gripped me, I finally made my way out of the white crowd and took my place with the Negro protestors. I knew none of them personally and none of them knew me. I nevertheless sensed an intense familiarity with each of them, as if we were all part of some great consciousness, far beyond ourselves" (p. 42). The emphasis on Peeples and his fears and doubts here serves to center him and to diminish the actions taken by blacks throughout the civil rights movement and throughout history. The dangers to them were surely greater than to Peeples, and yet his emphasis is on his own ability to stand up to racist laws and policies. Describing the civil war, Rubio (1993a) chooses stories that emphasize the centrality of the white roles in abolition societies and their efforts within the Underground Railroad. In a separate essay, Rubio (1994) interviews students at University of North Carolina, Chapel Hill about their efforts to obtain a Black cultural center. The struggle to get the center, which has been happening for over 20 years, has primarily involved African Americans students. Interestingly, this interview does not mention or include African American students, faculty, staff, or administrators.

Part of the danger in displaying the acts of these good whites is that the writers rarely discuss the ways in which their own practices maintain whiteness. Instead, they point out institutional racism and the racist comments they hear and see around them, but they almost never interrogate their own participation in whiteness. As C. Crenshaw (1997a) points out, such silences around whiteness are exactly what white scholars committed to anti-racism should work to uncover. Such narratives also maintain the centrality of the great white male hero, mark his actions as ones to be proud of, and trivialize the everyday dangers faced by blacks in their stances against such racism (other examples can be found in "Free to be Me," 1994; Johnson, 1999; Olson, 1995).

For race traitors, white celebratory acts seem to require black applause. For example, Mia (1998) writes a letter to the editors in which she describes her acts of race treason, which include breaking up with her racist boyfriend and finding acceptance from Black people:

"All my black friends hang around with this white guy, Chris, and he's cool. And I'm a white girl and they hang out with me" (p. 107). Power (1996) describes her involvement in teaching a literacy class composed of primarily black women. She describes in detail the responses of those women who affirmed her decision to tell them that her ancestors were slaveowners: "Ophelia…rose immediately to embrace me and some of the women followed suit. Some of the women did feel that they wanted to reassure me: "It's not your fault,' a few of them cried' " (1996, p. 11). Here, Power uses the respect and trust she receives from these black women as a kind of identification card that she is a good white. Power also notes that she has told this story many times, partly as encouragement to other whites to move past history. In another example, Dailey (1997) reports with pride his public disavowal of his white identity: "It was amusing to watch the reaction of the 'black' sales clerk. Bagging my purchase, she was grinning" (p. 85) (for other examples, see Olson, 1995; Peeples, 1994; Selena & Katrina, 1996).

Interestingly, this focus on celebratory acts of race treason allows for the denial of whiteness. In these examples, whiteness is positioned as a choice, as a state of mind. In this way, the argument among race traitors that whiteness is a social formation extends the social constructionist argument to its extreme, or to what K Crenshaw (1991) calls "vulgar constructionism." In the individual acts of race treason noted above, race traitors escape their whiteness, and thus, social accountability (C. Crenshaw, 1997a). Those individuals who try to oppose racism are now not white. As Kinchloe and Steinberg (1998) observe, "Whites alone can opt out of their racial identity, can proclaimed themselves nonraced. Yet no matter how vociferously they may renounce their whiteness, white people do not lose the power associated with being White. Such a reality renders many white renunciations disingenuous" (p. 22).

Within *Race Traitor* discourse, we have individual choice and intentional action as the foundations upon which we decide and determine who is, and is not, white. This desire to distance oneself from one's whiteness comes through in many letters to the editors. Paul Bollmeier (1998) writes, "This...(*Race Traitor*) has helped me immeasurably. I have white skin, but I can no longer be 'white.' I have been a member of the white club for 43 years, and here in Minnesota we have a very high degree of feeling as though we are open, progressive and 'nice' to all of those who are not 'white.' However, I have never trusted this feeling and now I need to find a way to break out of this 'white lie.' " (p. 105). In a response to a letter to the editors, the editors encourage this becoming unwhite: "For us, being white is not a skin color but a state of mind, and accepting the privileges of whiteness. We think that if you fight as hard as you can against those privileges, even to the point of risking your own ability to receive them, then you are on your way to becoming unwhite" (Editors' reply, 1998, p. 107). Once whiteness is reduced to a "state of mind," then the move from whiteness to a state of blackness is facilitated.

APPROPRIATION OF BLACKNESS

As we note earlier, abolitionists seek to create a new subjectivity for whites—that of race traitor. However, rather than stopping with the destruction of white subjectivity and reconstructing in its place some sort of "not-white" subjectivity through examples offered by mythic heroes, "race traitors" advocate an adoption of blackness. Reminiscent of white supremacist discourse, whiteness is constructed as an oppositional category in reference to blackness which, in turn, is depicted as the antithesis of whiteness (Harper, 1994). Although differing in intent, both white

supremacist and *Race Traitor* anti-whiteness discourses appropriate blackness to serve their own ideological and political agendas. In *Race Traitor* discourse, blackness as re-interpreted through the lens of whiteness is often reified. Consider the following excerpt from an interview with Ignatiev in the *Utne Reader*:

> Politically, whiteness is the willingness to seek a comfortable place within the system of race privilege. Blackness means total, implacable, and relentless opposition to that system. To the extent that so-called whites oppose the race line, repudiating their own race privileges and jeopardizing their own standing in the white race they can be said to have washed away their whiteness and taken in some blackness. ("Treason," 1994, p. 84)

The sentiment expressed by Ignatiev resonates with that of Roediger (1994) who advocates "becoming black" as a revolutionary alternative for anti-whiteness whites. In fact, many of the articles published in *Race Traitor* address the issue of whites "crossing over" into black culture or what Ignatiev has called "black assimilation" ("Treason," 1994, p. 84). Although Ignatiev acknowledges that blacks are right to question claims of "white assimilation into blackness," he does not appear to be concerned with, or even acknowledge, the contradiction inherent in the use of white privilege to appropriate and redefine blackness through a white lens as an anti-whiteness revolutionary strategy. Given Ignatiev's and other race traitors' admonitions to give up white privilege—to refuse whiteness—as well as their eschewal of essentialist discourses on race, this appropriation of Blackness is an especially troublesome tendency in *Race Traitor* discourse.

An uncritical celebration and valorization of an essentialistic Blackness occurs throughout this discourse. Often this manifests in explicit and implicit suggestions that whites become "black" or somehow locate their lost humanity in things Black. For example, Rubio (1993b) encourages white musicians to turn to Black jazz to find their lost humanity. Like jazz musicians, hip-hoppers (read: Black youth) have much to teach whites. In their rejection of the dominant value system, they suggest that whites need to rethink wisdom and knowledge, and opt for revolutionary change (Chicago Surrealist Group, 1993).

Black culture is frequently re-presented as a more authentic and humane culture. Day (1993) argues that Black youth have more cultural pride than white youth, and that white kids see the energy and cultural pride in black kids, and they want it. The image of the "noble savage" emerges in Zaido (1997) who writes about how he plays "black music" and of his interest in it: "I heard...a truth in black music only hinted at in others, an encompassing, exciting truth, clear and soaring" (p. 52). For him, this desire to play black music and be recognized as black comes from some kind of hunger. He writes "it is a spiritual hunger," or more specifically, "a White Nation hunger" (p. 58). In another example, Filemyr (1999) relates a time in which she and her lover Essie had come home from a Womyn's music festival and were making love when police banged on the door, demanding that they "open up." Essie goes outside to talk to the police and Ann remains inside. Ann describes their actions. Essie, whom Ann had always known as gentle, "stood defiantly, legs spread apart, refusing to cooperate...she remained rigid, refusing to flinch, her eyes fixed on his, unwavering" (p. 11). In playing up the "authenticity" of blackness and the silent strength of African Americans, race traitors reinforce an essentialist version of the "noble savage."

Ironically, in chronicling past white ripoffs of blackness especially in 19th century minstrel shows, Roediger (1993) notes the problematic appropriation of blackface. He writes, "Their 'taking-off' of Black culture involved both imitating it and ridiculing it. And, finally, their act rested on being able to 'take off' the blackface mask and to reveal that underneath they were as white as the audience" (p. 107). Unfortunately, his insights are rarely turned inward, and race traitors miss the parallel between the racism of their appropriation and that of white minstrel performers. In our view, race traitors construct a romantic notion of an eternally resisting "black community" in order to create a suitable location for escapees from whiteness. In this way, " 'black' people are condemned to reification as the price of 'white' people's liberation from the racialisation process" (Bonnett, 1996a, p. 105).

TOWARD AN INTERSECTIONAL WHITENESS

The recentering of whiteness that occurs throughout the discourse of *Race Traitor* emerges as another instance and variant of what Collins (1990, 1993) calls "the ideology of domination." Such domination thinking relies on and perpetuates binary conceptionalizations of social identity categories. The rigid juxtaposition of white oppressor/black victim that occurs in much *Race Traitor* discourse leaves little room for understanding of the fluid and complex workings of power (Bonnett, 1996a; Collins, 1990, 1993; Lorde, 1984; Winant, 1997). For example, K. Crenshaw (1993) shows how the imposition of such models impeded the outcomes of the Hill-Thomas hearings. Positioned historically as victims of oppression, Thomas, a Black man, could not, in this instance, be rewritten as oppressor.

Further, the emphasis on whiteness to the exclusion of other axes of domination that we see in much of *Race Traitor* sets up the subsequent argument that whiteness is the foundational source of oppression, and that once eradicated, social justice will emerge. Fundamental oppression claims have come under heavy criticism by female scholars of color, in particular, who argue that "domination operates by seducing, pressuring, and forcing" people to choose categorical loyalties (Collins, 1990, p. 229). In forcing people to choose categorical loyalties, antithetical relationships are established, precluding understandings of, and dialogues between, various movements. In addition, the struggle for social justice itself is effectively undercut as oppressive systems tend to be linked within relations of domination and subordination. Singling out only one aspect produces skewed visions of relations of power (Collins, 1990, 1993).

Moreover, by closing themselves off from alliances with other liberatory movements such as anti-racism, feminism, and the gay liberation, *Race Traitor* prevents dialogue and co-strategizing between themselves and other liberatory movements. This sort of coalitional work is absolutely crucial. The absence of dialogue either within or between activist movements encourages the taking on of what Bernice Johnson Reagon (1992) calls "mono-issue politics." As Reagon so aptly cautioned:

> Watch those mono-issue people. They ain't gonna do you no good. I don't care who they are. And there are people who prioritize the cutting line of the struggle. And they say the cutting line is this issue, and more than anything we must move on this issue and that's automatically saying that whatever's bothering you will be put down if you bring it up. You have to watch these folks. Watch these groups that can only deal with once thing at a time. (p. 509)

In contrast to such univocal approaches, we, following K. Crenshaw (1991, 1992, 1993) and C. Crenshaw (1997b), advocate an intersectional approach to whiteness studies. Intersectionality involves analyzing the interlocking nature of oppression (also see Collins, 1990, 1993; Volpe, 1996; Wildman, 1996). As C. Crenshaw (1997b) argues, race, class, gender, age, sexual orientation and other social

identity categories do not operate in isolation. We can no more talk about our experience as women, separate from our race or class, than we can identify those parts of our bodies that represent particular and singular identity positions (Collins, 1993; Spelman, 1988). Rejecting this "pop-bead" approach to identity, and advocating a movement from additive to multiplicative assessments of identity and power, Spelman (1988) highlights the tendencies to universalize and essentialize that undergird additive and foundational analyses of oppression. She argues that additive models (e.g., race + gender) contribute to silencing and erasing of the many different experiences and practices of privilege and domination (Spelman, 1988). Intersectionality becomes a strategy for minimizing such erasures because, as C. Crenshaw (1997b) notes, intersectionality requires that we look at both presence and absence. For example, K. Crenshaw (1991, 1992) identifies the ways in which battered women's shelters endanger women of color. She argues that policies designed to help women, such as requiring participation from shelter residents in group counseling, can be particularly risky when such policies preclude shelters from accepting women who do not speak English on the basis that these women would not be able to participate in group counseling. Similarly, Dace (1998) calls for intersectionality when she notes how the desire for racial solidarity among African Americans, seen in such instances as the Hill-Thomas hearings and the Tyson trial, ignores the complex interplay of race and gender in the lives of Black women. As an approach, intersectionality enables complex analyses of theory and practice by directing critical attention to the ways in which policies designed to empower can also disempower.

One strategy for engaging in intersectional analysis comes from Matsuda (1996), who advocates "asking the other question." Matsuda explains that we can examine, for instance, anti-racist practices for ways in which they might perpetuate sexism or hetero-sexism by asking the "other question." In the case of *Race Traitor*, we can look to the treasonous practices through this lens and perhaps avoid or minimize the tendency to recenter whiteness, and in particular, white men. For example, when race traitors encourage the cross-over to blackness, we can ask how the identification with blackness might reproduce racism and white privilege, and so avoid commodification and appropriation. When race traitors honor historic figures, such as John Brown, we can ask how the selection of heroes perpetuates sexism by absenting such heroes as Rosa Parks.

This analytic strategy then requires dialogue with and among various social movements, for it is often easy to miss the ways in which our own actions maintain oppression (Collins 1993). However, when anti-racists talk with abolitionists and feminists and queer theorists, we are likely to have more "other" questions being asked. If Collins (1993) is right when she argues that, "While many of us have little difficulty assessing our own victimization within some major system of oppression...we typically fail to see how our thoughts and actions uphold someone else's subordination" (p. 25), then we need to encourage and actively seek out conversations across groups. In these conversations and joint efforts, we can learn about the specifics of oppression as they are experienced by, for instance, Latina lesbians versus white lesbians versus straight Black men.

In this respect, intersectionality requires what C. Crenshaw (1997a), McKerrow (1989), Wander (1984), and others call critical self-reflexivity, or a holding up of our own practices to question and critique. *Race Traitor*, in generally avoiding such reflexivity, misses the corrective step necessary in strategizing social reform. As Ono and Sloop (1992) note, hegemony is sustained by static practices which are easily co-opted and used against social groups. Advocating a "contingent telos" Ono and Sloop (1992) argue that while we cannot avoid taking an action step, neither can we become so committed to our particular vision for change that we fail to see the possibility that every strategy for change can also become oppressive.

CONCLUSION

The last few years have witnessed an important growth in what is now commonly called "whiteness studies." As the tensions at the Berkeley conference highlight, however, whiteness studies scholars often disagree about what the goals and strategies of this work should be. While we appreciate the turn away from uncritical celebrations of whiteness that abolitionist white scholars offer, we hope in this essay to add another point of critique to the larger debate about whiteness studies. That is, whiteness projects, whether they be along the lines of making or unmaking, need to avoid the tendency to fall into monolithic and/or essentialist discourses. As the rhetoric of Race Traitor illustrates, even the attempt to destroy whiteness can unwittingly reinscribe white privilege when that attempt is not mediated with a healthy questioning of its own goals and beliefs.

Given the dangers that we identify in our analysis of *Race Traitor*, we offer intersectionality as a possible self-corrective for whiteness studies. As C. Crenshaw (1997b) and K Crenshaw (1991, 1992, 1993) illustrate, inter-sectionality highlights the multiple axes of oppression and the particular dynamics that emerge at the crossroads of race, class, gender, and sexual orientation. In their analyses and in our assessment of *Race Traitor*, we begin to see how, for example, anti-racist projects can perpetuate sexism, or how the destruction of whiteness is made possible only through a reductive and romanticized notion of blackness. In addition, Matsuda's (1987) directive to "ask the other question" can be a helpful tool for whiteness studies scholars and activists that can enable whiteness studies to continue efforts to build an emancipatory discourse.

An earlier version of this essay was presented at the National Communication Association conference, Chicago, IL, November 1997. The authors thank the reviewers and Paul Mongeau for their critical insights which helped shape this final draft. Dreama Moon (Ph.D., Arizona State University) is Assistant Professor, Communication Department, California State University, San Marcos, CA 92096-0001(dmoon@mailhost1.csusm.edu). Lisa A. Flores (Ph.D., University of Georgia) is Assistant Professor, Department of Communication and Ethnic Studies, University of Utah, Salt Lake City, UT 84112 (lisa.flores@mm.cc.utah.edu).

REFERENCES

Alcoff, L. M. (1998). What should white people do? *Hypatia,* 13(3), 6–26.

Autonomous Zone. (1997, Winter). Statement to Anti-racist network. *Race Traitor: Treason to Whiteness is Loyalty to Humanity,* 7, 21–24.

Bailey, A. (1998). Locating traitorous identities: Toward a view of privilege-cognizant white character. *Hypatia* 13(3), 27–41.

Baldwin, J. (1984, April). On being "white"…and other lies. *Essence,* 90–92.

Bollmeier, P. W. (1998, Winter). Breaking out [Letter to the Editor]. *Race Traitor: Treason to Whiteness it Loyalty to Humanity,* 8, 105.

Bonnett, A. (1996a). *Anti-racism and the critique of "white" identities. new community,* 22(1), 97–110.

Bonnett, A. (19966). "White studies": The problems and projects of a new research agenda. *Theory, culture, & society,* 13(2),145–155.

Boyer, D. C. (1998,Summer). Are you crazy? Mental illness & the belief in whiteness. *Race Traitor. Treason to Whiteness it Loyalty to Humanity,* 9, 117–119.

Bragg, E. (1998, Summer). Miserabdism and the new eugenics. *Race Traitor: Treason to Whiteness is Loyalty to Humanity,* 9, 87–90.

Burdman, P. (1997, April 12). Scholars gather in Berkeley to talk about whiteness, 3-day meeting on UC campus. *The San Francisco Chronicle,* A7.

Chao, J. (1997 April 12). Popular forum studying white folks; UC-Berkeley event aims to understand ethnicity, not foster guilt or supremacy. *The San Francisco Examiner,* A7.

Chas, T. (1997, Winter). Overjoyed. [Letter to the editor]. *Race Traitor: Treason to Whiteners it Loyalty to Humanity,* 7, 91.

Chicago Surrealist Group. (1993, Summer). Three days that shook the new world order: The Los Angeles rebellion of 1992. *Race Traitor: Treason to Whiteness is Loyalty to Humanity,* 2, 1–17.

Chicago Surrealist Group. (1998, Summer). Introduction. *Race Traitor: Treason to Whiteness is Loyalty to Humanity,* 9, 3–4.

Clifford, J. (1988). *The predicament of culture: Twentieth-century ethnography, literature, and art.* Cambridge, MA: Harvard University Press.

Collins, P. H. (1990). *Black feminist thought: Knowledge, consciousness, and the politics of empowerment.* New York: Routledge.

Collins P. H. (1993). Toward a new vision: Race, class, and gender as categories of analysis and connection. *Race, sex, and class,* 1 25–46.

Crenshaw, C. (1997a). Resisting whiteness' rhetorical silence. *Western Journal of Communication,* 61 253–278.

Crenshaw C. (19976). Women in the Gulf War: Toward an intersectional feminist rhetorical criticism. Howard *Journal of Communications,* 8, 219–255.

Crenshaw K. (1991). Mapping the margins: Intersectionality, identity politics, and violence against women of color. *Stanford Law Review,* 43, 1241–1299.

Crenshaw K. (1992). The import of the Anita Hill/Clarence Thomas hearings: Race, gender, and sexual harassment *California Law Review,* 65, 1467–1476.

Crenshaw, K. (1993). Whose story is it, anyway? Feminist and anti-racist appropriations of Anita Hill. In T. Morrison (Ed.), *Race-ing justice, en-gendering power: Essays on Anita Hill, Clarence Thomas; and the construction of social reality* (pp. 402–440). New York: Pantheon.

D'Andrea, C. (1993, Summer). Slaves, England, and the American word. *Race Traitor: Treason to Whiteness is Loyalty to Humanity,* 2, 52–59.

Dace K. L. (1998). "Had Judas been a Black man...": Politics race and gender in African America. In J. M. Sloop & J. P. McDaniel (Eds.), *Judgment calls: Rhetoric, politic, and indeterminacy* (pp. 163–181). Boulder, CO: Westview.

Dailey, J. (1997, Winter). Let them decide. [Letter to the editor]. *Race Traitor: Treason to Whiteness is Loyalty to Humanity, 7,* 85.

Day, C. (1993 Summer). Gangster rap: Live on the stage of history. *Race Traitor: Treason to Whiteness is Loyalty to Humanity, 2,* 29–38.

Day, C. (1994 Spring). Out of whiteness. *Race Traitor: Treason to Whiteners is Loyalty to Humanity, 3,* 55–66.

DeLuca, K. (1999). In the shadow of whiteness: The consequences of constructions of nature in environmental politics. In T. K. Nakayama & J. N. Martin (Eds.), *Whiteness: The communication of social identity* (pp. 217–246). Thousand Oaks, CA: Sage.

Demick J. R. (1995, Winter). This is me. [Letter to the editor]. *Race Traitor: Treason to Whiteness is Loyalty to Humanity, 4,* 111–112.

DuBois, W. E. B. (1997). *The soul of black folks* Boston: Bedford Books. (Original work published in 1903)

Dyer, R (1988). White. *Screen, 29,* 44–65

Dyer, R (1998). White. NY: Routledge

Eakins, P. (1995, Winter). Manifesto of a dead daughter. *Race Traitor: Treason to Whiteness is Loyalty to Humanity, 4,* 1–5.

Editorial: Abolish the white race—by any means necessary (1793, Winter). *Race Traitor: Treason to whiteness is Loyalty to Humanity, 1.* I-8

Editorial: When does the unreasonable act make sense? (1994, Spring). *Race Traitor: Treason to Whiteness is Loyalty to Humanity, 3,* 108–110.

Editorial: Aux armes! Formez vos bataillons! (1996a, Winter). *Race Traitor: Treason to Whiteness is Loyalty to Humanity, 5,* 1–3.

Editorial: Until it hurts. (19966 Winter). *Race Traitor: Treason to Whiteness is Loyalty to Humanity, 5,* 3–5.

Editors reply. (1994, Spring) *Race Traitor: Treason to Whiteness is Loyalty to Humanity, 3,* 114–115.

Editors' reply. (1998 Winter). *Race Traitor: Treason to Whiteness is Loyalty to Humanity, 8,*107–110.

Epperson, T. W. (1997, Winter). Whiteness in early Virginia. *Race Traitor: Treason to Whiteness is Loyalty to Humanity, 7,* 21–24.

Ervin, L K. (1994 Spring). Back from hell: Black power and treason to whiteness inside prison walls. *Race Traitor: Treason to Whiteness is Loyalty to Humanity, 3,* 13–19.

Exchange with a national socialist (1996, Winter). *Race Traitor: Treason to Whiteness is Loyalty to Humanity, 5,* 17–48.

Filemyr, A. (1999 Winter). Resisting arrest *Race Traitor. Treason to Whiteness is Loyalty to Humanity, 10,* 8–23.

Frankenberg, R (1993). *White women, race matters.* Minneapolis, MN: University of Minnesota Press.

Frankenberg, R (1997). Introduction: Local whiteness localizing whiteness. In R Frankenberg (Ed.), *Displacing whiteness: Essays in social and cultural criticism* (pp. 1–33). Durham, NC: Duke University Press.

Fraser. J. W. (1993, Winter). Two who said "no" to whiteness: Boston public schools, 1962–1975. *Race Traitor: Treason to Whiteness is Loyalty to Humanity, 1,* 9–20.

Frederickson, G. M. (1994, Spring). Reflections on the comparative history and sociology of racism. *Race Traitor: Treason to Whiteness is Loyalty to Humanity, 3,* 83–98.

Free to be me. (1994, Spring). *Race Traitor: Treason to Whiteness is Loyalty to Humanity, 3,* 33.

Fritschel, M. (1993, Summer). Huck Finn and the authority of conscience. *Race Traitor: Treason to Whiteness is Loyalty to Humanity, 2.* 46–51.

Garvey, J., & Ignatiev, N. (1997). Toward a new abolitionism: A Race Traitor manifesto. In M. Hill (Ed.), *Whiteness: A critical reader* (pp. 346–349). New York: New York University Press.

Gilbert, J. (1994, Spring). Who lost an American? *Race Traitor: Treason to Whiteness is Loyalty to Humanity, 3,* 1–12.

Giroux, H. A. (1997). White squall: Resistance and the pedagogy of whiteness. *Cultural Studies, 11,* 376–389.

Goodman, P. S. (1997, April 12). Conference seeks to clear up what it means to be white; Berkeley talks draw high turnout *The Washington Post* A16.

Harper, S. (1994). Subordinating masculinities/racializing masculinities: Writing white supremacist discourse on men's bodies. *Masculinities, 2,* 1–20.

Hasian, M., Jr., & Flores, L. A. (1997). Children of the stones: The Intifada and the mythic creation of the

Palestinian state. *Southern Communication Journal,* 62, 89–106.

Haynes V. D. (1998, March 1). "Whiteness studies" movement grows. *Las Vegas Review-Journal,* 10B.

Henson, B. (1999, Winter). Plowshares into swords: John Brown & the poet of rage. *Race Traitor: Treason to Whiteness is Loyalty to Humanity,* 10, 77–84.

Hill, B. B. (1998, Winter). Stir Fry. [Letter to the editor]. *Race Traitor: Treason to Whiteness is Loyalty to Humanity,* 8, 109.

Hill, M. (1997). Introduction: Vipers in Shangri-la, whiteness, writing and other ordinary terrors. In M. Hill (Ed.)., *Whiteness: A critical reader* (pp. 1–18). New York: New York University Press.

hooks, b. (1990). *Yearning: race, gender, and cultural politic.* Boston: South End.

hooks, b. (1992a). *Black looks: Race and representation.* Boston: South End Press.

hooks, b. (19926). Representing whiteness in the black imagination. In L Grossberg, C. Nelson, & P. Treichler (File.), *Cultural studies* (pp. 338–346). New York: Routledge.

Huckleberry Finn: *Race traitor. (1993, Summer). Race Traitor: Treason is Loyalty to Humanity,* 2, 39–41.

Hughes, L (1934/ 1969). *The ways of white folk.* New York: A. A. Knopf.

Ignatiev, N. (1993, Winter). The American intifada. *Race Traitor: Treason to Whiteness is Loyalty to Humanity,* 1, 45–49.

Ignatiev, N. (1994, Spring). The white worker and the labor movement in nineteenth-century America. *Race Traitor: Treason to Whiteness is Loyalty to Humanity,* 3, 99–107.

Ignatiev, N. (1996, Winter). Briefly noted. *Race Traitor: Treason to Whiteners is Loyalty to Humanity,* 6, 77–81.

Ignatiev, N. (1997, April). *The point it not to interpret whiteness but to abolish it.* The Making and Unmaking of Whiteness Conference, Berkeley, CA. [Online]. http:llwwwpostfun.com/racetraitor/features/thepoint.html

Ignatiev, N. (1999, Winter). Abolitionism and the white studies racket *Race Traitor: Treason to Whiteness is Loyalty to Humanity,* 10, 3–7.

Jackson II, R L (1999). White space, white privilege: Mapping discursive inquiry into the self. *Quarterly Journal of Speech* 85, 38–54.

Jacobs, H. (1994). The jealous mistress. In D. Ruediger (Ed.), *Black on white: Black writers on what it means to be white* (pp. 278–283). New York: Schocken Books. (Original work published in 1861)

Johnson, P. (1999). Reflections on critical white(ness) studies. In T. K. Nakayama & J. N. Martin (Eds.), *Whiteness: The communication of social identity* (pp. 1–12). Thousand Oaks, CA: Sage.

Johnson, T. (1999, Winter). My sentiments exactly. [Letter to the editor]. *Race Traitor: Treason to Whiteness is Loyalty to Humanity,* 10,105–107.

K., M. (1997, Winter). Another other. [Letter to the editor]. *Race Traitor: Treason to Whiteness is Loyalty to Humanity,* 7, 87–88.

Karcher, C. L. (1993, Winter). Lydia Marie Child and the example of John Brown. *Race Traitor: Treason is Loyalty to Humanity,* 1 21–44.

Katz, J. (1978). *White awareness: Handbook for anti-racism training.* Norman, OK: University of Oklahoma

Kaufman, C. (1996). The making and unmaking of whiteness. *Socialist Review,* 26(3/4), 195–201.

Kelley, S., Schuwerk, R, Krishnamurthy, P., & Kao, J. (1997, Winter). Abolitionism on the campus: Students for the abolition of whiteness: Chicago. *Race Traitor: Treason to Whiteness is Loyalty to Humanity,* 7, 1–6.

Kincheloe J. L, & Steinberg, S. R (1998). Addressing the crisis of whiteness: Reconfiguring white identity in a pedagogy of whiteness. In J. L Kincheloe, S. R Steinberg, N. M. Rodriguez, & R E. Chennault (Eds.), *White reign: Deploying whiteness in America* (pp. 3–29). New York: St Martin's.

Kurnick, D. (1993, Winter). Malcolm X beyond labels. *Race Traitor: Treason to Whiteness is Loyalty to Humanity,* 1, 108–113.

Large, J. (1999, January 17). Don't assume I'm white—their skin may be pale, but they want to overturn whiteness and the privilege that it confers. *The Seattle Times,* L1.

Lee, W. S. (1999). One whiteness veils three uglinesses: From border-crossing to a womanist interrogation of gendered colorism. In T. K Nakayama & J. N. Martin (Eds.), *Whiteness: The communication of social identity* (pp. 279–298). Thousand Oaks, CA: Sage.

Lipsitz, G. (1998). *The possesive investment in whiteness: How white people profit from identity politics.* Philadelphia, PA: Temple University Press.

Lorde, A. (1984). *Sister outsider: essays and speeches.* Freedom, CA: Crossing.

Marty, D. (1999). White andracist rhetoric as apologia: Wendell Berry's The Hidden Wound In T. K Nakayama &J. N. Martin (Eds.), *Whiteness: The communication of social identity* (pp. 51–68). Thousand Oaks, CA:

Matsuda, M. (1987). Looking to the bottom: Critical Legal Studies and reparations. *Harvard Civil Right-Civil Liberties Law Review,* 22, 323–339.

Matsuda, M. (1996). *Where is your body?: And other essays on race gender and the law.* Boston: Beacon Press.

McKerrow, R. E. (1989). Critical rhetoric: Theory and praxis. *Communication Monographs,* 56, 91–111.

Mia. (1998 Winter). Cool. [Letter to the Editor]. *Race Traitor: Treason to Whiteness is Loyalty to Humanity,* 8,107.

Miles, R (1989). *Racism.* New York: Routledge.

Moon, D. (1999). White enculturation and bourgeois ideology: The discursive production of "good (white) girls." In T. K. Nakayama & J. N. Martin (Eds.), *Whiteness: The communication of social identity* (pp. 177–197). Thousand Oaks CA: Sage

Morrison, T. (1992). *Playing in the dark: Whiteness and the literary imagination.* New York: Vintage Books.

Nakayama, T. K, & Krizek, R L. (1995). Whiteness: A strategic rhetoric. *The Quarterly Journal of Speech,* 81, 291–309.

Nakayama, T. K & Martin J. N. (1999). Introduction: Whiteness as the communication of social identity. In T. K Nakayama & J. N. Martin (Eds.), *Whiteness: The communication of social identify* (pp. vii–xiv). Thousand Oaks, CA: Sage.

Newitz, A., & Wray, M. (1997). Introduction. In M. Wray & A. Newitz (Eds.), *White trash: Race and loss in America* (pp. 1–12). New York: Routledge.

Niles, C. (1999, February). Why abolitionists are not anti-racists. *The New Abolitionist* 2(1), 3–4.

Olives J. (1995 Winter). Through the eyes of a villain [Letter to the editor]. *Race Traitor: Treason to Whiteness, is Loyalty to Humanity,* 4,116–117.

Olson, J. (1995, Winter). Police-assisted homicide. *Race Traitor: Treason to Whiteness is Loyalty to Humanity,* 4, 6–13.

Omi, M. & Winant, H. (1993). The Los Angeles "race riot" and contemporary U.S. politics. In R Gooding-Williams (Ed.), *Reading Rodney King/Reading urban uprising* (pp. 97–114). New York: Roudedge.

Omi, M., & Winant, H. (1994). *Racial formation in the United States from the 1960s to the 1990s* New York: Routledge.

Ono, K A. & Sloop, J. M. (1992). Commitment to telos—A sustained critical rhetoric. *Communication Monographs,* 59, 48–60.

Peeples, E. H. (1994, Spring). Richmond journal: Thirty years in black & white. *Race Traitor: Treason to Whiteness is Loyalty to Humanity,* 3, 34–46.

Power, K S. (1996, Winter). Beyond history. *Race Traitor: Treason to Whiteness is Loyalty to Humanity,* 5, 6–16.

Projansky, S., & Ono K A. (1999). Strategic whiteness as cinematic racial politics. In T. K Nakayama & J. N. Martin (Eds.), *Whiteness: The communication of social identity* (pp. 149–174). Thousand Oaks, CA: Sage.

Rawson, A. (1997, Winter). Zappatista. (Letter to the editor). *Race Traitor: Treason to Whiteness is Loyalty to Humanity,* 7, 90–91.

Reagon, B. J. (1992). Coalition politics: Turning the century. In M. L Andersen & P. H. Collins (Eds.), *Race, class, and gender: An anthology* (pp. 503–509). Belmont, CA: Wadsworth.

Renew the legacy of John Brown. (1999, Winter). *Race traitor: Treason to Whiteness is Loyalty to Humanity,* 10, 1–2.

Roediger, D. (1993, Winter). The white question. *Race Traitor: Treason to Whiteness is Loyalty to Humanity,* 1, 104–107.

Roediger, D. (1994). *Towards the abolition of whiteness.* New York: Verso.

Rosaldo, R. (1993). *Culture & truth: The remaking of social analysis.* Boston: Beacon.

Rosemont, F. (1998, Summer). Notes on surrealism as a revolution against whiteness. *Race Traitor: Treason to Whiteness is Loyalty to Humanity* 9 19–29.

Rubio, P. (1993a, Winter). Civil war reenactments and other myths. *Race Traitor: Treason to Whiteness is Loyalty to Humanity,* 1, 88–103.

Rubio, P. (19936, Summer). Crossover dreams: The exceptional white in popular culture. *Race Traitor: Treason to Whiteness is Loyalty to Humanity,* 2, 68–80.

Rubio, P. (1994, Spring). Can I get a witness? *Race Traitor: Treason to Whiteness is Loyalty to Humanity,* 3, 79–82.

Salahuddian. A. V. I. (1994, Spring). In the name of Allah, the gracious, the merciful (Letter to the editor]. *Race Traitor: Treason to Whiteness is Loyalty to Humanity,* 3, 115–119.

Segrest, M. (1994a). *Memoir of a race traitor.* Boston: South End.

Segrest, M. (1994b, Spring). When we don't get race, it kills us. *Race Traitor. Treason to Whiteness is Loyalty to Humanity,* 3, 23–32.

Selena, and Katrina (1996, Summer). Copwatch. *Race Traitor: Treason to Whiteness is Loyalty to Humanity,* 6, 18–23.

Shome R (1996). Race and popular cinema: The rhetorical strategies of whiteness in City of Joy. *Communication Quarterly,* 44, 502–518.

Shome, R. (1999). Whiteness and the politics of location. In T. K Nakayama &J. N. Martin (Eds.), *Whiteness: The communication of social identity* (pp. 107–128). Thousand Oaks, CA: Sage.

Sleeter C. E. (1995, Winter). White silence, white solidarity. *Race Traitor: Reason to Whiteness is Loyalty to Humanity,* 4,14–22.

Sloop, J. M. (1994). Apology made to whoever pleases": Cultural discipline and the grounds of interpretation. *Communication Quarterly* 42, 345–362.

Solomos, J. (1986). Varieties of Marxist conceptions of 'race,' class, and the state: A critical analysis. In J. Rex & D. Mason Eds.), *Theories of race and ethnic relations* (pp. 84–109). Cambridge, England: Cambridge University Press.

Spelman, E. V. (1988). *Inessential woman: Problems of exclusion in feminist thought.* Boston: Beacon Press.

Steyn M. (1999). White identity in context: A personal narrative. In T. K Nakayama & J. N. Martin (Eds.), *Whiteness The communication of social identity* (pp. 264–278). Thousand Oaks, CA: Sage.

Supriya, K E. (1999). White difference: Cultural constructions of white identity. In T. K Nakayama & J. N.

Martin (Eds.), *Whiteness: The communication of social identity* (pp 129–148). Thousand Oaks, CA: Sage.

Swayne, P. A. (1996 Summer). Don't assume I'm white. [Letter to the editor]. *Race Traitor: Treason to Whiteness is Loyalty to Humanity,* 6, 95–96.

Talbot, M. (1997, November 30). Getting credit for being white. *The New York Times,* p. 116.

Tenenbaum D. (1996, Summer). Race treason. (Letter to the editor). *Race Traitor: Treason to Whiteness is Loyalty to Humanity,* 6, 96–97.

Terry, R W. (1975). *For whites only.* Grand Rapids, MI: William B. Eerdman.

Treason to whiteness is loyalty to humanity: An interview with Noel Ignatiev of *Race Traitor* magazine. (1994, November/December). *Utne Reader,* 66, 82–86.

Volpe, L (1996). Talking "culture": Gender, race, nation, and the politics of multiculturalism. *Columbia Law Review,* 96,1573–1617.

Wander, P. (1984). The third persona: An ideological turn in rhetorical theory. *Central States Speech Journal* 35, 197–216.

Weiss, J. (1993, Summer). The law according to Huck. *Race Traitor: Treason to Whiteness is Loyalty to Humanity,* 2, 41–46.

Wildman S. M. (with Armstrong, M., Davis, A. D., & Grillo, T.). (1996). *Privilege revealed: How invisible preference undermines America.* New York: New York University Press.

Winant, H. (1997). Behind blue eyes: Whiteness and contemporary U. S. racial politics. In M. Fine L. Weis, L C. Powell, & L M. Wong (Eds.), *Off white: Readings on race, power, and society* (pp. 40–53). New York: Routledge.

Zaido, D. J. (1997, Winter). Blackface, jackstraws, & tin paneling. *Race Traitor: Treason to Whiteness is Loyalty to Humanity,* 7, 50–65.

The Evolution of Black Political Power

Eddie N. Williams and Margaret C. Simms

As we enter the 21st, century, African Americans have many of the same goals and aspirations they had going into the 20th century: to exercise their right to vote and make their votes count; to live in safe communities with healthy environments in which to raise their children; to work and be justly rewarded for that work; to accumulate wealth to enhance their quality of life, and to pass that wealth on to their heirs.

To achieve the last three goals during the 20th century, African Americans have relied greatly on the first goal-the exercise of political power. But over time, it has become increasingly clear that political and economic power are interrelated. It has long been recognized that, without political power, it is difficult for African Americans to make sustained economic gains. But it also is becoming clear that without economic power, it is difficult to make political power an effective tool for improving society.

Assessing progress toward achieving such goals depends on the point of comparison. Clearly, both political and economic advancement since the beginning, or even the middle, of the 20th century has been considerable. The impact of the Voting Rights Act of 1965 and Supreme Court rulings in the area of voting rights and representation is reflected in the sharp increase in the number of black elected officials. At the turn of the last century African Americans had little effective political power. Due to legal restrictions and physical and economic intimidation, African Americans were often denied the opportunity to vote, even though that right was granted to them by the 15th Amendment.

By 1960, political power had grown, but still was quite limited, with only an estimated 300 black elected officials in the nation, most in the northeastern and midwestern regions of the country. At the end of the 20th century, the Joint Center's 1998 *Roster of Black Elected Officials* counted nearly 9,000 African Americans in elective office, ranging from 25 holding statewide office to 4,277 holding municipal positions, such as mayors and city council members. The largest number of black elected officials can be found in the southern states, the region of the country where blacks were most politically oppressed during much of the last century.

African Americans have also gained power within party politics, though that has been one-sided. When President Clinton made his first State of the Union address in-the-new century to the U.S. Congress, the growth in black political power could be seen in the audience. The Clinton cabinet, which the president has touted as one that "looks like America," was seated in the front row. In their ranks were three African Americans: Secretary of Labor Alexis Herman, Secretary of Transportation Rodney Slater and Secretary of Veterans DMirs Togo West. Among the members of Congress were 39 African-American members of the House of Representatives including one Republican, J. C. Watts, who holds a leadership role in Congress as the Republican conference chairman in the House, the No. 4 position in the Republican leadership. Democratic members of the Congressional Black Caucus range in tenure from John Conyers (D-MI), who has served for 35 years, to Stephanie Tubbs Jones (D-OH), who replaced Congressman Louis Stokes last year. Four of the CBC are ranking members of congressional committees, including Congressman Charles Rangel, who sits on the powerful House Ways and Means Committee.

During his speech, President Clinton referred to the impact of the booming economy on all segments of the population, including African Americans, for whom unemployment and poverty rates are now the lowest they have been since such information has been recorded. While the picture painted by the president and by the diversity of the audience in front of him demonstrated the progress that had been made over the last half of the 20th century, the scene also revealed the fragility of that progress. Blacks hold high office in large numbers compared to the past, but they are still underrepresented relative to their proportion of the voting population. In addition, African Americans have been very closely affiliated with the Democratic Party, which means they are almost automatically excluded from the ranks of power when Republicans control the executive and/or legislative branches at both the federal and state levels.

The economic progress cited by the president in terms of low unemployment and poverty rates is partially overshadowed by large gaps

between the economic positions of African Americans and white Americans. Moreover, the political and social environment in which African Americans made their greatest gains was far different from the current environment. How, then, can we assess our accomplishments and adjust our strategies in the face of new and different challenges in the new century?

ACCOMPLISHMENTS OF THE 20TH CENTURY

African-American political progress in the second half of the 20th century would have been viewed as truly remarkable by people alive at the beginning of that century. When the United States entered the 1900s, the context for African-American political and economic life was shaped by the Supreme Court's separate-but equal ruling in *Plessy v. Ferguson* and the virtual absence of African Americans in elective office; the last African American to hold federal office in the 19th century left the U.S. House of Representatives in 1901.[1]

Table 1: Black Officials in the United States By Category of Office, 1970 and 1980

Year	1970	1998
Total Number	1,469	8,868
Federal	10	40
State	169	587
Substate Regional	–	17
County	92	930
Municipal	623	4,277
Judicial and Law Enforcement	213	998
Education	362	2,017

Source: *Black Officials: A Statistical Summary, 1998.* Joint Center for Political and Economic Studies.

While some gains were made between 1900 and 1960, real political momentum was achieved only with the passage of the Voting Rights Act of 1965 and its revisions in 1982.

Along with Supreme Court rulings in *Baker v. Carr* and *Thornburg v. Gingles,* that act gave real teeth to black voting power. As a result, the number of black elected officials rose from an estimated 300 in 1965 to 1,469 in 1970 and 8,868 in 1998.[2]

African Americans have also made progress in terms of party politics. During the last presidential campaign, they were well represented in the Democratic Party. Twenty percent of the Democratic National Committee was African American and 21.1 percent of the DNC executive committee was black.[3] Black Democrats were also prominent in state parties, putting them in good position to share in the benefits of electoral success in that presidential election year. African Americans have been far less active in Republican Party politics. Although a record number of black candidates ran for office as Republicans in 1994, their success in winning office was low. Moreover, blacks are virtually nonexistent in state Republican Party politics and leadership positions. The latter fact clearly has hampered the ability of blacks to use their political leverage as governorships and legislatures in many states have turned Republican.

Many expected growing political power to be reflected in greater economic power and improved quality of life within African-American communities, especially as political clout in the policy-making process was judiciously exercised. At the federal level, legislation could be reshaped, and budget allocations could be realigned to direct resources to worthy causes such as the War on Poverty and other social and economic programs. Political power also could be used to ensure that appointed officials would represent the values and expectations of disadvantaged communities. At the state and local levels, additional resources could be brought to bear to complete the process. African-American officials would have the power to appoint offcials who could make local programs work for minorities and disadvantaged populations of all ethnicities.

To some extent, the strategy worked well. African-American members of Congress, such as Adam Clayton Powell and Augustus Hawkins, played critical roles in the development of anti-poverty and education programs that benefitted black communities. African-American political activists worked with white policymakers to develop and implement equal opportunity and affirmative action programs. The two strategies together played major roles in economic advancement made by African Americans between 1960 and 1980.

Congressman Parren Mitchell spearheaded efforts to set aside a portion of transportation contract dollars for minority and women-owned businesses. At the local level, black mayors created and administered minority-business development programs that were instrumental in helping black-owned businesses to win and successfully execute government contracts. Similar efforts at state and local levels afforded new opportunities to businesses in many communities across the country. The role those programs played in the transformation of black-owned businesses has been documented in research completed by the Joint Center.[4]

As a result of the combination of social policy, affirmative action and individual initiative, the proportion of African Americans with a college degree tripled, increasing from 4 percent in 1960 to 14 percent in 1996. The proportion of African Americans in managerial, professional and technical jobs rose from 7 percent in 1960 to 23 percent in 1998. Black businesses grew tremendously over the two decades for which we have data. In 1972, the Census Bureau counted just under 195,000 firms in the entire country, mainly in "mom-and-pop" businesses. By 1992, the number of black-owned companies had tripled to almost 621,000. But that was just the tip of the iceberg, since many larger, more successful black-owned companies were not included in the 1992 numbers. Research by the Joint Center shows those latter firms are, in fact, very large in comparison to those actually included in the 1992 survey.

While the census survey presents a profile of the typical black-owned firm as having no employees and annual gross sales of only $52,000, our research identified many mufti-million-dollar companies with several hundred employees on their payrolls and much higher gross sales.[5] Without a doubt, the key to those firms' success was the hard work and entrepreneurial skill of their owners. However, many would not have been able to demonstrate those skills without minority-business programs in existence in both the public and private sectors.

Economic progress over the years has increased the proportion of African-American households with incomes at the upper end of the income distribution. In 1998, 22.8 percent of African-American households had incomes of more than $50,000, up from 9.1 percent with the same income (in 1998-adjusted dollars) in 1967. While the proportion of black households with incomes of more than $50,000 has increased about one-third since 1992, the proportion with incomes greater than $100,000 has increased nearly 50 percent. However, the gains have not substantially altered the relationship of black households to white and Asian households. Blacks were only one-half as likely as either white or Asian households to have incomes greater than $50,000. They were only one-third as likely as white households and only one-fourth as likely as Asian households to have incomes greater than $100,000.

Disparities persist as well at the low end of the income spectrum. The African-American poverty rate remains high and the black/white income ratio is little changed since 1960.

While the black poverty rate of 26.1 percent in 1998 was low by historic comparisons, it still was more than. twice the overall poverty rate. Poverty rates for black children (36.7 percent) were three and a half times the rate for non-Hispanic white children .[6]

Moreover, the current political environment is not supportive of efforts to keep open the doors of opportunity. Minority-business development programs have been under attack for the past decade, beginning with a 1989 Supreme Court decision in *Richmond v. Croson,* which ruled that certain minority-business set-aside programs were unconstitutional, and a 1995 decision in *Adarand v. Pena* that placed limits on federal business assistance programs. Affirmative-action programs in education and employment face similar threats. The passage of Proposition 209 in California was the beginning of a series of actions threatening to limit the extent to which state governments could provide opportunity through admissions policies that take account of race.

CHALLENGES FOR THE 21ST CENTURY

Added to the changed environment are several new or persistent challenges that African Americans face, including the ongoing issues of political representation, the growing diversity of the minority population within the United States, a newly identified divergence of opinion within the African-American population, and the growth of e-commerce and cyber-democracy.

One of the most immediate challenges to the African-American population will be the impact of the census on voting representation. A number of court rulings in the last decade of the 201 century left some significant questions unanswered with regard to minority representation, including the extent to which districts can be shaped to accommodate minority voting rights, and the definition and measurement of racially polarized voting. In addition, redistricting in 2001-2002 will be affected by the party composition of state legislatures. While blacks played significant roles in redistricting in a number of states after the 1990 census, Republican control of state legislatures in the current round of redistricting will restrict blacks' ability to influence the composition of political districts.

In addition to their declining influence in the legislative power structure, blacks may find their general political influence lessening as well. Until the end of the 1980s, African Americans were the dominant minority group in terms of population. Over the past decade, the growth of Hispanic and Asian populations has changed the way African Americans are viewed in society. As we enter the 21" century, African-American and Hispanic populations are similar in size, but over the coming decades African Americans will be a relatively constant share of the overall U.S. population, while Hispanic and Asian populations will grow rapidly. By the year 2045, the Hispanic population will be twice as large as the African-American population, and the Asian-American population will be slightly less, a difference that will be especially noticeable among younger cohorts Together, the three population groups will constitute a majority in terms of numbers by the year 2050, but so far they have not developed a collaborative agenda that will enable them to work as a cohesive political force. Indeed, significant differences have emerged within each of the racial/ethnic groups. Finding common ground on which a joint agenda for the three groups can be based will be a significant challenge during the coming decade.

Another challenge will be the management of what is likely to be a growing divergence of opinion within the African-American community. While such differences are not unique,

they are more striking because of the relative solidarity of opinion and party affiliation within the black population in the United States over the past 50 years. That solidarity has meant two things. First, it has enabled blacks to use their collective votes to provide the winning edge for political candidates, thereby increasing the chances of affecting policy decisions that benefit the African-American community. Second, the similarity of views made it easier for political representatives to work for their constituents, since a "one-view-fits-all" approach tended to prevail. When that commonality of views disappears, it could weaken the political clout of the African-American community.

The Joint Center has begun to document differences in political and social attitudes between older and younger African Americans. One of the most significant differences is in the area of education policy, where African Americans under the age of 35 have distinctly different views of the current quality of education available to children and the appropriate policies for improving educational outcomes. In particular, younger African Americans view school vouchers as an appropriate solution to poor educational outcomes in urban public schools. More than 70 percent of African-American respondents in the Joint Center's 1999 National Opinion Poll supported school vouchers. In contrast, only 49 percent of black respondents between the ages of 51 and 64, and 44 percent of those 65 and over, supported vouchers.

Compounding the growing diversity of opinion is the impact of differences in age on black voter participation. Younger people are less likely to vote than older citizens, regardless of race. Because the African-American population is younger than the white population, the impact of low black-voter participation has more of a negative impact on overall voting statistics. Young adults constitute 17 percent of the African-American voting age population (1 in 6 voters), compared to 12.6 percent of the white voting age population (1 in 8). Given the general cynicism of young voters, it will be a challenge to engage the new generation in the political process.

Another challenge will be the impact of new telecommunications technology on commerce, civic engagement and voter participation. While the Internet and related forms of electronic communication offer new means of low-cost information dissemination, they also can be a disadvantage to those without the means and inclination to use them. Recent studies of computer use and Internet connectivity reveal a very large "digital divide" between whites and Asian Americans on the one hand, and African Americans and Hispanics on the other. While nearly 38 percent of whites and 36 percent of Asian Americans used the Internet in 1998, only 19 percent of African Americans and fewer than 17 percent of Hispanics used the Internet at home, work or a community facility. That gap has been growing over the last two years, but there are significant differences in Internet use by age. In the Joint Center's 1999 National Opinion Poll, close to two-thirds (64.9 percent) of African Americans between the ages of 18 and 25 said they used the Internet, compared to only one-third (31.3 percent) of those between the ages of 51 and 64, and fewer than 10 percent of African Americans aged 65 or older. That would suggest cyberdemocracy has the potential to engage those who currently have the lowest levels of voter participation today.

The digital divide also threatens economic progress in the new century because of the growing importance of technological knowledge in both higher education and employment opportunity. The U.S. Bureau of Labor Statistics projects the fastest job growth will be in jobs requiring a college degree. And increasingly, entry into and good performance in college is dependent on good computer skills. Since African-American children are less likely to have been exposed to computer technology, they may face an additional disadvantage in applying to and performing in college. The same disadvantage will affect employment opportunities. As noted in the interim report of the President's Information Technology Advisory Committee, "…women and minorities are vastly underrepresented in both educational and workplace settings which require the development and/or use of information technology skills." Without those proficiencies, the report notes, individuals will lack the "skills needed to prosper in an information-rich society" While some of the burden for acquiring those competencies clearly lie with the individual, the public policy context will be important, especially for those with fewer family economic resources. The challenge will be how to exercise political clout in support of public programs of education and training when the locus of control for public policy has shifted from federal to state and local levels.

One of the rays of hope in the quest for political clout is the growing economic power of large minority-owned businesses, including a number of black-owned businesses. Entrepreneurs who have started some of the major businesses in the past 20 years came into business with considerable corporate experience and often brought clients with them. The growth of those firms and their potential influence in the policy arena is reflected in the newly formed Minority Business Round Table (MBRT). Founded in 1999 as a program of the Joint Center, the MBRT will provide opportunities for minority businesses to use their collective voice to speak out on policy matters affecting businesses and communities. To date, the Joint Center has identified more than 200 top-tier companies as potential members of MBRT Their annual gross sales range from $25 million to more than a billion dollars, and individually they employ between 80 and

4,000 people. Working together, they can be formidable proponents of good public policy. With the development of a business component to AfricanAmerican policy leadership, the marriage of political and economic power takes on a new meaning for the 21'° century. In that sense, the growing diversity within the black community only strengthens the power that can be wielded to improve its socioeconomic status. But it is likely that the prospect for success will be enhanced by expanding the coalition even more, working across racial and ethnic lines. The real challenge for African-American leaders is how to use diversity within the community and the nation as a whole in a positive, effective way.

NOTES

1. David A. Bositis, *African Americans and the Republican Parry,* 1996 (Washington, D.C.: Joint Center for Political and Economic Studies, 1996).

2. David A. Bositis, *Roster of Black Ekcted Offidals:1998* (Washington, D.C.: Joint Center for Political and Economic Studies, 1998).

3. David Bositis, *Blacks and the 1996 Democratic National Commotion* (Washington, D.C.: Joint Center for Political and Economic Studies, 1996).

4. Timothy Bates, *Banking on Black Enterprise* (Washington, D.C.: Joint Center for Political and Economic Studies, 1993).

5. Margaret C. Simms, "Community Development Issues in the 21st Century" in *Community Development. A Profitable Market Opportunity* (Washington, D.C.: Comptroller of the Company, 1997).

6. Margaret C. Simms, Economic Report, FOCUS, November 1999.

Part 5: Religion

African American Women's Definitions of Spirituality and Religiosity

Jacqueline S. Mattis

These two qualitative studies explore the meanings of spirituality for African American women and the distinctions that women make between spirituality and religiosity. In Study 1, content analyses of women's (N =128) written narratives reveal 13 categories of meaning that are assigned to spirituality. In Study 2, indepth interviews with a subsample of women (N= 21) reveal three key differences between religiosity and spirituality. First, whereas religiosity is associated with organized worship, spirituality is defined as the internalization of positive values. Second, religion is conceptualized as a path and spirituality as an outcome. Finally, whereas religion is tied to worship, spirituality is associated with relationships.

The terms spirituality and religiosity have been used interchangeably in much of social science research. The tendency to use these two terms as synonyms suggests that spirituality and religiosity name the same set of beliefs, values, and experiences. Although there are significant overlaps between spiritual and religious experience, empirical evidence suggests that lay people make important distinctions between these two constructs.

Perhaps the most persuasive evidence that there are substantive differences between spirituality and religiosity comes from self-report studies in which individuals indicate that they are more spiritual than religious (e. g., see Zinnbauer et al., 1997). Equally persuasive evidence of a difference between these constructs comes from research on the lives of African Americans. Research suggests that African American people make complex distinctions between spirits that exist as a part of the religious realm (e.g., God) and those that

exist within the secular realm of life (e.g., ancestors) (Jules-Rosette, 1980; Nelson, 1997). Although it appears that African Americans make distinctions between the religious and nonreligious realms of spiritual experience, at present, very little is known about the nature of those distinctions. Equally little is known about the meaning(s) that African American people assign to the terms spirituality and religiosity.

The importance of critically examining African American people's subjective definitions of spirituality and religiosity becomes clear when we consider the claims that are made about the functions of these two cultural constructs in African American life. Spiritual and religious beliefs have been shown to influence African American people's understandings of forgiveness, liberation, hope, justice, salvation, the meaning and purpose of life, and their responses to oppression (Cone, 1997; Lincoln & Mamiya, 1990; McKay, 1989; Wilmore, 1986).

Spirituality and religion play central roles in structuring African American people's interpersonal relationships, including their ideas about social obligations, their choice of romantic partners, and their definitions of community (for a review, see Mattis & Jagers, in press; see also Billingsley & Caldwell, 1991; Boykin & Ellison,1995; Scanzoni, 1971). Spirituality and religion have shaped African American people's notions of civic responsibility (Caldwell, Chatters, Billingsley, & Taylor, 1995; Dodson & Townsend Gilkes, 1986; Frazier, 1962; Lincoln & Mamiya, 1990; Moore, 1991; Townsend Gilkes, 1997), and have influenced their political beliefs and patterns of political participation (Calhoun-Brown, 1996; Harris, 1994; Reese & Brown, 1995). Furthermore, spirituality and religiousness have been shown to affect the physical and psychological well-being of African Americans (Blaine & Crocker, 1995; Brody, Stoneman, Flor, & McCrary, 1994; Handal, Black-Lopez, & Moergen, 1989; Knox, 1985; McAdoo, 1995; Stevenson, 1997), their folk healing practices (Jackson, 1997), and their efforts to cope with adversity (Lincoln & Mamiya, 1990; Neighbors, Jackson, Bowman, & Gurin, 1983; Taylor & Chatters, 1991). These findings suggest that spirituality and religiosity influence virtually every domain of African American life. However, the significance of these findings is limited by the fact that we do not have clear definitions of either spirituality or religiosity.

This qualitative study endeavors to achieve two goals. First, it aims to identify the definitions of spirituality that are privileged by African American lay women. Second, the study seeks to identify the distinctions that these women make between spirituality and religiosity. An ethnographic approach is taken in the effort to ground this study in the subjective experience and perspectives of African American women.

This study's focus on African American women is deliberate. Empirical evidence con-sistently demonstrates that African American women exhibit a greater overt focus on spirituality (Jagers & Smith, 1996) and religiosity than their African American male and White male and female counterparts (Conway, 1985–86; Taylor & Chatters, 1991). African American women are also more likely than men to attend worship services, participate in formal religious activities, and see religion as a salient and important part of their identity (Conway, 1985–86; Levin, Taylor, & Chatters, 1995; Mattis, 1997; Neighbors et al., 1983; Taylor & Chatters, 1991; Taylor, Mattis, & Chatters, 1999). These findings, considered in tandem with more general findings regarding the importance of religion and spirituality in the lives of African Americans, suggest a need for special attention to African American women's conceptualizations of spirituality and religiousness.

DEFINITIONS OF SPIRITUALITY

Within psychology, a number of definitions of spirituality have been offered (e.g., see Elkins, Hedstrom, Hughes, Leaf, & Saunders, 1988; Jagers & Smith, 1996; Kus, 1992; Potts, 1991). However, most of these definitions have developed out of the intellectual formulations of researchers rather than out of the direct experiences and articulations of lay people. Many scholars have grounded their definitions of spirituality in the etymology of the word. The word *spirituality* derives from the Latin word *spiritus,* which means "the breath of life" (Berdyaev,1939; Chaffers, 1994; MacQuarrie, 1972). A reading of the Old Testament of the Christian Bible indicates that this definition of spirituality is biblically consistent. In particular, the Creation text of the Old Testament provides some insight into Judeo-Christian approaches to the meaning and nature of spirituality:

The Lord God formed the man from the dust of the ground and breathed into his nostrils the breath of life, and man became a living being. (Genesis 2:7, New International Version)

This passage explicitly distinguishes between physical existence (i.e., the body) and a more ethereal force (i.e., the breath of life) that both symbolizes life and engenders it. The passage associates spirituality with life-giving power and with the capacity to create. Finally, it frames spirituality as a relationship between God and humans. More specifically, this passage of text suggests that spirituality can be defined as the active presence of the divine in the lives of humans.

In his comprehensive treatment of the meanings of spirituality, Berdyaev (1939) notes that the meanings assigned to the word depended in part on the historical moment and the cultural context in which it was used. At various points in history and in various cultures, spirituality has been used to describe myriad aspects of material as well as metaphysical existence. For example, spirit has been defined as a God-given life force, an elusive and insubstantial quality of existence, the soul, reason, rationality, and wisdom (Berdyaev, 1939).

Contemporary psychologists and sociologists have assigned various meanings to spirituality. For example, Tart (1975) defines spirituality as "that vast realm of human potential dealing with ultimate purposes, with higher entities, with God, with life, with compassion, [and] with purpose" (as cited in Benner, 1991, p. 3). Tart's definition of spirituality links spirituality with transcendent forces, life meaning, and core social values. Elkins, Hedstrom, Hughes, Leaf, and Saunders (1988) extend Tart's definition. More specifically, they assert that spirituality is "a way of being and experiencing that comes about through awareness of a transcendent dimension and that is characterized by certain identifiable values in regard to self, others, nature, life, and whatever one considers to be the Ultimate" (p. 7). Elkins et al. suggest

that the awareness of a nonmaterial (i.e., spiritual) dimension of life influences the ways that people relate to each other, God, ancestors, and the world around them. In short, spirituality affects the way that individuals perceive, interpret, and respond to their world(s) as well as significant social others.

In his definition of spirituality, Potts (1991) adds yet another important dimension to our understanding of this term. Potts argues that spirituality is a "belief that there is a sacred force that exists in all things." This definition, like others, points us to the transcendent nature of spiritual existence. However, Potts's definition is particularly important because it establishes a link between spirituality and sanctity. In short, Potts underscores the importance of sacredness as a defining feature of things spiritual.

Many of the points highlighted in these various definitions are effectively captured by Elkins et al.'s (1988) outline of the nine components of spirituality. Elkins and his colleagues suggest that spirituality includes a transcendent dimension, meaning and purpose in life, mission in life, sacredness of life, material values, altruism, idealism, awareness of the tragic, and beneficial outcomes and rewards (fruits). Although this conceptualization of spirituality appears to be comprehensive, it (like other definitions of spirituality) has an important shortcoming. It does not allow us to readily distinguish between spirituality and religiosity.

There are striking similarities between many existing definitions of spirituality and religion. Houf (1945), for example, asserts that there are three defining features of religion: a belief in transcendent, superhuman power(s); a yearning for certain material and spiritual values, including meaning and goodness; and a focus on specific behaviors, attitudes, and experiences that provide opportunities to secure important values. Batson and Ventis (1982) assert that religion is "whatever we as individuals do to come to grips personally with the questions that confront us because we are aware that we and others like us are alive and that we will die" (p. 7). Again, what Houf (1945) and Batson and Ventis (1982) presume to be defining features of religion are consistent with what Elkins et al. (1988) and others identify as defining characteristics of spirituality.

Chaffers (1994) offers a definition of spirituality that attempts to distinguish this construct from religiosity. He states that

> The spiritual...is not to be confused with the language and hierarchical structure of organized religion....Spiritual(i)ty [is]... the source of our (i)dentity, our individual(i)ty and our ind(i)vidual creative powers within a larger un(i)verse; i.e., the source of our inherent capacity to be self-validating, self-motivating, and self-directing....As such, it is the source of our capacity for optimism, personal enthusiasm, and passionate conviction...In sum, "spirituality" can be understood as an essential "inner-wellspring of energy" having the capacity to sustain our active participation in the whole of ever-evolving human and ecological systems. As such, it awakens us to the essence and greater potential of life as a self-transformative journey. (pp. 5–6)

Chaffers's definition is deliberately nonreligious in that it does not require a belief in the existence of a deity. It is also important to note that this definition does not explicitly require a belief in the existence of a transcendent, non-material dimension of life.

In his effort to distinguish between spirituality and religion, Chaffers (1994) contrasts the hierarchical structure of organized religion with the presumably fluid and individually determined (though not self-centered) arrangement that defines spirituality. Although he frames the distinction between spirituality and

religiosity in structuralist terms, in his effort to define spirituality, Chaffers takes a broad and distinctly functionalist approach. He asserts that spirituality allows individuals to experience passion, creativity, motivation, growth, and change. Implicit in his definition is the assertion that spirituality is both an individual and a communal phenomenon. Using an *i* in parentheses, Chaffers attempts to make the point that spirituality is not a self-centered or selfish pursuit. Taking an ecological approach, he argues that spirituality is the force that links individuals with the extant community. Chaffers's functionalist definition of spirituality is consistent with the Biblical definition of the term in that both suggest that spirituality is relational, and that it imbues life with passion, creativity, and direction. However, the extent to which African Americans endorse this functionalist definition of spirituality has not been examined systematically.

In a recent study of the distinctions between religiosity and spirituality, Zinnbauer and his colleagues (1997) concluded that whereas spirituality and religiosity are overlapping constructs, they do have distinct meanings. In their content analysis of the written narratives of a predominantly White sample of men and women, these researchers found that respondents' definitions of spirituality "most often included references to connection or relationship with a Higher Power of some kind, belief or faith in a Higher Power of some kind, or integrating one's values and beliefs with one's behavior in daily life" (p. 557). Although respondents' definitions of religion also included these points, they were distinct in that religiousness was often associated with the individual's level of adherence to the doctrines, beliefs, and ritual practices of religious institutions and level of organizational religious involvement (e.g., church attendance). The relevance of these definitions for African Americans has not, however, been explored.

The findings of two qualitative studies are presented here. Study 1 explores women's definitions of spirituality. This study provides a content analysis of African American women's written narratives to the question, "What does the term spirituality mean for you?" In Study 2, in-depth interviews were conducted with a subgroup of Study 1 participants, and the oral narratives were used to discern the ways in which women distinguish between spirituality and religion. Excerpts of written and oral narratives are used to highlight the findings of this work.

METHODS

STUDY 1

Participants in this study were African American women ($N = 128$) who were recruited from a large Midwestern university and surrounding communities, and from a large metropolitan center in the northeast. Participants were recruited through a variety of means: fliers circulated in communities, notices posted on electronic mail networks, and word of mouth. Each woman was informed that this was a two-part study, but that they could participate in Study 1 only, or in both Study 1 and Study 2. No monetary compensation was provided for participation in Study 1. A demographic description of the participants in Study 1 is provided in Table 1. The mean age of participants was 31.9 years ($SD = 12.9$). The majority of the women (64%) were single/ never married, 17% were married, and 19% were separated, divorced, or widowed. Although the women's annual incomes ranged from under $10,000 to $75,999, the group's modal income was under $10,000 (42%). This low modal income likely reflects the fact that at the time of the study many of the interviewees had returned to school to pursue their education.

DATA REDUCTION

To assess the meanings that each woman assigned to spirituality, participants were asked to provide written responses to the open-ended question, "What does the term spirituality mean for you?" Written responses varied in length and in narrative complexity. These responses were content analyzed using an open-coding process (Strauss & Corbin, 1990). In keeping with open-coding techniques, no a priori categories were imposed on the narrative data. Instead, themes were identified from the narratives. In the initial phases of the content analysis, two coders worked independently to identify themes from the written narratives. These themes were compared and organized into an initial set of coding categories. These categories were subsequently refined to yield clearly defined, nonoverlapping coding categories. To allow for the coding of multiple themes in any given narrative passage, phrases were used as the units of analysis. To control for differences in the length and stylistic complexity of the written responses, raters coded only for the presence or absence of endorsement of each of the response categories. Consequently, multiple mentions of a single theme in any given narrative response were coded only once. A randomly selected sample of narratives ($n = 10$) was coded to determine the use of the coding categories and the level of interrater reliability. An acceptable level of interrater reliability (90%) was achieved. Both raters then independently coded the remainder of the written narratives. After all narratives were coded, interrater reliability was again calculated. The 10 test narratives were not included in calculations of overall coding reliability. An overall interrater reliability of 92% was achieved.

RESULTS

Content analyses of women's written definitions of spirituality revealed 13 categories of

Table 1: Demographic Description of Study 1 Participants ($N = 128$)				
	M	**SD**	**PERCENTAGE**	**N**
Age	31.9	12.9		
Education				
Less than high school diploma			18	23
Some college			28	36
College degree			28	36
Graduate/professional degree			26	33
Marital status				
Single (never married)			64	82
Married			17	22
Separated			5	6
Divorced			12	15
Widowed			2	3
Personal income ($)				
0 to 9,999			42	54
10,000 to 19,999			24	31
20,000 to 29,999			10	13
30,000 to 49,999			15	19
50,000 to 75,999			9	12

responses. Table 2 lists these categories, their definitions, and the frequency with which women endorsed each category.

Of the respondents, 53% defined spirituality as a connection to and/or a belief in a higher external power. For example, one woman wrote, "My definition of spirituality involves one's conceptualization of a greater power than humankind." Beyond their focus on a belief in the existence of a higher power, many of the responses in this category focused on the existence of a relationship between a higher power (e.g., God) and humans. For example, one respondent asserted that "spirituality is a relationship between one and God. It is how that person relates to life situations through conscious efforts to find out God's plan for them." Another woman noted that, for her, spirituality is an "inspiration or the dominant influence of the Holy Spirit in humans." These responses collectively suggest that spirituality is both the belief in and the personal relationship between humans and God or a Higher Power.

Of the respondents, 24% defined spirituality as a belief in the transcendent or metaphysical nature of life. Responses in this category focused on the existence of beings (e.g., ancestors) and transcendent powers and abilities (e.g., intuition). For example, one respondent wrote

that spirituality has to do with energy. It is our spirit (mind), the part of us that is not biological. Psychological mechanisms, archetypes, after-death experiences, ESP, telekenesis (and more) all indicate that we have some sort of mind/energy that isn't always—or usually—tapped, but which still exists and will continue to exist after our bodies die.

Among these participants, the awareness of this transcendent dimension of life is associated with a belief that humans have access to knowledge and power that cannot easily be explained by science.

Table 2: Frequency of Endorsement of Categories of Definition of Spirituality (N + 128)

CATEGORY	DEFINITION	PERCENTAGE	N
Connection to or belief in a higher external power	Belief in the existence of a divine, sacred, and/or powerful force that is external to the individual (e.g., God, Allah). Reference to spirituality as a relationship with such a force.	53	68
Consciousness of metaphysicality	Awareness of the existence of forces or energies (e.g., soul, spirits) that indicate that life is not confined to physical existence. Reference to supernatural phenomena that are attributed to metaphysical/spiritual causes (e.g., telekenesis, ESP).	24	31
Understanding. accepting, being in touch with self	Spirituality defined as experience that influences self-awareness, self-knowledge, and self-acceptance.	23	29
Life direction, life instructions, guidance	Spirituality teaches individuals the steps by which to reach a given outcome. Spirituality serves as a compass.	22	28
Peace, calm, centerodness	Spirituality engenders (or manifests in) a sense of serenity, comfort, and/or groundedness.	13	17
Influences or affects relationships with others	Spirituality shapes or directs the nature or quality of social interactions, underscores the importance of social obligations, and/or promotes actions (e.g., forgiveness) that facilitate positive interpersonal relationships.	12	15
Life purpose, destiny, meaning	Spirituality provides understanding of the reason for one's existence and/or the ultimate goal of one's life.	10	13
Connection to or belief in higher power in self	Spirituality defined as an awareness of a divine or higher power resident in tie individual.	6	8
Support, strength, ability, and willingness to cope	Spirituality facilitates efforts to manage or survive adversity.	6	8
Faith, positive outlook. positive outcomes	Spirituality is associated with cognitive experiences such as faith, positive outlook, and perception of positive outcomes of events.	5	6
Nothing, very little, not sure	Respondent indicates that she is unsure of the meaning of spirituality.	5	6
Positive feelings	Spirituality is associated with positive affect (e.g., happiness, love, hope).	2	3
Clarity, wisdom, focus	spirituality provides knowledge, understanding, and insight, and ability to focus.	2	3

Of the respondents, 23% defined spirituality as an experience in which one understands, accepts, or is in touch with one's self. Responses in this category suggest that spirituality is a journey toward self-knowledge. This sensibility is reflected in the following statement made by one respondent:

> Spirituality to me means having an awareness of my inner self; knowing more than just the surface of myself; knowing the part of me that's connected to the rest of the world.

This journey toward self-knowledge includes efforts to understand the motivation for one's thoughts and actions. However, the movement toward self-knowledge, as described by the participants, is not to be confused with self-absorption. Respondents uniformly emphasized that self-knowledge is spiritual insofar as it promotes an appreciation of the relationship between self and external others. Self-knowledge allows individuals to behave empathetically, and facilitates understanding of one's obligations to proximal and distal others.

Of the participants, 22% associated spirituality with life direction and life instructions. For example, one respondent asserted that spirituality means "guidance for your life." The responses in this category suggest that guidance and direction are often provided by transcendent forces (e.g., God or ancestors). There were 13% who defined spirituality as an experience of peace, calm, and/or centeredness. In contrast, the absence of spirituality is believed to manifest in persistent frustration, confusion, and angst.

Of the respondents, 12% defined spirituality as a force that directly influences or affects relationships with others. One woman noted that, for her, spirituality means "feeling connected to people everywhere." Beyond notions of connectedness to others, responses in this category were concerned with social obligations and with engaging in and modeling behaviors that promote positive social relationships. These ideas are evident in the following response: "[spirituality means] caring for others and using my life as a Christian to be an example for others."

For 10% of the women, spirituality was defined as life purpose, destiny, and meaning. That is, spirituality was associated with the conviction that life has meaning and that life experiences and outcomes are nonrandom. Less frequently endorsed responses included the notion that spirituality is a connection to or belief in higher power in one's self (6%); support, strength, ability, and willingness to cope (6%); faith, positive outlook, and positive outcomes (5%); and positive feelings such as love and hope (2%). Two percent of the participants defined spirituality as a sense of clarity, wisdom, or focus. Approximately 5% of the respondents were either unsure of what spirituality meant for them, or indicated that spirituality had no meaning. Chi-square analyses revealed no systematic age, education, or income differences in women's endorsements of the 13 categories.

Although a phrase-by-phrase content analysis of these narratives allowed for the development of various categories of definition of spirituality, there are clear benefits to examining the written responses in their full context. Attention to the full prose of women's responses underscores the reality that many participants hold multiple definitions of spirituality. For example, in response to the question, "What does the term spirituality mean for you?" one respondent wrote that

> it means my ability to see beyond the material [consciousness of metaphysicality]; the depth of my relationship with the Lord [connection to or belief in a higher external power]; my personal stability/ability to cope in any circumstance [support, strength, ability, and willingness to cope].[1]

Like this woman, 59% of respondents in Study 1 offered definitions of spirituality that were coded in more than one category. This pattern of multiple responses underscores the complexity and multidimensionality of women's definitions of spirituality.

DISCUSSION

The findings of Study 1 are consistent with the findings of Zinnbauer et al. (1997). For the majority of respondents, spirituality is associated with a belief in the existence of a transcendent, nonmaterial dimension of life. For many women, spirituality refers in part to ideologies, practices, and experiences that reflect both a belief in a Higher Power (e.g., God) and evidence of the active presence of that Higher Power in daily life. Furthermore, many women define spirituality as a belief in the existence and active presence of spirits (e.g., ancestors) in daily life, and to abilities and experiences (e.g., near-death experiences) that defy scientific explanation.

First, many interviewees argue that although spirituality refers to the internalization and consistent expression of key values, religiousness is an individual's embrace of prescribed beliefs and ritual practices related to God. Second, many interviewees assert that religious values and practices serve as conduits for achieving spirituality. That is, religiosity is a tool, whereas spirituality is a desired outcome. Finally, although religion was associated with doctrines and rituals, spirituality was defined as a relational phenomenon.

SPIRITUALITY AS THE INTERNALIZATION AND EXPRESSION OF KEY VALUES

In general, interviewees ($n = 11$) asserted that religiosity is one's adherence to predefined beliefs and rituals. In contrast, spirituality was defined as the internalization of positive values

and the effort to manifest goodness in one's daily life. This distinction is evident in Adair's narrative.[2]

> Spirituality for me has nothing to do with organized religion. It's the way a person lives....That to me is spirituality.

A key element in this distinction between spirituality and religiosity is the element of conscious choice. Spirituality denotes a conscious decision to live in accordance with values that promote goodness, and that preserve the sanctity and integrity of life. One interviewee, Grace, reinforces this point:

> Religiosity is more doing what you're told because somebody else told you whether you believe it or not....It's doing what man said do....Spirituality, I do believe, is a central core of religions....Spirituality is just a wonderful guide, a source. I've been involved with religious people who weren't spiritual, and I didn't know this before I really understood the difference....We can go to church together and all that, however the bottom line is are you spiritual? Spirituality is fundamentally important. Otherwise I can't—I don't know how you can have any trust without that in another person.

Adair's and Grace's conceptualizations of spirituality are, in part, reactions against the perceived hypocrisy and rigidity of organized religion. They, like other interviewees, suggest that religious people may be pious during periods of formal worship, but may deviate from their presumed religious commitments once formal worship has ended. In contrast, interviewees indicate that spiritual values, commitments, and identity are contextually and situationally stable. In short, they insist that individuals who are spiritual accept certain values and beliefs, and consistently endeavor to live in accordance with those values and beliefs. Because of its association with positive values and situational and contextual consistency, spirituality has implications for the development of intimacy and genuine trust in interpersonal relationships. Spirituality, with its focus on ethics and moral integrity, is contrasted with societal focus on materialism, individualism, and superficiality. These ideas are evident in a statement made by Cassandra: "[We are] really getting down to the bare basics of what spirituality means—we're not on parade here. Whatever I've got—that should be fine, you know. And, whatever you've got that's cool too."

RELIGION AS THE CONDUIT FOR ACHIEVING SPIRITUALITY

A second perspective regarding the distinction between spirituality and religiosity holds that religion, church life, and formal devotional rituals are conduits for achieving spirituality. This perspective was clearly expressed by six interviewees. One such interviewee, Grace, stated that

> For me one of the ways that I get in touch with spirituality sometimes is through practice of a religious organization, or the choir that I sing in. It'll allow the spirit to fill me, and so I feel my spirituality on a deeper level. I don't confuse spirituality with religiosity, though religious practices are important for me. Spirituality's...critical. That's the difference.

Grace and other interviewees who share her perspective assert that worship and praise activities (e.g., singing, dancing, and praying) provide venues for creativity, the experience of freedom, and an intimate experience of connection with others and the divine. Through these public modes of religious expression, these women experience spirituality (i.e., the vital, passionate presence of the divine and living as well as ancestral others) in deeply personal ways.

SPIRITUALITY AS A RELATIONAL PHENOMENON

Although interviewees defined religiosity as one's adherence to formal religious doctrines and rituals, the majority ($n = 11$) defined spirituality in relational terms. Spirituality was variously conceptualized as one's relationship with God, with self, and/or with transcendent forces, including nature.

The relationship with God or a Higher Power was associated with the experience of power, freedom, wisdom, and creativity and the transcendence of limits. This perspective is expressed by Diana:

> Spirituality is power....Until that point where that inner being comes together with the consciousness I call God—when I tap into that power there is no limit to what I can do....I look at that as being in alignment. When you are out of alignment you run up against walls. You don't even run up against walls, you're hitting walls all the time, and you're bouncing off the walls. And, you're totally feeling like your life is spiraling down into a morass.

Diana suggests that the relationship with a divine source of power leads to outcomes that previously were construed as unachievable. Such a direct, personal relationship inspires faith and trust, and reinforces beliefs in ways that abstract and indirect encounters with the divine do not. Furthermore, the personal nature of the relationship allows God or a Higher Power to confront, challenge, and effect change in the lives of individuals. In short, it is the personal and intimate nature of the relationship that imbues spirituality with its power to transform. The absence of such a relationship, and/or the disruption of this relationship, is associated with negative experiences and negative life outcomes.

Some women define spirituality as an individual's relationship to and knowledge of herself. The notion is clearly articulated by Lena.

> Spirituality means really being in touch with your inner self. Knowing what your fears are, what those may come from, what your beliefs, and values, and those types of things are.

Self-knowledge was conceptualized as a dynamic and interdependent process. For these women, spirituality is the dynamic experience of both going inward and going outward. The journey inward is associated with a number of ends including reflectiveness, self-awareness, inner strength, emotional fortitude, centeredness, calm, self-awareness, self-criticism, and clarification of core values and beliefs. Participants consistently noted that the relationship with one's self provides the context for understanding and improving relationships with others.

Many interviewees also associated spirituality with a sense of connectedness to others, and with a belief that they do not have to face the challenges of life alone. Corinthian states, for example, that "[Spirituality means] just kind of knowing, just knowing that you are not alone. Just knowing that somebody has your back." Spirituality, then, is associated with the perceived existence of a network of support that includes God, ancestors, and living others.

For some women, spirituality is defined as a quest toward an ordered and harmonious relationship between all things, including nature and the inanimate world. This point is expressed by Lena.

> Lately [spirituality] means to me—I sort of developed this understanding that I'm in harmony with nature, and the universe. And, that sort of answers any questions that I have when I'm confused about a situation, and not knowing what to do. I think

about what's natural in terms of how the universe is run.

For some women, this belief in the relatedness of, and harmonious connection between, all things is associated with a philosophy that all events happen for a greater good and/or as a part of destiny. Sonya defines spirituality in a way that is consistent with these beliefs.

> I'm not really religious. But, I have a weird spirituality. I believe in more of like destiny and kind of like a force kind of thing. But, I do believe that there's something out there that's greater than us, because I do believe that when things happen they were meant to be.

Many of the interviewees report that they live with a sense of assurance that even seemingly serendipitous events are connected as a part of a larger plan. Their trust in this larger plan, and in the benevolence of God or a Higher Power, leaves these women with the conviction that they will prevail in spite of the challenges that they may encounter in life.

DISCUSSION

Do spirituality and religiosity name distinct experiences, or are they simply two words that describe the same set of experiences? From a methodological standpoint, the question can be restated as, To what extent does the analysis of discourse about religiosity and spirituality reveal conceptual differences between the terms? To what extent does analysis of discourse about spirituality and religiosity reveal that the two terms are synonymous (i.e., that the existence of these two terms is merely an artifact of language)? The findings of these two studies suggest that the terms spirituality and religiosity do, indeed, describe distinct experiences.

The results of the narrative analyses indicate that by themselves, none of the broad definitions of spirituality offered by Potts (1991),

Elkins et al. (1988), and Chaffers (1994) adequately represent the conceptualizations of spirituality offered by the women in this study. However, each of these definitions gestures toward the complex ways in which participants conceptualize spirituality. For most women, spirituality is, as Potts (1991) suggests, a belief in the sacred force that resides in all things. However, this definition does not capture women's focus on spirituality as a relational enterprise. The conceptualizations of spirituality offered by Chaffers (1994), Tart (1975), and Elkins et al. (1988) direct our focus to spirituality's connection with sacredness, meaning, purpose, morality, prosocial values, goodness, hope, creativity, and the like. However, these definitions do not adequately reflect women's beliefs about the religious dimensions of spirituality. Nor do they effectively capture women's beliefs about ancestors (and other spirits) and capacities (e.g., extrasensory perception) that comprise the transcendent dimension of spirituality.

Differences in the content of the coding categories and coding procedures used in this study and the study conducted by Zinnbauer et al. (1997) preclude a direct comparison of findings. However, in general, it appears that the findings of the two studies are consistent. Both studies yielded multiple categories of definition of spirituality. Furthermore, both studies find that although religiousness and spirituality are intertwined experiences, there are key factors that distinguish the two. For many participants, religiosity is defined as one's adherence to prescribed rituals and beliefs about God (or a set of gods). Whereas religiousness may involve participation in prescribed rituals, spirituality is defined as the internalization of, and the genuine and consistent commitment to, particular beliefs and values (e.g., quest for goodness). For many women, spirituality is defined as an intimate relationship between God, the individual, and others. Spirituality also denotes a journey of self-reflection, self-criticism, and self-awareness that culminates in a greater understanding of the relationship between self, God, and the larger community (including the community of ancestors). Finally, many interviewees insist that religion and church life provide an entrée into the experience of spirituality.

Given these definitions of spirituality, and given the distinctions between spirituality and religiosity, it is imperative that researchers interested in the study of African American spirituality exercise care in the ways in which they measure each construct. More specifically, it is imperative that researchers who are interested in the study of spirituality avoid the common practice of using measures of religiosity to assess spirituality.

Taken together, the findings of Study 1 and Study 2 point to the need for a refined, multidimensional measurement of spirituality. First, spirituality must be measured in terms of the extent to which individuals believe in a transcendent dimension of life. Second, spirituality must be measured in relational terms. That is, this construct must be measured in terms of a relationship with one's self (i.e., self-awareness, self-acceptance), as well as a sense of intimacy between oneself, others, and external metaphysical forces (e.g., God, spirits). Importantly, this sense of intimacy should be understood as both cognitive (i.e., perceived closeness) as well as affective (i.e., love, adoration, awe). Third, measures of spirituality must assess the extent to which individuals attempt to discern and live in accordance with the will of God or a Higher Power. Finally, measures of spirituality must assess the extent to which individuals have internalized beliefs and values that are demonstrative of the active presence of the divine in the life of the individual. These beliefs and values include, but are not limited to, a belief in the sacredness, purposefulness, and mutuality of all life; commitment to moral action; and a pursuit of goodness (e.g., self-sacrifice, charity, and caring).

This study has an important limitation. The participants report a much higher level of educational attainment than is representative of the broader African American community. Furthermore, the sample is relatively homogenous (particularly with regard to income, education, and religious identification). Certainly, the inclusion of a more diverse sample of African American women will add significantly to our understanding of the ways in which spirituality and religiosity are experienced and defined by members of this group. However, it is important to note that despite their relative homogeneity, the respondents in this study offered various definitions of spirituality. This suggests that people's conceptualizations of spirituality are influenced by an array of factors. These may include education and social class, as well as such factors as age, gender socialization, cultural background, and life experience.

A review of the findings of this research leads to an important point of consideration. It may be the case that a significant part of the confusion about the meaning of spirituality (and about the distinctions between spirituality and religiosity) owes to two related and equally important factors. First, the confusion about the meaning of spirituality may emerge from the complex ways in which the term is used. When defining this construct, people may refer to one or more of the various dimensions of spirituality that were identified in this research. For example, in defining spirituality, a given individual may refer to both her conviction that her life has purpose and to her sense of connection to a divine or Higher Power.

Second, the confusion about the definition of spirituality may be a consequence of the act of attempting to define an elusive term. When asked to define abstract terms (e.g., love, joy, or spirituality), individuals are called upon to bridge the gap between experience and language. In their effort to bridge this gap, individuals may employ a variety of cognitive strategies. One such strategy might involve translating the original question. In short, when asked, "What does spirituality mean?" individuals may respond by addressing more answerable questions, such as "What does spirituality do?" or "How is spirituality experienced?" Such translations do not detract from the value or veracity of people's responses. However, they do underscore the limitations of our ability to fully depict this complex experience in language.

Given the powerful influence that spirituality and religion are believed to have in the lives of African American people, it is imperative that we endeavor toward empirical precision in the study of these two constructs. As such, researchers must explore methodologies that will permit increasingly sophisticated studies of the meaning(s) and functions of spirituality and religion in the lives of African Americans. In particular, there may be benefits to conducting longitudinal studies of religion and spirituality. Such approaches will provide a clearer understanding of the nature of African American religious and spiritual development. In addition, researchers may benefit from the use of multimethod approaches that allow for examination of religiosity and spirituality within and across various relational and institutional contexts (i.e., in family and peer groups, churches, and secular institutions).

NOTES

1. Bracketed text reflects codes applied to each preceding phrase.

2. Pseudonyms are used to protect the identity and confidentiality of each of the interviewees.

REFERENCES

Batson, D., & Ventis, W. (1982). *The religious experience: A social psychological perspective.* New York: Oxford University Press.

Benner, D. (1991). Understanding, measuring and facilitating spiritual well-being: Introduction to a special issue. *Journal of Psychology and Theology,* 19, 3–5.

Berdyaev, N. (1939). *Spirit and reality.* London: The Centenary Press.

Billingsley, A., & Caldwell, C. H. (1991). The church, the family and the school in the African American community. *Journal of Negro Education,* 60, 427–440.

Blaine, B., & Crocker, J. (1995). Religiousness, race and psychological well-being: Exploring social psychological mediators. *Personality and Social Psychology Bulletin,* 21,1031–1041.

Boykin, A. W., & Ellison, C. M. (1995). The multiple ecologies of Black youth socialization: An Afrographic analysis. In R. L. Taylor (Ed.), *African American youth: The social and economic status in the United States* (pp. 93–128). Westport, CN: Praeger.

Brody, G., Stoneman, Z., Flor, D., & McCrary, C. (1994). Religion's role in organizing family relationships: Family process in rural, two-parent African American families. *Journal of Marriage and the Family,* 56, 878–888.

Caldwell, C., Chatters. L., Billingsley, A., & Taylor, R. (1995). Church-based support programs for elderly Black adults: Congregational and clergy characteristics. In M. Kimble, S. McFadden, J. Ellor, & J. Seeber (Eds.), *Aging, spirituality and religion* (pp, 306–324). Minneapolis, MN: Fortress.

Calhoun-Brown, A. (1996). African American churches and political mobilization: The psychological impact of organizational resources. *Journal of Politics,* 58(4), 935–953.

Chaffers, J. (1994, May 25). *Spirituality—the missing "i" in mass product(i)on: Or why "mass quality" need not be an oxymoron.* Conference proceedings of the Association of Collegiate Schools of Architecture European Conference: The Urban Scene and the History of the Future, London.

Cone, J. (1997). *God of the oppressed.* New York: Orbis Books.

Conway, K. (1985–86). Coping with the stress of medical problems among Black and White elderly. *International Journal of Aging and Human Development,* 21(1), 39–48.

Dodson, J., & Townsend Gilkes, C. (1986). Something within: Social change and collective endurance in the sacred world of Black Christian women. In R. Reuther & R. Keller (Eds.), *Women and religion in America: Volume 3: 1900–1968. A documentary history* (pp. 80–130). New York: Harper and Row.

Elkins, D., Hedstrom, L., Hughes, L., Leaf, J., & Saunders (1988). Toward a humanistic-phenomenological spirituality: Definition, description and measurement. *Journal of Humanistic Psychology,* 28, 5–18.

Frazier, E. (1962). *The Negro church in America.* New York: Schocken Books.

Handal, P., Black-Lopez, W., & Moergen, S. (1989). Preliminary investigation of the relationship between religion and psychological distress in Black women. *Psychological Reports,* 65, 971–975.

Harris, I? (1994). Something within: Religion as a mobilizer of African American political activism. *Journal of Politics,* 56(1), 42–68.

Houf, H. (1945). *What religion is and does: An introduction to the study of its problems and values.* New York: Harper and Brothers.

Jackson, B. (1997). The other kind of doctor: Conjure and magic in Black American folk medicine. In T. Fulop & A. Raboteau (Eds.), *African American religion: Interpretive essays in history and culture* (pp. 417–431). New York: Routledge.

Jagers, R., & Smith, P. (1996). Further examination of the Spirituality Scale. *Journal of Black Psychology,* 22, 429–442.

Jules-Rosette, B. (1980). Creative spirituality from Africa to America: Cross-cultural influences in contemporary religious forms. *Western Journal of Black Studies,* 4, 273–285.

Knox, D. (1985). Spirituality: A tool in the treatment and assessment of Black alcoholics and their families. *Alcoholism Treatment Quarterly,* 2, 33–44.

Kus, R. J. (1992). Spirituality in everyday life: Experiences of gay men of Alcoholics Anonymous [Special issue]. *Journal of Chemical Dependency Treatment,* 5(1), 49–66.

Levin, J., Taylor, R., & Chatters, L. (1995). A multidimensional measure of religious involvement for African Americans. *Sociological Quarterly,* 36(1), 157–173.

Lincoln, C., & Mamiya, L. (1990). *The Black church in the African American experience.* Durham, NC: Duke University Press.

MacQuarrie, J. (1972). *Paths in spirituality.* London: SCM Press.

Mattis, J. (1997). *Spirituality and religiosity in the lives of African American women.* African American Research Perspectives, Institute for Social Research, University of Michigan, 3(2), 56–60.

Mattis, J., & Jagers, R. J. (in press). Toward a relational framework for the study of religion and spirituality in African American life. *Journal of Community Psychology.*

McAdoo, H. (1995). Stress levels, family help patterns, and religiosity in middle- and working class African American single mothers. *Journal of Black Psychology,* 21(4), 424–449.

McKay, N. (1989). Nineteenth-century Black women's spiritual autobiographies: Religious faith and self-empowerment. In Personal Narratives Group (Ed.), *Interpreting women's lives: Feminist theory and personal narrative* (pp. 139–154). Bloomington: Indiana University Press.

Moore, T. (1991). The African American church: A source of empowerment, mutual help, and social change. *Prevention in Human Services,* 10(l), 147–167.

Neighbors, H., Jackson, J., Bowman, P, & Gurin, G. (1983). *Stress, coping, and Black mental health: Preliminary findings from a national study.* Newbury Park, CA: Sage.

Nelson, T. (1997). He made a way out of no way: Religious experience in an African American congregation. *Review of Religious Research,* 39(1), 5–26.

Potts, R. (1991). Spirits in the bottle: Spirituality and alcoholism treatment in African-American communities. *Journal of Training & Practice in Professional Psychology,* 5(1), 53–64.

Reese, L., & Brown, R. (1995). The effects of religious messages on racial identity and system blame among African Americans. *Journal of Politics,* 57(1), 24–43.

Scanzoni, J. (1971). *The Black family in modern society.* New York: Allyn & Bacon.

Stevenson, H. (1997). Managing anger: Protective, proactive, or adaptive racial socialization identity profiles and African American manhood development. *Journal of Prevention and Intervention in the Community,* 16(1–2). 35–61.

Strauss, A., & Corbin, 1. (1990). *Basics of qualitative research: Groundea theory procedures and techniques.* Newbury Park, CA: Sage.

Taylor, R., & Chatters, L. (1991). Religious life. In J. S. Jackson (Ed.). *Life in Black America* (pp. 105–123). Newbury Park, CA: Sage.

Taylor, R., Mattis, J., & Chatters, L. (1999). Subjective religiosity among African Americans: A synthesis of findings from five national samples. *Journal of Black Psychology.*

Townsend Gilkes, C. (1997). The roles of church and community mothers: Ambivalent American sexism or fragmented African familyhood? In T. Fulop & A. Raboteau (Eds.), *African American religion: Interpretive essays in history and culture* (Vol. 25, pp. 524–543). New York: Routledge.

Wilmore G. (1986). *Black religion and Black radicalism: An interpretation of the religious history of Afro-American people.* New York: Orbis Books.

Zinnbauer, B., Pargament, K., Cole, B., Rye, M., Butter, E., Belavich, T., Hipp, K., Scott, A., & Kadar, J. (1997). Religiousness and spirituality: Unfuzzying the fuzzy. *Journal for the Scientific Study of Religion,* 36(4), 549–564.

Cultural Resources and Psychological Adjustment of African American Children: Effects of Spirituality and Racial Attribution

Marcelle D. Christian and Oscar A. Barbarin

This study explored the relationship of a family's sociocultural resources to adjustment in a sample of low-income African American children from Ohio and Southeastern Michigan. Children of parents attending church at least weekly had fewer problems compared to those whose parents attended less frequently. Furthermore, the use of racial attributions to explain negative life outcomes was related to more frequent behavior problems. These data confirm the importance of religion as a sociocultural resource in African American families, one that potentially contributes to resilience of children at risk for behavioral or emotional mal-adjustment as a function of growing up in poor families and communities. In contrast, the data point out the complexity in the effects of reliance on racial attributions to explain outcomes. Although many have argued that such attributions may be a protective factor, they did not protect against children's behavior problems.

Although many children grow up in environments that allow them to develop into socially competent and emotionally adjusted adults (Barbarin & Soler, 1993), not all children do. The presence of factors such as community violence (Pynoos & Eth, 1984; Shakoor & Chalmers, 1991) and domestic violence (Graham-Bermann,1996) place children at risk for impaired school performance, substance abuse, emotional disturbances, and behavior problems. In addition, other sociocultural factors such as ethnic minority status and poverty put developing children at risk for emotional and behavioral problems (Barbarin, 1993b). In the state of Michigan, for example, 18.2% of all children but 46.2% of African American children lived in poverty (Gregory, 1993). Because both minority status and poverty may be related to the presence of child behavior problems, African American children raised in impoverished communities deserve further attention and are the focus of the current study. A brief look at census data underscores why psychologists should be concerned with the development of low-income children. Furthermore, a brief look at the literature pertaining to risk and resiliency for children, specifically African American children, permits us to speculate on those coping styles that exacerbate and buffer against the negative effects of poverty. All of this leads up to the present study, an investigation of low-income African American children and parental factors that are related to their reports of child behavior problems.

Certain parental factors, such as individual differences and life circumstances of the child, are associated with the probability of psychological disorders among children. A literature review reveals a number of parental factors that serve as risk and protective forces in behavior problems, and two specific constructs taken from the literature review will be the focus of the current study. Parental religiosity and parental racial attributions and their effects on reports of behavior problems are the specific variables to be studied. In general, this study examines whether parents who use religiosity as a coping strategy and racial attributions to explain events will report less frequent behavior and emotional problems than parents who do not employ these coping strategies. If religiosity/spirituality and a strong tendency to use racial attributions in explaining the plight of African Americans are associated with decreased risk of behavior problems, then perhaps these natural resources, already found within African American communities, can be tapped and further developed. First, however, an overview of the condition of African Americans in the United States and a brief overview of the childhood risk and resiliency literature are in order.

By 2000, African Americans were projected to constitute 12.9% of the U.S. population (U.S. Bureau of the Census, 1992, cited in Aponte, Rivers, & Wohl, 1995). As a group, they are confronted by a variety of challenges to life that include high infant mortality, chronic disease, HIV infection, and homicide (Hammond & Yung, 1993; O'Hare, Pollard, Mann, & Kent, 1991, both cited in Aponte et al., 1995). The diminished life expectancy due to violence is most disturbing because it reaches down to touch even the lives of children. In a study conducted in Chicago by Shakoor and Chalmers (1991), 75% of the African American boys in their study and 70% of girls had seen someone shot, stabbed, robbed, or killed. In Baltimore, Maryland, adults perceived random violence as having increased over time, and parents were concerned about drugs and the use of firearms in the victimization of innocent people (Kaljee, Stanton, Ricardo, & Whitehead, 1995). Not only were parents concerned about the pervasive lack of safety in their communities, but they had lost all confidence in the ability of the government to protect them and their children.

With large numbers of minority and specifically African American children currently living in the United States under stressful conditions, one suddenly understands why researchers should be concerned with the development of African American children. African American children appear with a host of problems, including difficulty concentrating, peer conflict, suspension from school, and antisocial behaviors (Barbarin & Soler, 1993). If researchers can identify the stressful situations of African American children that render them vulnerable to emotional and behavioral problems and identify parental factors that can buffer against the negative effects of these stressors, this would have an important impact on the body of knowledge related to child development. What is interesting in this story is not just that many African American children may be poor and maladjusted but that many poor African American children are not maladjusted and seem resilient in the face of the stressors they face in life. The story of resilient children becomes just as important as the story of children with behavior problems.

ADVERSITY, RISK AND RESILIENCY: CHARACTERISTICS OF CHILDREN AND ADOLESCENTS

Resiliency has become a popular theme in the literature. In one study (Gordon, 1995), 40 African American high school students all came from homes with low socioeconomic status and high stress. In the study, high academic achievement was the operational definition of resiliency. The resilient students, when compared with the nonresilient students, had healthier self-concepts. They felt more positively about their cognitive abilities and placed more emphasis on extracurricular activities and on material gain than did their nonresilient counterparts. Furthermore, the ability to focus on future financial security and to think about increasing one's independence were characteristics of students who achieved academically despite high levels of stress in their environment. Gordon also discussed the merits of biculturality. Maintaining an identity with one's own culture while allowing oneself to be socialized into the mainstream White American culture may be effective in overcoming obstacles, adapting, and achieving.

Resiliency, however, as Barbarin (1993a) pointed out, is not only a quality of individuals but can be attributed to social contexts that provide protective factors. Community structures such as schools, churches, and neighborhood organizations, for example, can buffer children against the negative effects of poverty. In addition to these institutions, one must examine the social context in which children receive their earliest experiences—the family. Family characteristics seen as risk factors and family characteristics that can buffer against stress also should be investigated.

FAMILY CHARACTERISTICS AND THEIR ROLE IN BEHAVIOR PROBLEMS: RISK FACTORS

In an excellent review article, McLoyd (1990) discussed poverty and economic decline among Black children. Economic hardship, marital distress, and the rising incidence of female-headed households all present themselves as important factors in understanding the development of ethnic minority children. In addition, the author discussed the assertion that racism further complicates poverty for African Americans, making barriers to housing, jobs, and educational institutions that much more difficult. Keeping in mind joblessness, poverty, poorer health, and various other stressors for African Americans, the familial context in which many African American children are raised becomes clearer.

The mechanisms by which poverty affects the family and the children, however, are not as clearly understood. What is it about the low-income family that makes children susceptible to behavior problems? Several possible explanations have been presented in the literature. First, the assertion that poverty affects marital functioning, which in turn affects parent-child interactions, has been presented. Vinokur, Price, and Caplan (1996) demonstrated that financial strain had significant effects on depressive symptoms of both the unemployed job seeker and that individual's spouse. These depressive symptoms, in turn, led to the spouse's withdrawal of social support and increased social undermining within the marriage. Poverty may affect developing children by altering parental functioning, thus worsening marital relations and depleting parents of their resources to form bonds with and care for their children. Ge et al. (1992) found evidence that some of the negative effects of poverty on children are indeed mediated by marital quality. In a study of 451 families, the researchers found that economic pressures had a negative influence on marital quality, which in turn had a negative effect on parent-child relations. Much of the relationship between economic pressure and parent-child relationship quality was indirect and mediated by marital quality. Poorer parent-child relationships put these adolescents at greater risk for adolescent emotional distress. One way in which poverty affects children, then, is through weak marital bonds.

One might take this information and assume that single parenthood might be the answer, eliminating the possible detrimental effects of weak marital bonds on child development.

Single parenthood, however, is not the answer. The strains and additional burdens of single parenthood often are accompanied by anxiety, depression, and health problems in the parent (Guttentag, Salasin, & Belle, 1980, as cited in McLoyd, 1990), which in turn have their own detrimental effects on the ability to raise children.

Another family variable implicated in the presence of child behavioral problems is maternal social support. To begin, perceived social support has been shown to be a significant buffer of stress in the mental health of Black women (Brown & Gary, 1987). With Black women using a support network, this would presumably allow more energy and resources for child rearing and have an effect on the types of parenting behaviors they use. That social support has an impact on maternal behavior has indeed gained support. One example is in a study by Whaler (1980). In this study, maternal social support played a role in preventing child behavior problems. In this study of low-income families, days marked by high proportions of friend contacts were correlated with fewer child behavior problems, defined as oppositional behaviors rated by an independent observer. In addition, on those days marked by greater social interaction, compared with those days in which the mothers were more insular, mothers were significantly less aversive in their child interactions. The findings from this early study suggest that on those days where social contacts are few, the mother's sustained ability to change troublesome interactions with her children could be seriously hampered, thus resulting in more oppositional behaviors from her children.

Other studies have focused more directly on maternal functioning and its role in maternal behavior and maternal reports of child behavior problems. For example, demographic variables indicative of environmental stress (such as being on public assistance) have been found to be positively related to maternal distress,

authoritarian child-rearing values, and negative perceptions of children, and those variables were inversely related to positive maternal behaviors (Conger, McCarty, Yang, Lahey, & Kropp, 1984). In another study by Whaley and O' Hara (1989), maternal depression was positively correlated with maternal reports of internalizing forms of child behavior and child somatic problems. Myers, Taylor, Alvy, Arrington, and Richardson (1992) also addressed maternal distress and other variables related to behavior problems in boys and girls. In this study as in others, high maternal distress was related to behavior problems in a sample of inner-city African American boys and girls. In this study, as in others, high maternal distress was related to behavior problems in a sample of inner-city African American boys and girls and explained 33% of the variance. Furthermore, high family stress load (measuring both acute and chronic life experiences) consistently accounted for a small portion of the variance.

Sameroff and Fiese (1992) continued the research on parental factors that account for child maladjustment. In a report on their study with low-income preschool children, the authors identified many of the familial risk factors associated with poorer socioemotional and cognitive competence scores. Within the family, a history of maternal mental illness, high maternal anxiety, minimal maternal education, the presence of the head of a household in an unskilled occupation, and disadvantaged minority status were related to lower intelligence and emotional functioning. No single variable was determinant of outcomes, however. Only in families with multiple risk factors was the child's competence jeopardized. For African American children, Barbarin and Soler (1993) found that single parenthood was an important element related to behavior problems. Younger children from biological-mother-only households exhibited a greater number of antisocial behaviors, behaviors related to peer conflict, and total number of behavior problems than did children in two-parent families.

To the extent that parents themselves are distracted by financial need and report deterioration in both personal functioning and interpersonal relationships, their capacity to reinforce and stimulate their children is diminished. This decrease in resources can affect a variety of domains, including children's academic performance (Slaughter & Epps, 1987), and parent-related adversity has been associated with an increase in children's conduct problems (Gest, Neeman, Hubbard, Masten, & Tellegen, 1993). A parent living in an impoverished environment may experience a decreased ability to provide the various forms of behavioral and emotional support necessary for the social and cognitive development of the children (Barbarin, 1993a). Just as a number of factors have been implicated in the presence of increased behavior problems, however, there are family factors that seem to be related to resiliency in children, and these factors deserve as much attention as do those risk factors.

FAMILY CHARACTERISTICS AND THEIR ROLE IN BEHAVIOR PROBLEMS: RESILIENT FAMILIES

One factor that might be associated with resiliency is parental religiosity or spirituality, and this will be investigated in the current study. Barbarin (1993a) speculated that religiosity might influence socialization styles toward firmer control, greater maturity demands, and greater acceptance of personal responsibility for behavior. Religious parents might teach children to cope with emotional arousal by stoically accepting the situation or by reaching out to other people or to a Supreme Being through prayer. Barbarin (1993a) continued that these family values teach children to endure suffering and delay gratification, which might prepare them well for success in academic settings and other situations.

Racial identity also might be another resiliency factor, buffering against the negative effects of environmental stress for minority children. Barbarin (1993a), in speculating about a firm racial identity, wrote that identity might influence coping strategies and influence affect regulation, self-esteem, and self-efficacy, all thought to be related to more positive developmental outcomes for African American children. In addition to racial identity, however, the ability to use racial attributions to explain why one's group is oppressed also might serve to protect the psychological functioning of parents, which allows them to be effective parents.

This racial attribution is the second focus of the current study. A review article by Crocker and Major (1989) summarized various articles related to stigmatized groups and coping strategies that serve to protect self-esteem. Not only can minority groups compare their outcomes with those in the in-group rather than with out-group members to protect self-esteem, but they can selectively devalue those dimensions on which their group fares poorly and value those dimensions on which their group excels. In addition, Crocker and Major argued that members of stigmatized groups can attribute negative feedback to prejudice against their group rather than to internal, global, and stable reasons that might serve to undermine self-esteem. The present study will serve to explore some of these external attributions for the plight of African Americans and see if these potentially self-protective attributions contribute to a lower number of reported child behavior problems. If parents identify strongly with their African American heritage, find fault with the system, and attribute the plight of African Americans to a racist culture, these attributions, much like religion, could have positive effects on the socialization of children. These attributions, perhaps passed on to children, might allow children to deal more easily with adversity, to place external attributions on their own failures, and thus be less discouraged and better behaved. It is not likely that researchers are advocating blindly attaching racial attributions for all situations; however, particularly in a situation where the feedback is ambiguous, external attributions for failure may be self-protective.

HYPOTHESES

A number of factors have been associated with behavioral problems in children, and a variety of factors have been correlated with resiliency. In this study of low-income African American boys and girls from areas of Southeastern Michigan and Ohio, only two of these factors will be chosen. We investigated the effect of parental religiosity and racial identity on parental reports of child behavior problems.

First, greater endorsement of religiosity as important in the parent's life was hypothesized to be associated with lower parental reports of child behavior problems. In addition, the use of racial attributions to explain the plight of African Americans was hypothesized to be associated with decreased reports of child behavior problems. Gender differences also were explored. As suggested by Barbarin and Soler (1993), boys were hypothesized to be at greater risk for behavior problems compared to girls.

METHOD

PROCEDURE

Data were collected from 1989 through 1991 as part of the University of Michigan Family Development Project, a study of families coping with sickle cell disease. The data used in this study were collected on a comparison group of children who were not living with sickle cell disease. Trained interviewers using structured interviews and questionnaires gathered data. Interviewers were graduate students in psychology and social work or paid, full-time research assistants. Interviews were completed individually in the family homes, and parents and children were interviewed separately.

SAMPLE

Children ranged in age from 5 to 18 and were referred to the study by the families of children coping with sickle cell disease or were recruited to the study from posters in local supermarkets. The children resided in areas of Southeastern Michigan and Northern Ohio. All children come from low-income families. The word *children* is used throughout the article to describe all participants. However, when looking at the data, we distinguished between older and younger children, referring to older children (those age 12 and older) as adolescents when appropriate.

MEASURES

Sociodemographic variables. Sociodemographic variables were collected from the families. Information on ethnicity, parental education, parental occupation, and the number of and ages of children in the family was collected. Although parents rarely volunteered information on precise yearly income, participants had all been previously identified as low income.

Child adjustment. The Behavior Problem Index (BPI) (Zill, 1985) was used. Behavior and affective adjustment were measured using 32 brief symptom items assembled by a panel of developmental consultants. Items relating to child adjustment, previously used in a study by Barbarin and Soler (1993), were selected to cover the domains included in the Child Behavior Checklist, a widely used measure of child functioning. In the measure used for the current study, the parent is asked to answer 32 items, which are read to him or her by an interviewer and recorded. For each item, parents indicated whether the items read were *often true, sometimes true,* or *not true* of the target child or adolescent. In the scoring, *sometimes true* and *often true* were coded as 1 and not true was coded as 0. The remaining items assessed academic adjustment. Parents indicated whether the target child or adolescent repeated a grade and experienced suspension or expulsion, ranked the student (5-point rating from the top to the bottom of the class), and rated the quality of overall performance (1= *doing really well,* 2 = *about as well as he or she can,* 3 = *could be doing better*). The evidence supporting the construct validity and reliability of the BPI scales is substantial (Peterson & Zill, 1986; Zill, 1985). Seven subscales for the BPI were developed using a principal components analysis of items. Estimates of internal consistency average about .85 for young children (Bussing, Halfon, Benjamin, & Wells, 1995).

The antisocial subscale assessed the occurrence of symptoms related to socially disapproved, aggressive, and delinquent behavior. The scale, only for adolescents, consists of six items assessing lying, cheating, bullying and being mean, disobeying at school, lacking remorse for misbehavior, and not getting along with teachers.

The anxiety/depression subscale assessed symptoms relating to internalizing disorders. The scale contains five items assessing mood changes, feeling unloved, fear, worthlessness, and sadness. For younger children, there is a sixth item.

The headstrong subscale, common to all children regardless of age, refers to those items typically falling under oppositional behaviors. Scores indicate the degree to which the target child or adolescent is noncompliant and diffi-

cult to influence. The subscale contains five items addressing stubbornness, disobedience at home, strong temper, arguing, and being high strung.

The hyperactivity subscale refers to those behaviors often associated with attention deficit disorder. The subscale contains five items pertaining to inability to concentrate, being easily confused, and being impulsive, obsessive, and restless.

Peer conflict/social withdrawal refers to problems in social functioning. This three-item scale taps into difficulty in getting along with other children, being liked by other children, and being withdrawn. There is a fourth question for older children.

Immaturity/dependence refers to an excessive reliance on others, particularly adults. It is characterized by a lack of independence and autonomy and is a scale only used with children younger than age 12.

Because the aim of this study is to look at children and adolescents together (and separately) and how behavior problems relate to the independent variables, it makes more sense to find the mean score of behavior problems on each subscale rather than the total sum. The number of questions differs depending on the age of the child, and thus, the total possible score changes depending on age, making it impossible to compare the younger and older children's scores. Consequently, the mean score (ranging from 0 to 1), instead of the sum, was obtained on each subscale for each participant.

Parental religiosity. Using structured questionnaire items, participants were asked a variety of questions about their religion and religious practices. They were asked to identify their religion. They also were asked to evaluate the importance of religion in their lives on a 5-point scale. They rated how often they usually attended religious services on a 5-point scale (from *nearly everyday—four or more times a week* to *less than once a year*). In addition, they rated how often they prayed (same 5-point scale) and were asked to rate how religious they felt they were (4-point scale).

Group and personal identity and racial attribution. Several questions measured racial identity and attributions for the life outcomes of African Americans. One question directly assessed personal identification (Black vs. African American). Another question explored group identification and solidarity by asking whether the respondent felt Blacks should always vote for Black candidates (5-point scale ranging from *strongly agree* to *I don't know*) and whether Blacks should shop in Black-owned stores whenever possible. In addition, participants were asked about preferred means for attaining social justice and social change. Would they prefer political or confrontational means? They were asked whether voting and politics were preferable to demonstrations and boycotts for gaining equal rights in this country. They were asked to decide whether Blacks should work together as a group or work independently to improve the position of Black people in the United States. Last, parents were asked to endorse one of two explanations when Black people fail to do well in life. One explanation ascribed failure to not working hard enough to get ahead, and a second explanation referred to being kept back because of racism.

RESULTS

Data were analyzed using SPSS 7.5 for Windows. A series of one-way ANOVAs was performed to assess the relationship of parental religiosity and racial attribution to child behavioral and emotional problems. Results of the statistical analyses appear in Tables 1, 2, and 3. Tables 4, 5, and 6 illustrate sample characteristics. Most mothers were employed and 45% of mothers ($n = 18$) were at least high school graduates. All participants identified themselves as Black, and most were Protestant and considered religion to be very important. Table 6 illustrates responses to a variety of questions assessing group and personal ethnic identity. Of the mothers, 65% responded that Blacks should work together as a group to improve power ($n = 26$), and 67.5% ($n = 27$) of mothers felt that Blacks should work to gain equal rights in this country by voting.

EFFECTS OF PARENTAL RELIGIOSITY ON BEHAVIOR PROBLEMS

We examined the relationship of parental religiosity to reports of child behavior problems. Parents were asked to comment on their religion, the importance of religion in their lives, religious service attendance, frequency of prayer, and how religious they were. The significant findings were observed with respect to religious service attendance. Participants were assigned to one of three categories based on their frequency of church attendance: almost daily, once a week, and less than weekly. Data are summarized in Table 1. For the 40 cases with complete data, the main effect of church attendance on headstrong behaviors was significant, $F(2, 38) = 5.455, p \le 01$. Scheffe post hoc analyses revealed that children and adolescents of weekly church attendees had lower scores on the headstrong subscales ($M = .36$) than did those who attended infrequently ($M = .66$). Thus, parents who attend church frequently report fewer problems of oppositional behavior in their children than do parents who attend infrequently. There was no significant difference between weekly and daily attendees or between daily and infrequent attendees. In addition, there was a main effect of church attendance on peer conflict/social withdrawal. Those who attended a religious service once a week reported fewer peer conflict problems ($M = .02$) than did those who attended infrequently ($M = .25$). The group attending nearly every day did not

Table 1: Behavioral Problems and Church Attendance

Behavior Problem	Mean Group Comparisons			Total Means	Standard Deviation	ANOVA F Value	Post Hoc Analysis		
	Almost Daily (D)	Weekly (W)	Infrequently (I)				D vs. I	W vs. D	I vs. W
Anxiety/depression (children, n = 29)	.0833	.1296	.3299	.2299	.2671	2.250	ns	ns	ns
Anxiety/depression[a] (all, n = 39)	.0889	.1690	.3772	.2581	.2897	3.771	p < .10	ns	ns
Headstrong[a] (all, n = 40)	.5143	.3571	.6632	.5300	.2919	5.455	ns	ns	p < .01
Hyperactive[a] (all, n = 40)	.3429	.2143	.3579	.3050	.2679	1.259	ns	ns	ns
Peer conflict (children, n = 29).	.2500	.0000	.2292	.1609	.2763	2.453	ns	ns	ns
Peer conflict[a] (all, n = 39)	.1667	.0179	.2456	.1517	.2592	3.540	ns	ns	p < .05
Immature (children, n = 29)	.6875	.1667	.4063	.3707	.3697	3.415	113	p < .10	ns

[a] Includes children and adolescents.

Table 2: Behavioral Problems and Racial Attribution

Behavior Problem	Mean Group Comparisons		Total Means	Standard Deviation	ANOVA F Value	Analysis I vs. E
	Internal (I)	External (E)				
Anxiety/depression (children, n = 21)	.1250	.2949	.2302	.2861	1.817	ns
Anxiety/depression[a] (all, n = 28)	.1571	.3452	.2512	.3069	2.805	ns
Headstrong[a] (all, n = 29)	.4533	.5857	.5172	.3140	1.301	ns
Hyperactive[a] (all, n = 29)	.1867	.3714	.2759	.2695	3.737	p < .10
Peer conflict (children, n = 21)	.0000	.2564	.1587	.2910	4.524	p < .05
Peer conflict[a] (all, n = 28)	.0000	.2738	.1369	.2686	9.591	p < .01
Immature (children, n = 21)	.1563	.4231	.3214	.3459	3.284	p < .10

[a] Includes children and adolescents.

Table 3: The Interaction Between Church Attendance and Racial Attributions (N = 29)

	n	M Headstrong Behavior Problem (SD)
Internal Racial Attributions		
Daily attendance	4	.4500 (.1000)
Weekly attendance	6	.4333 (.1506)
Infrequent attendance	5	.4800 (.3899)
External Racial Attributions		
Daily attendance	1	.4000 (0)
Weekly attendance	5	.2000 (.2449)
Infrequent attendance	8	.8500 (.207)

Table 4: Sample Characteristics (N = 40)

	Response	Percentage
Ethnicity	Black (N = 40)	100
Number of target child's siblings	0 (n = 4)	10.0
	1 (n = 17)	42.5
	2 (n = 7)	17.5
	3 (n = 4)	10.0
	4 (n = 5)	12.5
	5 (n = 2)	5.0
	No response (n = 1)	2.5
Mother's education	Trade school (n = 7)	17.5
	High school graduate (n = 18)	45.0
	Some high school (n = 7)	17.5
	No response (n = 8)	20.0
Mother's employment	Unemployed (n = 6)	15.0
	Employed (n = 30)	75.0
	No response (n = 4)	10.0

Table 5: Religiosity Variables (N = 40)

	Response	Percentage
Religious affiliation	Protestant (n = 33)	82.5
	Islam (n = 1)	2.5
	No response (n = 6)	15.0
Importance of religion	Important (n = 37)	92.5
	Unimportant (n = 3)	7.5
Church attendance	Almost daily (n = 7)	17.5
	Weekly (n =14)	35.0
	Infrequently (n =19)	47.5
How religious	Very (n =13)	32.5
	Fairly (n = 23)	57.5
	Not too religious (n = 1)	2.5
	Not religious at all (n = 3)	7.5
Frequency of prayer	Nearly everyday (n = 26)	65.0
	At least once a week (n = 10)	25.0
	A few times per year (n = 4)	10.0

differ from either the weekly or the infrequent church-attending groups.

A main effect for church attendance also was observed for immature behaviors in children, $F(2, 28) = 3.42$, $p \leq 05$. However, the mean difference between daily attendees ($M = .69$) and weekly attendees ($M = .17$), according to Scheffe post hoc analyses, was significant at only the $p \leq 10$ level. Daily versus infrequent attendance did not yield a significant difference, and infrequent attendees did not differ from weekly attendees on the immature subscale. There was also a main effect of service attendance on the anxiety/ depression means for all children, $F(2, 38) = 3.77$, $p \leq 05$. Scheffe post hoc tests, significant at the $p \leq 10$ level, suggest that the difference between the daily attendees ($M = .09$) and the infrequent attendees ($M = .38$) accounts for this effect. Daily and weekly church attendees did not differ on reports of anxiety and depression, and there was no difference between infrequent and weekly church attendance.

EFFECTS OF PARENTAL GROUP IDENTITY AND ATTRIBUTIONAL STYLE ON PARENTAL REPORTS OF CHILD BEHAVIOR PROBLEMS

Analysis of variance tests were used to assess the relationship of identity variables to behavior problems. Parents were asked a number of questions pertaining to racial group identification and internal or external explanations for Blacks failing in life. ANOVA tests found that racial group identity, assessed by questions about voting preferences, shopping at Black-owned stores, using political demonstrations, and working together as a group or independently, was unrelated to child behavior problems. However, attributional styles about Black life outcomes were significantly related to problems. Specifically, parents categorized as internal ascribe Blacks' failure to insufficient effort and persistence and to not working hard enough. Participants categorized as external felt that Blacks were kept back because of race and racial prejudice. Some parents did not answer or said "both." The children (children and adolescents) of these groups of parents differ significantly on peer conflict/social withdrawal, $F(2, 27) = 9.59$, $p \leq 01$. Those ($n = 28$) whose parents endorsed an internal attributional style had a mean social conflict score of .00. The mean conflict score for those with an external attributional style, by contrast, was .27 (see Table 2). This is contrary to the hypotheses. The effect for peer conflict/social withdrawal data also is significant for young

children when we look at the data that excludes adolescents, $F(2, 20) = 4.524$, $p \leq 05$. Young children whose parents endorsed an external attributional style had a mean peer conflict score of .26, whereas young children whose parents endorsed an internal style had a mean peer conflict score of .00.

Noteworthy but only significant at the $p \leq 10$ level, parents with an external attributional style reported greater hyperactive means for all children ($M = .37$) than did those with an internal attributional style ($M = .19$), $F(2, 28) = 3.737$. Parents with an external attributional style reported greater problems on the immaturity subscale for young children ($M = .42$) than did those with an internal attributional style ($M = .16$), $F(2, 20) = 3.284$, $p \leq .10$. Finally, although there may be a main effect for racial attributions of parent on anxiety and depression scores of adolescents, a closer look at how the cases are distributed reveals that there are only seven cases, making these data too small to interpret. Six of these cases have parents with the internal style and only one case was with the parent with the external style. In summary, internal attributional styles tend to be associated with fewer behavior problems as measured by the peer conflict, hyperactive, and immaturity subscales. Parents with external racial attributional styles reported more problem behaviors in their children. There were no significant gender effects.

INTERACTIONS

We explored possible interactions between church attendance and attributional styles on children's behavior problems. To preserve the number of participants, one-way ANOVAs were reported throughout the article. However, two-way ANOVAs were performed to investigate the interaction effects between church attendance and racial attributions, which cut the total number of participants greatly. Only 29 cases answered both the church attendance

Table 6: Racial Identity and Attribution Variables—Sample Characteristics (N = 40)

	Response	Percentage
Personal identification	Black/African American (n = 13)	32.5
Which is more important to you?	American (n = 2)	5.0
	Both equally important (n = 21)	52.5
	Don't know (n = 1)	2.5
	Other or no response (n = 3)	7.5
If Black people don't do well it's because . . .	They don't work hard to get ahead (n = 15)	37.5
	They are kept back because of their race (n = 14)	35.0
	No response (n = 11)	27.5
What should Blacks do to gain equal rights?	Work through present system by voting (n = 27)	67.5
	Use demonstrations, boycotts, group protests (n = 11)	27.5
	No response (n = 2)	5.0
What should Blacks do to improve power and position?	Blacks should work together as a group (n = 26)	65.5
	Each Black person should work to get ahead on his or her own (n = 13)	32.5
	No response (n = 1)	2.5
Black people should shop in Black-owned stores whenever possible	Strongly agree (n = 17)	42.5
	Agree (n = 10)	25.5
	Disagree (n = 6)	15.0
	Strongly disagree (n = 3)	7.5
	Don't care/don't know (n = 3)	7.5
	No response (n = 1)	2.5
Black people should always vote for Black candidates	Strongly agree (n = 2)	5.0
	Agree (n = 1)	2.5
	Disagree (n = 21)	52.5
	Strongly disagree (n = 14)	35.0
	Don't care/don't know (n = 1)	2.5
	No response (n =1)	2.5

and the racial attribution questions. The noteworthy finding is that on the headstrong subscale, religious service attendance and racial attributions interacted significantly. The relationship between church attendance and headstrong behaviors was different for those with an external versus an internal attributional style, $F(3, 26) = 4.80$, $p \leq 05$. Among those with an internal style, the amount of headstrong behavior did not vary with church attendance. However, among those parents with an external attributional style, headstrong behavior was greatest among those with infrequent church attendance ($M = .85$) and lowest among those who attended church weekly ($M = .20$) (see Table 3 for details).

DISCUSSION

The central issue in this study was the relationship of parental religiosity and racial attributions to child behavior problems. Several of the relationships may not have been significant due to insufficient power, but several very interesting comments can be made about the relationships that were significant. Regular church attendance by their parents was related to fewer reports of problems with opposition and peer conflict, depression, headstrong behaviors, and with immaturity for young children. There are several plausible explanations for this relationship. First, regularly attending church services might serve as a coping strategy, which reduces parental distress and makes them more effective and accessible parents. Alternatively, the church community itself may be a source of spiritual, emotional, and instrumental support that aids both parent and child. For example, membership in a religious community might provide a parent with community members available to assist with child rearing. Religiosity also might be passed on to children and enhance their capacity for self-regulation by teaching and reinforcing the virtues of obedience, patience, delay of gratification, and control of anger.

The strength of racial identity and the use of racial attributions to explain negative outcomes was originally thought to be a protective factor for parents, improving their functioning and allowing them to avoid self-blame. For example, racial attributional styles might actually somehow be passed to children, particularly older children, resulting in greater self-esteem and an ability to brush off adversity and attribute it to external factors, which might result in better behavior. Our findings, however, did not support this speculation. Those parents with an external racial attribution style reported more problem behaviors in the peer conflict/social withdrawal realm. Although not significant, even the data concerning hyperactivity and immaturity point to an association between behavior problems and externalizing racial attributions. Use of racial attributions to account for hypothetical failure actually might be indicative of an inability to accept that failure might be a result of an inability to mobilize personal resources effectively to manage problem behavior. Moreover, a generalized externalizing style may cause parents to ignore signs of problems in their child because problems themselves are not viewed as inherent in and under the control of the child.

Last, the interaction effect indicates that the relationship between church attendance and headstrong behaviors varies depending on parental attribution style. Furthermore, weekly church attendance is related to fewer headstrong behaviors for those with the external attributional style, but for those with this external attributional style, infrequent attendance is more of a risk, leading to more headstrong behaviors. Perhaps for regular church attendees, the external attributions are transformed and incorporated into a religious belief in which African Americans are seen as a suffering but chosen people who will ultimately prevail either through their own struggle or with the help of a higher power. Alternatively, the institutional support from a church or religious institution may protect against oppositional and defiant behavior on the part of the children. Having the support of the institutional church magnifies the power of parents in the eyes of their children and may induce children to be more compliant.

Several very obvious limitations of the study exist, including subjectivity of measures and correlated method error. The children's behavior is assessed through parental reports and is not cross-validated by teacher reports or some other measure. Moreover, the same participant provides the information on church attendance, racial attributions, and child behavior. Despite the study's limitations, it is linked to a growing body of research on risk and protective factors in children and specifically addresses the population of low-income African American children. Exploring religiosity and racial attributions, which is rarely studied explicitly in empirical research, this study has the potential to make a contribution to the literature on risk and resiliency in minority populations.

Providing affordable mental health to African American families and building up the existing spiritual resources in the community might be effective because parental reports of religious service attendance are related to decreased reports of behavior problems in children. The present study can serve as a guide in the development of programs targeted to children at risk for problem behavior. It suggests that reinforcing the strong African American spiritual resources already in existence might be useful in decreasing behavior problems, and parents of boys may be targets of attention. This is neither an argument nor an apology for spirituality. Instead, it points to the use of resources that already exist within African American communities and families. For example, Hurd, Moore, and Rogers (1995) found that in their sample of 50 African American families, 37 identified spirituality as an important theme within the family. The need to nourish the spiritual dimensions of their children was cited by the parents. Parents in this study derived comfort from participating in religious activities such as attending church, reading the Bible, and praying. Therefore, it is clear that religious and spiritual resources are already present in a large number of African American families; the present study merely would support the notion that nourishing and supporting the continuation of these resources is a good idea. Also, it is important to keep in mind that religiosity may not be a key factor—it may be the case that spirituality, which is different, is the factor. Some belief in a higher being or beings might be just as effective as participation in an organized religion when raising children. There does appear to be something especially important about attending services, however.

The importance of research on the development of African American children is important. This study, an investigation of family factors that may be playing a role in the presence of child problems, will hopefully lead to further, more controlled studies on those characteristics of parents that lead to fewer behavior and emotional problems. It is surprising that an external racial attributional style led to more reports of behavior problems. The idea that blaming failure on a racist system is protective may still be true for other age groups and for other outcomes (e.g., unemployment). This finding is intriguing. Hopefully, more research on individual differences, community factors, and societal institutions can be combined with this research on family factors to make real strides in improving the lot of African American children, teasing out those parental attributes that lead to more effective and less effective parenting.

REFERENCES

Aponte, J. F., Rivers, R. Y., & Wohl, J. (1995). *Psychological interventions and cultural diversity.* Needham Heights, MA: Allyn & Bacon.

Barbarin, O. A. (1993a). Coping and resilience: Exploring the inner lives of African American children. *Journal of Black Psychology,* 19, 478–492.

Barbarin, O. A. (1993b). Emotional and social development of African American children. *Journal of Black Psychology,* 19, 381–390.

Barbarin, O. A., & Soler, R. E. (1993). Behavioral, emotional, and academic adjustment in a national probability sample of African American children: Effects of age, gender, and family structure. *Journal of Black Psychology,* 19, 423–446.

Brown, D. R., & Gary, L. E. (1987). Stressful life events, social support networks, and the physical and mental health of urban Black adults. *Journal of Human Stress,* 13, 165–174.

Bussing, R., Halfon, N., Benjamin, B., & Wells, K. (1995). Prevalence of behavior problems in U.S. children with asthma. *Archives of Pediatrics and Adolescent Medicine,* 149, 565–572.

Conger, R. D., McCatty, J. A., Yang, R. K., Lahey, B. B., & Kropp, J. P (1984). Perception of child, child rearing values, and emotional distress as mediating links between environmental stremors and observed maternal behavior. *Child Development,* 55, 2234–2247.

Crocker, J., & Major, B. (1989). Social stigma and self-esteem: The self-protective properties of stigma. *Psychological Review,* 96, 608–630.

Ge, X., Conger, R., Lorenz. F O., Elder, G. H., Montague, R. B., & Simons, R. L. (1992). Linking family economic hardship to adolescent distress. *Journal of Research on Adolescence,* 2, 351–378.

Gest, S. D., Neeruan, J., Hubbard, J. J., Masten, A. S., & Tellegen, A. (1993). Parenting quality, adversity, and conduct problems in adolescence: Testing process-oriented models of resilience. *Development and Psychopathology,* 5, 663–682.

Gordon, K. E. (1995). Self-concept and motivational patterns of resilient African American high school students. *Journal of Black Psychology,* 21, 239–255.

Graham-Betmann, S. A. (1996). Family worries: Assessment of interpersonal anxiety in children from violent and nonviolent families. *Journal of Clinical Child Psychology,* 25, 280–287.

Gregory W. C. (1993, January 22). Other voices: Michigan's silent depression. *Detroit Free Press,* p. A13.

Hurd, E. P, Moore, C., & Rogers, R. (1995). Quiet success: Parenting strengths among African Americans. *Families in Society,* 76, 434–443.

Kaljee, L. M., Stanton, B., Ricardo, I., & Whitehead, T. L. (1995). Urban African American adolescents and their patents: Perceptions of violence within and against their communities. *Human Organization,* 54, 373–382.

McLoyd, V. C. (1990). The impact of economic hardship on Black families and children: Psychological distress, patenting, and socioeconomic development. *Child Development,* 61, 311–346.

Myers, H. F, Taylor, S., Alvy, K. T, Arrington, A., & Richardson, M. A. (1992). Parental and family predictors of behavior problems in inner-city Black children. *American Journal of Community Psychology,* 20, 557–576.

Peterson, J., & Zill, N. (1986). Marital disruption, patent-child relationships, and behavior problems in children. *Journal of Marriage and the Family,* 48, 295–307.

Pynoos. R. S., & Eth, S. (1984). The child as witness to homicide. *Journal of Social Issues,* 40, 87–108.

Sameroff, A. J., & Fiese, B. H. (1992). Family representations of development. In I. E. Sigal, A. V. McGillicuddy-DeLiss, & J. J. Goodnow (Eds.), *Parental beliefs systems: Psychological consequences for children* (pp. 347–369). Hillsdale, NJ: Lawrence Eribaum

Shakoor, B., & Chalmers, D. (1991). Co-victimization of African American children who witness violence: Effects of cognitive, emotional, and behavioral development. *Journal of the National Medical Association,* 83, 233–238.

Slaughter, D. T, & Epps, E. G. (1987). The home environment and academic achievement of Black American children and youth: An overview. *Journal of Negro Education,* 56, 3–20.

Vinokur, A. D., Price, R. H., & Caplan, R. D. (1996). Hard times and hurtful partners: How financial strain affects depression and relationship satisfaction of unemployed persons and their spouses. *Journal of Personality and Social Psychology,* 71, 166–179.

Whaler, R. G. (1980). The insular mother. Her problems in parent-child treatment. *Journal of Applied Behavior Analysis,* 13, 207–219.

Whaley, A. L., & O'Hara, E. J. (1989). Negative emotions and maternal report of behavior problems in clinic-referred children: A preliminary report. *Child & Family Therapy,* 10, 41–47.

Zill, N. (1985). *Behavior Problem Scales, developed from the 1981 Child Health Supplement to the National Health Interview Survey.* Washington, DC: Child Trends, Inc.

Good as Gospel

Michelle Bearden

Individually, they represent a range of professions: college teacher, occupational therapist, national sales manager, optometrist, domestic queen.

Together, they are the Sweet A-Chord.

On Saturday, these Bay area singers will join other local gospel groups in a rare opportunity to show their stuff before thousands during the welcoming ceremony of the 36th annual Gospel Music Workshop of America at the Tampa Convention Center.

"This is a chance to get on a national platform and expand our horizons beyond Florida," said Sweet A-Chord member Angela August. "Something like this doesn't come around every day. We have to make the most of it."

Anybody who is anybody in gospel music will be here, from record producers and business managers to agents and teaching instructors.

Choirs from as far away as Japan and Brazil will perform, joining a star-studded lineup that includes Kirk Franklin, CeCe Winans, Dorothy Norwood, Tramaine Hawkins and Donnie McClurkin. On Wednesday, 73-year-old Albertina Walker, the legendary "first lady of gospel" who helped build the foundation for today's musicians, will be honored in a ceremony.

Up to 20,000 delegates are expected to attend the weeklong event, which comes to Tampa for the first time. For the host city, it will mean at least a $10 million boost to the economy, according to Tampa Bay Convention & Visitors Bureau estimates.

Michelle Chester Pruitt, a national sales manager with the bureau and a member of Sweet A-Chord, expects the convention will trigger business from some of the smaller organizations involved.

"This kind of exposure is priceless," she said. "And it's coming in the slower season, filling rooms that normally wouldn't be filled."

For gospel music enthusiasts, Tampa is the place to be come Saturday, when the event opens with the 22nd annual Gospel Music Excellence Awards. The black-tie gala, patterned after the Grammy Awards, will honor the best of gospel in 26 categories. The subsequent week includes more than 100 classes and plenty of live gospel music.

BREAKING DOWN WALLS

"It's the greatest music this side of heaven," said Al "The Bishop" Hobbs, record producer, broadcaster and vice chairman of Gospel Music Workshop of America. "There's no doubt that gospel music has broken through the traditional walls. Yes, it's still about worship and inspiration, but it's not just in the sanctuary anymore."

GMWA was founded in Detroit in 1967 by the late Rev. James Cleveland, who wanted to bring the growing industry together. He envisioned an annual convention where enthusiasts could gather for networking, learning and performing. Hobbs said Cleveland would be proud of what GMWA has done for gospel music, once relegated to church choirs and school auditoriums.

The gathering has become such a huge draw, it's a coup to be selected as the host city, Hobbs said.

"We not only bring our own people, but we make a point to inspire the local folks and generate greater awareness of our music," he said. "When we leave our convention cities, we want to leave a lasting impression of this wonderful music."

Limousine driver Carlton Brown has a lifelong passion for gospel music. He grew up singing gospel with the choir at New Mount Zion Missionary Baptist Church in Tampa. He's still there.

"I joined at age 7, and I just kept moving up the line," he said. "I can never get tired of it. It helps me in the worst of times, and it gives me even greater joy in the best of times."

Brown serves as his church's assistant minister of music and directs the 45-member choir for GMWA's Tampa Bay chapter. He's waited 10 years for the convention to come to Tampa.

"For local citizens not to be a part of this would be a huge disappointment and mistake," Brown said. "It won't be back for at least 15 years. I would encourage everyone to take advantage of this."

When Albertina Walker accepts her honor at the tribute Wednesday, the audience will get a firsthand glimpse of one of gospel's greats.

Walker began her storied career at age 4 with the West Point Baptist Church in Chicago, where she still sings.

In 1951, she founded The Caravans, which achieved world recognition and spawned some of the biggest names in gospel, including Cleveland, Cassietta George and Shirley Caesar.

"Oh Lord, the music has changed but the lyrics are still the same," she said. "And I can tell you why gospel is here to stay. We're just singing the word, right from the Bible, and that's a universal language that will never die."

"IN THROUGH THE BACK"

She had no idea gospel music would rise to such heights, she said, particularly among mainstream audiences. In her day, she and group members traveled from city to city by car, slept in boardinghouses designated for "Negroes" and used restrooms marked "Colored People Only."

"We couldn't even afford to stay in the hotels where we performed," she said, with a laugh. "And for sure, we couldn't go through the front doors. We had to come in through the back."

Still, she doesn't regret those days because "I didn't know any better. I just loved the music so. We were building a foundation for the folks today, only we didn't know it. We just thought we were serving the Lord."

The Rev. Moses Brown of Tampa serves as master of ceremonies at Saturday's musical, after the awards program. He's founder of Feed Our Children Ministries, and writes and produces his own gospel music. Profits from his CD "Second Chances" help fund his ministry, which supports disadvantaged families in the Bay area.

He says faith and music were what kept him together after learning he was adopted—and his birth mother was a rape victim.

"Knowing I was the product of that caused me a lot of emotional distress. I began to think I wasn't supposed to be in this world," he recalled.

Like slaves before him in another century, he turned to gospel spirituals for comfort. The music gave him the peace he needed.

"It has an intense message that's persistent and consistent," he said. "And it gives people the satisfaction there is hope beyond situations and circumstances in their lives.

"Most important, it soothes my heart and connects me with my maker, Jesus Christ."

Sing Praise: "Y'all Better Clap Your Hands"; Superstars of Worship, Music Ministers Often Set Tone in Today's Black Churches

John Blake

Dorsey Hammond marches through a tunnel and struts to the center of the stage as the crowd rises to greet him.

Nodding to the drummer, he slides behind his keyboard as the band launches into a James Brown groove. Hammond sways his head like a bobblehead doll as his backup singers, executing synchronized dance steps, chime in.

"You better move your feet!" one of the singers tells the crowd of about 5,000 people. "Y'all better clap your hands!"

The crowd cheers in response. Hammond beams at his musicians. A woman bolts to the front of the stage where Hammond is playing and thrusts her arms joyously into the air.

But this isn't a concert—it's a Sunday morning church service at World Changers Church International in College Park.

And it's orchestrated by a new superstar in the world of worship—the choir director. In the contemporary black church, choir directors, or music ministers, now rival the prestige of preachers.

Pastors bid for their services like baseball team owners vie for coveted free agents. Top music ministers make six-figure salaries. They have recording contracts. They tour.

And Atlanta, with many of the nation's top music ministers, is a key player in this transformation.

The music ministers' superstar status has helped them reshape choirs from a volunteer "come as you are" ministry to professional organizations that record, audition and even punish members who can't keep up.

But their popularity has also caused tension. Some pastors feel threatened by their acclaim. And some congregations view top music ministers as musical mercenaries—hired gospel guns who bounce from church to church seeking the highest salaries.

The growing stature of music ministers marks a break from black church tradition. Churches typically paid them little attention—or money. Some would simply pay them with a "love offering" of a couple of bills tossed into a collection plate.

Now churches consider them the Pied Pipers of Praise—the crucial person who lures in the Sunday morning crowds.

"A lot of people will come to church just because of the music," says Hammond, music minister of metro Atlanta's second-largest church. "If you have a choir that isn't kicking, if it isn't ministering, half of the time they won't come to your church."

These music ministers are also riding a boom in black gospel music. While overall music sales have slumped, Christian and gospel music sales rose 18 percent during the first half of 2002, according to the Christian Music Trade Association. Black gospel crossover acts such as Kirk Franklin and Yolanda Adams have gone platinum since they've targeted a mainstream audience—and especially youth.

"If you look at the gospel artists, especially the younger artists, you cannot tell if you see their picture if they're a gospel artist or an R&B artist," says Rhonda Baraka, a Billboard magazine columnist.

SOME HAVE SIX-FIGURE INCOMES.

Token love offerings won't pay for Kevin Bond.

Bond is the music minister for metro Atlanta's largest church, New Birth Missionary Baptist Church in Lithonia. A stylish dresser with an earring, he has recorded with the gospel greats such as Franklin, Adams and Walter Hawkins.

"I know people who make as little as $15,000 and I know people who make as much as $200,000," says Bond, who declined to disclose his salary ("I would never tell you that."). The church also would not divulge his pay.

And pastors aren't offering just money, he says.

"You get full health plans," Bond says. "You get benefits. Some people get car allowances. Some people get housing allowances."

Because the black church has been traditionally decentralized and informal, there is no national or regional tracking of the salaries or benefits music ministers make.

Also, associations and universities that follow the pay of musicians are at a loss to say what an "average" compensation package might look like for a choir director.

But those in the business say top music ministers can become personal conglomerates. They can branch off into public speaking, staging seminars and writing music for films.

And what they make depends on their skill and business acumen.

"The beauty of what we do is we're not limited to just this church house," Bond says. "Most of us are able to go outside and make a secondary income."

Byron Cage, New Birth's previous music minister, has done just that. He says it's "not uncommon at all" for a nationally known music minister to make six figures.

"I do," he says, although he also declined to give specifics.

Cage, 39, directs the music ministry for Ebenezer AME in suburban Washington. He's also a nationally known recording artist who performs around the county.

When Cage directed his first choir in Atlanta 20 years ago, he received $60 a week. Now, in addition to his church salary, he's on the road about three days a week playing at other churches for a fee that includes travel, hotel costs plus an "honorarium." He wouldn't reveal his fee.

Some music ministers are in such demand that they simultaneously work for different choirs. One is Ricky Dillard. He directs the choir at Mount Carmel Baptist Church in Atlanta. But he also flies to Chicago every fourth Sunday to direct his recording choir, Ricky Dillard & New Generation Chorale.

Plenty of opportunity outside church The Rev. Timothy Flemming Sr., Mount Carmel's pastor, says he doesn't mind Dillard splitting his duties.

"In Atlanta, with so many megachurches, it's hard to find a qualified minister of music," Flemming says.

Flemming says it's even harder to keep a top music minister.

"If you find one, the competition is so great that someone can offer more money than you and you can easily lose a minister of music," he says. "I don't think Ricky Dillard will stay here that long—too many opportunities," he says.

When Dillard was told what Flemming said, his only response was, "We'll see what the Lord says."

Dillard, like most directors of recording choirs, says his recording chorale members do not get paid.

"Patti LaBelle doesn't get paid what the LaBelles get paid," he says. "It's Patti's show. It's Ricky Dillard and the Chorale. It's Ricky's show. I started this, and this is my thing."

Those in the business agree that's usually how it works. Celebrity music ministers typically do not pay choir members—even those who record for them, says the Rev. Milton Biggham, president of Savoy Records and founder of the Georgia Mass Choir (featured in the film, "The Preacher's Wife").

Biggham says he's even heard of choir directors who demand that their choir members pay them to take them on tours. These choir directors persuade their members to do so by saying that they'll get a chance to travel and sing a lot. Choir members accept this because they don't get into choirs to make money but to exercise their spiritual gifts, Biggham says.

"Church people are sheep," Biggham says. "You can take sheep and do anything you want with them. That's why those of us who are leaders must be trustworthy."

Biggham says he made sure that all the singers received a flat rate for appearing in "The Preacher's Wife" and participating in the soundtrack. Others got more lucrative deals. When his group tours, he also pays their travel and lodging. Recording mass choirs that do not have a celebrity choir director tend to share their profits with the director and their churches, he says.

Rashad Henderson, a member of the Open Door Outreach Center recording choir in College Park, says if he writes a song that becomes a huge hit, he expects to get paid. But he doesn't expect payment for just participating in his choir's recording.

"It's not about the money for me," he says. "It's a passion for me and that's where my blessings come from, to be obedient to the gift that God has given me."

PREACHER VS. MUSIC MINISTER

One of the most fragile relationships in the black church is between the pastor and the music minister. The problem arises when a pastor thinks a music minister isn't "submitting to the pastor's authority."

Cage says Bishop Eddie Long, New Birth's senior pastor, once became angry with him after he drove the congregation to a frenzy with a song. Long told him that the audience was too stirred up for him to preach the message he intended.

"He was angry," Cage says. "He thought I was rebelling against him….In my mind, I thought he was just upset and jealous because I got the better response."

Long says some music ministers compete against their pastors instead of complementing their sermons. He and Cage, though, clashed in that incident only because of miscommunication, he says.

"I'm a Baptist boy and Byron is Pentecostal," Long says. "I remember asking Byron to give me an up-tempo song but Baptist up-tempo is a little slower than Pentecostal up-tempo. I thought he was getting out of line but he was actually in line with his tradition."

Some pastors alienate music ministers when they try to control the church's music, says Reggie Gay, a choir director and disc jockey for the Kiss 104.1 (WALR-FM) morning gospel show.

"The choir director may say we need to be an audition choir. And the pastor will say, 'Naw, we've been this way for 50 years and that's it,'" Gay says. "The minister of music should not be above the pastor. But in a lot of cases, churches are mediocre because they won't allow the music minister to embellish the choir."

Flemming, Mount Carmel's pastor, says he's had to fire several music ministers because they tried to turn the choir against him. Some don't leave quietly.

"A lot of times they will leave to show you need them," he says. "Sometimes they might do a lot of nasty things like saying if they leave, the choir will fall."

A good pastor can prevent a choir coup by staying close to them, he says.

"You can't turn your back on them" Flemming says. "Stay on them. Let them know that you are concerned about them and love them."

SINGERS HELD TO HIGH STANDARDS

Hammond, who grew up listening to Motley Crue and Def Leppard, gives his choir plenty of attention, but it's of the tough-love variety.

When people audition for World Changers' choir, Hammond tests their ability to match piano notes with their voice. He checks for vocal control and diction. His choirs rehearse at least six hours a week and people who chronically skip rehearsal are fired.

Some people cry when they fail auditions, Hammond says.

"We break it to them gently," he says. "We'll say, 'Well brother or sister, we understand. Maybe you need to join the usher board or the parking lot staff.'"

Hammond also has a financial stake in how well his choir sings. He says the profits from the choir's recordings go to the church but he gets royalties from them as well.

Malik Jones, a member of Hammond's "Praise Team" (singers who lead the choir on Sundays), says choir members appreciate Hammond's insistence on excellence.

"It's like in the army," he says. "When a drill sergeant is in your face, it's nothing personal. He's pushing you to be the best fighter you can be."

Hammond's high standards may anger some traditionalists. The black church has typically demanded exuberance—not excellence—from its choirs. And many smaller black churches still don't see the need to pay for a top music minister, Gay says.

"Sometimes I go to some churches and I just want to go up there with a fly swatter and beat everybody—'You ought to be ashamed of yourself for tearing up that song like that,' " he says.

Bond, New Birth's music minister, says the greatest reward for a music minister isn't the money, the music or the prestige.

It's watching your music change lives.

"I've written songs that people have later come up to tell me, 'My life was changed by that song you wrote,' " Bond says. "There is no greater reward than knowing that something you birthed blessed somebody. It's like your child growing up to be Martin Luther King."

Performing Blackness Down Under: The Café of the Gate of Salvation

E. Patrick Johnson

This essay examines the performance of black American gospel music by white Australian gospel choirs. Focusing primarily on the choir The Café of the Gate of Salvation, the essay examines how the medium of gospel music facilitates a dialogic performance of "blackness." The essay also addresses the politics of appropriation, highlighting the ways in which Australians explain their interest in and performance of gospel music and the ironies that underlie these explanations. Further, the essay explores the complexities of cultural usurpation by focusing on how the author's role as an "authentic" black American singer affected Australians' performances and vice versa. The analysis, then, demonstrates the problematic aspects of cross-cultural gospel performance, as well as the mutual benefits garnered when self and Other performatively engage one another via gospel music. Keywords: gospel music, cross-cultural performance, appropriation, authenticity

I put it [a gospel record] on, and I just began to howl. I began to weep. I just thought, this it extraordinary—the intensity, the surrender, the joy, the yearning everything that I could hear in it. (J. Backhouse)

I've always sung music that comes from a black tradition. So, if it's not soul, it's funk or reggae. So, I think African music touches me in some way. I don't know why that is—a white Jewish girl from Sydney, what can I say? Them's [sic] my roots. (Greenberg)

It's that once a week singing with other people and recognizing that we all have things to overcome, and being uplifted, and I just think music is universal. It conquers the language barrier. (Kerr)

In a black church, you know who[m] you're singing to. They believe every word you're going to say, and it's a fantastic opportunity to get in touch with yourself. And also, because they're far more responsive, as you know, it's like "whoa." (T. Backhouse)

An all-white, mostly atheist, Australian gospel choir—at first it sounds contradictory. Yet, when situated within the contested contexts of "blackness" and "performance," white Australian, atheist gospel singers are no more contradictory than black, gay Republicans. We live out the contradictions of our lives, and an aversion to religion does not exclude persons from making personally meaningful connections to gospel music that sometimes resemble, sometimes contradict, and sometimes supersede gospel music's functions in the United States. Once signs—or, in this case, *sounds*—of "blackness" are "let loose" in the world,

259

they become the site at which cultures contest and struggle over meaning. Gospel music, as a sign/sound of "blackness," functions as one such contested site.

This essay examines the performance of black American gospel music by white Australian gospel choirs. Research for this study occurred over the three-year period from 1996 to 1999 and included four trips to Australia, with each trip lasting from three to six weeks. During these trips, I formally interviewed fifteen members of an Australian gospel choir called The Café of the Gate of Salvation and informally interviewed twenty-seven Australian gospel singers at workshops I conducted in Sydney, Canberra, Wollongong, Newcastle, Melbourne, Adelaide, and Perth.[1] I focus initially on the formation and performances of The Café of the Gate of Salvation and then move to a more general discussion of gospel performance in Australia, examining how the medium of gospel music facilitates a dialogic performance of "blackness." Given the racial, cultural, and religious composition of The Café and other Australian choirs, this essay necessarily addresses the politics of appropriation, highlighting the ways in which Australians explain their interest in and performance of gospel music and the ironies that underlie these explanations. Further, I explore the complexities of cultural usurpation by focusing on how my role as an "authentic" black American singer affected Australian choir members' performances and vice versa. The analysis, then, demonstrates the problematic aspects of cross-cultural gospel performance, as well as the mutual benefits garnered when self and Other performatively engage one another via gospel music.

"COULDN'T HEAR NOBODY PRAY": DISCOVERING GOSPEL DOWN UNDER

I learned of The Café of the Gate of Salvation through Houston Spencer, a former classmate in graduate school. One of the things he and I share is a love of gospel music. Houston immigrated to Australia in 1991 but kept in touch through letters. Many of his letters included requests that I send him gospel tapes because they were hard to find in Australia. Then, in the spring of 1992, he wrote to let me know that he had discovered a gospel choir in Sydney. This was not just any gospel choir. It was an *a cappella,* predominately non-Christian or atheist gospel choir. I refused to believe him until he sent me a recording of the choir's self-titled compact disc.[2] A couple of years later I secured a grant to travel to Sydney to begin conducting research.

Though I had listened to the choir's recording and had been amazed by the power of their voices, upon my arrival in Australia, I nevertheless held a condescending attitude. As an African American who had been raised in a black southern Baptist church, I had doubts about the abilities of an all-white, Australian gospel choir. My attitude began to change, however, the first time I attended one of their rehearsals. Had I closed my eyes on that occasion, I would have sworn I was back home at my church in western North Carolina. The choir had not only accomplished a "black" sound, they had also had created the ethos of a black devotional service. When they stood, hand-in-hand in a circle in the middle of the sanctuary singing "I Woke Up This Morning With My Mind Stayed on Freedom," an anthem from the civil rights movement of the 1960s, I was impressed.

During the three weeks of that first visit, I interviewed various choir members, and, without exception, all were both willing to share their experiences in the choir and curious about my impressions of their performance. Specifically, they wanted to know if I thought they were "good," if they sounded the way gospel music "should" sound. My response was always encouraging but usually noncommittal. "I was *really* impressed," I often told them. Although I thought they had a great sound and, to some extent, had mastered the gospel idiom, I nevertheless felt that something was missing. I realize now what I did not then: that I was waiting to hear an "authentic" voice in their music. I was listening for the conviction, the expression of faith, that fuels much black American music in general and gospel music in particular.[3] Because I did not hear this "authentic" sound, I did not fully appreciate The Café's music—or, I should say, I did not *allow* myself to appreciate it fully. My initial response was one of admiration coupled with skepticism. I admitted the choir's performance as a good approximation, yet I dismissed it as definitely not the "real" thing. In retrospect, I recognize that I entered this ethnographic encounter with an "ax to grind rather than feeling for the organism."[4] Compounding this, my first visit was only three weeks in length, not nearly enough time to get a sense of Australia's cultures, day-to-day rituals, politics, and ways of being in the world. Later, I discuss how subsequent visits complicated my initially ambivalent attitude toward Australian gospel music. First, however, I provide a brief history of how The Café of the Gate of Salvation came into being and who the members of this gospel choir are.

"BLACKNESS" IN THE MAKING

Tony Backhouse, a native New Zealander, formed The Café of the Gate of Salvation in 1986, after years as a guitarist and vocalist in the Crocodiles, a New Zealand rock band. His interest in gospel music began when he heard "You Don't Know What the Lord Has Done For Me," a track on the album *Sorrow Come Pass Me Around.* A record shop owner whose store was located near the Badde Manners Café that Tony managed gave the recording to Judy Backhouse who, at the time, was Tony' wife. When Judy played the song for Tony, both were powerfully affected. Tony recalls:

> The voices were so strange on it, and the feeling was just fantastic. To me, it was weird, like it was very exotic and, at the same time, kind of earthy and truthful....There was one strong singer, the alto, and then there was somebody else who sounded like someone's dying grandmother who was, sort of, seemingly, singing a soprano part or sort of set soprano tone, but she was actually singing lower than the alto in this kind of strange voice that was not always kind of hitting the same harmonies as someone else. And then there was a sort of bass voice that you could barely hear, so voices didn't blend, and half of it was inaudible, and that just added a fantastic character to it, and I just wanted to find out more about it.[5]

Though this song piqued Tony's interest in gospel music, he did not begin singing gospel right away.

It was four years later that Tony "got a 'calling'" to start a choir. The idea came to him during a ten-day Buddhist meditation retreat, and soon after the retreat, he put up signs in the café where he worked, in other cafés around Sydney, and in the Conservatory of Music. The signs read: "Singers Wanted for Gospel Choir. Buddhists Welcome" (T. Backhouse). Forty people showed up for the first meeting, a meeting which occurred in the living room of Tony's and Judy's one bedroom flat. Judy recalls, "He had no idea what he was going to do really. He'd prepared one song, 'How I Got Over,' Aretha Franklin's version, and that was it—the choir was born." The liner notes to the choir's first compact disc alludes to this initial meeting: "The idea was to see if there was a bunch of singers around ready to go down a passionate, exhilarating spiritual, but culturally specific and little known byway; i.e., to form a choir inspired by the Afro-American religious singing tradition. When we started to rehearse in Tony and Judy's lounge room we had few expectations. It was an experiment that could have lasted 20 minutes or 20 years." In the months that followed, Tony continued to learn about gospel music. He obtained gospel music recordings from Australian disc jockeys; he corresponded with white music scholars in the United States; and he read articles on gospel music, as well as the liner notes of gospel recordings.

Regarding how the choir got its name, Tony remembers, "I was reading a book on coffee at the time. It [The Café of the Gate of Salvation] is the name of an actual café out of Istanbul. It's been there since the 13th century or the 16th century. Just the ring of it sounds kind of nice. It's a terrible name. You can't fit it on any decent sized poster. We should have called it 'Punk' or something, a little bitty, one-word [name] would have done a lot better." Nonetheless, the name stuck, and now, two recordings later, the choir enjoys a reputation as, arguably, the best gospel choir in Australia. Today, Tony is known throughout the country for his voice and gospel music, and gospel music workshops he has organized have generated other Australian gospel choirs.

At the time of my first visit to Australia, The Café of the Gate of Salvation included approximately 35 singers. All of the choir's members were white except Cheryl, an African American woman from Detroit whose hospital transferred her to Sydney, and William, a Maori from New Zealand.[6] Cheryl sang with the choir from 1993 to 1997 before leaving the group to star in musicals and form her own female singing group. Until 1999, William

sang in both the choir and Tony's quartet, the Heavenly Light Quartet. Other than Cheryl, no African American has ever been a part of the choir. The choir is slightly more diverse in its religious affiliation and includes practicing Buddhists, Jews, and "spiritualists," as well as agnostics and atheists. Based on formal interviews and informal conversations with the members, it appears that most fall into the latter two categories. Addressing this, Tony speculates, "I suppose you could say it's serving a therapeutic purpose, not necessarily a religious purpose, but…there has to be a place for non-specific spirituality, spirituality that doesn't necessarily attach itself to a label or a Messiah." When I asked the obvious question of how one does that while singing about Jesus, Tony responded, "Well, I don't know. I mean there are Jews in the choir who have a little bit of trouble with the 'J' word, but they get around it by, I guess, making a mental flip in their mind—retranslating the word 'Jesus' to mean 'my highest welfare,' or 'my highest good,' or 'mankind's highest good,' [do you] know what I mean?" The choir—comprised of working-class and middle-class people; heterosexuals, bisexuals, and homosexuals; Baby Boomers, Generation Xers, leftists, hippies, and political activists—is the site at which multiple identities converge.

Much of the gospel music aesthetic in the United States is lost in the Australian translation. In addition to the absence of the call-and-response dynamic,[7] other traditional features of the American gospel aesthetic are also lost. Clapping, rocking, discipline in rehearsals, and dress—all extremely important in black American gospel performance—are not The Café's strongest suits. Unlike the billowing robes and "flashy" outfits donned by African American choirs, The Café's attire is eclectic. Most of the time, the choir's members wear whatever they wish to, and even when a dress code is enforced, the singers wear all black costumes, accented with a colored sash or scarf.

While The Café, in general, has competent clappers and rockers, some of them are what I call "rock and clap challenged." I often teased members of The Café and those attending my workshops about their lack of rhythm, and I regularly found myself spending as much time teaching them how to rock and clap at the same time as I did teaching them songs. Judy Backhouse half jokingly noted,

> We clap and rock, but we're not very good. We can't get that hard, solid clap. We can't get it. None of us have that sharp voice that cuts through, those sharp women's voices that sound like boy's voices. That's what a woman's voice should sound like in my book. There are some great solo singers in the choir, but they don't sound the same. We don't move in time. We don't clap in time. God knows what we're really doing really.

For the most part, the choir does not try to replicate the sound of American gospel music and does not necessarily try to sound "black." In fact, this was never Tony's goal. According to him, gospel was a "starting point for developing our own musical language and our own nonspecific spiritual kind of music." However, as I detail later, some of the members' motivations for wanting to travel to the United States was to experience the "real" thing so they could sound "better." While one might argue that this does not necessarily translate into trying to sound "black," it does register a desire on the part of at least some of the choir's members to sound more "authentic."

When asked about what motivated them to sing gospel music, all but a few of the members cited the music's centrality in African American history. For example, Scot Morris stated:

The whole thing about gospel is the release that it gives you…in terms of freeing your spirit, and the joy and sharing that goes on is universal even though it comes from those (slave) roots.…A lot of the songs are a metaphor for the freedom that people were longing for from the oppression that they found themselves in, and, I think, part of the reason that we do a lot of the original sort of gospel numbers—and do them in a fairly traditional style—is out of respect [for] that tradition.

It appears that the singers not only revere the music but also the history of the struggle out of which it comes. They seem to find a transcendent quality in the struggle of African Americans that allows them to generalize this experience to struggles over other forms of oppression, and in this transcendence of struggle, they discover a message of hope. According to one member of The Café, "There is a common thread in terms of recognizing the spirituality and the universality of the messages that gospel music brings, and the joy" (Morris). Similarly, another choir member explains:

> As I understand it, it [gospel music] came from the slave time and was what got them through those hard times, and I think a lot of people can relate to that because suddenly people go—doesn't matter what race, religion, or color, whatever—everybody goes through their own constant, personal dramas, and that music is, like, you can overcome…whatever. I know you can overcome adversity, and you can overcome things, and the strength from the unity just makes you, just empowers you, I guess. (Kerr)

A common theme that runs throughout these statements is that gospel music is a universal language that transcends difference in order to help others overcome their own "personal dramas" and adversities.[8]

Some choir members link their history as descendants of convicts to African Americans' history as descendants of slaves. For these singers, the music becomes a vehicle through which to express repressed sorrow and grief. Grant Odgers, a member of both The Honeybees and The Café states, "We do have the same history of cruelty and brutality [as African Americans], but we don't express it. I think that's why it [gospel music] becomes so big, because we need the catharsis" (qtd. in Martin). The "history of cruelty and brutality" to which Odgers refers is the "settlement" of Australia—then known as "Botany Bay"—by the British in order to "contain" their "criminal" population. In *The Fatal Shore,* Australian historian Robert Hughes chronicles the exportation of English convicted felons to what is now Australia. He notes that "in the whole period of convict transportation, the Crown shipped more than 160,000 men, women and children (due to defects in the records, the true number will never be precisely known) in bondage to Australia. This was the largest forced exile of citizens at the behest of a European government in pre-modern history. Nothing in earlier penology compares with it" (2). The fact that these criminals were excommunicated by their "own" further complicates the already ambivalent feelings many Australians harbor toward Britain. For example, at one of the gospel music workshops I conducted, a woman who wishes to remain anonymous told me, "We know what it means to be treated like scum. Just like black Americans, we, too, have been put down because we're not of royal stock. We're the descendents of people who[m] the upper crust of England banished. So, in a way, we connect with black Americans and their fight to be legitimate. Singing gospel is the closest we come to making that happen." While Robert Hughes maintains that this feeling of "illegitimacy" persisted until the 1960s, this woman's statement suggests very clearly that traces of this feeling persist today.

These feelings of illegitimacy stem from at least two factors: first, the English often reminded Australians of their criminal ancestry, and, second, the history of criminality in Australia forged a mythology around which working-class Australians could claim a history of oppression. Thus, English ridicule of Australians sent "upper-middle-class Australians into paroxysms of social embarrassment," while the working class created a stereotype of convict identity that said that "convicts were innocent victims of unjust laws, torn from their families and flung into exile on the world's periphery for offenses that would hardly earn a fine today" (Hughes 158–59). These two stances—denial/embarrassment and victim mythology—shape many Australians' current views of England and their relationship to British subjects, and one result has been the fomenting of Australian nationalism. In the past few years, for instance, the Australian government has engaged in heated debates about whether to break away from the monarchy and become a self-governing republic. Another result has been a longing to reconcile the past with the present. Gospel music, some singers argue, has helped bring about that reconciliation.

ROMANTICIZATION OR IDENTIFICATION?: UNIVERSAL BLACKNESS

Although I was moved by the conviction with which members of The Café and other Australian choirs express the love for humankind that gospel music brings them, I kept wondering how they justify white Australia's treatment of Aborigines. Their romanticization of African American culture and history exists uneasily beside the virtual obliteration of Aboriginal culture. In fact, very few of the singers I interviewed discuss the white privilege they enjoy in relation to the subjugation of the Aboriginal community. As one anonymous storekeeper put it in a 1996 interview, "We don't have an Aboriginal problem because we don't talk about it." This sentiment typifies the general attitude regarding the oppression of Aboriginal people. On the one hand, these gospel singers identify with an oppressed group thousands of miles away and condemn their oppressors. On the other hand, they fail to acknowledge the ways in which they participate in the subjugation of the "blacks" of their own country.

This cross-identification with African Americans represents one instance of a denial of privilege. I was struck, for instance, by how many white Australians lamented: "I just do not understand the racism in America. Why are people so mean?" And, tine and again, this sentiment was juxtaposed against scenes of Aboriginal homelessness and destitution around Sydney. Those who don't live on the streets are confined to a section of Sydney called "Redfern," known as an Aboriginal "ghetto" where crime and alcoholism are a mainstay. I remember trying to hail a cab one evening at a Sydney train station not too far from the Redfern area. After half an hour of watching empty taxis pass me by, an Asian driver stopped for me. When I communicated to him what had happened, he said that the other taxis did not stop because it was dark and they thought I was "black," meaning Aboriginal. It turns out some taxi drivers had been robbed in that area, and, therefore, they did not stop near that particular train station or for Aborigines in general. While I understand the taxi drivers' concern for safety, I cannot overlook the unacknowledged racism underlying their actions. Unfortunately, it seems that racism, like the message of gospel music, is also "universal."

Like many white Americans, many white Australians do not feel responsible for the past—at least in terms of acknowledging how they benefit, on a daily basis, from the subjugation of Australia's indigenous people. Thus, it was odd for me, as an African American, to

have an Australian shake his or head in disdain at what white Americans have "done to me." When I addressed the problem of racism in Australia with members of the choir or Australians in general, they seemed uncertain as to what to say. I do not wish to imply that none of the Australian gospel singers or no Australians more generally are concerned about or actively fight for the rights and welfare of the Aborigines. Rather, I want to make note of the fact that rarely was the plight of Australia's indigenous population a topic of conversation and that when it was, it was brief.

Another problem associated with Australian singers' universalizing the ethos of gospel music is that this practice fails to acknowledge the specificity of African American history. African Americans who sing gospel music do so from a place of struggle *and* faith. For them, the music functions not only as a testimony of their secular struggles of living in a white supremacist society, but also of their sacred faith in a God who has delivered them and continues to sustain them through those struggles. Therefore, when Australian gospel singers state that they identify with African Americans who sing gospel music, the comparison seems misplaced and inappropriate. Their rationale for singing gospel music fails to recognize that the "struggle" they inherit as descendents of convicts differs markedly from the struggle African Americans inherit in the move from chattel slavery to freedom. In light of the white privilege they enjoy in their own country in relation to the Aborigines, their "struggles" seem decidedly different from African Americans. This is not to suggest that white Australians do not carry the pain of their criminal heritage. Rather, I believe that this history and its long-term material effects are distinct from and do not have the same impact as the history of oppression for either black Americans or black Australians. White Australians do not experience their bodies through the same racial lens as black

Australians and black Americans, and to romantically dissolve the specificity of the history of "black" bodies remains problematic.

Nevertheless, the psychological wounds of convict heritage and second class citizenship may allow these singers to connect to the African American experience. As much as spirituals and gospel music were a survivalist strategy to physically escape oppression, they also provided and provide a psychological escape from oppression. That psychological release stems from both the shared witnessing of joy and pain and the corresponding cathartic moment generated in gospel performance. The rhythm, syncopation, repetition, and call-and-response coalesce as a generative force that facilitates a psychological release. Among African Americans, that release is most often manifested physically. Whether through the waving of hands, dancing, rocking, crying, shouting, praying or laying on of hands, the catharsis comes through corporeal and verbal expression. Further, it is a communal act of experiencing this gestalt in the presence of others in that moment of mutual affirmation of faith and witnessing.

When members of The Café and other Australian gospel music singers talk about how gospel music makes them "feel better" and "picks them up," they, too, are naming the cathartic power of gospel. I argue, however, that their catharsis is brought on not by the universality of gospel "touching" them in the same way it does African Americans, but rather by the shedding of residual traces of British propriety. The physicality, emotionality, and self-display inherent in gospel performance does not accommodate self-consciousness, timidity, or taciturnity. Because Australian culture often devalues self-display and thwarts creativity in youngsters, when Australians sing gospel music, they cannot help but feel a release. It is as if they are discovering for the first time a hidden part of themselves. What they are "connecting with,"

however, is not the oppression of African Americans but rather a part of themselves that has been underdeveloped or lying dormant. Not surprisingly, the release Australians experience when they sing gospel music brings about a sense of joy and happiness. All of the testimonies chronicled earlier suggest that singing gospel amounts to a transformative experience. According to Judy Backhouse, the emergence of gospel singing groups in Australia represents the "first full community, the tribal thing, the group thing…for expressing creativity." She also believes that singing gospel music has an impact at the level of the individual. "There are very few ways in which people can authenticate themselves as singers or as artists of any kind," she said. "Usually, no one would come out and say, 'I'm a singer, I'm an artist,' even in this gospel community. But if they stand in a group and sing, they can sing without having to say anything about themselves. So it's a vehicle for their creativity, and it's a vehicle for belonging, for joining." The community that is created, however, is, I maintain, based less on a superficial connection with African Americans than on the communal feeling stimulated when a group of people come together to share previously unexpressed parts of themselves with one another.

AUTHORIZING BLACKNESS: SINGING BLACK INTO BEING

During my second trip to Australia, Grant Odgers asked me if I would consider conducting a workshop or two around Sydney, and I happily agreed. What began as something to do for "fun" materialized into something much more as I became a sort of a gospel music icon in the country. I appeared on several national radio and television programs and was asked to perform at concerts around the country. These programs positioned me as the "authentic" black gospel singer, and often people requested that I sing on command to demonstrate how gospel "should" sound. Many of the radio and television commentators, as well as their listening audiences and those who came to my workshops, had preconceived notions about me before I sang a note: I am a black American; therefore, I can sing. Or, so the stereotype goes. Ironically, once I did sing, I only reinforced their beliefs. The more I was interviewed and the more workshops I conducted, the more quickly the news spread about the black singer from the United States who could sing "authentic" gospel. The Sydney *A Cappella* Association, which sponsored and organized many of my workshops, circulated flyers that read "E. Patrick Johnson, Direct From the USA, Black Gospel Workout." The posters, featuring a picture of me that had been taken without my knowledge and used without my permission, not only emphasized my "authentic" talents but also served as a palimpsest of flyers that circulated during the slave trade, flyers that might have read "Direct from Africa" in order to increase the market value of the "merchandise" by emphasizing the authenticity of the enslaved persons.[9] These images became one of several ways in which my own blackness affected the ethnographic field. Indeed, my black and American identities were deployed in ways that I no longer controlled. Thus, as I moved from ethnographer to teacher to performer, I was catapulted into the center of identity politics. Because I am a singer raised in the gospel tradition, my workshops only worked to further the often racist perception of me as the authentic, black, exotic Other.

When I traveled to Adelaide to conduct a workshop, my host, Briar Eyers, a 67-year-old, white Australian woman with dreadlocks, told me: "When Rhonda rang and said that you would be willing to come down, I wasn't too sure of the response because of everything going on at the moment. But I've had a great response because you're black, you see, and they've never seen you, and they want the real thing." At the second workshop I conducted in

Adelaide, Briar introduced me in the following fashion: "We're fortunate to have Patrick Johnson with us tonight. He's the authentic thing from the States. I'm just [grabbing and shaking her dreadlocks], you know, and came to the music through the CDs, but Patrick, he's the real thing." That same evening, a woman came up to me after the workshop and said, "If I'm listening to the radio, I can tell if it's a black singer in the first two notes. I heard it tonight in your voice—what is that?" I responded, "my mama." (While my Signifyin' was totally lost on her, it nevertheless gave me a great deal of satisfaction!)

During the course of my fieldwork, I became increasingly aware of my role in how "blackness" got disseminated in Australia vis-a-vis my workshops and the media. I grew self-reflexive about teaching gospel songs to non-believers whose only connection to the music might be a secular/romantic one. Was I not accountable to African American communities that regard this music as sacred? At the same time, however, I was also aware of how I, an "outsider," was beginning to essentialize Australian culture in general and Australian gospel singers specifically, while simultaneously holding a condescending attitude toward their notion of the sacred. By viewing Australians as fixed subjects and by juxtaposing that view against my own authenticating narratives of "blackness," I began to fall prey to the same essentializing discourse I found among those who attended my workshops.

Nowhere was my complicity in this construction of "authentic blackness" more present than in my television and radio interviews. Often, I would authenticate my blackness and my authority on gospel by narrativizing my experience of growing up in the south in the black church and singing in the choir since age five, and by emphasizing the physicality of gospel singing. These experience narratives ontologically linked race, region, and religion as epistemological sites, foregrounding "blackness,"

"Southemness," and "Christianity" as authenticating features of gospel expertise.

Each radio announcer assumed that Australians could not sing gospel well and that this "fact" was my motivation for coming to teach them how to do it "right." Often, in Australian singers' defense, I would suggest that there are indeed "good" gospel singers and that they can sing gospel as well as anyone else. Ultimately, however, I wound up implicitly reifying the essentialist position that framed the interview by suggesting that white Australians had to be coached in order to sing the music, by speaking as an "expert" on the history of gospel, and by singing on air. Consider, for example, the following excerpt from an interview with Peter Adams, a radio talk show host:

Adams: His name is Patrick Johnson, and he sings gospel music. And he's been doing that since he was, well, five years old, in Hickory, North Carolina. Patrick is an African American. He's professor of literature and choir director at Amherst College, and I welcome him to the program....As well as performing here, you're also teaching people how to sing gospel. Can white people sing gospel?

EPJ: Of course they can. Anybody can sing gospel.

Adams: But can they sing it *great?*

EPJ: Of course they can...with a little...help.

Adams: From you.

EPJ: [laughter] From me or from other capable hands.

Adams: Well, hands are important aren't they because you've got a teaching technique that involves parts of the body? Can you briefly explain that?

EPJ: Yes. Gospel music is very physical. You can't just stand and sing. You have to use the diaphragm. You have to use your hands. You have to use the voice. And in the States, choreography is also very important—clapping and moving and swaying and stomping. Adams: Are you going to do all of that tonight?

EPJ: No

Adams: [sighing disappointedly] Awwwww.

EPJ: [laughter]

Adams: I want the choreography. I want the stomping and the clapping. Oh dear oh dear.

I[n] addition to Adams' exoticization and fetishization of gospel and of me, what stands out in this interview is how complicitous I am in the construction of the authenticating narrative of gospel. I was invited on the show as a scholar on the topic, and, as such, I spoke with scholarly authority on a subject about which I was conducting research; however, in the context of a public interview where the assumption was that white Australians cannot sing gospel music well (or worse, that they can't sing it at all), my scholarly authority registered as cultural and social authority rooted in my blackness. No matter how I tried to undermine that authority, the fact of my blackness carried more cultural capital than the fact of my scholarship. Adams' initial inquiry regarding whether *white* people can sing gospel—not whether Australians can sing gospel—underscored the cultural capital of race in this context. The lack of a qualifying ethnic or national identity of whiteness is telling here, for the underlying assumption in his question is that if all white people cannot sing gospel music, then all black ones can. My singing in the studio and my "lecture" on gospel, coupled with my thoughts and comments on Australian singers as novices, secured the legitimacy of not only my own (black) authority, but the discursive representation of Australian gospel singers as inauthentic.

Another interview indicates how my "stardom" around Sydney began to effect my integrity. In this instance, I pander to the stereotype of the theatrical preacher and black churchgoer by affirming the authenticity of the problematic representation of a church service in a scene from *The Blues Brothers*. Richard Glover, one of Sydney's more popular news radio personalities conducted the interview.

Glover: He's a great singer. He can teach the history of gospel music, but he can also sing it. Now in Australia to conduct choir and lead workshops, Patrick Johnson joins us in the studio. G'day.

EPJ: G'day.

Glover: In those *Blues Brothers* films, which many Australians have seen, we got an image of the black southern church with the preachers singing and dancing. Realistic or not at all?

EPJ: Not only is it realistic, but there are some churches that are even more charismatic than those in those *Blues Brothers* films.

Glover: Including the priest, the Reverend singing the whole sermon virtually, and sort of doing high kicks and all of that?

EPJ: Yes, that's what we call a chant, when a preacher will begin speaking as I'm speaking to you, and then it will [begins chanting] go into a little hum-huh—somethin' a little like that—huh. Ohhhhhh yeeeeaaaahhh. So, it's kind of a singsong chant, and that really gets the congregation going.

Glover: Do a little bit more of that. What would they then go on to say? Would they go on to sing or to give a sermon in a sense?

EPJ: Well, it's both a song and a sermon. Most of the time these preachers will call upon formulaic expressions that the congregation is quite familiar with, things like "I was sick and I couldn't get well. The Lord healed my body, now I can tell. I went to the valley, but I didn't go to stay. My soul got happy and I stayed all day."

Glover: Can you do that as they would do it? Or is it outside your range:'

EPJ: Well, not on the spot I can't. But sometimes when I'm goofing off I can do it.

Glover/EPJ: [laughter]

Following the interview, I sang Thomas Dorsey's "Precious Lord" with all of the fervor I could muster. Glover, seemingly amazed by the power of my voice, responded with "Wow. You really have a fantastic voice." In retrospect, as I reflect back on the interview, I realize how insidious my performance was. Rather than critique the racist stereotype captured in the film, I perpetuated it with the confidence of a seasoned minstrel. In fact, the interview was such a success—the station was inundated with calls—that I was invited back to the program to sing before a live studio audience and to lead them in a song or two, an invitation I accepted.

Each of the radio personalities positioned me as an exotic, racial other that they wanted to put on display for their radio audience, and I was both consciously and unconsciously complicit with that positioning. Nevertheless, my goal in this discussion is not to demonize the announcers or myself. Rather, my aim is to point out that there are no innocents in the perpetuation of narratives of black authenticity. The reference to *The Blues Brothers* in the interview context underscores Paul Gilroy's claim that "the discourse of authenticity has been a notable presence in the mass marketing of successive Black folk-cultural forms to white audiences" (105). That this marketing has been at the hands of non-blacks as well as blacks should come as no surprise. In either case, a premium is placed on black authenticity. In regard to gospel music in Australia, it seems that the most productive way to rise above the identity politics that singing the music incurs is to look to the music not as an universalizing agent or as an essential one but as an opportunity to engage in a conversation with the Other and the self so that both may be better understood.

BLACKNESS AND DIALOGIC PERFORMANCE

There is no easy way to avoid the identity politics that arise when one group or culture appropriates another group or culture's art form and when members of the "indigenous" culture, the appropriating culture, and critics from both cultures articulate conservationist or pluralistic arguments. Conservationists argue in essentialist ways that totalize and reduce black culture, most often in the name of Black Nationalism, while many pluralists explode the notion of any coherent organizing principal of blackness or black cultural production. There is, however, an alternative to either of these positions, particularly in reference to black music. Paul Gilroy writes:

> Music and its rituals can be used to create a model whereby identity can be understood neither as a fixed essence nor as a vague and utterly contingent construction to be re-invented by the will and whim of aesthetes, symbolists and language gamers. Black identity is not simply a social and political category to be used or abandoned according to the extent to which the rhetoric that supports and legitimizes it is persuasive or instantly powerful. Whatever the racial constructionists may say, it is lived as a coherent (if not

always stable) experiential sense of self. Though it is often felt to be natural and spontaneous, it remains the outcome of practical activity: language, gesture, bodily significations, desires. These significations are condensed in musical performance, though it does not, of course, monopolize them. In this context, they produce the imaginary effect of an internal racial core or essence by acting on the body through the specific mechanisms of identification and recognition that are produced in the intimate inter-action of performer and crowd. This reciprocal relationship serves as strategy and an ideal communicative situation even when the original makers of the music and its eventual consumers are separated in space and time. (108–109)

Key to Gilroy's demolition of the essentialist/anti-essentialist binary is the primacy he places on the relationship between the body and discourse as a complex, dynamic, intricate web of significations and meanings that are simultaneously both experienced as real and imaginatively produced. This view of "black" performance opens up new possibilities for interpreting the performance of gospel music by Australians.

One way to view the Australians' performance of gospel is as an instance of cultural performance, wherein their performances provide a space for social and cultural reflection and critique. Although they are performing an Other's culture, their engagement with the music emerges from a cultural site specific to their own history as well—namely, the legacy of British propriety and the secularity of contemporary Australian culture. Because their gospel performances are in striking contrast to socially and culturally sanctioned Australian cultural performances, they hold the potential of transgressing the strictures of hegemonic systems that sanction behaviors, beliefs, and attitudes. It is specifically the liminal space of performance that provides this occasion for cultural reflection and critique, this space where "the past is momentarily negated, suspended, or abrogated, and the future has not yet begun, an instant of pure potentiality when everything, as it were, trembles in the balance" (Turner, *From Ritual* 44). In this liminal state, "cultural performance holds the potential for negation, as well as affirmation" but nonetheless "[induces] self-knowledge, self-awareness, [and] plural reflexivity" (Conquergood, "Performaing Cultures" 59). When, for instance, The Café of the Gate of Salvation members speak of the joy, love, and sense of belonging they experience when they perform, they are naming the process of self-knowledge and self-awareness facilitated by gospel. The fact that such self-awareness is induced by a cultural discourse (gospel music) that transgresses the cultural milieu of Australia highlights the political nature of cultural performance. Turner suggests that cultural performances set in motion "a set of meta-languages whereby a group or community not merely expresses itself, but more actively, tries to understand itself in order to change itself" (Rev. of *Ethnopoetics* 338).

This change is facilitated by what Dwight Conquergood calls "dialogic" performance. Through dialogic performance, the performer comes to know the self by performing the Other. According to Conquergood, dialogic performance

> resists closure and totalizing domination of a single viewpoint, unitary system of thought. The dialogical project counters the normative with the performative, the canonical with the carnivalesque, Appollonian rationality with Dionysian disorder. [...]Dialogicalism strives to bring as many different voices as possible into the human conversation, without any of them suppressing or silencing the other. ("Between Experience and Meaning" 47–48).

The dialogic performance paradigm foregrounds the tensions between self and Other such that, despite evidence to the contrary, self and Other temporally and spatially unite. This productive view of performance elides narrow essentialist views of performance while, at the same time, acknowledging difference. Indeed, "dialogic performance celebrates the paradox of 'how the deeply different can be deeply known without becoming any less different'" (Conquergood, "Performing As A Moral Act" 10).

In "Performance, Personal Narratives, and the Politics of Possibility," D. Soyini Madison theorizes the politics, benefits, and limits of performance with regard to three subject positions that comprise dialogic performance: the audience, the performers, and the subjects being performed. For each of these subject positions, Madison highlights what she calls the "performance of possibilities" in order to articulate a politicized practice of dialogic performance. In what follows, I relate each of these three subject positions to Australian gospel performance.

In Australia, the audiences of gospel performance are usually comprised of everyday folk who are not invested in musical performance of any kind. During most of the gospel performances I attended, the audience lacked the cultural capital to respond to the performance in ways that conform to the black gospel aesthetic of call and response, hand clapping, standing, hand waving, and so on. However, because the singers are familiar with the cultural aesthetic of gospel in the United States, they would often encourage the audience to participate, sometimes to no avail and at other times with much success. As some of the performers revealed to me, reactions to gospel performance vary from venue to venue, ranging from a response of total disinterest to lukewarm reception, from appreciation to interrogation of the history of the music. No matter what the "goal" of gospel performance, the engagement of the audience speaks to the possibilities that such performances create. For Madison, the audience's engagement with the performance is a critical component of political and social action:

> Action, particularly, new action requires new energy and new insight. In the *performance of possibilities,* when the audience member begins to witness degrees of tension and incongruity between the Subject's life-world and those processes and systems that challenge and undermine that world, something more and new is learned about how power works. The question to what extent these life-worlds are threatened and, in turn, resist, is only partially captured in the space and time of performance; however, the audience, as involved citizens, both disturbed and inspired, may seek the answer long after the final curtain. This is a pursuit of possibility, a gift of indignation and inspiration, passed on from the Subject to the audience member. In the *performance of possibilities,* the expectation is for the audience member to continue, reaffirmed, or, to at least begin honing her skills toward "world travel." In the *performance of possibilities* both performers and audiences can be transformed. They can be themselves and more as they travel between worlds. (285; emphasis in original)

As regards Australian audiences, their witnessing a gospel music performance provides them a glimpse into the lives and history of a geographically and racially distant Other, a glimpse that may motivate them to join in the Other's struggle for humanity and equality. Although this is an idealistic view of audience, the performance of gospel in Australia nonetheless opens the "possibility" for political action.

Self-reflexivity is one by-product of cultural performance, and this is particularly true for the performer who performs the Other. In the meeting of self and Other in performance, the performer "is transported slowly, deliberately, and incrementally, at each rehearsal and at each encounter toward knowledges and life-world of the Subject" and, thus, "creatively and intellectually taking it all in[,] internalizing and receiving partial 'maps of meaning' that reflect the subject's consciousness and context" (Madison 285). If the performer "tak[es] it all in," then he or she cannot helped but be transformed. "The process of being transported, or receiving meanings and generating meanings is a more intimate and, potentially, a more traumatic engagement for the performers than for the audience members, because the transportation is mentally and viscerally more intense..." (283). The intimacy and visceral and mental intensity inherit in cross-cultural performance implies that an internal dialogue between self and Other is inevitable. This "felt-sensing" (Bacon) experience energizes, inducing self-reflexivity, self-knowledge and empowerment. Judith Carson, for example, an elderly woman who sings with the gospel choir The Honeybees discovered her own singing voice again after having been discouraged from singing in her younger years. Now in her 70s, Judith is rediscovering that part of herself that she thought she had lost, a rediscovery facilitated by her willingness to engage the Other. In an email, she narrates the joy of her discovery:

Dear Patrick,

This is your most enthusiastic Sydney student. I am dotty about singing, as you probably realise. All my life it has been my dearest interest. Tragically for me, in 1952 I started having singing lessons. The teacher said, "Do it from the diaphragm," and "Lift your palate." Never, "Listen to that awful noise you are making." I broke my voice and could not sing at all for years. It was too important to me to give up, and I tried teacher after teacher. It has been disastrous.

I love the power of your sweet voice, and the beauty of the music you made. Since you left, I have sung with your tapes, copying the sound and lilt of the music, and my body responds to the music I make[,] and I am beginning to sing with my own voice. Perhaps you can imagine what this means to me? It's all a bit of a miracle. If you come to Sydney again soon[,] I should enjoy very much singing with you again.[…]

Much affection,

Judith

Judith's testimony exemplifies Madison's call for the performer to be "committed—doing what must be done or going where one must go—to 'experience the felt-sensing dynamics' of the social world of the Other: it's tone and color—the sights, sounds, smells, tastes, textures, rhythms—the visceral ethos of that world" (284). When Judith placed those sights, sounds, and rhythms in her body, her body responded in ways that empowered her to find her own voice by singing with and through Others' voices. Her "broken" voice was "healed" through the "miracle" and power of performed blackness.

Judy Backhouse reports a similar self-discovery when she was persuaded to perform in New Orleans. In this instance, however, she and the Subjects she performed mutually benefited from the performance due, in part, to the space in which the performance occurred. Borrowing from Lawrence Grossberg's notion of "spatial territorialization," Madison argues that identities are "constituted by identification with certain cultural practices and connect to certain locales that are often ripe with struggle, conflict, and difference just as they are with creation, empowerment, and belonging" (284). In the following story, Judy Backhouse under-

scores the importance of place in relation to identity and dialogic performance:

It was one of the most harrowing nights of my life. [. . .] I was in this church. I made friends with this choir called John Lee and the Heralds of Christ in New Orleans. They said come to their church, they were giving a program, and I went along, and I was sitting in the audience. They were singing and everything was great: there was call and response, when, suddenly, John Lee said, "We have a good friend here from Australia, Ms. Judy Backhouse and she's going to come up and sing." And I said, "Oh No! I'm not a soloist. I'm not a soloist, really." And he said, "Oh no, you're going to come up." And I said, "No, no, no." And I was very certain that I wasn't going to have to go up. I'm a strong person. No one's going to make me do what I don't want to do. However, I just couldn't not go up because it would have been an insult to everybody—everybody was wanting me to go up. And I had to go up. I was so scared, cause I thought, "I can't sing, they'll see that I can't sing. It will be the worst insult to them to sing badly in this great place where everybody is singing." Everything crossed my mind. I had to go up, I had to sing "Precious Lord." They said, "What do you want to sing?" and the only song I really love more than anything else in the world is "Precious Lord." Well, I've got a tape of this, and it just sounds like someone on their deathbed, their last gasp, you know. But there they were, starting to encourage me: "alright," "go on," "do it." And that encouragement and that love they directed toward me, encouraged me really, it really emboldened me. By the end of the song, I was singing it, instead of just gasping it and panting it. I was singing it, and I just thought what it gives the performer, just makes you feel like you're in Heaven. And

I wish we did that here in Australia, it will probably come in time.

Clearly, Judy was transformed by this experience. Her repeated emphasis on the place in which the performance occurred speaks to the fact that "identity is definable yet multiple, contested yet affirmed, contextual yet personal and a matter of difference and a matter of identification" (Madison 286). Judy's reluctance to perform was based on her own rigid notion of identity and performance, especially within the culturally prescribed space of the black church. She briefly assumed the stance that Conquergood calls the "Skeptic's Cop-out, in which the performer refuses to perform the Other because of empirical and biological difference ("Performance as a Moral Act" 8). Quickly swept up in the centripetal energy of the church space, however, she moved to the center of dialogic performance. Once she began the performance, that liminal space where self and Other converse began to emerge, generating a powerful, dynamic, and transformative space. The encouragement of the audience whose art and cultural history was being performed helped Judy to "travel" in their world and, thus, provided her with a sense of belonging such that "by the end of the song, [she] was singing it, instead of just gasping it and panting it."

The words of the song that Judy sang were also crucial to the transformative power of this performance. Thomas Dorsey's classic hymn exclaims: "Precious Lord, take my hand. Lead me on, let me stand. I am tired. I am weak, I am worn." Because Judy is a nonbeliever, her singing of this song takes on mythic status insofar as she calls upon the trope of the anthropomorphic God to take her hand and help her through the song, to "take her hand and lead her on." With the encouragement of the black Subjects in the church, and despite her status as non-Christian, Judy appropriated an Other's religious myth to empower herself to sing "in this great place where everybody is

singing." The performed myth aided Judy in this moment of personal crisis. Conquergood writes, "It is through the liminal and transformative act of performance that myth and reality dissolve into a molten power that charges life with meaning and purpose" ("Between Experience and Expression" 2).

Witnessing this performance was meaningful to the black Subjects in the church as well. Their personhood, history, culture, and spirituality were affirmed and validated. This kind of validation is key to the "performance of possibilities" because it presents and represents "Subjects as made and makers of meaning, symbol, and history in their fullest sensory and social dimensions" (Madison 285). It acknowledges their existence in the eyes of others. The reflection of our selves through others is elemental to understanding the "performance of possibilities." As the events chronicled above attest, space, place, and time are each important in the making of the "performance of possibilities." Still, for "the deeply different" to become "deeply known," there must be a move "beyond the *acknowledgement* of voice within experience to that of actual *engagement*" (Madison 284). Performers and their audiences must engage the Others' political, social, cultural landscape, their contextually constituted subjectivities within contested spaces. Through this process of dialogic engagement, "subjectivity linked to performance becomes a poetic and polemic admixture of personal experience, cultural politics, social power, and resistance" (Madison 283).

In the "performance of possibilities," when this sharing of two worlds occurs, both the Subjects and performers benefit, as was the case when The Café of the Gate of Salvation visited the United States. In April of 1999, The Café made their first journey to the U.S. as a choir. Many individual members of The Café had come to the U.S. with Tony on his many "tours," but this was the first time that most of the choir's members together came to tour black churches here. Traveling from New York City to Birmingham to New Orleans, Tony arranged for the choir to give concerts, attend choir anniversary programs and rehearsals, church services, as well as experience the New Orleans Jazz Festival. I managed to arrange a trip to witness one of the choir's performances in New York. I was curious about how they would be received by African American churchgoers and how, in turn, the choir would react to that reception. I was especially anxious to experience the choir's performance in Harlem at the United House of Prayer, an unlikely place, I thought, to invite a group of non-believing, white Australians to sing gospel music.

Located on 125th Street, the United House of Prayer is a typical storefront church. It was Easter Sunday—the evening service—and an array of fuchsia, canary, and white wide-brimmed hats were sprinkled around the sanctuary. The crowd was small, but the pews gradually filled as the preprogram testimonies wore on. The devotional service continued for at least an hour and a half before the program officially began. Then, the master of ceremony welcomed everyone to their Easter concert, featuring their special guests all the way from Australia: The Café of the Gate of Salvation. The choir gathered in front of the altar. All were dressed in black, but each member had added his or her own tie or scarf, a splash of brilliant color—red, purple, blue, yellow. A nervous energy filled the air as they stood before the church. No one, including the choir members, knew quite what to expect.

Then, Tony Backhouse greeted the congregation with his consummate charm and graciousness, expressing the choir's gratitude for the invitation to sing. Their journey there had not been easy, he said, as they had to leave several fellow singers behind due to family commitments or because they could not afford to make the trip. But one member, Deborah, had joined the tour despite her brother's death just days before the choir left Sydney. Deborah stepped forward and addressed the congregation. "He told me to come. 'Sing your heart out,' he said. Then he died the next day," she said tearfully, prompting cries of "Have mercy" and "Bless the Lord" from the congregation.

Then the choir lifted their voices to sing.

The congregation appreciated the first few numbers, but I had a sense that the choir was not really reaching them. Then something broke. The basses set an upbeat tempo, their heads bobbing in time and their faces lighting up. The tenors, altos and sopranos joined the basses in harmony and rhythm. Soloist Tracey Greenberg stepped up to the microphone and launched into "You Brought the Sunshine," a song by the Clarke Sisters of Detroit that was popular in the early 1980s. The church pianist began to play, and there was uproar as the congregants rose to their feet and began to sing along: "You made my day/You paved my way/You heard me, every, every time I prayed. You brought the Sunshine (You brought the sunshine) In my life (You are the lifeline)." The choir beamed as the congregation's enthusiasm intensified in shouts of "Hallelujah' " and "Saaaaaannnng choir" syncopated by clapping hands, rocking bodies, and stomping feet that shook the church's creaky, wooden floorboards. At that moment, as the melodious voices lifted in the air, the United House of Prayer fell under the spell of the spirit that moved the foundation of the church.

During and after dialogic performance—and specifically within the "performance of possibilities," —performer, Subject, and audience are transformed. Each comes away from the performance changed. They traverse the world of the Other, glimpse its landscape, and this "sighting" leaves a lasting imprint on the consciousness of all who experience this symbolic journey. Indeed, they "[enter], albeit symbolically and temporarily, in [the Others'] locations of voice within experience" (Madison 280). The performance of "You Brought the Sunshine" tapped into the Others' voice within experience, due in part to the Cafés execution of and enjoyment of the song. This particular song registered with the congregation as a "difficult" song, and The Café's performance of it demonstrated their commitment to, investment in, and reverence for gospel music. The choir's performance competence initiated genuine dialogue in that contested space where identities and subjectivities conjoin, converse, commune, and contrast. According to Madison, "Performance becomes the vehicle by which we travel to the worlds of Subjects and enter domains of intersubjectivity that problematize how we categorize who is 'us' and who is 'them,' and how we see ourselves with 'other' and different eyes" (Madison 282). This blurring of subjectivities in the symbolic space of performance foregrounds the discursive nature of identity, such that during their performance in the United House of Prayer, the Australian choir and the black listening audience participated in the coproduction of blackness. Thus, for all intents and purposes, The Café of the Gate of Salvation, in the face of evidence to the contrary, "became" black. This is not to suggest that outside this symbolic space of performance and within the specific confines of the black church that the choir does not enjoy white skin privilege. On the contrary, as soon as they stepped foot outside the church and onto the streets of New York City, they enjoyed the material fruits of their skin's color. Nonetheless, their performance inside the church and during this particular song foregrounded the arbitrariness of black signification as well as the possibilities created by means of performance. Indeed, the choir was engaging in what Richard Schechner calls "believed-in theatre," where "at site specific event-specific, audience-specific performances, people gather as cocreators, participants, actors, spectators, witnesses, citizens, activists

[. . .] doers. The occasions are frequently more social or personal or quasi-religious (ritual-like) than aesthetic. Sincerity and making an honest effort are appreciated" (89–90).

One should never underestimate the transformative power of dialogic performance. For the members of The Café of the Gate of Salvation, their experiences during their tour were life altering, collectively and individually. Four months after their tour, I traveled to Sydney to conduct more research and follow-up interviews after the choir's U.S. tour. What I found was a choir "transfixed" —to borrow Judy Backhouse's term—by the power of their intercultural exchange. Their relationship to one another and to the music had changed. For example, half an hour before their rehearsals, they held an optional meditation session to set the tone for the rehearsals. This newly introduced ritual was a version of devotional services and/or prayer meetings they had attended while on tour. Although optional, the institution of the meditation period, according to some of the choir members, proved to be divisive. Members who did not go on the tour, for example, resented what they felt to be a new "religiosity" taking over the choir, which, according to them, flew in the face of the choir's past stance on fundamentalist dogma.

Moreover, a few of the members became "saved" on the tour. Judith Foster, in particular, told me that her life had been changed on the tour, that she was no longer a nonbeliever. In fact, she and one other member asked me to interview them again because they no loner felt the same way about issues of spirituality and God. The emergence of rituals and practices and shifts in beliefs by members of The Café suggests the malleability of the human spirit as well as the mobilizing force of performance. Despite their resistance to the spiritual ethos enlivened by gospel, the choir, through performance, came to realize as Judy Backhouse had done already, that the music "does something to you" or, as Tony Backhouse put it, that it "changes you for the better."

CONCLUSION

In their 1989 hit single, Huey Lewis and the News proclaim, "It's Hip to Be Square." In some instances, the same can be said of blackness. In recent times, blackness seems to have particular currency in popular culture, whether represented by middle class white youths who embrace hip hop or by well-intentioned liberals who, in an attempt at interracial bonding, appropriate black vernacular (e.g., "you go, girl"). On the other side of the coin, African Americans themselves circulate blackness in as many troubling ways, often grounding it in biological essence or confining it to a particular brand of politics as an agent of social efficacy. Whatever the case blackness has definitely become a "hip" signifier of identity and difference.

As a national and global commodity, black music has penetrated the boundaries between and among cultures around the world. As such, it becomes bound up in an intricately spun web of cultural, social, and political battles over origin, ownership, circulation, and performance. Until fairly recently, gospel music existed on the margins of this political minefield, due in part to its relatively limited circulation and popularity among mostly southern blacks. As it is has found currency among a younger audience—a currency made possible due to a shift in how it is marketed and, more importantly, how it is produced—gospel music, like rhythm and blues, has become more popular intra- and inter-continentally. It has, indeed, made its way over and "down under."

Like other black cultural art forms let loose in the world, gospel has become enshrouded in identity politics. The instance oɪ The Café of the Gate of Salvation is one example of how "messy" these politics may become. Like all identity politics and notions of "authenticity," the choir members' appropriation of blackness is both/and rather than either/or. Each time the choir performs gospel music they participate in what has become one of the most recognizable signifiers of black culture. In that regard, they perform blackness when they sing. On the other hand, their performance of blackness does not diminish the white skin privilege they enjoy in their country or in the U.S. Their performance of their own and the Other's identity, however, is never a static process. Rather, it is always in flux and flow, a performance of *possibilities*.

Negotiating any identity is a dangerous adventure, particularly in a postmodern world where we have come to recognize that identities are made, not given. We also must realize that the postmodern push to theorize identity discursively must be balanced with theories of corporeality and materiality. In other words, "blackness" may exist as a floating signifier in various cultures, but the consequences of its signification vary materially, politically, socially, and culturally depending on the body upon which it settles. I, for instance, walk this precarious tightrope of identity politics each time I conduct ethnographic research on Australian gospel.

NOTES

1. This essay is part of a larger book-length project, and not all of the interviews I conducted are referenced in this essay. Except where indicated, the subjects interviewed all consented to using their real, full names.

2. In addition to the choir's first compact disc, *The Café of the Gate of Salvation,* the group has subsequently released a second recording, *A Window in Heaven.*

3. For more on the notion of "voice" as a personal and cultural text connected to the body and lived experience, see Barthes.

4. I credit Emily Toth with this phrase.

5. What Tony is describing here is "heterophony," a musical term used to describe singing that is not in harmony but rather is a mixture of voices singing in unison with one or two harmonizing in between. This style of singing is common in African

American worship services, particularly in rural, southern churches.

6. Cheryl and William wished to be identified only by their first names.

7. For more on the role of audience in African and African American performance, see Ogunba and Elam.

8. In fact, this focus on the history of gospel music and the "empowerment" gleaned from that history was one of the factors that motivated the choir to organize a trip to the United States. According to Judy Backhouse, she and Tony wanted the choir to "see what they're representing and which tradition they're relating to. I don't think they really realize. We think they'd be really inspired, and it would make a huge difference in their singing, to their heart relationship to it." Eventually, the choir did travel to the United States, visiting churches in New York, Alabama, and New Orleans. As I discuss later, the trip did "change" them in ways that complicated their earlier tendency to universalize gospel music.

9. I do not mean to suggest that the circulation of these flyers announcing my gospel music workshops functioned in exactly the same manner as flyers that reduced enslaved Africans to objects. Rather, I merely make the point that the two flyers are discursively interconnected insofar as they "authenticate" black bodies by fetishizing and commodifying them.

REFERENCES

Backhouse, Judy. Personal interview. 10 January 1998.

Backhouse, Tony. Personal interview. 8 June 1996.

Bacon, Wallace. *The Art of Interpretation* New York: Holt, Rinehart and Winston, 1979.

Barthes, Roland. "The Grain of the Voice." Image/Music/Text. Trans. Stephen Heath. NY: Hill and Wang, 1977. 179–89. The Café of the Gate of Salvation. *A Window in Heaven.* Polygram, 1995.

———. *The Café of the Gate of Salvation.* Polygram, 1991.

Carson, Judith. Email to the author. 20 April 1998.

Conquergood, Dwight. "Performing as a Moral Act: Ethical Dimensions of the Ethnography of Performance." *Literature in Performance* 5 (1985): 1–13.

———. "Between Experience and Expression: The Performed Myth." Speech Communication Association Convention. Chicago, Illinois. November 1986.

———. "Between Experience and Meaning: Performance as Paradigm for Meaningful Action." *Renewal and Revision: The Future of Interpretation.* Ed. Ted Colson. Denton, TX: NB Omega, 1986. 26–59.

———. "Performing Cultures: Ethnography, Epistemology, and Ethics." *Miteinander Sprechen Und Handelm: Festschrift Fur Hellmut Geissner.* Ed. Edith Sembek. Frankfurt: Seriptor, 1986. 55–66.

Elam, Harry. *Taking It to the Streets: The Social Protest Theater of Luis Valdez and Amiri Baraka.* Ann Arbor: U of Michigan P, 1997.

Foster, Judith. Personal interview. 8 September 1999.

Gilroy, Paul. "Sounds Authentic: Black Music and Ethnicity." *Imagining Home: Class, Culture, and Nationalism in the African Diaspora.* Eds. Sidney Lemelle and Robin D. G. Kelley. New York: Verso, 1994. 93–117.

Hughes, Robert. *The Fatal Shores.* New York: Knopf, 1987.

Johnson, E. Patrick. Interview with Philip Adams. *Late Night Live,* ABC Radio National Sydney, 17 Aug. 1999.

———. Interview with Richard Glover. 2BL ABC Sydney, 19 Aug. 1999.

Kerr, Deborah. Personal interview. 1996.

Madison, D. Soyini. "Performance, Personal Narratives, and Politics of Possibility," *The Future of Performance Studies: The Next Millennium.* Ed. Sheron J. Dailey. Annandale: National Communication Association, 1998. 276–286.

Martin, Lauren. "A Black and White Gospel." Sydney Morning Herald 13 Sept. 1999: 399.

Morris, Scot. Personal Interview. 8 June 1996.

Ogunba, Oyin. "Traditional African Festival Drama." *Theatre in Africa.* Eds. Oyin Ogunba and Abiola Irele. Nigeria: Ibadan UP, 1978. 3–26.

Schechner, Richard. "Believed-In Theatre." *Performance Research* 2.2 (1997): 76 J1.

Turner, Victor. *From Ritual to Theatre: The Human Seriousness of Play.* New York: Performing Arts Journal Publications, 1982.

———.Review of Ethnopoetics, *Symposium of the Whole: A Range of Discourse Toward an Ethnopoetics.* Eds. Jerome Rothenberg and Diane Rothenberg. Berkeley: U of California P, 1983. 337–339.

Appendix

Statement of the American Sociological Association on the Importance of Collecting Data and Doing Social Scientific Research on Race

RACIAL CLASSIFICATIONS AS THE BASIS FOR SCIENTIFIC INQUIRY

Race is a complex, sensitive, and controversial topic in scientific discourse and in public policy. Views on race and the racial classification system[1] used to measure it have become polarized. In popular discourse, racial groups are viewed as physically distinguishable populations that share a common geographically based ancestry. "Race" shapes the way that some people relate to each other, based on their belief that it reflects physical, intellectual, moral, or spiritual superiority or inferiority. However, biological research now suggests that the substantial overlap among any and all biological categories of race undermines the utility of the concept for scientific work in this field.

How, then, can it be the subject of valid scientific investigation at the social level? The answer is that social and economic life is organized, in part, around race as a social construct. When a concept is central to societal organization, examining how, when, and why people in that society use the concept is vital to understanding the organization and consequences of social relationships.

Sociological analysis of the family provides an analogue. We know that families take many forms; for example, they can be nuclear or extended, patrilineal or matrilineal. Some family categories correspond to biological categories; others do not. Moreover, boundaries of family membership vary, depending on a range of individual and institutional factors. Yet regardless of whether families correspond to biological definitions, social scientists study families and use membership in family categories in their study of other phenomena, such as well-being. Similarly, racial statuses, although not representing biological differences, are of sociological interest in their form, their changes, and their consequences.

THE SOCIAL CONCEPT OF RACE

Individuals and social institutions evaluate, rank, and ascribe behaviors to individuals on the basis of their presumed race. The concept of race in the United States—and the inevitable corresponding taxonomic system to categorize people by race—has changed, as economic, political, and historical contexts have changed

(19). Sociologists are interested in explaining how and why social definitions of race persist and change. They also seek to explain the nature of power relationships between and among racial groups, and to understand more fully the nature of belief systems about race—the dimensions of how people use the concept and apply it in different circumstances.

SOCIAL REALITY AND RACIAL CLASSIFICATION

The way we define racial groups that comprise "the American mosaic" has also changed, most recently as immigrants from Asia, Latin America, and the Caribbean have entered the country in large numbers. One response to these demographic shifts has been the effort (sometimes contentious) to modify or add categories to the government's official statistical policy on race and ethnicity, which governs data collection in the census, other federal surveys, and administrative functions. Historically, changes in racial categories used for administrative purposes and self-identification have occurred within the context of a polarized biracialism of Black and White; other immigrants to the United States, including those from Asia, Latin America, and the Caribbean, have been "racialized" or ranked in between these two categories (26).

Although racial categories are legitimate subjects of empirical sociological investigation, it is important to recognize the danger of contributing to the popular conception of race as biological. Yet refusing to employ racial categories for administrative purposes and for social research does not eliminate their use in daily life, both by individuals and within social and economic institutions. In France, information on race is seldom collected officially, but evidence of systematic racial discrimination remains (31, 10). The 1988 Eurobarometer revealed that, of the 12 European countries included in the study, France was second (after Belgium) in both anti-immigrant prejudice and racial prejudice (29). Brazil's experience also is illustrative: The nation's then-ruling military junta barred the collection of racial data in the 1970 census, asserting that race was not a meaningful concept for social measurement. The resulting information void, coupled with government censorship, diminished public discussion of racial issues, but it did not substantially reduce racial inequalities. When racial data were collected again in the 1980 census, they revealed lower socio-economic status for those with darker skin. (38).

THE CONSEQUENCES OF RACE AND RACE RELATIONS IN SOCIAL INSTITUTIONS

Although race is a social construct (in other words, a social invention that changes as political, economic, and historical contexts change), it has real consequences across a wide range of social and economic institutions. Those who favor ignoring race as an explicit administrative matter, in the hope that it will cease to exist as a social concept, ignore the weight of a vast body of sociological research that shows that racial hierarchies are embedded in the routine practices of social groups and institutions.

Primary areas of sociological investigation include the consequences of racial classification as:

- A sorting mechanism for mating, marriage and adoption.

- A stratifying practice for providing or denying access to resources.

- An organizing device for mobilization to maintain or challenge systems of racial stratification.

- A basis for scientifically investigating proximate causes.

Race as a sorting mechanism for mating, marriage, and adoption. Historically, race has been a primary sorting mechanism for marriage (as well as friendship and dating). Until anti-miscegenation laws were outlawed in the United States in 1967, many states prohibited interracial marriage. Since then, intermarriage rates have more than doubled to 2.2 percent of all marriages, according to the latest census information (14, 28). When Whites (the largest racial group in the United States) intermarry, they are most likely to marry Native Americans/American Indians and least likely to marry African Americans. Projections to the year 2010 suggest that intermarriage and, consequently, the universe of people identifying with two or more races is likely to increase, although most marriages still occur within socially designated racial groupings (7).

Race as a stratifying practice. Race serves as a basis for the distribution of social privileges and resources. Among the many arenas in which this occurs is education. On the one hand, education can be a mechanism for reducing differences across members of racial categories. On the other hand, through "tracking" and segregation, the primary and secondary educational system has played a major role in reproducing race and class inequalities. Tracking socializes and prepares students for different education and career paths. School districts continue to stratify by race and class through two-track systems (general and college prep/advanced) or systems in which all students take the same courses, but at different levels of ability. African Americans, Hispanics, American Indians, and students from low socioeconomic backgrounds, regardless of ability levels, are over-represented in lower level classes and in schools with fewer Advanced Placement classes, materials, and instructional resources (11, 13, 20, 23).

Race as an organizing device for mobilization to maintain or challenge systems of racial stratification. Understanding how social movements develop in racially stratified societies requires scholarship on the use of race in strategies of mobilization. Racial stratification has clear beneficiaries and clear victims, and both have organized on racial terms to challenge or preserve systems of racial stratification. For example, the apartheid regime in South Africa used race to maintain supremacy and privilege for Whites in nearly all aspects of economic and political life for much of the 20th century. Blacks and others seeking to overthrow the system often were able to mobilize opposition by appealing to its victims, the Black population. The American civil rights movement was similarly successful in mobilizing resistance to segregation, but it also provoked some White citizens into organizing their own power base (for example, by forming White Citizens' Councils) to maintain power and privilege (2, 24).

Race and ethnicity as a basis for the scientific investigation of proximate causes and critical interactions. Data on race often serve as an investigative key to discovering the fundamental causes of racially different outcomes and the "vicious cycle" of factors affecting these outcomes. Moreover, because race routinely interacts with other primary categories of social life, such as gender and social class, continued examination of these bases of fundamental social interaction and social cleavage is required. In the health arena, hypertension levels are much higher for African Americans than other groups. Sociological investigation suggests that discrimination and unequal allocation of society's resources might expose members of this racial group to higher levels of stress, a proximate cause of hypertension (40). Similarly, rates of prostate cancer are much higher for some groups of men than others. Likewise, breast cancer is higher for some groups of women than others. While the proximate causes may appear to be biological, research shows that environmental and socioeconomic factors disproportionately place at greater risk members of socially subordinated racial and ethnic groups. For example, African Americans' and Hispanics' concentration in polluted and dangerous neighborhoods result in feelings of depression and powerlessness that, in turn, diminish the ability to improve these neighborhoods (35, 40, 41). Systematic investigation is necessary to uncover and distinguish what social forces, including race, contribute to disparate outcomes.

RESEARCH HIGHLIGHTS: RACE AND ETHNICITY AS FACTORS IN SOCIAL INSTITUTIONS

The following examples highlight significant research findings that illustrate the persistent role of race in primary social institutions in the United States, including the job market, neighborhoods, and the health care system. This scientific investigation would not have been possible without data on race.

JOB MARKET

Sociological research shows that race is substantially related to workplace recruitment, hiring, firing, and promotions. Ostensibly neutral practices can advantage some racial groups and adversely affect others. For example, the majority of workers obtain their jobs through informal networks rather than through open recruitment and hiring practices. Business-as-usual recruitment and hiring practices include recruiting at predominantly White schools, advertising only in suburban newspapers, and employing relatives and friends of current workers. Young, White job seekers benefit from family connections, studies show. In contrast, a recent study revealed that word-of-mouth recruitment through family and friendship networks limited job opportunities for African Americans in the construction trades. Government downsizing provides another example of a "race neutral" practice with

racially disparate consequences: Research shows that because African Americans have successfully established employment niches in the civil service, government workforce reductions displace disproportionate numbers of African American—and increasingly, Hispanic—employees. These and other social processes, such as conscious and unconscious prejudices of those with power in the workplace, affecting the labor market largely explain the persistent two-to-one ratio of Black to White unemployment (4, 5, 9, 15, 32, 39, 42, 43).

NEIGHBORHOOD SEGREGATION

For all of its racial diversity, the highly segregated residential racial composition is a defining characteristic of American cities and suburbs. Whites and African Americans tend to live in substantially homogenous communities, as do many Asians and Hispanics. The segregation rates of Blacks have declined slightly, while the rates of Asians and Hispanics have increased. Sociological research shows that the "hyper-segregation" between Blacks and Whites, for example, is a consequence of both public and private policies, as well as individual attitudes and group practices.

Sociological research has been key to understanding the interaction between these policies, attitudes, and practices. For example, according to attitude surveys, by the 1990s, a majority of Whites were willing to live next door to African Americans, but their comfort level fell as the proportion of African Americans in the neighborhood increased. Real estate and mortgage-industry practices also contribute to neighborhood segregation, as well as racially disparate homeownership rates (which, in turn, contribute to the enormous wealth gap between racial groups). Despite fair housing laws, audit studies show, industry practices continue to steer African

American homebuyers away from White neighborhoods, deny African Americans information about available loans, and offer inferior property insurance.

Segregation profoundly affects quality of life. African American neighborhoods (even relatively affluent ones) are less likely than White neighborhoods to have high quality services, schools, transportation, medical care, a mix of retail establishments, and other amenities. Low capital investment, relative lack of political influence, and limited social networks contribute to these disparities (1, 6, 8, 9, 17, 21, 22, 25, 30, 35, 36, 37, 42, 44).

HEALTH

Research clearly documents significant, persistent differences in life expectancy, mortality, incidence of disease, and causes of death between racial groups. For example, African Americans have higher death rates than Whites for eight of the ten leading causes of death. While Asian-Pacific Islander babies have the lowest mortality rates of all broad racial categories, infant mortality for Native Hawaiians is nearly three times higher than for Japanese Americans. Genetics accounts for some health differences, but social and economic factors, uneven treatment, public health policy, and health and coping behaviors play a large role in these unequal health outcomes.

Socio-economic circumstances are the strongest predictors of both life span and freedom from disease and disability. Unequal life expectancy and mortality reflect racial disparities in income and incidence of poverty, education and, to some degree, marital status. Many studies have found that these characteristics and related environmental factors such as over-crowded housing, inaccessibility of medical care, poor sanitation, and pollution adversely impact life expectancy and both overall and cause-specific mortality for groups that have disproportionately high death rates.

Race differences in health insurance coverage largely reflect differences in key socio-economic characteristics. Hispanics are least likely to be employed in jobs that provide health insurance and relatively fewer Asian Americans are insured because they are more likely to be in small low-profit businesses that make it hard to pay for health insurance. Access to affordable medical care also affects health outcomes. Sociological research shows that highly segregated African American neighborhoods are less likely to have health care facilities such as hospitals and clinics, and have the highest ratio of patients to physicians. In addition, public policies such as privatization of medicine and lower Medicaid and Medicare funding have had unintended racial consequences; studies show a further reduction of medical services in African American neighborhoods as a result of these actions.

Even when health care services are available, members of different racial groups often do not receive comparable treatment. For example, African Americans are less likely to receive the most commonly performed diagnostic procedures, such as cardiovascular and orthopedic procedures. Institutional discrimination, including racial stereotyping by medical professionals, and systemic barriers, such as language difficulties for newer immigrants (the majority of whom are from Asia and Latin America), partly explain differential treatment patterns, stalling health improvements for some racial groups.

All of these factors interact to produce poorer health outcomes, indicating that racial stratification remains an important explanation for health disparities (3, 12, 16, 18, 21, 27, 33, 34, 40, 41).

SUMMARY: THE IMPORTANCE OF SOCIOLOGICAL RESEARCH ON RACE

A central focus of sociological research is systematic attention to the causes and consequences of social inequalities. As long as Americans routinely sort each other into racial categories and act on the basis of those attributions, research on the role of race and race relations in the United States falls squarely within this scientific agenda. Racial profiling in law enforcement activities, "redlining" of predominantly minority neighborhoods in the mortgage and insurance industries, differential medical treatment, and tracking in schools, exemplify social practices that should be studied. Studying race as a social phenomenon makes for better science and more informed policy debate. As the United States becomes more diverse, the need for public agencies to continue to collect data on racial categories will become even more important. Sociologists are well qualified to study the impact of "race" —and all the ramifications of racial categorization—on people's lives and social institutions. The continuation of the collection and scholarly analysis of data serves both science and the public interest. For all of these reasons, the American Sociological Association supports collecting data and doing research on race.

REFERENCES

1. Alba, Richard D., John R. Logan, and Brian J. Stults. 2000. "The Changing Neighborhood Contexts of the Immigrant Metropolis." *Social Forces* 79:587–621.

2. Bloom, Jack M. 1987. *Class, Race and the Civil Rights Movement.* Bloomington, IN: Indiana University Press.

3. Bobo, Lawrence D. 2001. "Racial Attitudes and Relations at the Close of the Twentieth Century," Pp. 264–201, in *America Becoming: Racial Trends and Their Consequences,* vol. 2, edited by Neil J. Smelser, William J. Wilson, and Faith Mitchell. Washington, DC: National Research Council.

4. Bobo, Lawrence D., Devon Johnson, and Susan Suh. 2002. "Racial Attitudes and Power in the Workplace: Do the Haves Differ from the Have-Nots?" Pp. 491–522, in *Prismatic Metropolis: Inequality in Los Angeles,* edited by Lawrence D. Bobo, Melvin J. Oliver, James H. Johnson, Jr., and Abel Valenzuela Jr. New York, NY: Russell Sage Foundation.

5. DiTomaso, Nancy. 2000. "Why Anti-Discrimination Policies Are Not Enough: The Legacies and Consequences of Affirmative Inclusion—For Whites." Presented at the 95th annual meeting of the American Sociological Association, August 16, Anaheim, CA.

6. Drier, Peter, John Mollenkopf, and Todd Swanstrom. 2001. *Place Matters: Metropolitics in the 21st Century.* Lawrence, KS: University of Kansas Press.

7. Edmonston, Barry, Sharon M. Lee, and Jeffrey Passel. (in press). "Recent Trends in Intermarriage and Immigration, and Their Effects on the Future Racial Composition of the U.S. Population," in *The New Race Question,* edited by Joel Perlmann and Mary C. Waters. New York, NY: Russell Sage Foundation.

8. Farley, Reynolds. 1996. *The New American Reality: Who We Are, How We Got Here, Where We Are Going?* New York, NY: Russell Sage Foundation.

9. Farley, Reynolds, Sheldon, Danzinger, and Harry Holzer. 2001. *Detroit Divided.* New York, NY: Russell Sage Foundation.

10. Galap, Jean. 1991. "Phenotypes et Discrimination des Noirs en France: Question de Methode." *Intercultures* 14 (Juillet): 21–35.

11. Hallinan, Maureen T. 2001. "Sociological Perspectives on Black-White Inequalities in American Schooling." *Sociology of Education* (Extra Issue 2001): 50–70.

12. Hayward, Mark D, Eileen M. Crimmins, Toni P. Miles, and Yu Yang. 2000. "Socioeconomic Status and the Racial Gap in Chronic Health Conditions." *American Sociological Review* 65: 910–930.

13. Heubert, Jay P., and Robert M. Hauser, eds. 1999. *High Stakes: Testing for Tracking, Promotion, and Graduation.* Washington, DC: National Research Council.

14. Jones, Nicholas A., and Amy Symens Smith. 2001. *The Two or More Races Population 2000: Census 2000 Brief.* U.S. Bureau of the Census (November). Retrieved June 19, 2002, (http: www.census.gov/population/www/cen2000/briefs.html.)

15. Kirshenman, Joleen, and Kathryn M. Neckerman. 1992. "We'd Love to Hire Them, But....The Meaning of Race for Employers," Pp. 203–234, in *The Urban Underclass,* edited by C. Jencks and P. Peterson. Washington, DC: The Brookings Institution.

16. Klinenberg, Eric. 2002. *Heat Wave: A Social Autopsy of Disaster in Chicago.* Chicago, IL: University of Chicago Press.

17. LaVeist, Thomas. 1992. "The Political Empowerment and Health Status of African Americans: Mapping a New Territory." American *Journal of Sociology* 97: 1080–1095.

18. LaViest, Thomas A., C. Diala, and N.C. Jarrett. 2000. "Social Status and Perceived Discrimination: Who Experiences Discrimination in the Health Care System and Why?," Pp. 194–208, in *Minority Health in America,* edited by Carol J.R. Hogue, Martha A. Hargraves, and Karen Scott-Collins. Baltimore, MD: Johns Hopkins University Press.

19. Lee, Sharon M. 1993. "Racial Classifications in the U.S. Census: 1890–1990." *Ethnic and Racial Studies* 16: 75–94.

20. Lucas, Samuel Roundfield. 1999. *Tracking Inequality: Stratification and Mobility in American High Schools.* New York, NY: Teachers College Press.

21. Massey, Douglas S. 2001. "Residential Segregation and Neighborhood Conditions in U.S. Metropolitan Areas, " Pp. 391–434, in *America Becoming: Racial Trends and Their Consequences,* vol. 1, edited by Neil J. Smelser, William J. Wilson, and Faith Mitchell. Washington, DC: National Research Council.

22. Massey, Douglas S., and Nancy Denton. 1993. *American Apartheid: Segregation and the Making of the Underclass.* Cambridge, MA: Harvard University Press.

23. Mikelson, Roslyn A. 2002. "What Constitutes Racial Discrimination in Education? A Social Science Perspective." Prepared for workshop on Measuring Racial Disparities and Discrimination in Elementary and Secondary Education, National Research Council Committee on the National Statistics Center for Education, July 2002. For a grant from the Ford Foundation and National Science Foundation.

24. Morris, Aldon D. 1986. The Origins of the Civil Rights Movement: Black Communities Organizing for Change. New York, NY: The Free Press.

25. Oliver Melvin L., and Thomas J. Shapiro. 1995. *Black Wealth? White Wealth?: A New Perspective on Racial Inequality.* New York, NY: Routledge.

26. Omi, Michael. 2001. "The Changing Meaning of Race." Pp 243–263, in *America Becoming: Racial Trends and Their Consequences,* edited by Neil J. Smelser, William J. Wilson, and Faith Mitchell. Washington, DC: National Academy Press.

27. Quadagno, Jill. 2000. "Promoting Civil Rights through the Welfare State: How Medicare Integrated Southern Hospitals." *Social Problems* 47: 68–89.

28. Qian, Zhenchao. 1997. "Breaking the Racial Barriers: Variations in Interracial Marriage Between 1980 and 1990." *Demography* 34: 263–276.

29. Quillian, Lincoln. 1995. Prejudice as a Response to Perceived Group Threat: Population Composition and Anti-Immigrant and Racial Prejudice in Europe. *American Sociological Review* 60: 586–611.

30. Rankin, Bruce H., and James M. Quane. 2000. "Neighborhood Poverty and Social Isolation of Inner-City African American Families." *Social Forces* 79: 139–164.

31. Raveau, F., B. Kilborne, L. Frere, J. M. Lorin, and G. Trempe. 1976. "Perception Sociale de la Couleur et Discrimination." *Cahiers d' Anthropologie* 4: 23–42.

32. Reskin, Barbara F. 1998. The *Realities of Affirmative Action in Employment.* Washington, DC: The American Sociological Association.

33. Rogers, Richard, Robert Hummer, Charles B. Nam, Kimberly Peters. 1996. "Demographic, Socioeconomic, and Behavioral Factors Affecting Ethnic Mortality by Cause." *Social Forces* 74: 1419–1438.

34. Ross, Catherine E. and John Mirowsky. 2001. "Neighborhood Disadvantage, Disorder, and Health." *Journal of Health and Social Behavior* 42: 258–276.

35. Sampson, Robert J., Gregory D. Squires, and Min Zhou. 2001. *How Neighborhoods Matter: The Value of Investing at the Local Level. Washington,* DC: The American Sociological Association.

36. Schuman, Howard, Charlotte Steeh, Lawrence Bobo, and Maria Kryson. 1997. *Racial Attitudes in America.* 2 ed. Cambridge MA: Harvard University Press.

37. Squires, Gregory D., and Sally O'Connor. 2001. *Color and Money: Politics and Prospects for Community Reinvestment in Urban America.* Albany, NY: SUNY Press.

38. Telles, Edward. 2002. "Racial Ambiguity among the Brazilian Population." *Ethnic and Racial Studies* 25: 415–441.

39. Waldinger, Roger. 1996. *Still the Promised City? African-Americans and New Immigrants in Postindustrial New York.* Cambridge, MA: Harvard University Press.

40. Williams, David R. 2001. "Racial Variations in Adult Health Status: Patterns, Paradoxes, and Prospects," Pp. 371–410 2 in *America Becoming: Racial Trends and Their Consequences,* vol. 2, edited by Neil J. Smelser, William J. Wilson, and Faith Mitchell. Washington, DC: National Research Council.

41. Williams, David R. and Chiquita Collins. (in press). "Racial Residential Segregation: A Fundamental Cause of Racial Disparities in Health." *Public Health Reports.*

42. Wilson, William J. 1996. *When Work Disappears: The World of the New Urban Poor.* New York, NY: Alfred A. Knopf, Inc.

43. Woo, Deborah. 2000. *Glass Ceilings and Asian Americans: The New Face of Workplace Barriers.* Walnut Creek, CA: AltaMira Press.

44. Yinger, John. 1995. *Closed Doors, Opportunities Lost.* New York, NY: Russell Sage Foundation.

NOTES

1. The federal government defines race categories for statistical policy purposes, program administrative reporting, and civil rights compliance, and sets forth minimum categories for the collection and reporting of data on race. The current standards, adopted in October 1997, include five race categories: American Indian or Alaska Native; Asian; Black or African American; Native Hawaiian or Other Pacific Islander; and White. Respondents to federal data collection activities must be offered the option of selecting one or more racial designations. Hispanics or Latinos, whom current standards define as an ethnic group, can be of any race. However, before the government promulgated standard race categories in 1977, some U.S. censuses designated Hispanic groups as race categories (e.g., the 1930 census listed Mexicans as a separate race).

Eminem:
The New White Negro

Carl Hancock-Rux

*"From the Negro we take only the magical-liturgical bits, and
only the antithesis makes them interesting to us."*
—Hugo Ball

*"There is a zone of non-being,
An extraordinary sterile and arid region,
An utterly naked declivity
Where an authentic upheaval can be born.
In most cases the Black man lacks the advantage
Of being able to accomplish this descent
Into a real hell."*
—Frantz Fanon, from "Black Skin, White Masks"

REVENGE OF PENTHEUS

Pentheus, the protagonist of Euripides' *The Bacchae,* was a young moralist and anarchical warrior who sought to abolish the worship of Dionysus (god of tradition, or perhaps better said, god of the re-cyclical, who causes the loss of individual identity in the uncontrollable, chaotic eruption of ritualistic possession). When Pentheus sets out to infiltrate the world of the Bacchae and explore the mysteries of savage lore, his intention is to save the possessed women of Thebes (from themselves), who engage in hedonistic practices somewhere high in the mountains. Dionysus derails the young warrior's lofty mission by titillating his sexual curiosity (inviting him to take a quick glimpse of the drunken women as they revel in their lesbian orgy). In order to witness firsthand the necromancy of the inhumane, Pentheus must disguise himself as *one of* the inhumane. Ultimately the young moralist's disguise mirrors the appearance of Dionysus, the very god he seeks to subjugate. The transformed soldier, now possessed by the spirit of his nemesis, is set on the highest branch of a fir tree, elevated above all and visible to none—or so he is led to believe.

Pentheus' disguise is as transparent as his voyeuristic fetish, and it is because of this very visible elevated space he inhabits that he is brutally dismembered by the gang of possessed women on the mountain (led by his own mother), who see him for what he is.

Historically, academics have neatly interpreted the characters of *The Bacchae* as belonging to themes of good versus evil, rational versus reason, nobility versus paganism. In the casual study of classical realism, Pentheus is noble in his efforts to eradicate paganism, and Dionysus is an all-powerful demonic and *immoral* force. But in a more careful study (or at least, an alternate one), we may learn that Dionysus is a traditional Olympian god, neither good nor bad. His powers are *amoral;* they are powers informed only by the powers that control human existence. Real life—death, sex, grief, joy, etc.—in its entire splendor. Dionysus and his worshipers cannot be controlled or converted. Their humanity *has been perceived as* inhumane, and in defense of their right to preserve an identity and a culture for themselves, an extreme cruelty befitting of inhumanity is enacted. The mother's murder of her son is a necessary *evil;* we accept the death of Pentheus as the inevitable defeat of his judgmental and moral idealism, but because this act of brutality is performed by the mother of its victim, we also question the value of human existence above the existence of humanity (couldn't she have just given ham a slap on the hand and a good talking—to and said, "Baby, some people live differently than others, but ain't nobody better than the rest…"?). Perhaps the moral of the story is: The identity of the individual is most often sacrificed for the identity of the collective, so we must now all live and speak in broad familiar terms and forsake our sons and daughters for the ultimate good of humanity as we see it. The evolution of human existence is propelled by a constant narcissism; a struggle to negotiate one's perception of self and one's percep-

tion of the other, and some of the most (historically) flawed (though pervasive) acts of negotiating a collective identity are politicized oppression and cultural mimicry of the other—both of which seek agreement. Inevitably, collective agreement regarding identity produces a common design for humanity, or a morality relative to the perceptions of a particular group. Hierarchical notions of humanity are formed, and, eventually, once the tracks are laid, people will have to pitch their tents on either side. Conflict. War. Somebody (or bodies) in opposition to the populace will have to be dismembered so that new orders of identity can be formed.

Fast-forward a few thousand years to a more contemporary but parallel heroic-antiheroic protagonist—Eminem, the platinum-domed, Caesar-hair-cut, pop-prince bad-boy superstar of late-twentieth/early-twenty-first-century postmodern hip-hop culture. Like Pentheus, Eminem may also be seen as a rebellious and beardless icon with disdain for the majority, and like Pentheus, he dresses himself in the garments of the outcasts, has learned their language, their songs and rituals. But unlike Pentheus, Eminem is no moralist martyr with a secret desire to objectify. The real Slim Shady does not make the mistake of re-creating the Theban soldier's vain attempt to destroy the god of mass appeal. He accepts the unholy ghost as his personal savior, and with a slight flip of the Greek tragedy script (with hip-hop flare), introduces to us his first sacrifice—his own mother, whom he publicly debases and strips of all garments of integrity, drags nude into the spotlight, and ritualistically murders hit single after hit single. Though savagery is expected to call for misogyny of magnanimous proportions, Eminem's humiliation of the maternal figure is not just limited to his *own* mother, but extends itself to she who is also the mother of his own child (or in ghetto fabulous vernacular, his *baby mama*). In one of his first award-winning acts of hit-single hedonism, the real Slim Shady murders his baby mama right in front of his baby (for our entertainment pleasure)—and later, in his sophomore phase, morphs into a fan of himself who is inspired to do the same. A continuum, thereby raising the inhumane status of outcast culture to new bacchanalian heights.

The postmodern pop-culture icon of the outlaw is complete and to be carried into the new millennium; Eminem does not *seek* to know pagan lore—he was *born* into it, has always spoken the language of it, has always danced to the music of it, has always dressed himself in the latest pagan wear, has never used this language, this music, or this apparel to *disguise* his true identity or to disguise his race, and he has never tried to dissociate himself from the source of his performance, the black male outlaw or outcast of hip-hop fame. Rappers Big Boi and Dre may go by the moniker Outkast, but Eminem proves that a *real* outcast has got to do more than make *Miss Jackson's* daughter cry—you got to fuck the bitch, kill the bitch, dump the bitch's dead body in the river, and not apologize for any of it.

Eminem's politically incorrect vaudeville routine (an oxymoron) is not to be attempted by everyone. Even his protégés, D-12, failed miserably as horror rappers on their debut album *Devil's Night* (if poor record sales and bad reviews are any indication). With boasts of slapping around handicapped women, gorging pills, and sodomizing their grandmothers, the effect is less tongue-in-cheek than tongue-in-toilet. And, when old-school mack daddy of hip-hop cool, Slick Rick, made a cameo appearance on the recently released Morcheeba album, *Charango,* derivatively flowing à la Eminem style ("Women Lose Weight") about murdering his overweight wife in order to hook up with his sexy blond secretary, MTV did not come-a-calling. The result is derivative at best. Incidentally, not long after the Morcheeba album release, Slick Rick found himself arrested by the INS and await-

ing deportation from this country (because somebody *just* found out that he has been an illegal resident for over thirty years). Not to suggest that his penal consequences are the direct result of imitating Eminem, but so far, only Eminem gets away with *being* Eminem, perhaps because he uses his visors and disguises to disguise his split personality as undisguised—raising the questions, who is the real outcast, who is the real Slim Shady, what has he inherited from culture to achieve his bad-boy, outcast minstrel, rebel superstar status, and *exactly* what identity crisis is being performed?

FANON HAD A (SEMANTIC) DREAM

Frantz Fanon tells us that the oppressed must identify an oppressive archetype in order to overcome historical oppression. But before the oppressed can achieve acts of true upheaval, they must first realize that they have yet to achieve "non-being" status. The oppressed may have attempted prior acts of resistance, but have never actually "descended into a real hell" that will scorch into the very nature of seeing an *effective* upheaval that brings the non-being into being. For now, the oppressed continue to live in the dream of identity, the dream that (in reality) the oppressed are, in fact, Negro, Colored, Black, Minority, Afro or African American, Hispanic, Oriental, Dykes, Queers, Bitches, Hos, Niggaz. All accepted as real identities. The acceptance of these identities further compels a performance of these identities, whether compliant or rebellious.

The oppressed identity performance relies upon a collective agreement informed by a historical narrative that either supports the validity of, or opposes the construct of, these identities. Before a revisionist identity can be forged, there was an inheritance and an acceptance of a construct—thus, even when the oppressed think they are revising their identities, updating the language of their identities, or endeavoring to better the circumstances of their identities, they are not—not completely and not actually—because no language in the American polyglot has ever been subscribed to by the collective that points to the very nature of human identity beyond elementary categorizations, and no accurate language regarding race-identity exists in our collective agreement. We are comfortable with vague concepts of identity, and the ghettos and empires these concepts create.

What the oppressed figure in America has been working with as an identity is actually an archetypal construct born out of a dream (as in aspirations and imaginings) belonging to an oppressive figure who is not only the architect of the dream that oppresses us, but is also the Dionysian-like landlord of our realities—both good and bad—neither real nor unreal, and completely exempt from being vanquished from our realities. We inhabit an oppressive dream, and until that descent into Fanon's "real hell," the oppressed will continue to pay a high price to rent substandard space in the dream that we call *race* in America.

EMINEM, THE OTHER WHITE MEAT

"...If all the Niggers
Started calling each other Nigger,
Not only among themselves...but among Ofays...
Nigger wouldn't mean anymore than 'Good night,'
'God bless you,' or 'I promise to tell the whole truth
And nothing but the whole truth so help me God'...
When that beautiful day comes,
You'll never see another Nigger kid
Come home from school crying
Because some Ofay motherfucker called him
Nigger."

 —Lenny Bruce

Eminem, a.k.a. Marshall Mathers, was born in St. Joseph, Missouri (near Kansas City),

spending the better part of his impoverished childhood in Detroit, Michigan—which, by the way, is about 90 percent *ethnic minority* and has one of the highest concentrations of African Americans in the nation, at 83 percent, while non-Latino whites comprise only 12 percent of the city's population. Detroit's recent dip below one million is largely attributed to continuing *white flight,* and 10 percent of the state's population has lived in poverty for more than twenty years (a family of three with an income of a little more than $9,300 earns too much to qualify for welfare in Michigan—but is about $4,000 below the federal poverty guideline), according to the American Community Survey released by the U.S. Census Bureau. Translation: Eminem may have been *born* white but he was socialized as *black,* in the proverbial hood—and the music of the proverbial hood in America for the last twenty-five years has been hip-hop music. The same inner-city struggles and impoverished circumstances that brought us blues, jazz, rhythm and blues, doo-wop and soul, brought us hip-hop music—it began as a form of identity-boosting vocal scatting over pulsating beats and progressed to become a means of expressing the social realities of African-American urbanity. By the time it became a major moneymaker in the music industry, the genre of hip-hop transformed into a bodacious representation of gangsta life and gangsta obsessions replete with murder, money, sex, alcohol and drug consumption—and, when this got tired, narrowed itself down and preoccupied itself with the glam of capital gain.

The legend of Eminem, a.k.a. Slim Shady, a.k.a. Marshall Mathers (and his psychotic nasal slapstick trips of alienation) begins with his Detroit exposure to rap, performing it at the age of fourteen and later earning notoriety as a member of the Motor City duo Soul Intent. The legend is that he dropped out of high school, worked minimum-wage jobs, practiced beat boxing and freestyling his lyrics on home recordings, and worshipped rap groups like NWA—he admits he "wanted to be Dr. Dre and Ice Cube," wore big sunglasses while "lip-syncking to their records in the mirror." He also honed his style in the company of five black Detroit MC's (D12). Together, the racially integrated posse decided that each of them would invent an alter ego, thus the six MC's were to be thought of as twelve MC's—dubbing themselves, the Dirty Dozen. When Eminem emerged as a solo artist in 1996 with the independent release *Infinite,* he was accused of trying to sound "too much like Nas," so he perfected a nasal white-boy, horror-rap cadence, following *Infinite* with *The Slim Shady LP,* which led the hip-hop underground to dub him hip-hop's "great white hope."

The legend of his discovery varies. Allegedly, Dr. Dre discovered Eminem's demo tape on the floor of Interscope label chief Jimmy Iovine's garage. Another story goes that Dre first heard Eminem on the radio and said, "Find that kid whoever he is! I'm gonna make him a star!" or something like that. Either way, not until Eminem took second place (who won first?) in the freestyle category at 1997's Rap Olympics MC Battle in Los Angeles did Dre agree to sign him, producing the bestselling triple-platinum *Slim Shady LP* in early 1999. With controversial yet undeniable talent (the right mix for stardom of any kind), Eminem became the white-boy cartoon god of surreal white-trash humor and graphic violence, a stratum of Roseanne Barr-meets-Quentin Tarrentino-meets-Mickey Mouse Club-cum Snoop Dogg and beatnik Dobie Gillis. The *Marshall Mathers LP* followed and sold close to two million copies in its first week of release, making it one of the fastest-selling rap albums of all time, and his latest album, *The Eminem Show,* was the first album since 'N Sync's *Celebrity* and the September 11 terrorist attacks to sell over one million copies in its debut week. To top it all off, Eminem's roman

à clef feature film debut, *8 Mile,* is described as a story about "the boundaries that define our lives and a young man's struggle to find the strength and courage to transcend them." In his great struggle to transcend boundaries, the surrealist rap icon has also managed two weapons charges, an assault charge, a lawsuit from his mother for humiliating her in his lyrics, and his baby mama's attempted suicide—all to keep it real, as they say

But Eminem does not offer us the real, he offers the *surreal*—several alter egos further immersing our bacchanalian notions of race-inclusive hip-hop lore. We all want to be Bacchus or Dionysus. Especially black people, especially Niggaz, who have invented the alter ego of a New Savage God—a gun-toting nationalist radical with supreme sexual prowess and unsurpassable talent to counter Bill Cosby's 1980s middle-class Negrodum. We, who are members of the so-called ethnic minority and belong to a hip-hop generation, have inherited an imposition and elaborated on it until it has become an opportunity, borrowing our new black character from a relevant history of slavery, reconstruction, ghetto realism, black civil rights, arts and radical movements, and mythic Blaxploitation heroes like Shaft and Foxy Brown. But lest we get high-minded about it all, the badass thug and gangsta bitch are not purely the inventions of inner-city urban imagination. They are also products of Hollywood's imaginary American heroes: second-generation immigrants turned Depression-era gangster moguls, as portrayed by Edward G. Robinson, James Cagney, Humphrey Bogart; John Wayne's cocky cowboy; Sean Connery's hyper-heterosexual sci-fi upper-class guy, "James Bond." Hip-hop inventors have grown up with these archetypes on their television screens, and incorporated them into a contemporary gothic myth set in the housing projects they know America to be. In order for this merger of white and black icons to evolve, there had to be in place a basic understanding of race among a contemporary generation. The new power brokers of culture had to inherit an inherited concept of race and form vaguely similar ways of seeing the construct of race. If it appears that the history of race in America means less to the new generation of pop-music icons and their fans—socially, politically, and psychologically—than the performance of class and outlaw status, it is because a race-inclusive product for the American cultural marketplace demands short-term memory.

What has emerged from an old system of cultural supremacy and inferiority is a new superpower contingent upon our informed (and uninformed) race perception. The final incarnations of the black male figure in a century that began with sharecroppers and first-generation free peoples trying to avoid the hanging tree are their gun-toting, dick-slinging capitalist descendants. The black male outlaw identity is a commodifiable character open to all who would like to perform it. In order for the oppressed figure's dream of attaining ostentatious wealth and fame while defying conventional structures of morality to come into fruition, the dream *had to* be race-inclusive, race-accessible, and dangerous enough to pose an idealistic threat to a conservative society— translation: like jazz, white people had to like it, buy it, invest in it, and benefit from it, and above all, identify with it too. And the seduction had to appeal to a fascination with and fear of a complex figure they'd been taught to disdain. Not unlike Pentheus's objectifying curiosity, white culture watched the evolution of the hip-hop character from afar before the hip-hop character knew they were watching at all. Thus, hip-hop culture has evolved into another classic ready-to-wear American original, like rock 'n' roll—except this time, the black hip-hop artist participates in the profit and control of the industry (to some extent) more so than ever before. But it is still an outsider culture, perpetuating its own outsider mythology, and if there are non-black, eco-

nomically privileged teenagers who wear their oversized jeans pulled down around their knees and sleep beneath posters of self-proclaimed rapists, gang members, and murderers with record deals, it is because every generation of youth culture since Socrates has identified with outsider/outcast/radicalism, and typically pursued some kind of participation in it. Because radicalism, whether political or not, is a multicultural and universal sentiment.

Some may contend that white artists who pioneer their way into so-called black music forms take the privilege of being allowed to do so seriously and pursue lofty goals of destroying race barriers, thereby bridging gaps of new race perception in America. But others may contend that race *inclusivity* (*sic*) diminishes the organic intention of race music (*sic*) until it simplifies into yet another popular entertainment form in the marketplace, where its inventor will compete for a right to exist (i.e., if Eric Clapton, Bonnie Raitt, or Lyle Lovett stopped playing the blues, what would it mean to B. B. King or Keb' Mo's pop chart eligibility?).

Race performance in America—however guilty we all are of it (and we *all* are guilty of it)—has suffered an uneven exchange. There are allowances made for some to a greater degree than others. From jazz to rock 'n' roll, white representation in black music forms is completely acceptable and rarely questioned (even if contemporary black representation in rock, alternative rock, or any kind of rock warrants front page *New York Times* explanations), but some have questioned whether or not white representation in black music ultimately diminishes the sentiment of black music, or distracts a critical audience from narrowly perceiving black music innovations *as* black music. Whom does music or race belong to? Whether or not race is to stake its claim in music, race performance prevails as much now as it did in the good ol' Al Jolson days. One can easily see a careful study in the color-line cross-over iconography of artists like Vanilla

Ice, the first popular hip-hop "wigger" to top the charts, who cooked his character with the main ingredients of authentic angry black male aggression, by promising dope hits and throats slit (from "*Livin'*"), further validating himself with essential sociopolitical blues lamentations of existential thug life, screaming his hatred at society (from *A.D.D.*), and offering us some insight to the familial dysfunction of ghetto life that produced his incredulity, blaming an abusive father and excusing his mother from all responsibility for his compulsive and unexplainable brain-blasting (from *Scars*).

But Vanilla Ice's middle-class white-childhood reality emerged and ruined the authenticity of his performance—though his hip-hop icon still left an indelible mark on hip-hop culture. As with all great rock stars or rock-star hopefuls, it is the image of these icons and their proclamations of themselves that reach beyond them, creating a mass of followers who are inspired by their belief in the performance, not the person. In this way, those few artists fortunate enough to achieve superstar status become ancient, distant arche-types that appeal to our psychic dispositions, like Jesus or Gatsby—the icon we believe in helps us validate what we believe about ourselves and the world as we see it, whether it's real or not.

THE GOOD, THE BAD, AND THE NIGGA

"It's not right to start penalizing good people....We need a humane monitoring system to search out the good and bad."

—Slick Rick, while awaiting deportation in a Florida detention facility

Both Eminem and Vanilla Ice take their cues from a savage model, and it is this savage model that has informed everyone from the Surrealists to the Bohemians. If there is an eternal plan, it is a primitive one with no bearing on virtue. Their performances are rooted in

a supposed realism. Realism places God in heaven, makes distinct social classes where moral law distinguishes between good and evil—an orderly world with gradual changes: wars, revolutions, inventions, etc. One can belong to the outcasts of this world and still be a realist. It's all in the style of your performance. Style becomes the only authentic instrument of classic realism, and an important elemental style of hip-hop realism involves daily mortal danger. However, within one's own existence, one is influenced not only by the current circumstances of life but by the style of life where we are experiencing it. Style both replicates reality and takes us away from our reality. Style also heightens and produces a counterbalance to the realism of life (i.e., your hip-hop icon du jour may live with a sense of daily mortal danger—like you do—but unlike you, he drives a Mercedes jeep, wears diamonds and furs, and maintains a harem of scantily clad women with bodies endowed according to his fickle fetish fantasies).

Those of us who choose to deny that we now live in a society psychically impacted by hip-hop realism may still embrace the changing styles of hip-hop realism because it removes us from our actual reality (as all good forms of entertainment should). If the edict of early hip-hop lore shifted its weight from the innocence of Sugarhill Gang's party babble to Public Enemy's urban radicalism and political consciousness, it seemed to be a call to arms—an insistence that the oppressed figure recognize something about his status-elevation potential. If hip-hop again shifted its weight from Suge Knight's heyday of East Coast/West Coast rivalry and gangbanging to Puffy's epoch of Versace gear, Cristal champagne, and Harry Winston diamond-encrusted platinum jewelry, it read as an attempt to break from the tradition that celebrated the kind of violence that produced the sudden and actual deaths of Biggie Smalls and Tupac Shakur—an attempt to make a gradual transference from ghetto realism toward escaping conventions of death. An oppressed capitalist's bargaining with life.

The antisymbolic nature of the savage archetype from which Eminem creates his character is different from Vanilla Ice's invention. Vanilla's performance was classic in nature—a form of modern realism where human truth was more important than the poetry of words. Eminem's eminence rarely attempts to address serious social or political ills, nor is it obsessed with hypercapitalism. Eminem does not attempt to perform the authentic Nigga as much as he performs a New White Nigga. He maintains his whiteness with quirky vocal Jerry Lewis-like phrasing and a bright Greek-god bleached-blond buzz cut; and the classic hip-hop realism he was initially influenced by when he first studied the style of Naughty by Nature and Nas has been replaced by his own brand of contemporary Surrealism that abstracts and exaggerates hip-hop lore more so than any of his authentic heroes or contemporaries dare try.

Eminem's lyrics speak to the wayward descendants of Fanon's Negroes: Niggaz. Niggaz hear him and Niggaz understand him; still, he comes as a representative of what Niggaz have produced in their dreams—someone who is not them but worships them and belongs to them and, by virtue of socialization, is one of them. He confounds Niggaz and white people alike in the multicultural schoolyard with his mastering of Nigga language and assumption of Nigga style. His presentation is not overtly authentic, but infused with authenticity because he has lived in Nigga neighborhoods and listened to Nigga music and learned Nigga culture—and the integrity of his performance does not overtly attempt mimicry, like those culture bandits who came before him, after him, or share pop-chart status with him. He frowns at white people like Moby, Christina Aguilera, Fred Durst, and Everlast, who poorly adapt yet successfully co-opt the aesthetics,

ideologies, and style of Niggaz. He comes already revered by a relevant society of new and old royalty—Dr. Dre who discovered him, Busta Rymes who once dubbed him "the baddest rapper out here," Madonna and Elton John who have knighted him their heir apparent. But before we give him the NAACP Image Award, it should remain clear that Eminem's race performance is not (solely) intended to impress the oppressed. He's already done that and moved on.

Eminem takes the mythology of the oppressed—identifying himself as impervious, armed and dangerous, sexually superior, economically privileged, radical—and turns this dream on its head. Makes it a macabre comedy of internal warfare. We must laugh at our anger and still be angry, he says. We must be offensive and still be funny, he says. Our enemy is not race…our enemy is everybody and anybody who is not "us," and "us" is defined as outsiders who have grown up disenfranchised with strange, irreverent dreams—the problem with "us" Niggaz is we don't take our irreverence far enough, lyrically speaking. We talk about killing each other and celebrate our daily drug and alcohol consumption, but we still get up at the MTV awards and *thank and praise my Lord and Savior Jesus Christ* for small favors like best rap video. We aspire to make millions of dollars any way we can, to get rich quick and stay rich forever, but as soon as we sign our souls to a record contract, we take our advance to the nearest check-cashing place, lay away sneakers with diamond soles, slam a deposit down on any house Cher once owned, (equipped with gold-leaf toilet paper) and wait for MTV Cribs to drop by (At least Eve promises to buy herself a Warhol every year for her birthday.)

Niggaz may talk bad about bitches and they baby's mama—Eminem brutally murders his. Niggaz may have issues regarding absent fathers or dysfunctional mothers—Eminem comically exposes their dysfunctions, and hangs his mother's pussy high up on a wall for all the world to see. Niggaz may be misogynist, may boast of sexual superiority and sexual indiscretions with a multitude of women, may commonly relegate women to *just another piece of ass prime for the taking status*—but Eminem drugs the bitch, fucks the bitch, moves on to the next bitch. This horror-rapping member of the oppressed nation has won. He has proven to the oppressed that he is not one of us, but he is down for us—and he has proven to the oppressor that he is not one of them, but he is the product of their extreme idea of "us" —and, by virtue of neutralizing the nebulous medium, Eminem *becomes* us with supernatural powers beyond us. Ultimately, he *replaces* us, paying homage to an old abstract idea.

THE NEW SURREALIST MANIFESTO

The early-twentieth-century European movement of white male artists who attempted to perform a poetic, political, revolt by way of anti-cortical [sic] understanding, insisted that there was to be no distinction made between what they considered to be abstract and what they considered to be real. In "Surrealist and Existentialist Humanism," Ferdinand Alquie wrote, "To claim that reason is man's essence is already to cut man in two, and the classical tradition has never failed to do so. It has drawn a distinction between what is rational in man (which by that sole fact is considered truly human); and what is not rational (instincts and feelings) which consequently appears unworthy of man." Freud also spoke of the mortal danger incurred for man by this split, this schism between the forces of reason and deep-seated passions—which seem destined to remain unaware of each other. Surrealism wanted to save impulses and desires from repression.

Like Eminem, the Surrealists borrowed the sinister dreams of the oppressed—aspirations for economic success outside of traditional structures; achieved narcissism born to overwhelm self-loathing and inherent existentialism; illusions of grandeur used to counter inescapable depressed circumstances; dismissal of history in order to fashion a new reality in a present tense.

The Surrealist as well as the early Modernist movements fashioned themselves after their associations with the outcasts of society—in most cases, the outcasts were either of Spanish or African descent, and in all cases, the outcasts (or savages) were economically and socially disenfranchised. Gautier and Alexander Dumas traveled through Spain and wore gypsy costumes as if to make their willed identification more real, and this escape into the exotic became the trend of many pre- and post World War II European writers, artists, and autodidacts, or White Negroes.

It was Verlaine who first coined the phrase "White Negro" when describing Rimbaud, calling him "the splendidly civilized, carelessly civilizing savage," though the origin of the phrase is usually ascribed to the title of a Norman Mailer essay, in which he attempts to explain the impulse of the white man who dares to live with danger by attempting the art of the primitive.

"The White Negro," written in 1959, was Mailer's response to William Faulkner on the topic of school segregation, and the relationship between blacks and whites. He insists, "Whites resist integration and the prospect of equality" because whites secretly know "the Negro already enjoys sensual superiority.... The Negro has had his sexual supremacy and the White had his white supremacy." Mailer further identified himself as a "near-Beat adventurer" who identified with Negroes and "urban adventurers," those who "drifted out at night looking for action with a Black man's code to fit their facts." "The hipster," he said, "had absorbed the existentialist synopsis of the Negro and could be considered a White Negro" because "any Negro who wishes to live must live with danger from his first day...the Negro knew life was war....The Negro could rarely afford the sophisticated inhibitions of civilization, and so he kept for survival the art of the primitive. The Black man lived in the enormous present, he subsisted for his Saturday night kicks, relinquishing the pleasures of the mind for the more obligatory pleasures of the body, and in his music he gave voice to the character and quality of his existence, to his rage and the infinite variations of joy, lust...and despair of his orgasm..."

Mailer's pronouncement of Beat culture (a mid-century replication of radical Bohemian culture) as "the essence of hip" further emphasized that "the source of hip is the Negro, for he "has been living on the margin between totalitarianism and democracy for two centuries...the Bohemian and the juvenile delinquent came face to face with the Negro...the child was the language of hip, for its argot gave expression to abstract states of feeling." James Baldwin countered Mailer's racist and myopic views in his essay "The Black Boy Looks at the White Boy," calling Mailer's sentiments "so antique a vision of the Blacks at this late hour." But countering Baldwin, Eldridge Cleaver called Mailer's view "prophetic and penetrating in its understanding of the psychology involved in the accelerating confrontation of Black and White in America."

Fifty years before Mailer's ethnographic fantasy, Flaubert traveled to Egypt out of a desire for a "visionary alternative," for something "in contrast to the grayish tonality of the French provincial landscape"—resulting in his "labored reconstruction of the other." Baudelaire said true civilization was comprised of "...hunters, farmers, and even cannibals—all these...superior by reasons of their energy and their personal dignity to our western races." Gautier (whose best friend was a Negro from Guadalupe, Alexandre Privat d'Anglemont) when commenting on the Algerian influence on turn-of-the-century French fashion, said, "Our women already wear scarves which have served the harem slaves...hashish is taking the place of champagne...so superior is primitive life to our so-called civilization." Before Josephine Baker reared her beautiful black ass in Paris in the 1920s, European Bohemia was already fascinated with their perceptions of Negroes, and as explained by Firmin Maillard, Bohemians were "philosophers who couldn't have cared less what their philosophy was based on...[they were] brave searchers for infinity, impudent peddlers of dreams..." And Erich Muhasm admitted, "It emerged that all of us without single exception were apostates, had rejected our origins, were wayward sons." Maurice de Vlaminck was already collecting African art as early as 1904, and Picasso ennobled the command of African sculpture on his own work by stating, "I understood what the Negroes used their sculpture for...to help people avoid coming under the influence of spirits again."

In 1916, Hugo Ball, founder of the Dada movement, opened a cabaret in the red-light district of Zurich, called the Café Voltaire, where prostitutes and Africans commingled freely with starving European artists, like Jean Arp, Tristan Tzara, and Walter Serner, who became infamous for their illogical simultaneous poems—explained by them to be "elegiac, humorous, bizarre." They wore black cowls and played a variety of exotic drums, titling their performance the "Chant Nègres." Ten years later, in Paris, Surrealist artists Robert Desnos and André de la Rivière moved into studio apartments next door to the Bal Nègre, a bar frequented by Negroes who lived in hostels on the same street. Hugo Ball explained, 'We drape ourselves like medicine men in their insignia and their essences but we want to ignore the path whereby they reached these bits of cult and parade."

These "bits of cult and parade," co-opted by European Bohemians, leaked into the mass culture of modernity, much in the same way hip-hop and R&B have produced Eminem, Britney Spears, and 'N Sync. The result is not associated with race as much as it is associated with an abstraction of culture. Alfred Jarry (author of the infamous nineteenth-century French play *Ubu*) also re-created himself as an avant, but the invention was so abstract that it could not directly be linked to the Negro—Jarry lived in a room with nothing except a bed and a plaster cast of a huge penis (his ode to both poverty and the wealth of hypersexuality). He perfected a staccato speech for himself, a Negro slang of sorts, without directly impersonating the Negro. He publicly performed the fictional character he'd invented for himself by walking up and down the boulevards or attending the opera in white clown masks, cycling clothes, or dirty white suits and shirts made of paper on which he had drawn a tie—demanding outcast inclusion in a formal world. Heseltine, a writer who possessed a sweet, boyish face and closely cropped blond hair, was described by D. H. Lawrence (in *Women in Love*) as "degenerate," "corrupt," married the beautiful Puma (who eventually committed suicide—much like Em's baby mama tried to do—an ode perhaps to the tragic *grisette,* or working girl, of Paris who loved the self-indulgent Bohemian savage artist), and composed music under the nom de plume Peter Warlock. Heseltine was also known to smoke a lot of weed, and delve into the occult. Eventually, he gassed himself to death—death by suicide translated into immortality for most existentialist Bohemians, much like death by driveby once meant the same for hip-hop dons.

Fifty years or so after the European Bohemian era, the Beat generation invented itself with Jack Kerouac, Allen Ginsberg, Neal Cassidy, and William Burroughs at its forefront (LeRoi Jones is often omitted from the history of insurgent Beat culture—most likely because any true Beat poet is to be remembered as a *performer* of savagery, not an *actual* savage). When a young Allen Ginsberg admitted in an interview that while growing up he "developed a tremendous tolerance for chaos," and described the world as "absolutely real and final and ultimate and at the same time, absolutely unreal and transitory and of the nature of dreams...without contradiction," he easily validated Verlaine and Norman Mailer's theoretical view of the Negro and their psychological profile of the White Negro.

Like hip-hop culture, Beat culture emerged in an era of economic prosperity and political paranoia. If the mid-twentieth-century American White Negro emerged in a postwar era of convention, in which hip and cool Negro icons created a counterculture of style, immorality, and self-destruction, the latter twentieth-century American New White Negro patterned himself after hip-hop culture's era of rebellion, taking him on an uncharted journey prone to danger. Ronald Reagan and Rodney King were good reasons to re-create a new generation of Charlie Parkers and Billie Hollidays—undeniably gifted icons of artistic genius, personal style, and self-destruction. If the Negro hipster lived without a definable past or future, the hip-hopster never let you forget his past and elaborately decorated his present with excess in anticipation of a life without a future—which elevated him to the status of potential martyr. He (or she) emulated Robert De Niro (in *Taxi Driver*) or, the hip-hop favorite, Al Pacino (in *Scarface*)—an outlaw feared for his enormous ferocity, and survivor skills, or revered for his unsurpassable stolen wealth, and for living daily with the threat of assassination or mutiny. Beat culture produced popular icons that offered a more abstract version of the White Negro. Its superstar, Jack Kerouac, was a Dionysian figure whose impulses toward the primitive conflicted with his tendency toward culture, education, and ego.

Ultimately, Jack was not as interested in being an outlaw as he was interested in being a star—the celebrity that white status could afford him. And as Baldwin pointed out, the Beat hipster could, at the end of the day, "return to being white." The threat of daily living could never mean as much to him as it did the Negro because the hipster's was an avant-garde performance of cool. Vanilla Ice has returned to the beach, has formed a heavy-metal band, and reflects on the days when Suge Knight hung him by his ankles over a balcony railing—Ice has escaped the danger of hip-hop lore by returning to the comfort of fundamental whiteness. Eminem escapes the actual danger of hip-hop lore by maintaining fundamental whiteness in the context of comical blackness. As Sir Elton John assuaged us all, we mustn't "take him seriously"

LIVING IN THE DREAM
(TYPES & TROPES, SYMBOLS & SIGNS)

In the reality that is our daily human existence, Eminem does not exist. He never did. But he is a real product of the American dream—a character born out of our nation's collective unconscious, our inborn predilection to produce parallel images or identical psychic shapes common to all men. He is conjured from what we think of ourselves and what we think of others. He is born out of *The Jerry Springer Show, South Park,* Jack Kerouac, Carl Van Vechten—all part of a dream, and within this dream there is a dream. Singling out Eminem as an archetype of race perception and performance in America is a shallow undertaking—the composition of his character has its history within the context of the American dream, which is now a conundrum of dreams within dreams. Dreams may be difficult to interpret—because they are, after all, indistinct metaphors and allegories of fantasy—but the dream of race

and its performance in American culture is not difficult to track. It has a history, and that history comes with presupposed rules and presupposed character traits that are familiar to us all.

In the dream that is identity, there are archetypal conflicts between the free will of the human maker (his savage creative impulses—an unconscious state of being) and what is the human thinker's intellect (culture, and historical perspective—a conscious state of being). The landscape of democracy and freedom for all men is also the invention of a dream—a utopian impulse, a way of perceiving an eternal plan in the contingencies of time; a creation of the human will born out of fiction where there is no transcendental dimension or registration of the infinite "I am."

Race is a recent historical invention used to make a distinction between people for purposes of colonization. C. Loring Brace, professor of anthropology at the University of Michigan, explains that the concept of race "does not appear until the Trans-Atlantic voyages of the Renaissance." But the prevalence of race as a concept—and its relationship to appearance, human status, and identity formation—is actually more significant today than it ever was. Our obsession with race is surpassed only by our seemingly polite and progressive neutrality regarding race. The Racial Privacy Initiative, a ballot promoted by black businessman Ward Connelly (who also successfully ended affirmative action in the state of California), is designed to obliterate the "race box" on school and government forms because it forces us to "pay attention to immutable and meaningless characteristics like skin color and ancestry" ("When Color Should Count," Glenn C. Loury *New York Times*). But even if race does not accurately identify a people, the concept is firmly in place and forces a social dynamic as well as pinpoints a social perception of a people. We don't see each other as one in the same. Never did. Never will. The perceived image of race is based on individual (or collective) sight, which has been re-created and reproduced. It is an appearance, or a set of appearances, which has been detached from the place and time in which it first made its appearance and preserved (in language and colloquialism) for a few moments or a few centuries. Once we are aware that we can see, we are aware that we can be seen, and "the eye of the other combines with our own eye,"…we are always looking at the relation between things and ourselves…our perception of what we see depends on our way of seeing. Images, for instance, were first made to conjure up the appearance of something that was absent. Gradually, it becomes evident that an image can outlast what it once represented, but the verbalized perception of image arrests the object in a perceived context for as long as the perception and the original language for the perception are upheld (*Ways of Seeing* by John Berger). In the case of race in America, it is physiology and the historical perceptions of and common terminology used to describe physiology that most often informs the individual's sense of defining race.

The dream of race as identity is born only in a perceived land of diversity (or difference). Race is a regenerated fantasy owing its genesis to neurosis (or as Freud said, "some early trauma repressed") and our need to achieve psychic balance. What is actual is what we produce from our dreams—symbols and signs of our expressions and intuitive perceptions. Our response to what we *think* we see. Identity. Race. Identity is an invented thing. Race is an invented thing. They are not real, but they are *actual*. Race and identity are based on perception and performance and are relative only to the perceptions and performances of the individual and the collective understanding of existence and the activity of being within the context of the dream. These symbols and signs cannot be expressed differently by us or better said by us. Language fails us—and the individual or collective mind is forced into over-

drive in order to invent language and behaviors for archetypes of identity. Apertures into nonordinary reality.

It is therefore less significant that Eminem, easily identified as "white" (a nonspecific race term for people of European descent), identifies himself with "black" culture (a nonspecific race term for people of African descent, "black culture" being that which is socially produced by the collective of people of African descent). That is not what makes his archetype of nonordinary reality a significant landmark in the landscape of the American dream. Rather, it is how he has refashioned an old symbol that appeals to popular culture and its boilerplate concepts of race, class, and identity, to fit a new generation in a new yet strangely redundant way—and how that old symbol has transmogrified in the last one hundred years, owing its present-day existence not to the historical performance of *blackness* but to the historical performance of *whiteness* and the ingenuity of human dreams.

There is something called *black* in America and there is something called *white* in America and I know them when I see them, but I will forever be unable to explain the meaning of them, because they are not real even though they have a very real place in my daily way of seeing, a fundamental relationship to my ever-evolving understanding of history, and a critical place in my interactive relationship to humanity. If one believes in the existence of race, it is because one needs to believe in the existence of self (within a culture that relies on race as an important variable of human existence). One needs to believe in culture, and the products of culture that define identity and inform history. The concept of race has long been one of the most vital sources of cultural product (as well as cultural conflict) because race has as its square root a hierarchical structure of being expressed in symbolism. A semiotics of identity that has yet to be solved. These tropes and signs are produced from the unconscious as revelation: The collective unconscious creates them in order to survive (by confrontation) the present archetypal structure. Conveniently forgotten in our race sentimentality are the ever-changing faces of race. Whiteness *became* something one had to attain in America. Being of Nordic or European ancestry did not automatically translate into whiteness. Whiteness had more to do with class privilege than some notion of nationality or physiology (and class is a better definition). Whiteness was purchased and fought for by Jews, Catholics, the Irish, Italians, Polish, indentured servants...all considered to be, at one time or another in America, non-white (and even today, depending on whose definition of whiteness you subscribe to). Blackness was never something one had to attain, at least not outside of Bohemian circles. Today, it seems...it is.

If we look to Eminem's archetype to appeal to what we know about ourselves now, we do it without referring to what we know about the identity of the other. The Eminem show is supposed to make us forget about race and think about how rigid this society is. How we have never really loosened up, and just had barnyard fun with our sacred cows. He uses the vernacular of black hip-hop culture, as well as the psychoanalytical vernacular of the white intellectual—and this invention of character is transferable to any race. The old White Negro may have worn cork and Afro wigs, soaked up Harlem culture and delivered the talented tenth to the mainstream, given race music a haircut, tuxedo jacket, and orchestration, may have learned to shake his narrow white hips in the snakelike manner of the Negro, thereby creating just enough soul to gain Hollywood movie-star musical status, and may have heroicized Negro jazz musicians in his literature, proudly proclaiming to have actually shared a joint or some smack with one or two at the height of Bohemian subculture's race mixing—but the new White Negro—like Eminem—has not *arrived* at black culture....He has *arrived* at white culture with an authentic performance of whiteness, influenced by a historical concept of blackness.

And there is a difference...?

REFERENCES

Arrowsmith, William. "Introduction to *The Bacchae*." In *Euripides V Three Tragedies*, edited by David Grene and Richard Lattimore. Chicago: University of Chicago Press, 1969.

Berger, John. *Ways of Seeing*. New York: Viking Press, 1995.

Wilson, Elizabeth. Bohemians: *The Glamorous Outcasts*. New Brunswick, N.J.: Rutgers University Press, 2001.

Key Websites

http://www.asanet.org/

The American Sociological Association is a nonprofit membership association dedicated to advancing sociology as a scientific discipline and profession serving the public good..

http://www.alternet.org

AlterNet.org is a project of the Independent Media Institute, a nonprofit organization dedicated to strengthening and supporting alternative journalism.

http://www.inequality.org/

Inequality.Org provides data and essays on various aspects of inequality in the United States.

http://www.census.gov/statab/www/

The Statistical Abstract of the United States. It contains a collection of statistics on social and economic conditions in the United States.

http://www.ins.usdoj.gov/graphics/aboutins/statistics/gbpage.htm

The Immigration and Naturalization Services statistics page.

http://www.nul.org

The Urban League is the nation's oldest and largest community-based movement devoted to empowering African Americans to enter the economic and social mainstream.

http://www.ssc.wisc.edu/irp/

The Institute for Research on Poverty at the University of Wisconsin is a national, university-based center for research into the causes and consequences of poverty and social inequality in the United States.

http://www.arc.org/

The Applied Research Center. This website focuses on the consequences of welfare reform.

http://www.pbs.org/wgbh/aia

The Africans in America–PBS Online website is a companion to "Africans in America," a six-hour public television series

http://www.naacp.org/links/

NAACP List of Recommended Links: The NAACP (National Association for the Advancement of Colored People) is the oldest, largest, and strongest civil rights organization in the United States.

http://www.census.gov/pubinfo/www/hotlinks.html

U.S. Census Bureau–Minority Links provides some quick and easy links to the latest data on racial and ethnic populations in the United States.

http://www.hsph.harvard.edu/grhf/WoC/

Women of Color Web explores the intersection of gender and race. It provides a considerable amount of material on blacks.

http://www.webcom.com/~intvioce

Interracial Voice (IV) is an independent information-oriented, networking newsjournal, serving the mixed-race/interracial community in cyberspace.

http://www.census.gov/apsd/www/wepeople.html

A link to a series of U.S. Census groups on various groups in the United States, this series is called "We the Americans" and profiles racial and ethnic groups, women, the elderly, and immigrants, to name a few.

http://www.bls.gov/

The Bureau of Labor Statistics provides a comprehensive picture of the U.S. economy at any given moment in time.

http://www.ncfr.org/

The National Council on Family Relations (NCFR) "provides a forum for family researchers, educators, and practitioners to share knowledge about families."

http://www.nafeo.org/

National Association for Equal Opportunity in Higher Education (NAFEO) is the national umbrella and public policy advocacy organization for 118 of the nation's historically and predominantly black colleges and universities.

http://www.omhrc.gov/

The Office of Minority Health (OMH) was created by the U.S. Department of Health and Human Services to improve the social, physical, and psychological health of minorities in the United States.

Acknowledgements

CREDITS

Appendix 22. 279: American Sociological Association, 2003. THE IMPORTANCE OF COLLECTING DATA AND DOING SOCIAL SCIENTIFIC RESEARCH ON RACE. Washington, DC: American Sociological Association.

Appendix 23. 289: "Eminem: The New White Negro" from EVERYTHING BUT THE BURDEN WHAT WHITE PEOPLE ARE TAKING FROM BLACK CULTURE, edited by Greg Tate, copyright (c) 2003 by Greg Tate. Used by permission of Broadway books, a division of Random House, Inc.

Chapter 1. 3: "21st Century African American Family" by Dr. C.O. McDaniel, University of North Carolina at Wilmington, Department of Sociology and Criminology, 2003.

Chapter 2. 19: From Annette Lareau, "Invisible Inequality: Social Class and Child Rearing in Black Families," AMERICAN SOCIOLOGICAL REVIEW, Vol. 67 (October) 2002. Copyright (c) 2002 the American Sociological Association (ASA). WAITING ON OFFICIAL CREDIT

Chapter 3. 53: Audrey Edwards, "Bring Me Home a Black Girl" ESSENCE, Vol. 33, No. 7, 2002, pp. 176-179. Used by permission of the author.

Chapter 4. 57: "Black Power Backlash to the New Amalgamationism" from INTERRACIAL INTIMACY: SEX, MARRIAGE, IDENTITY, AND ADOPTION, by Randall Kennedy, copyright (c) 2003 by Randall Kennedy. Source: Pantheon Books, a division of Random House, Inc.

Chapter 5. 91: "Does Multicultural Education Warrant Reconstruction for the 21st Century?" by Dr. Charles C. Jackson, Augusta State University, Department of Education, 2002.

Chapter 6. 101: M. Placier, P.M. Hall, S. Benson McKendall, & K.S. Cockrell, "Policy as the Transformation of Intentions: Making Muliticultural Education Policy," EDUCATIONAL POLICY, vol. 14, No. 2, 2000, pp. 259-289. Copyright (c) 2000 Corwin Press, Inc. Reprinted by permission of Corwin Press, Inc.

Chapter 7. 123: From "African American Men and Women in Higher Education: 'Filling the glass' in the New Millennium" by K. Edelin-Freeman, 2000, pp. 61-90. Source: The National Urban League.

Chapter 8. 139: From P. Burdman, "Voice of Dissent" in BLACK ISSUES IN HIGHER EDICATION, Vol. 18, No. 6, 2001, pp. 28-31. Reprinted with permission from Black Issues in Higher Education, www.blackissues.com.

Chapter 9. 145: D. Rhym, "Losing the Race" from JOURNAL OF AFRICAN AMERICAN MEN, Vol. 6, No. 2, 2001, pp. 88-90. Used by permission of Transaction Publishers.

Chapter 10. 149: From D. Leonard, "The Decline of the Black Athlete: An Online Exclusive: Exteneded Interview with Harry Edwards," COLOR LINES, Vol. 3, No. 1, 2000. Used by permisson.

Chapter 11. 155: A.O. Adebayo, A.A. Adekoya, & O.F. Ayadi, "Historicaly Black Colleges and Universities: (HBCUs) as Agents of Change for the Development of Minority Businesses," JOURNAL OF BLACK STUDIES, Vol. 32, No. 2, 2001, pp. 166-183. Copyright (c) 2001 Sage Publications, Inc. Reprinted by permission of Sage Publications, Inc.

Chapter 12. 167: From C. Hayes, "Media Meltdown: With Urban Marketing so Hot, Black-Owned Ad Agencies are Prime Targets for Acquisitions and Mergers," BLACK ENTERPRISE, June 2000, pp. 179-185.

Chapter 13. 175: From D. Horowitz, "Ten Reasons Why Reparations for Slavery is a Bad Idea for Blacks--and Racists Too," THE BLACK SCHOLAR, Vol. 31, No. 2, 2001, p. 48. Used by permission.

Chapter 14. 179: From E. Allen & R. Chrisman, "Ten Reasons: A Response to David Horowitz," THE BLACK SCHOLAR, Vol. 31, No. 2, 2001, pp. 49-55. Used by permission.

Chapter 15. 187: From D. Moon & L.A. Flores, "Antiracism and the Abolition of Whiteness: Rhetorical Strategies of Domination Among 'Race Traitors,'" COMMUNICATION STUDIES, Vol. 51, No. 2, 2000, pp. 97-115. Source: Department of Speech Communication/Eastern Illinois University.

Chapter 16. 207: From E.N. Williams & M.C. Simms, "The Evolution of Black Political Power," THE STATE OF BLACK AMERICA: BLACKS IN THE NEW MILLENNIUM, 2000, pp. 91-120. Source: The National Urban League.

Chapter 17. 215: J.S. Mattis, "African American Women's Definitions of Spirituality and Religiosity," JOURNAL OF BLACK PSYCHOLOGY, Vol. 26, No. 1, 2000, pp. 101-122. Copyright (c) 2000 Association of Black Psychologists/Sage Publications, Inc. Reprinted by permission of Sage Publications, Inc.

Chapter 18. 233: M.D. Christian & O.A. Barbarin, "Cultural Resources and Psychological Adjustment of African American Children: Effects of Spirtuality and Racial Attribution," JOURNAL OF BLACK PSYCHOLOGY, Vol. 27, No. 1, 2001, pp. 43-63. Copyright (c) 2001 Association of Black Psychologists/Sage Publications, Inc. Reprinted by permission of Sage Publications, Inc.

Chapter 19. 249: "Good as Gospel" by Michelle Bearden from TAMPA TRIBUNE, August 8, 2003.

Chapter 20. 253: ATLANTA JOURNAL AND CONSTITUTION [STAFF PRODUCED COPY ONLY] by J. BLAKE . Copyright 2002 by ATLANTA JOUR-CONSTITUTION. Reproduced with permission of ATLANTA JOUR-CONSTITUTION in the format Textbook via Copyright Clearance Center.

Chapter 21. 259: "Performing Blackness Down Under: The Café of the Gate of Salvation" by E.P. Johnson, TEXT AND PERFORMANCE QUARTERLY, (2002) Vol. 22 no. 2, pp. 99-119. Used by permission of Taylor & Francis Ltd, http://www.tandf.co.uk/journals/titles/10462937.html